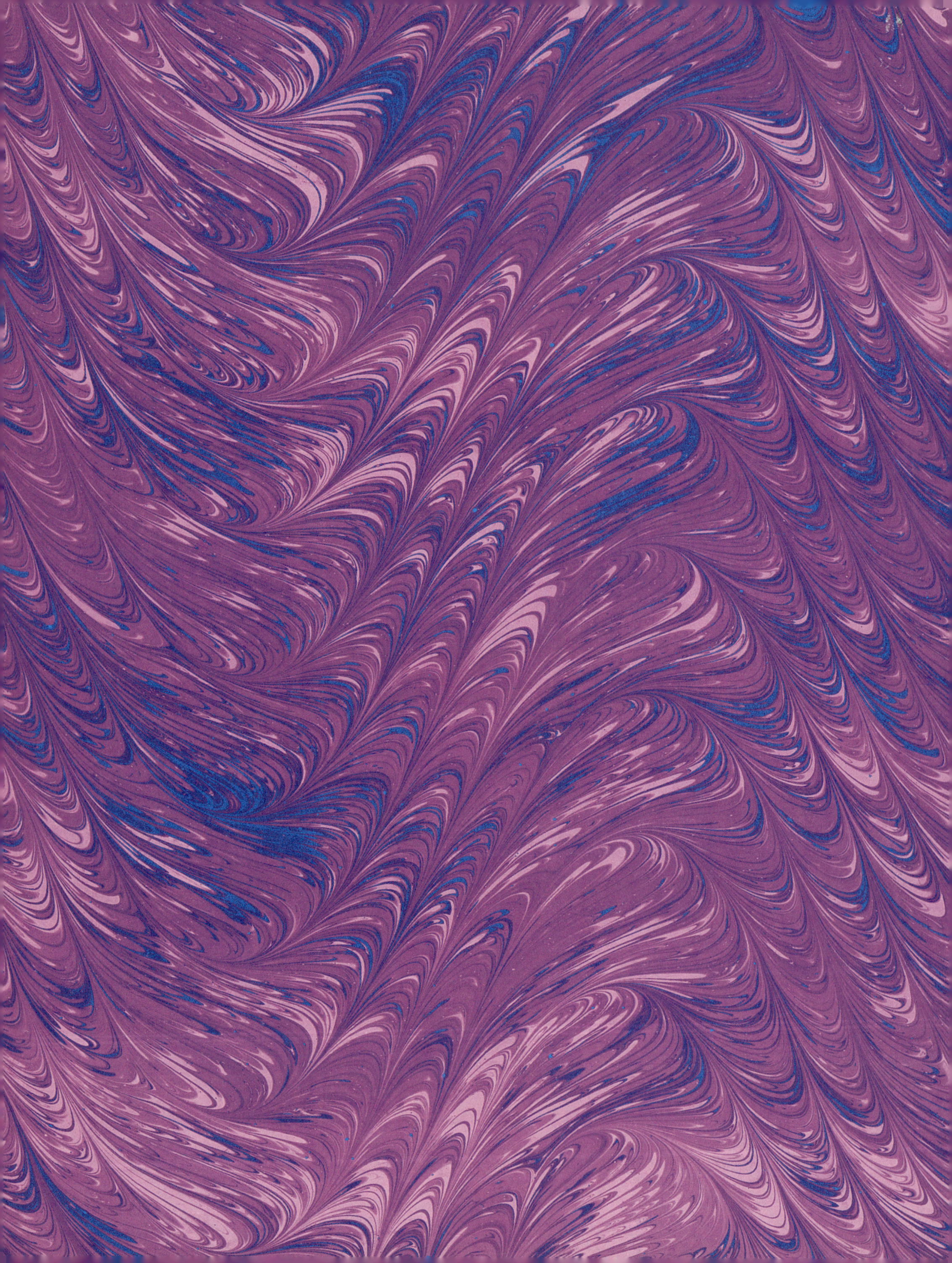

HARCOURT TROPHIES

A HARCOURT READING/LANGUAGE ARTS PROGRAM

LEAD THE WAY

SENIOR AUTHORS
Isabel L. Beck ◆ Roger C. Farr ◆ Dorothy S. Strickland

AUTHORS
Alma Flor Ada ◆ Marcia Brechtel ◆ Margaret McKeown
Nancy Roser ◆ Hallie Kay Yopp

SENIOR CONSULTANT
Asa G. Hilliard III

CONSULTANTS
F. Isabel Campoy ◆ David A. Monti

Orlando Boston Dallas Chicago San Diego

Visit *The Learning Site!*

www.harcourtschool.com

Printed in the United States of America

ISBN 0-15-345256-0

4 5 6 7 8 9 10 0868 10
4500239294

HARCOURT

TROPHIES

A HARCOURT READING/LANGUAGE ARTS PROGRAM

LEAD THE WAY

Dear Reader,

We all can think of people who inspire us. They may be historical figures, friends, or family members. We look up to people who are not afraid to move ahead in a new direction.

In **Lead the Way,** you will read about people who are working toward their goals by taking bold strides. Some travel to distant lands to study rare plants, while others simply plant a garden in their neighborhood. Some help those around them, while others work to improve themselves. Some even brave the dangers of the frontier to lead the way west.

As you read this book, you will see how both real people and story characters solve problems and make the most of changes. You may find someone here to inspire you!

Now, keep your eyes and your mind wide open, turn the page, and prepare to read about people who lead the way.

Sincerely,

The Authors

The Authors

THEME 1

CONTENTS

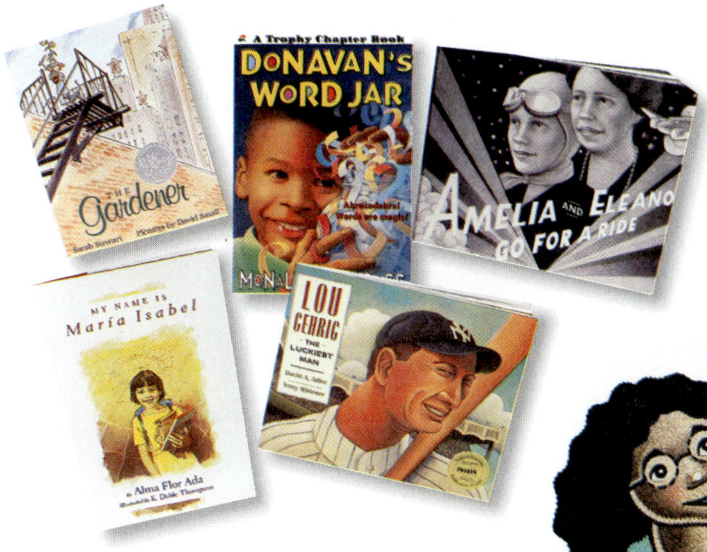
THE Gardener
A Trophy Chapter Book
DONAVAN'S WORD JAR
AMELIA AND ELEANOR GO FOR A RIDE
MY NAME IS María Isabel
Alma Flor Ada
LOU GEHRIG THE LUCKIEST MAN

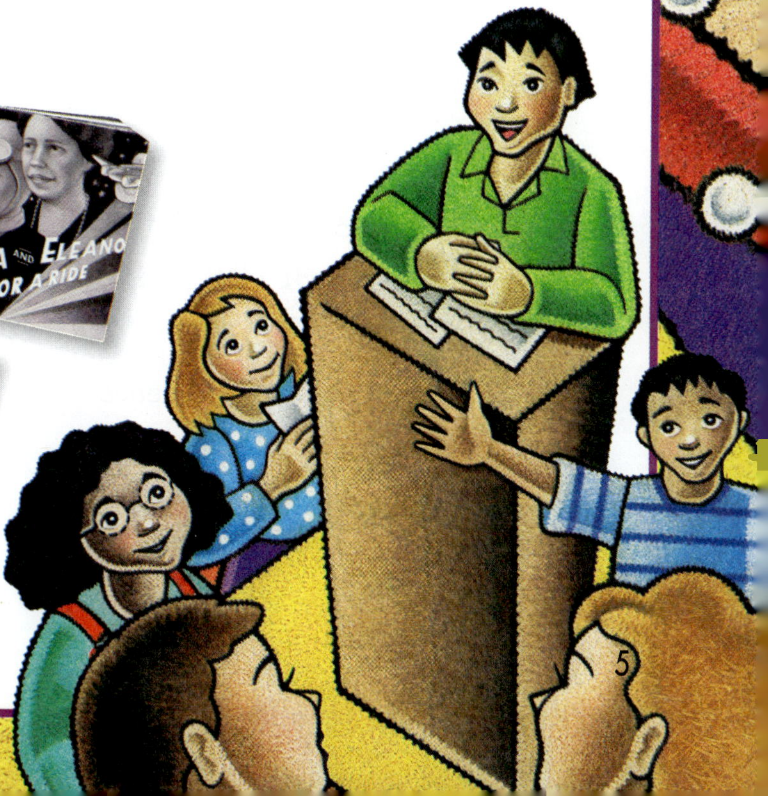

THEME 2

SIDE BY SIDE

CONTENTS

The Baker's Neighbor
The Emperor and the Kite
How to Babysit an Orangutan
Nights of the Pufflin
ERIKA TAMAR
The Garden of Happiness

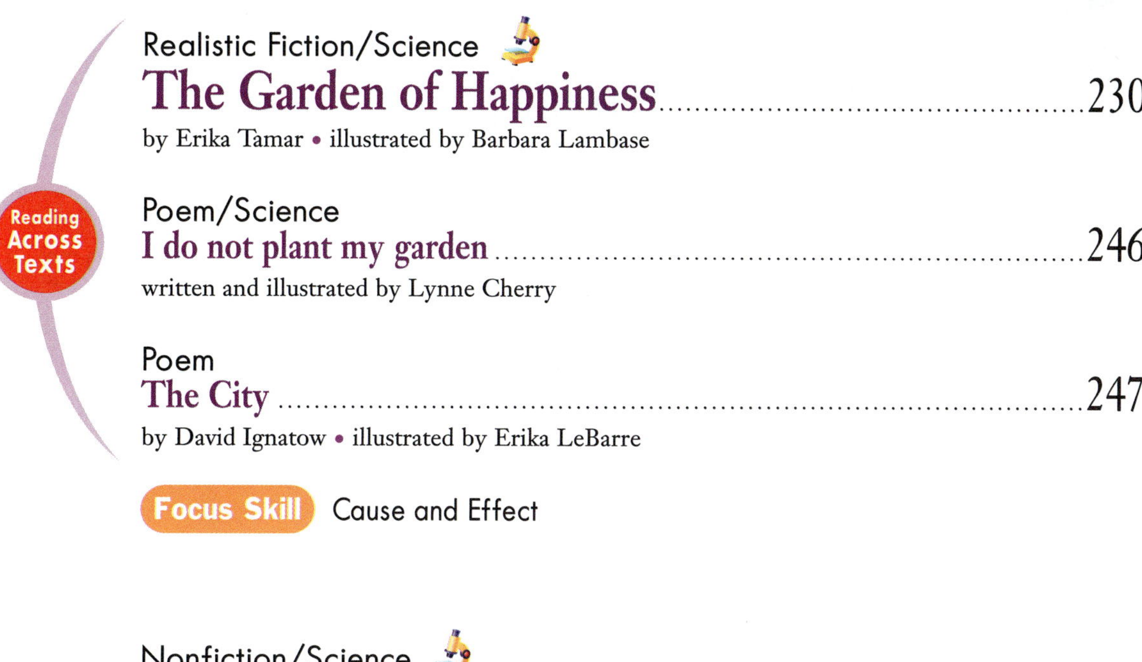

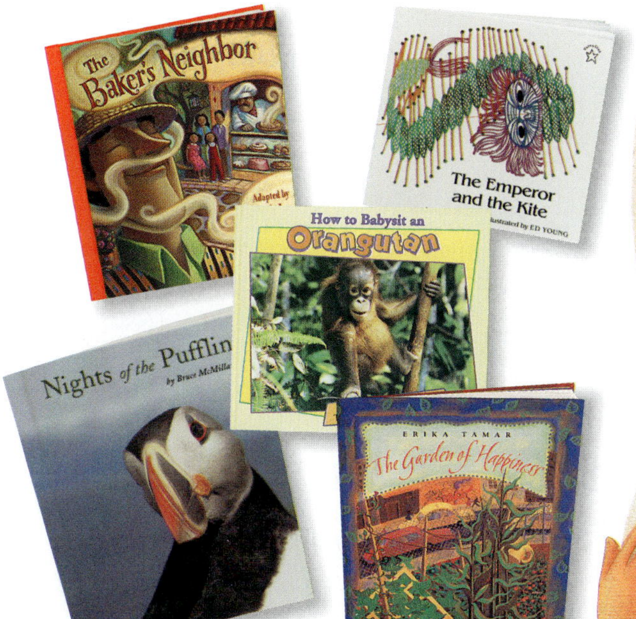

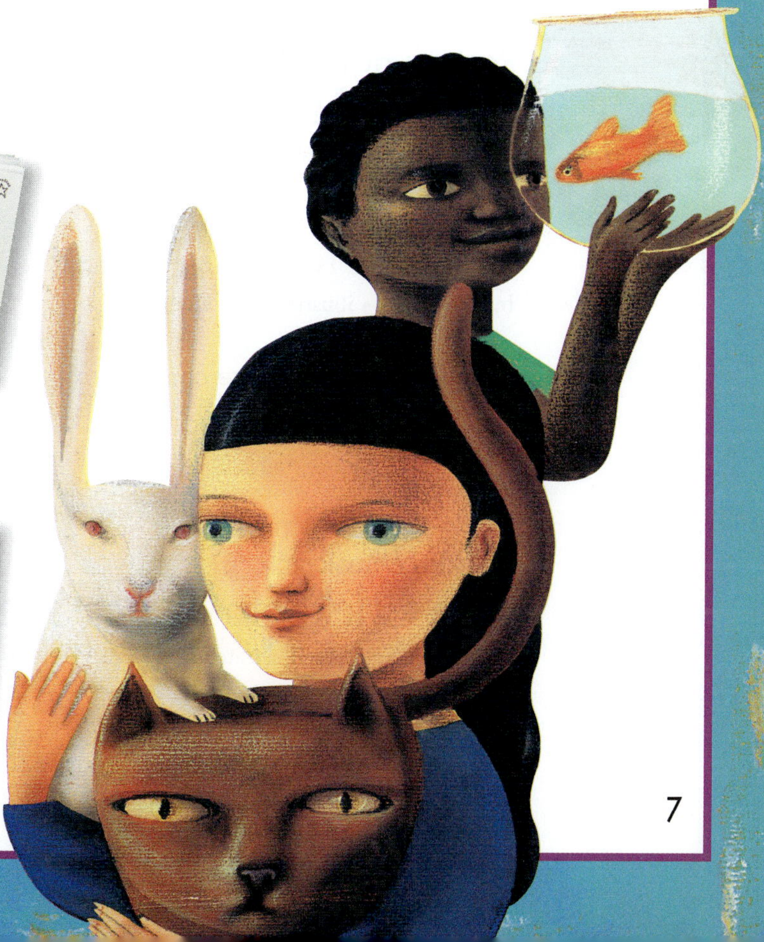

THEME 3

Make Yourself at Home

CONTENTS

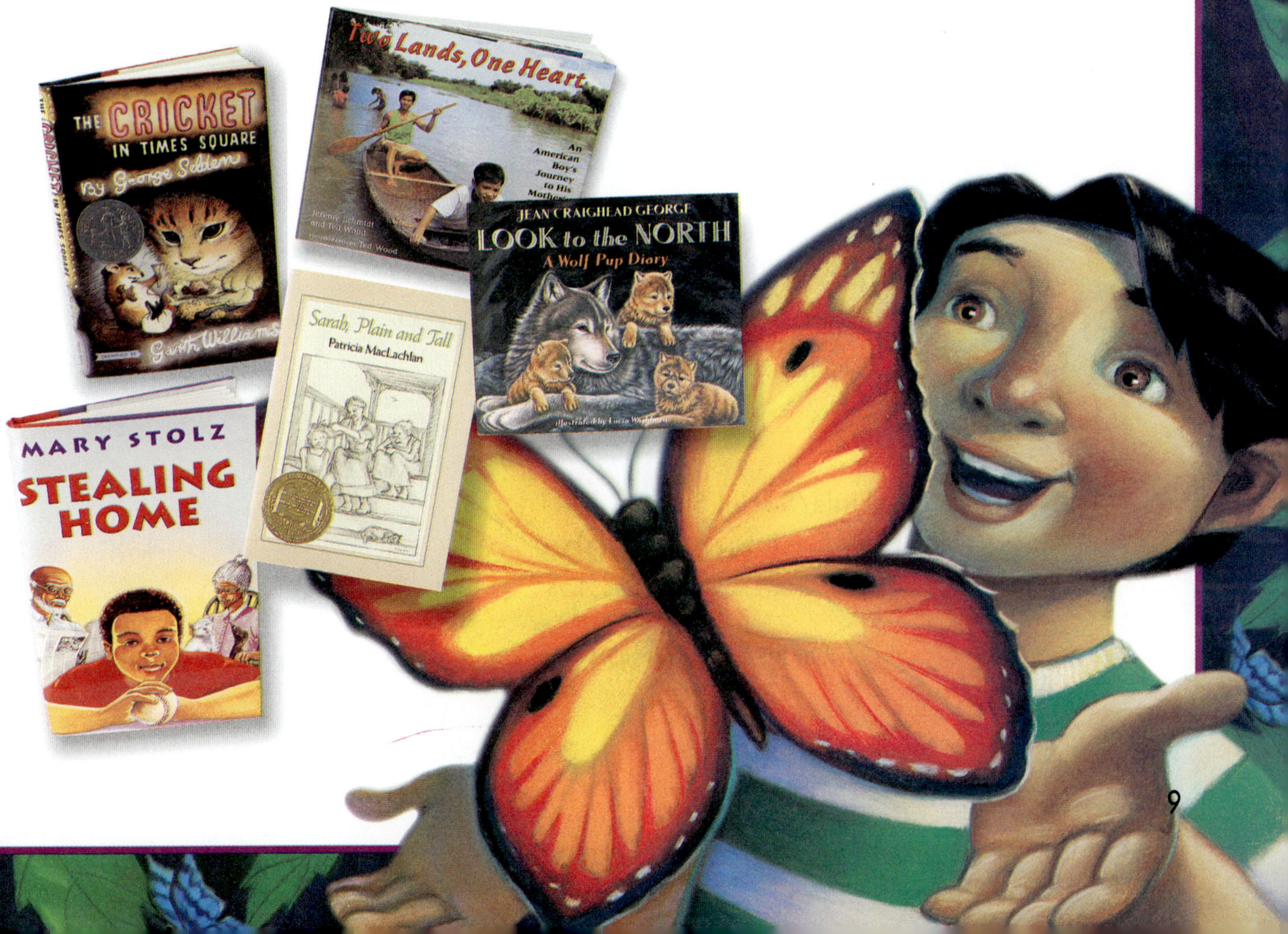
The Cricket in Times Square
By George Selden
Garth Williams
Two Lands, One Heart
An American Boy's Journey to His Mother's
Jean Craighead George
Look to the North
A Wolf Pup Diary
Sarah, Plain and Tall
Patricia MacLachlan
Mary Stolz
Stealing Home

THEME 4

CREATIVE MINDS

CONTENTS

Red Writing Hood
THE CASE OF PABLO'S NOSE
In the Days of King Adobe
One Grain of Rice
Demi
The Kids' Invention Book

THEME 5

Community Ties

CONTENTS

A Very Important Day
Maggie Rugg Herold
Catherine Stock
FIRE!
Saguaro Cactus
Paul and Shirley Berquist
Puffin Newbery Library
Blue Willow
Doris Gates
In My Family
En Mi Familia
Carmen Lomas Garza

THEME 6

NEW LANDS

CONTENTS

The Gold Rush
Johanna Hurwitz
The Down & Up Fall
Paul Bunyan
and Babe the Blue Ox
Fly Traps!
Plants That Bite Back
Read and Wonder
Martin Jenkins
David Parkins
I Have Heard of a Land

Using Reading Strategies

A strategy is a plan for doing something well.

You probably already use some strategies as you read. For example, you may **look at the title and illustrations before you begin reading** a story. You may **think about what you want to find out while reading.** Using strategies like these can help you become a better reader.

Look at the list of strategies on page 17. You will learn about and use these strategies as you read the selections in this book. As you read, look back at the list to remind yourself of the **strategies good readers use.**

Strategies Good Readers Use

- Use Decoding/ Phonics
- Make and Confirm Predictions
- Create Mental Images
- Self-Question
- Summarize
- Read Ahead
- Reread to Clarify
- Use Context to Confirm Meaning
- Use Text Structure and Format
- Adjust Reading Rate

Here are some ways to check your own comprehension:

✔ Make a copy of this list on a piece of construction paper shaped like a bookmark.

✔ Have it handy as you read.

✔ After reading, talk with a classmate about which strategies you used and why.

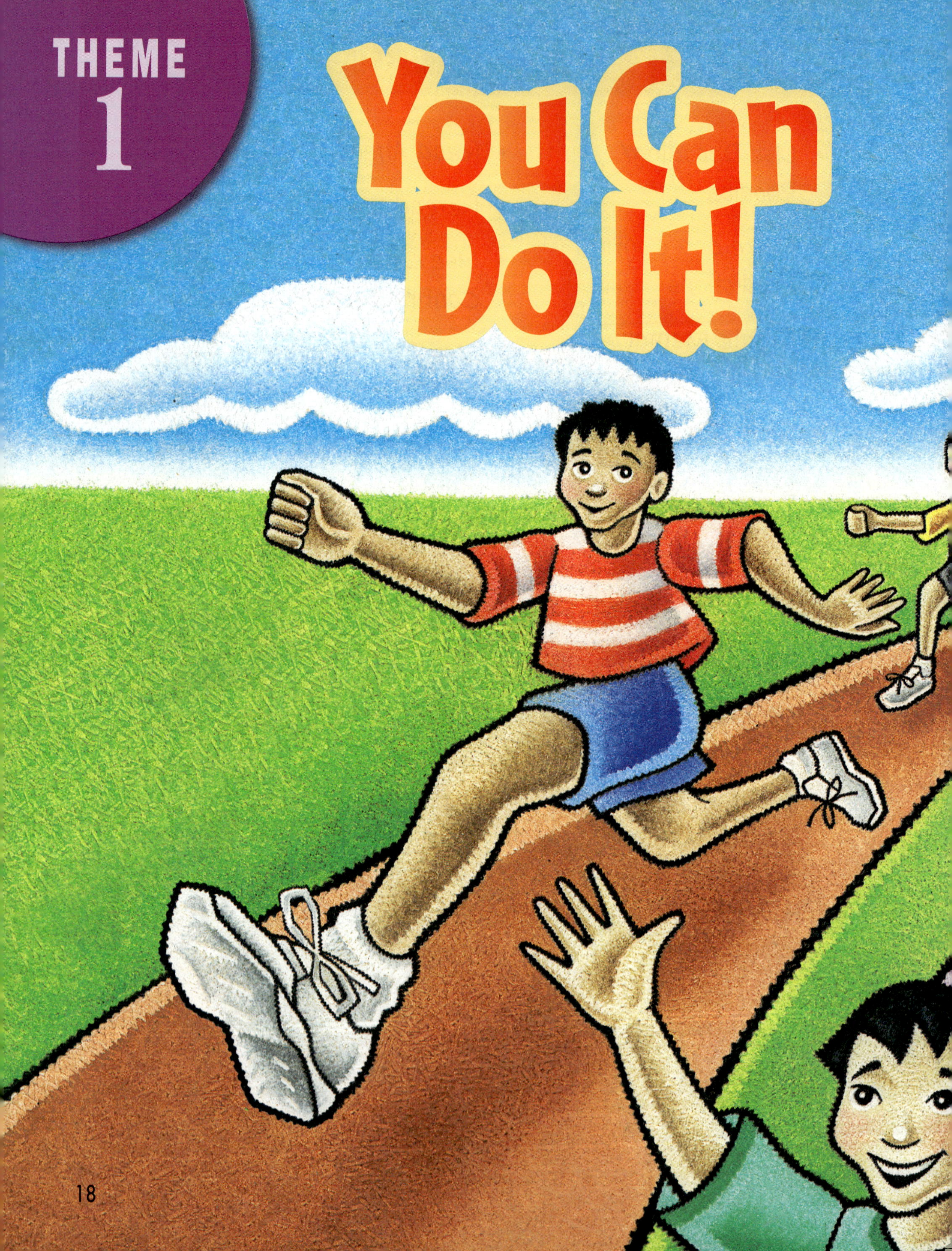
THEME
1
You Can Do It!

CONTENTS

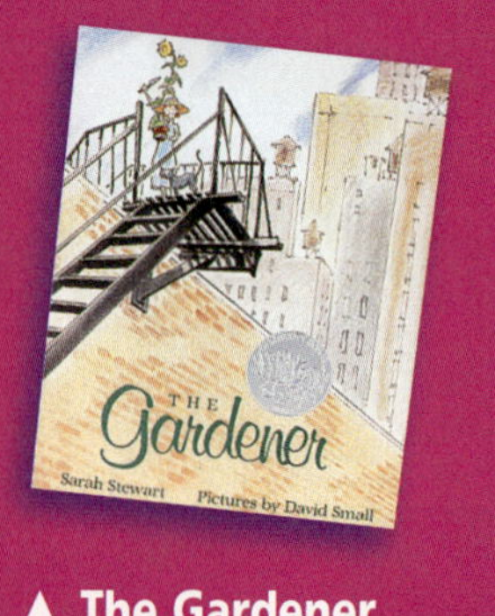

▲ The Gardener

Vocabulary Power

In the selection "The Gardener," Lydia Grace and her grandmother share an interesting hobby. The following journal entry tells about a boy who also has a special relationship with his grandmother.

anxious

recognizing

adore

retire

vacant

sprucing

Saturday

What an exciting day! Mom and I went to the airport to pick up Grandma. I was **anxious** because her plane was late. Mom was as nervous and excited as I was.

Finally the plane landed. I hadn't seen Grandma in a long time, but I had no trouble **recognizing** her. I knew who she was the minute I saw her. She recognized me right away, too, even though I've grown a lot.

She brought me a new soccer ball. She knows I **adore** soccer because I always e-mail her to tell her how many goals I've scored.

Now here's the best news of all. Grandma says she is going to work at her job for just one more year. Then she plans to **retire** and move here to Mayville! She wants to find a **vacant** store that nobody is using so she can open a little flower shop. She says she will need some help **sprucing** up her shop. It will be fun helping Grandma clean it and decorate it. I can't wait for next year!

Vocabulary–Writing
CONNECTION

Who is someone that you **adore**? Write a paragraph telling about your relationship with that person.

Genre

Realistic Fiction

Realistic fiction has characters and events that are like people and events in real life.

In this selection, look for

- **A setting that could be a real place**
- **Realistic characters and events**

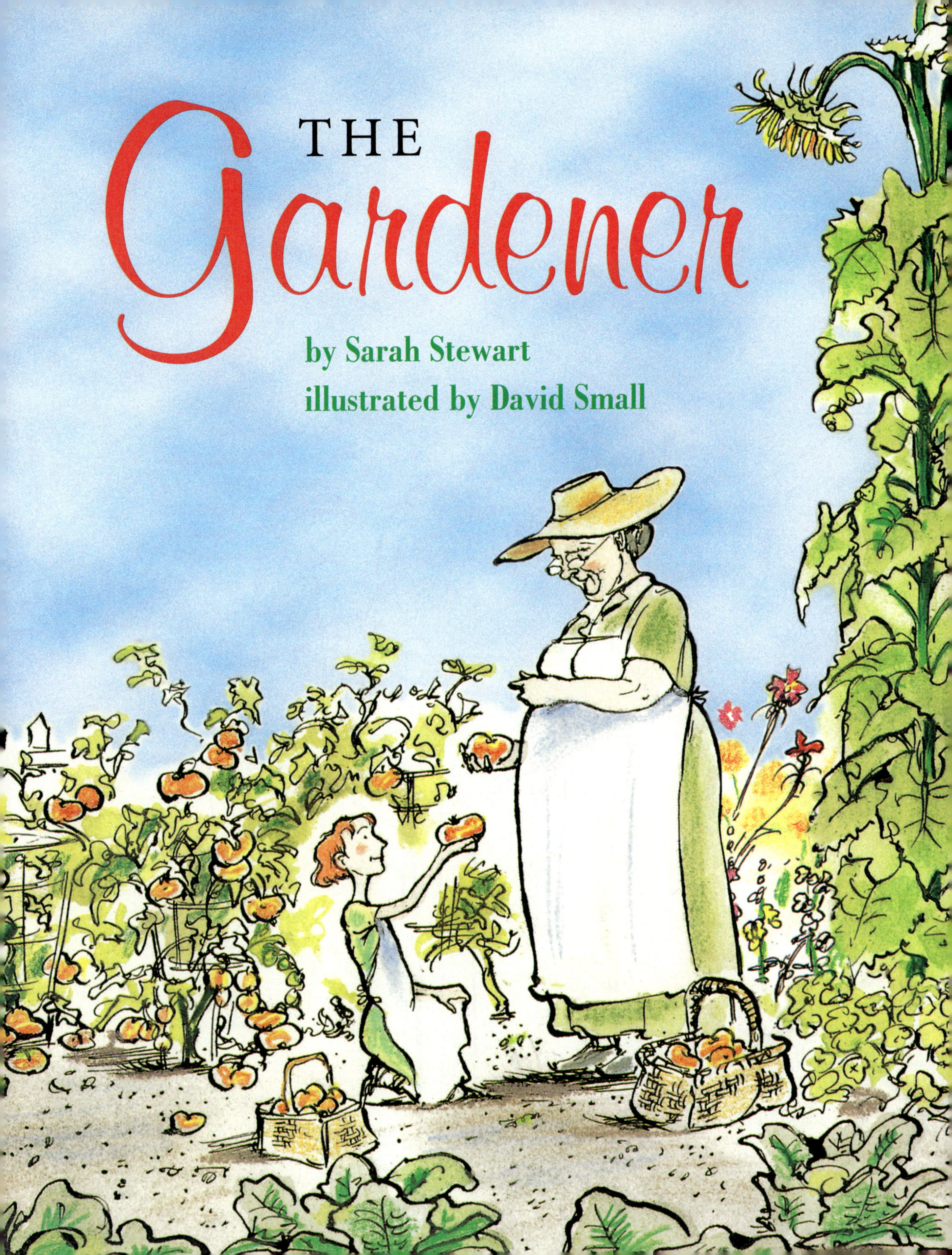
THE
Gardener
by Sarah Stewart
illustrated by David Small

August 27, 1935

Dear Uncle Jim,

Grandma told us after supper that you want me to come to the city and live with you until things get better. Did she tell you that Papa has been out of work for a long time, and no one asks Mama to make dresses anymore?

We all cried, even Papa. But then Mama made us laugh with her stories about your chasing her up trees when you were both little. Did you really do that?

I'm small, but strong, and I'll help you all I can. However, Grandma said to finish my schoolwork before doing anything else.

Your niece,
Lydia Grace Finch

September 3, 1935

Dear Uncle Jim,

I'm mailing this from the train station. I forgot to tell you in the last letter *three important things* that I'm too shy to say to your face:

1. I know a lot about gardening, but nothing about baking.
2. I'm anxious to learn to bake, but is there any place to plant seeds?
3. I like to be called "Lydia Grace"—just like Grandma.

Your niece,
Lydia Grace Finch

On the train
September 4, 1935

Dear Mama,

I feel so pretty in your dress that you made over for me. I hope you don't miss it too much.

Dear Papa,

I haven't forgotten what you said about recognizing Uncle Jim: "Just look for Mama's face with a big nose and a mustache!" I promise not to tell him. (Does he have a sense of humor?)

And, dearest Grandma,

Thank you for the seeds. The train is rocking me to sleep, and every time I doze off, I dream of gardens.

Love to all,
Lydia Grace

BAKERY

September 5, 1935

Dear Mama, Papa, and Grandma,

I'm so excited!!!

There are window boxes here! They look as if they've been waiting for me, so now we'll both wait for spring.

And, Grandma, the sun shines down on the corner where I'll live and work.

Love to all,
Lydia Grace

P. S. Uncle Jim doesn't smile.

December 25, 1935

Dear Mama, Papa, and Grandma,

I adore the seed catalogues you sent for Christmas. And, Grandma, thank you for all the bulbs. I hope you received my drawings.

I wrote a long poem for Uncle Jim. He didn't smile, but I think he liked it. He read it aloud, then put it in his shirt pocket and patted it.

Love to all,
Lydia Grace

February 12, 1936

Dearest Grandma,

Thank you again for those bulbs you sent at Christmas. You should see them now!

I really like Ed and Emma Beech, Uncle Jim's friends who work here. When I first arrived, Emma told me she'd show me how to knead bread if I would teach her the Latin names of all the flowers I know. Now, just half a year later, I'm kneading bread and she's speaking Latin!

More good news: We have a store cat named Otis who at this very moment is sleeping at the foot of *my* bed.

Love to all,
Lydia Grace

P. S. Uncle Jim isn't smiling yet, but I'm hoping for a smile soon.

July 4, 1936

Dearest Mama, Papa, and Grandma,

I am bursting with happiness! The entire city seems so beautiful, especially this morning.

The secret place is ready for Uncle Jim. At noon, the store will close for the holiday, and then we'll bring him up to the roof.

I've tried to remember everything you ever taught me about beauty.

Love to all,
Lydia Grace

P. S. I can already imagine Uncle Jim's smile.

YOU'VE ARRIVED!
PLEASE GO UP

July 11, 1936

Dear Mama, Papa, and Grandma,

My heart is pounding so hard I'm sure the customers can hear it downstairs!

At lunch today, Uncle Jim put the "Closed" sign on the door and told Ed and Emma and me to go upstairs and wait. He appeared with the most amazing cake I've ever seen—covered in flowers!

I truly believe that cake equals one thousand smiles.

And then he took your letter out of his pocket with the news of Papa's job!

I'M COMING HOME!

Love to all, and see you soon,
Lydia Grace

P. S. Grandma, I've given all of my plants to Emma. I can't wait to help you in your garden again. We gardeners never retire.

Think and Respond

1. How does Lydia Grace show strength during her year away?
2. What information do readers learn from the pictures that Lydia Grace does not tell in her letters?
3. What does Lydia Grace's family do to help her feel less **anxious** about the changes in her life?
4. Do you think Uncle Jim is a good uncle to Lydia Grace, even though he hardly ever smiles? Explain your answer.
5. When did you use context to confirm the meaning of a word?

Meet the Author Sarah Stewart

Sarah Stewart grew up in Texas. As a young girl, she found strength in "safe places" like the library and the garden. She believes both places are full of hope. Books make readers think of all the things they can be and do, and it is inspiring to watch seeds grow into plants. At home today, Sarah has a library—and five gardens! She has written poetry and speeches as well as books for children. Her suggestions for writers include studying Latin, reading poems, and taking time to be quiet.

Sarah Stewart

NET WT.
200 mg.
SEEDS
$1.59

Meet the Illustrator David Small

David Small grew up in the large city of Detroit, Michigan. He remembers being glad to get away from all the factory buildings when he spent vacations with his grandmother in the country. There was no television, so he played outside a lot when he was there. One day he saw a mural by Diego Rivera in a Detroit museum. It showed something that was part of the real world around him—workers making cars. He decided he would try art himself. David Small has written and illustrated a number of books for children. He is married to Sarah Stewart.

Visit *The Learning Site!*
www.harcourtschool.com

▲ The Gardener

Making Connections

Text to Self • Text to Text • Text To World

Compare Texts

NC STANDARDS: ELA 2.04b identify theme, 3.01b interpret/evaluate text/examine characters' actions/motives, 3.02 analyze/compare texts

1. How does "The Gardener" fit the theme of facing challenges? INTERPRETATION / EVALUATING
2. Look at the letter on page 29. Compare it to the last letter, on page 43. What is the most important change you see in Lydia Grace? INTERPRETATION / ANALYZING
3. What can you tell from the letters on pages 26 and 27 about how Lydia Grace is feeling? INTERPRETATION / EVALUATING
4. Think of another story you know about a family that makes it through hard times. How is the family in that story like Lydia Grace's family? CONNECTIONS / ANALYZING
5. What would you like to grow in a garden? How could you learn how to care for your garden? INTERPRETATION / EVALUATING

Write to Explain

Lydia Grace tries to think of ways to make Uncle Jim smile. Write about a time when you cheered someone up. Explain what you did to make that person feel better. Organize your steps in a sequence diagram like this one. Then use your sequence diagram to help you write your paragraph.

Writing CONNECTION

NC STANDARD: ELA 3.06 conduct research using a variety of tools

Compare and Contrast Time Periods

Social Studies CONNECTION

"The Gardener" takes place many years ago during the Great Depression. Do research to find out when the Great Depression was and what happened during that time. Then use the information you found and your knowledge of life in the present to compare and contrast life during the Great Depression with present-day life. Organize your information in a Venn diagram.

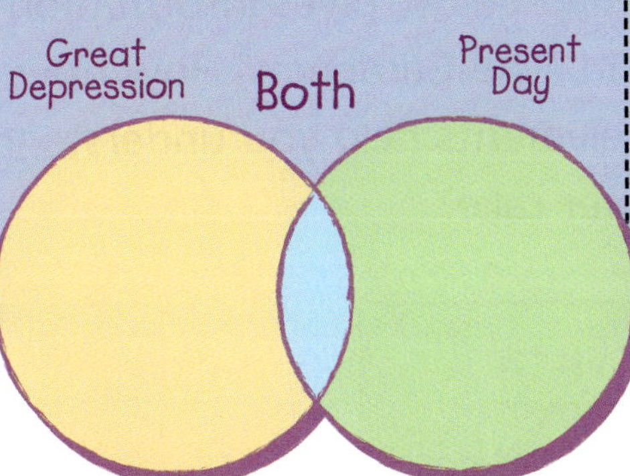

NC STANDARD: ELA 3.06 conduct research using a variety of tools

Research Growing Conditions

Use an encyclopedia or a nonfiction book about gardening to find out what conditions each of the following plants needs to grow: cactus, orange tree, apple tree, redwood. Then use what you know about the conditions where you live to decide how well each of these plants would grow in your community. Use a line scale like the one below to show which plants would be the most successful and which ones would be the least successful.

Least successful — Most successful

▲ The Gardener

NC STANDARDS: ELA 2.04a identify plot, 2.04c identify main idea/details

Narrative Elements

The most important elements in a story, or narrative, are **setting**, **characters**, and **plot**. Thinking about the narrative elements in a story helps you understand why the characters act as they do.

The story map below gives information about the narrative elements in "The Gardener." How does thinking about the narrative elements help you understand why Uncle Jim bakes the flower cake?

Characters
Lydia Grace, Mama, Papa, Grandma, Uncle Jim, Ed Beech, Emma Beech

Setting
1935—1936
A city in the United States

Plot
Lydia Grace has to stay with her Uncle Jim in the city.
Uncle Jim never smiles.
Lydia Grace plants a rooftop garden to surprise Uncle Jim.
Uncle Jim bakes a cake covered with flowers for Lydia Grace.

Visit *The Learning Site!*
www.harcourtschool.com

See *Skills and Activities*

Test Prep
Narrative Elements

NC STANDARD: ELA 2.04a
identify main idea/details

▶ **Read the story. Then answer the questions.**

"It's so dark and quiet out here in the country," Sam thought. He missed the noise and excitement of the city. He knew he needed to get used to the long days and quiet nights because he would be here all summer while his mom went back to school.

In the morning, Sam asked Aunt Susan how he could help around the farm. She showed him how to feed the chickens. Sam decided he'd write a letter to his mom. He wouldn't tell her how dark and quiet the nights were, though.

CRITICAL STANCE / ANALYZING

1. Why is Sam staying with his Aunt Susan?

A He wants to live on a farm.

B His mom wants him to experience farm life.

C His mom is going to school.

D He is doing a report about farms for a school project.

Tip

Important information about the plot of a story is often given at the beginning. Reread the first paragraph to help you find the answer.

CRITICAL STANCE / ANALYZING

2. Knowing that Sam is from the city helps you understand his feelings because —

F he doesn't like chickens

G life in the city is very different from life in the country

H he's afraid of the dark

J he is not used to hard work

Tip

Decide how Sam feels. Then you can identify what it is about the setting that makes him feel this way.

▲ Donavan's Word Jar

Vocabulary Power

In the selection "Donavan's Word Jar," a boy named Donavan learns to understand people better. One way to find out about people is to ask them questions.

- leisure
- disappointment
- perseverance
- uneasy
- compromise
- chortle

Roving Reporter's

Question of the Day:

How do you like to spend your **leisure** time?

Roberto Fernandez, age 39

I play volleyball in my free time. When I don't play as well as I'd like, it's a **disappointment**, but I don't let that stop me. A sport like volleyball takes **perseverance**. You have to keep trying in order to improve.

I like to climb mountains, but my hobby made my family **uneasy**. They were worried that I might get hurt. We decided to **compromise**. We agreed that they wouldn't worry about me as long as I never climb alone.

Sarah Swanson, age 27

Harry Collins, age 65

What do I do in my spare time? I sit on this bench and watch the world go by. Let me tell you, I see some funny sights. Sometimes I chuckle to myself, and sometimes I **chortle** right out loud!

Vocabulary-Writing CONNECTION

Sometimes it is necessary to **compromise** in order to get along with others. Write a paragraph telling about a compromise you made with a friend or a family member.

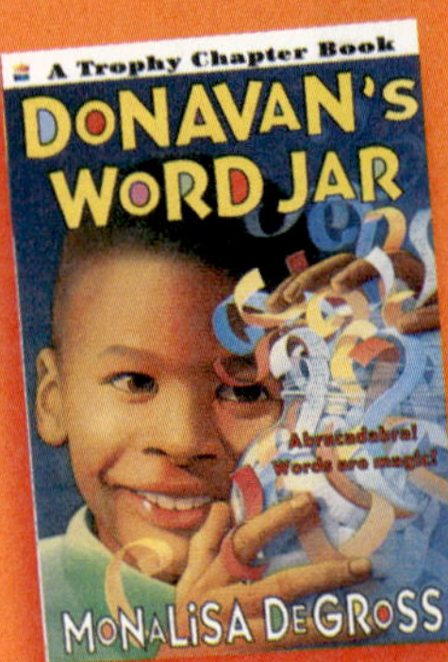

Genre

Realistic Fiction

Realistic fiction tells about characters and events that are like people and events in real life.

In this selection, look for

- **Characters that have feelings that real people have**
- **A plot with a beginning, a middle, and an ending**

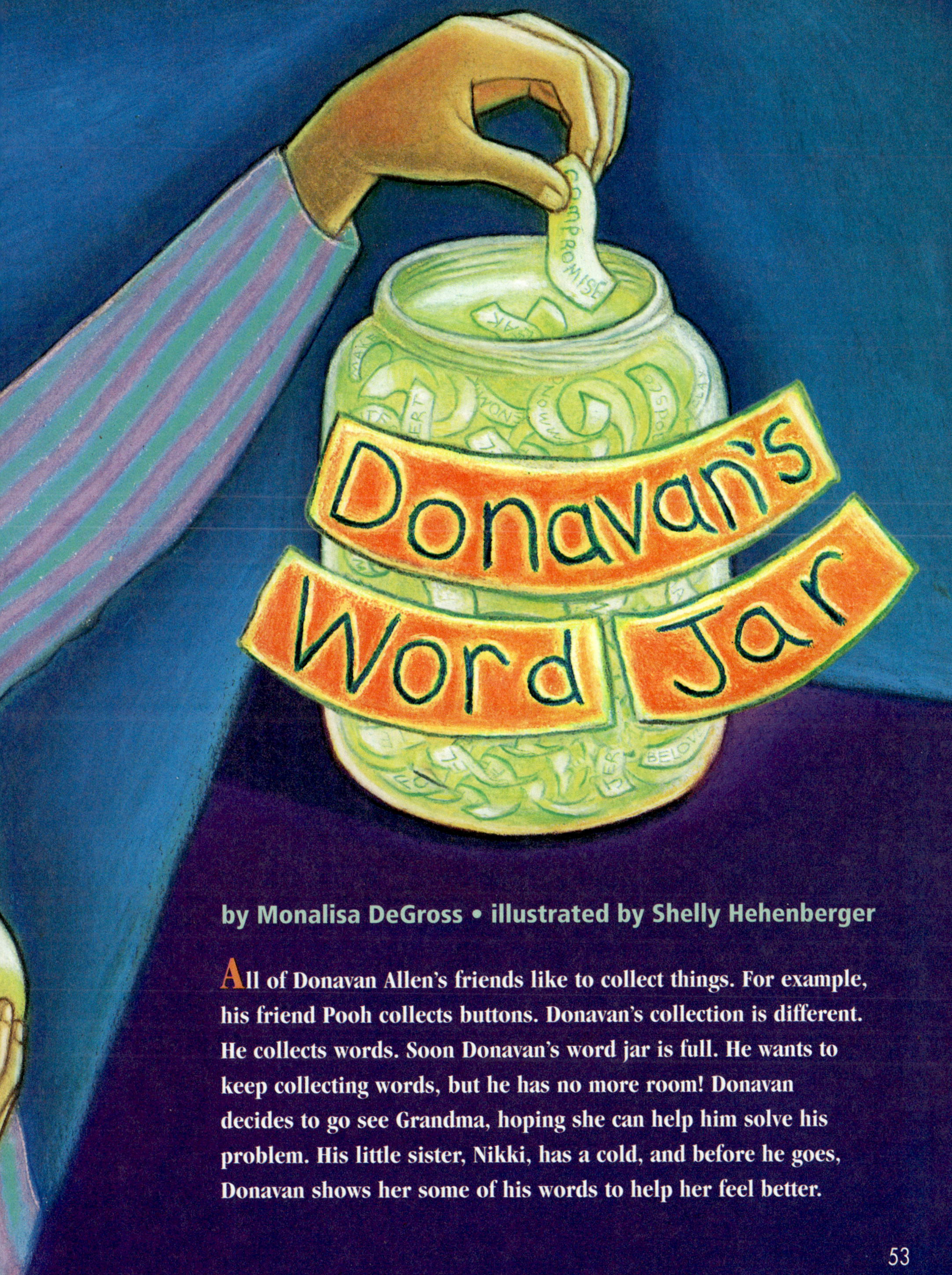

by Monalisa DeGross • illustrated by Shelly Hehenberger

All of Donavan Allen's friends like to collect things. For example, his friend Pooh collects buttons. Donavan's collection is different. He collects words. Soon Donavan's word jar is full. He wants to keep collecting words, but he has no more room! Donavan decides to go see Grandma, hoping she can help him solve his problem. His little sister, Nikki, has a cold, and before he goes, Donavan shows her some of his words to help her feel better.

Donavan was reading when he heard his father's footsteps in the hall. He got up from his chair and tiptoed across the room. He didn't want Nikki to wake up. They had played with his words until she picked the word LULLABY. To give her a hint, Donavan sang her a song. Nikki was so tired from playing that she fell asleep.

Donavan's father opened the door and peeped into Nikki's room. Donavan put his finger to his lips to keep his father from speaking. He picked up his jar and followed his father down the stairs and into the kitchen.

"How are you doing, partner?" his father asked.

"Fine, and Nikki's feeling a lot better," Donavan said quickly. Before his father could ask another question, Donavan rushed on. "Can I go over to Grandma's and visit? It's really important." Donavan didn't want to waste another minute. He had had fun keeping Nikki company, but now he wanted to get his problem solved.

"Okay, but you watch yourself crossing the streets in the rain," his dad said. "And Donavan, why don't you ask your grandma if she's free to come to dinner tonight? Tell her I'm doing the cooking," he added.

"I will," Donavan called over his shoulder. He was already pulling on his shiny green slicker, rain hat and yellow rubber boots. He tucked his word jar in the crook of his arm. He thought if his grandma could see his problem, it might help her to come up with a great idea. Donavan opened the kitchen door and stepped out into the steady drizzle.

Donavan pushed open the heavy glass doors to the Mellow View Apartments. He smiled at Mr. Bill Gut, the security guard, as he signed his name in the guest book.

After lunch, Donavan set his jar on the dining room table and explained his problem to his grandma. When he finished talking, he sat back in his chair and waited for her solution.

Grandma reached over and plucked a few slips of paper from Donavan's jar. She looked at a slip of paper and laughed.

"Donnie," Grandma said, "do you remember when Pooh traded your ice-cream cone for a broken kite?"

"I won't ever forget that," Donavan said, frowning. Grandma showed him the word BAMBOOZLE, and they both laughed. "And this word EMPORIUM," Grandma said shaking her head slowly. "It makes me think of long ago, when I was a young girl. I used to buy licorice at Mr. McCready's store." She selected another word from the jar. "Donnie, where did you get this word?" she asked. She was surprised to see KALEIDOSCOPE written on the slip of paper. "I haven't seen one of those in years. I wonder if kids still play with them."

"I have never seen a kaleidoscope, Grandma, but I saw a picture of one in an old catalog. That's where I found the word," Donavan answered.

Grandma read several more words before she looked at Donavan over the rims of her wire glasses.

"Donnie," she said, "you sure have got yourself a treasure here. This is a wonderful collection of words." Donavan smiled and sat up a little straighter.

Grandma's praise made him feel good, but Donavan still needed a solution to his problem.

"Do you see my problem, Grandma?" he asked. "I thought of getting a larger jar, but that would only get full, too."

"Well, honey, what do other collectors do when their collections grow too large?" she asked.

"I dunno," Donavan said. He thought about it for a minute. "Well, Pooh collects buttons, but he never gets too many because he trades them for other things."

"Like what?" Grandma asked.

"Sometimes he trades for a poster, or for a few comics. Once he traded three buttons for a T-shirt," Donavan explained.

"You think you could do that?" Grandma asked.

"No, Grandma, I can't think of anything I could get worth my words," he said. "And I really don't want to give any of my words away," he added.

Grandma settled back in her chair. She didn't say anything for a long while, and Donavan began to feel a little uneasy. Maybe, just maybe, his grandma didn't have a solution. She dipped her hand back into the word jar and pulled out a few more words.

"There are some words in this jar that I know folks living here could use," she said. Donavan slipped to the edge of his chair and wondered what his grandma was going to say. She continued.

"Now, I like the word PERSNICKETY. That word fits Miz Marylou to a T. That woman has to have everything she does just right." Grandma slipped another word from the jar. "CANTANKEROUS—that's a perfect word for our guard, Bill Gut.

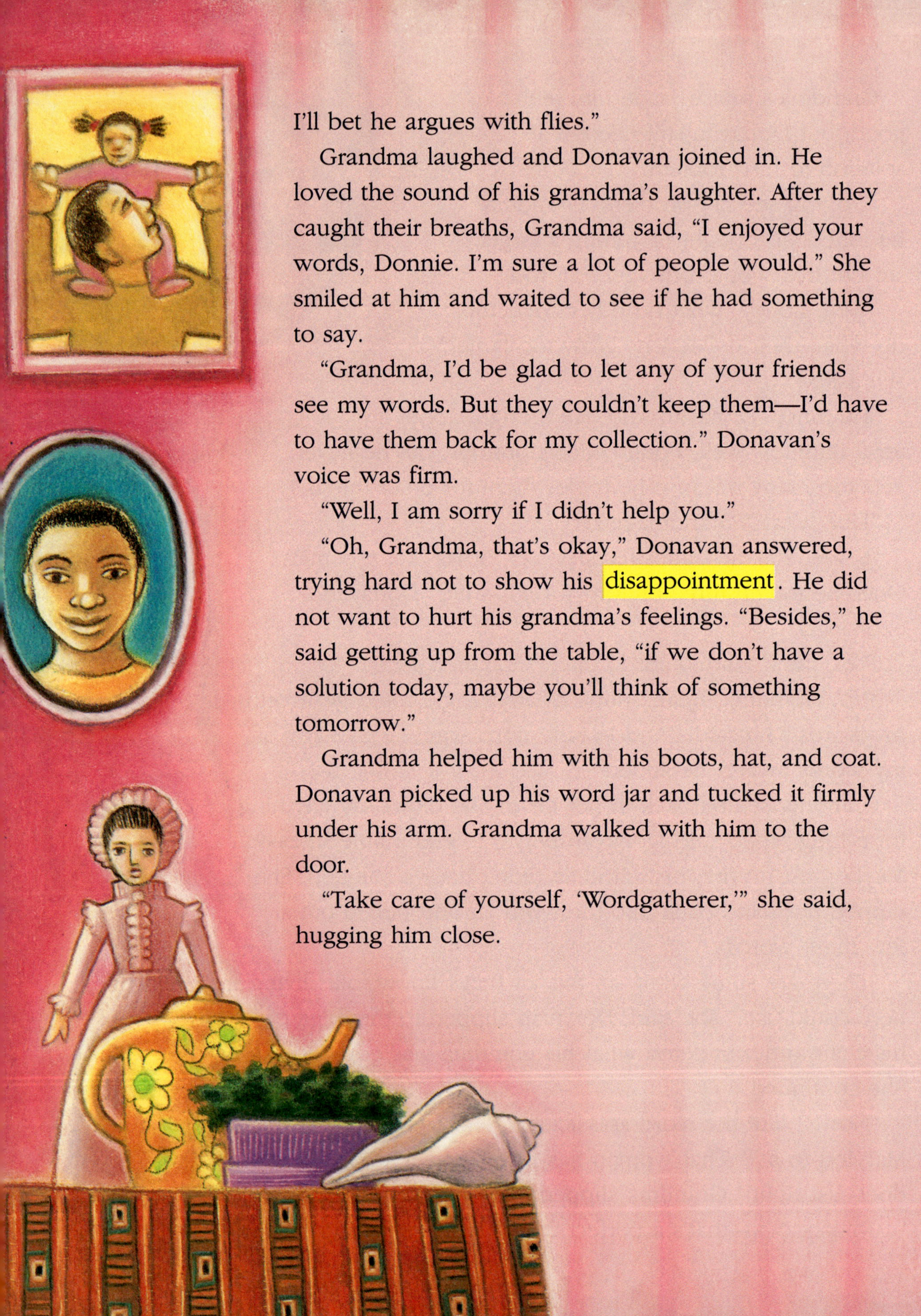

I'll bet he argues with flies."

Grandma laughed and Donavan joined in. He loved the sound of his grandma's laughter. After they caught their breaths, Grandma said, "I enjoyed your words, Donnie. I'm sure a lot of people would." She smiled at him and waited to see if he had something to say.

"Grandma, I'd be glad to let any of your friends see my words. But they couldn't keep them—I'd have to have them back for my collection." Donavan's voice was firm.

"Well, I am sorry if I didn't help you."

"Oh, Grandma, that's okay," Donavan answered, trying hard not to show his disappointment. He did not want to hurt his grandma's feelings. "Besides," he said getting up from the table, "if we don't have a solution today, maybe you'll think of something tomorrow."

Grandma helped him with his boots, hat, and coat. Donavan picked up his word jar and tucked it firmly under his arm. Grandma walked with him to the door.

"Take care of yourself, 'Wordgatherer,'" she said, hugging him close.

Welcom

In the elevator, Donavan thought about his word jar. It had taken months, weeks, days, and hours to fill it. Deciding which words to keep was hard. Then Donavan checked the spelling and made sure he understood what each new word meant. What had his grandma been thinking of? It seemed like she wanted him to just give his words away. He loved his word collection. But he had to think of a way to handle it, now that it was growing so large.

The elevator doors opened, and Donavan stepped into the lounge. He saw three of Grandma's neighbors sitting around the television set. They didn't seem to care much what was on. And there was Mr. Perkins, sitting by the window, looking at the raindrops hitting the windowpane. Miss Millie had a magazine opened on her lap, but she wasn't reading it. Mr. Crawford, the mailman, was sitting on a hassock rubbing his feet. He looked as if he couldn't take another step. No one in the room was talking to or looking at each other, except Miz Marylou and Mr. Bill Gut.

They were standing at the security guard's desk arguing very loudly. No one else was paying any attention to them. As Donavan walked closer he could hear every word they said.

"Miz Marylou, this lounge will open or close when I say so," Mr. Bill Gut said in a gruff voice.

"Well, I am telling you, Bill, that's a mistake. That should be decided by the people who live here," she answered back.

"I'm the guard, and I say what goes on in this lounge," Mr. Bill Gut bellowed.

"Well, I live here and I say that people who live here should set the time," Miz Marylou said almost as loudly.

Donavan looked from one to the other. They both began to shout at the same time, since neither one was listening to what the other was saying. Donavan set his word jar on the corner of the desk and dug around inside the jar until he found a certain word. He tugged Miz Marylou's sleeve and then Mr. Bill's jacket. They both looked down, surprised to see Donavan standing there.

"I think you two need this word," Donavan said in a stern voice.

They both looked at the yellow slip of paper in Donavan's hand. Miz Marylou giggled, and Mr. Bill Gut smiled.

"Well, Marylou, what time do you think is a good time to open?" Mr. Bill Gut asked, scratching his head.

"Bill, I checked with a couple of people and they suggested ten o'clock. What do you think of that?" Miz Marylou asked, smiling at Mr. Bill Gut.

Donavan let out a loud sigh of relief. He had come at just the right time—they needed the word COMPROMISE. Miz Marylou and Mr. Bill weren't shouting anymore. They were talking to each other quietly; they were coming to an agreement. That sure made Donavan feel good. His word had been just what they needed.

Donavan suddenly remembered that his father had asked him to invite Grandma to dinner. He ran back to the elevator and pushed the UP button.

"Back so soon?" Grandma asked, opening the door. "I thought you had gone home."

"I forgot to invite you to dinner tonight. Dad is going to cook. Do you want to come around?" Donavan asked.

It didn't take Grandma long to make up her mind. She loved Donavan's father's cooking.

"Well, I certainly do—in fact, why don't I just get my coat and walk with you?" Grandma suggested. "Maybe we could talk about your word jar a little bit more," she said.

Donavan waited while Grandma got her coat and locked her apartment door. She was carrying a big brown paper sack, and he wondered what was in it. As they walked down the hall, Donavan began to tell Grandma about how he had helped Miz Marylou and Mr. Bill Gut.

When Grandma and Donavan got to the lounge, Donavan could not believe what he saw. Grandma's neighbors were up and around, laughing and talking. They all seemed excited. He looked around to see what was going on. Donavan saw that they were waving little yellow slips of paper in their hands.

"MY WORDS! THEY HAVE MY WORDS!" Donavan shouted.

Some people had one slip of paper in their hands, others had two. Mr. Avery was no longer slumped in front of the TV. He was tacking one of Donavan's words up on the bulletin board. Miss Millie was looking up the word on her slip of paper in a pocket dictionary. Donavan looked over at the desk and saw Mrs. Agnes digging into his word jar. There were people in a line behind her laughing and talking. They were waiting to get a word from his jar.

"WHAT'S GOING ON?" Donavan asked, as loud as he could. "GRANDMA! STOP THEM. THEY ARE TAKING MY WORDS!" He turned to his grandma, but she looked just as surprised as he felt.

"Donnie, calm down. They didn't know. You left the jar on the desk," she said in a quiet voice.

"I AM GOING TO GET MY WORD JAR," Donavan said firmly. "EXCUSE ME," he shouted. "EXCUSE ME, MAY I GET PAST?" he yelled, moving through the crowd. He pushed a little, he even shoved a bit. It was no use. Donavan couldn't stop what was happening.

Mr. Crawford, the mailman, passed Donavan and waved his word over his head. "PERSEVERANCE," he called out. "That's just the word I need. Some days I get so tired, I

can hardly make it. I'm going to try just a little harder to keep going," he said, tucking the word in his shirt pocket.

Donavan stopped pushing and stood still.

"Wow! One of my words made Mr. Crawford feel better," Donavan said. He looked around and saw Miss Millie talking to Mr. Foote. Donavan was surprised.

"BOISTEROUS," he heard Miss Millie say in her soft voice. Grandma always told Donavan that Miss Millie was so shy that she hardly ever spoke to anyone.

Mr. Foote, on the other hand, spoke to everyone. "Well, I'll be darned," Mr. Foote said in surprise. "My word is TIMID!"

"Perhaps we should exchange words," Miss Millie suggested.

"Oh, no. Maybe I need to quiet down some. Sometimes I am a bit loud," Mr. Foote said softly.

"You're right, I think I'll keep my word too. I am going to start speaking to people more. I am going to change my ways." Miss Millie's voice sounded like she meant it.

"Did my words do that, make them want to change?" Donavan asked himself in surprise.

All around him, Grandma's neighbors were laughing and talking to each other. They had never acted so lively before.

"Nikki was right. Words can make people feel better," Donavan said quietly.

"Donavan!" Miz Marylou called out, as she walked over and stood next to him. "Your words are wonderful. I just couldn't help myself, after you gave Bill and me a word, I . . . I . . . well, I got carried away. I just gave Mr. Kincaid the word LEISURE. That man works entirely too hard," she said smiling. "And Donavan, people just started coming up and asking for words, and if they didn't get one they wanted, they just traded it." She looked so pleased, it was hard for Donavan not to smile.

Mr. Bill Gut came over and pinched Donavan's cheeks. Mr. Perkins patted his shoulders. Everyone wanted to thank him for sharing his words. Donavan felt as if the sun had come out inside him. Mr. Bill Gut pointed to the empty jar on the desk and said, "Looks like we cleaned you out, young fellow."

When Grandma pushed through the crowd, she looked worried.

"Donnie, are all of your words gone?" she asked. "Honey, I am so sorry, I know you didn't want to give your words away. Maybe you could ask for them back?" she said.

Donavan looked up at her and smiled.

"Grandma, they love my words. The words made them talk to each other. Look," he said, pointing to Mr. Foote and Miss Millie. "They are talking to each other." Donavan was so excited. "And Grandma, Mr. Crawford the mailman doesn't look so tired anymore." Grandma looked around the room and smiled.

"Donnie, you know, Mr. Mike got the word CHORTLE, and I actually heard him giggle," she said laughing. "But, Donnie, they didn't give you anything for your words." Grandma was still worried.

"Yes, they did. They made me feel like a magician. My words changed them." The sunshine Donavan felt inside was shining all over his face.

1. What decision does Donavan make about his word collection? What causes him to change his mind?
2. What idea do you think the author wants readers to get from this story?
3. Why does Donavan feel **disappointment** after he talks to Grandma?
4. Which of the words from Donavan's jar do you like best? Why do you like this word?
5. When did you use a reading strategy to figure out a word in this story? Give an example to show how the strategy was helpful to you.

Monalisa DeGross

"How did you become a writer?"

When I was younger, I was always trying to create something. As an adult, I found that when I created stories in my head and wrote them down, I was creating stories for picture books and chapter books.

"Your new book is* Grandaddy's Street Songs. *Is there a message in that?"

Yes. I want kids to understand the wonderful and powerful relationship that can be found from knowing and interacting with someone from another generation.

Shelly Hehenberger

As a child, Shelly Hehenberger began telling stories through pictures. She enjoys illustrating children's books and has received much praise for her artwork.

Shelly Hehenberger is also a part-time instructor for children and adults at the Cincinnati Art Academy. She loves art and says, "I don't know what it would be like not to be an artist."

Genre
Poem

I Love the Look of Words

Popcorn leaps, popping from the floor
of a hot black skillet
and into my mouth.
Black words leap,
snapping from the white
page. Rushing into my eyes. Sliding
into my brain which gobbles them
the way my tongue and teeth
chomp the buttered popcorn.

When I have stopped reading,
ideas from the words stay stuck
in my mind, like the sweet
smell of butter perfuming my
fingers long after the popcorn
is finished.

I love the book and the look of words
the weight of ideas that popped into my mind
I love the tracks
of new thinking in my mind.

by Maya Angelou
illustrated by Tom Feelings

ALA Notable Book
Coretta Scott King Award

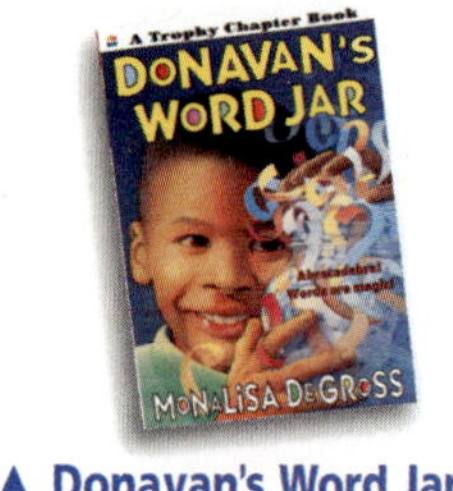

▲ Donavan's Word Jar

Making Connections

Text to Self • Text to Text • Text To World

Compare Texts

NC STANDARDS: ELA 2.04b identify theme, 3.02 analyze/compare texts, 3.06 conduct research using a variety of tools

1. What challenge does Donavan face, and what does he learn from it? INTERPRETATION / EVALUATING
2. Compare the illustration on page 61 with the illustration on page 69. What change does the artist show? CRITICAL STANCE / ANALYZING
3. What viewpoint is shared by the authors of the story and the poem? CRITICAL STANCE / EVALUATING
4. Think of another story in which a character learns something about sharing. How is that story like and unlike this one? CONNECTIONS / ANALYZING
5. If you wanted to start your own word collection, where might you look for interesting and unusual words? INTERPRETATION / EVALUATING

Explain an Idea

Writing CONNECTION

Donavan helps the senior citizens in his grandmother's apartment building. How could you help the senior citizens in your community? Choose your best idea, and write a paragraph explaining what you could do and why it would be helpful. Use a graphic organizer like this one to plan.

Ways to Help Senior Citizens

NC STANDARDS: ELA 2.02e interact with text/connect text to own experiences, 4.02a use oral language to communicate with others

Create a Postcard

Social Studies CONNECTION

Donavan's grandmother keeps postcards that friends have sent her from faraway places. Create a postcard that a visitor to your region might send to someone who lives far away. On one side of an index card, draw a picture of a special feature of your region. On the other side, write a brief description of the picture and tell why the feature it shows is important.

Make a Line Graph

Math CONNECTION

After Donavan has given away all of his words, he will have to rebuild his word collection. If Donavan adds 10 words to his collection each day, in 10 days he will have 100 words. On a sheet of graph paper, set up a graph like the one below. Then make a line graph to show how Donavan's word collection grows over the 10-day period.

Number of Words: 100, 90, 80, 70, 60, 50, 40, 30, 20, 10

Days: 1, 2, 3, 4, 5, 6, 7, 8, 9, 10

NC STANDARDS: Math 3.01 use coordinates to locate points and draw figures, 4.01 collect/organize/analyze/display data to solve problems

▲ Donavan's Word Jar

Prefixes, Suffixes, and Roots

A **prefix** is a word part added to the beginning of a root word or a root. A **suffix** is a word part added to the end of a root word or a root. A **root** is the basic part of a word that gives the word its meaning. It must be added to other word parts to make a word.

Look at the underlined words in these sentences:

Donavan likes it when Grandma retells his favorite story.
Donavan has a word collection.

Each underlined word is formed by adding a word part to the beginning or end of a word.

Prefix	Root Word	Suffix	New Word
re ("again")	tell ("to say aloud")		retell—"to say aloud again"
	collect ("to gather")	-ion ("the act, process, or result of")	collection—"the result of gathering"

Now look at the underlined word in this sentence.

Donavan's dad talks to Grandma on the telephone.

This word is made by combining two roots. *Telephone* is made up of the root of *tele* ("from afar") and the root *phon* ("sound").

Visit *The Learning Site!*
www.harcourtschool.com

See *Skills and Activities*

Test Prep

Prefixes, Suffixes, and Roots

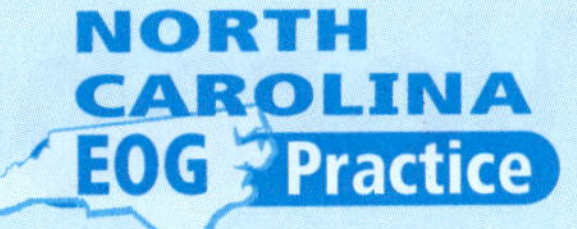

NC STANDARDS: ELA 1.02 use roots/prefixes/suffixes to decode meanings

Focus Skill

▶ **Read the passage. Then answer the questions.**

When Karonna comes upon an interesting word, she writes it down in her notebook. Last week her friend Lucy got a new microscope to help her study small insects. Karonna's grandma told her that the word was formed from the Greek roots micro, which means "small," and scope, which means "see."

Sometimes Karonna's notebook gets untidy because she has too many words. It's a good thing the notebook is refillable. She just takes out the old pages and puts in new ones.

COGNITION / KNOWLEDGE

1. What does the word microscope mean?

A a person who studies insects

B a kind of insect

C an instrument used to see small objects

D an instrument used to hear quiet sounds

Tip Reread the part of the passage that tells the meanings of the roots that are combined to form the word.

COGNITION / KNOWLEDGE

2. What does the word untidy mean?

F not tidy

G tidy again

H more tidy

J too tidy

Tip Identify the prefix and the root word. Then think about how the prefix changes the meaning of the root word.

▲ My Name Is María Isabel

- pageant
- rehearsals
- restless
- tropical
- troublesome
- attentively

Vocabulary Power

Putting on a play can be a lot of fun, but it isn't always easy. Look at the steps these fourth graders took to make their play a success.

Anna: Let's put on a **pageant**!

Kyle: What's a pageant?

Anna: It's a show about events or stories from long ago.

Marco: I have another idea. We can make up a play about space travel!

Kyle: That sounds like fun.

Anna: Let's get started!

(One week later)

Kyle: I'm getting tired of having **rehearsals** every day. How many of these practices are we going to have, anyway?

Marco: I wish we could move around more. I get **restless** when I have to sit still.

Kyle: This spacesuit is too hot! I'm so warm that I feel I'm in a **tropical** country.

Anna: Why is everybody being so **troublesome**? Let's stop causing problems and get back to work!

(After the play)

Kyle: I think the audience really liked our play!

Marco: Yes, you could tell they were interested. They listened **attentively** so they wouldn't miss a word.

Anna: Let's do another show soon!

Vocabulary-Writing
CONNECTION

Think about a **pageant** you saw or one in which you had a part. Write a paragraph describing the pageant.

Genre

Realistic Fiction

Realistic fiction tells about characters and events that are like people and events in real life.

In this selection, look for

- **A main character who overcomes a challenge**
- **Challenges and problems that might happen in real life**

My Name Is María Isabel

by Alma Flor Ada • illustrated by José Ortega

María Isabel Salazar López is proud of being named for her Puerto Rican grandmothers. She has a problem, though. Her teacher calls her Mary López because there are two other Marías in the class. María Isabel sometimes doesn't recognize her new name. She does not have a part in the play *Amahl and the Night Visitors* because the teacher called on Mary López when she assigned parts, and María Isabel didn't respond. The play is the main part of the school's Winter Pageant. Every day, the pageant draws closer, and María Isabel knows her parents are eager to see her in the show.

Everything at school now revolved around plans for the Winter Pageant. The class was making wreaths and lanterns. The teacher explained to the class that Christmas is celebrated differently in different countries, and that many people don't celebrate Christmas at all. They talked about Santa Claus, and how he is called Saint Nicholas in some countries and Father Christmas in others. The class also talked about the Jewish feast of Hanukkah that celebrates the rededication of the Temple of Jerusalem, and about the special meaning of the nine candles of the Hanukkah menorah.

The teacher had asked everyone to bring in pictures or other things having to do with the holidays. A lot of kids brought in photographs of their families by their Christmas trees. Mayra brought in pictures of New Year's Day in Santo Domingo. Michelle brought in a picture of herself sitting on Santa's lap when she was little. Gabriel brought in photos of the Three Kings' Day parade in Miami, Florida. He had been there last year, when he went to visit his Cuban grandmother. Marcos brought in a piñata shaped like a green parrot that his uncle had brought back from Mexico. Emmanuel showed everyone a photo album of his family's trip to Israel, and Esther brought in cards her grandfather had sent her from Jerusalem.

One day, Suni Paz came to the school. She sang Christmas songs from different countries and taught the class to sing a Hanukkah song, "The Candles of Hanukkah."

María Isabel went home humming softly "Hanukkah . . . Hanukkah . . . Let us celebrate." The bus trip seemed a lot shorter as the song ran through her head. It almost felt as if she had traveled to all those different countries and had celebrated all those different holidays.

María Isabel was still singing while she made dinner and set the table:

"With our menorah,
Fine potato latkes,
Our clay trumpets,
Let us celebrate."

Her voice filled the empty kitchen. María Isabel was so pleased she promised herself that she'd make a snowman the next time it snowed. And she'd get it finished before the garbage men picked up the trash and dirtied up the snow.

But after Suni Paz's visit to the school, the days seemed to drag by more and more slowly. María Isabel didn't have anything to do during rehearsals, since she didn't have a part in *Amahl*.

The teacher decided that after the play the actors would sing some holiday songs, including María Isabel's favorite about the Hanukkah candles. Since she didn't have a part, María Isabel wouldn't be asked to sing either.

It didn't seem to matter much to Tony and Jonathan, the other two kids who weren't in the play. They spent rehearsal time reading comics or whispering to each other. Neither boy spoke to María Isabel, and she was too shy to say anything to them.

The only fun she had was reading her library book. Somehow her problems seemed so small compared to Wilbur the pig's. He was in danger of becoming the holiday dinner. María Isabel felt the only difference was that the characters in books always seemed to find answers to their problems, while she couldn't figure out what to do about her own.

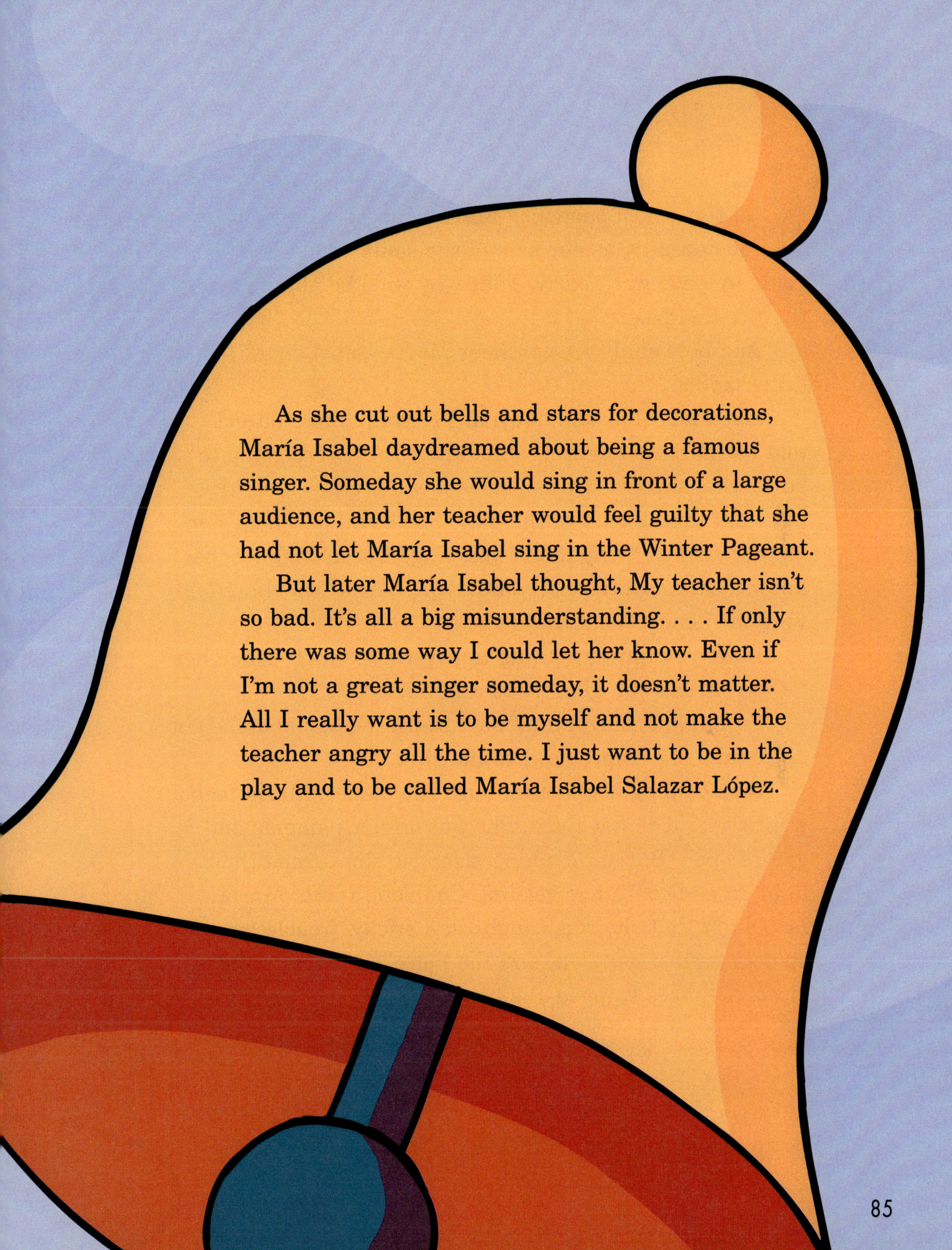

As she cut out bells and stars for decorations, María Isabel daydreamed about being a famous singer. Someday she would sing in front of a large audience, and her teacher would feel guilty that she had not let María Isabel sing in the Winter Pageant.

But later María Isabel thought, My teacher isn't so bad. It's all a big misunderstanding. . . . If only there was some way I could let her know. Even if I'm not a great singer someday, it doesn't matter. All I really want is to be myself and not make the teacher angry all the time. I just want to be in the play and to be called María Isabel Salazar López.

"I've asked my boss if I can leave work early the day of the school pageant," María Isabel's mother said one evening as she served the soup. "Papá is also going to leave work early. That way we'll be able to bring the rice and beans."

"And best of all, we can hear María Isabel sing," her father added.

María Isabel looked down at her soup. She had not told her parents anything. She knew they were going to be very disappointed when they saw the other kids in her class taking part in the play. She could just hear her mother asking, "Why didn't you sing? Doesn't the teacher know what a lovely voice you have?" María Isabel ate her soup in silence. What could she say?

"Don't you have anything to say, Chabelita?" asked her father. "Aren't you glad we're coming?"

"Sure, Papá, sure I am," said María Isabel, and she got up to take her empty bowl to the sink.

After helping her mother with the dishes, María Isabel went straight to her room. She put on her pajamas and got into bed. But she couldn't sleep, so she turned the light on and continued reading *Charlotte's Web*. María Isabel felt that she was caught in a sticky, troublesome spider's web of her own, and the more she tried to break loose, the more trapped she became.

When the librarian had told her that she would like the book, María Isabel had felt that they were sharing a secret. Now as she turned the pages, she thought that maybe the secret was that *everyone* has problems. She felt close to poor little Wilbur, being fattened up for Christmas dinner without even knowing it. He was a little like her parents, who were so eager to go to the pageant, not knowing what was waiting for them.

"It just isn't fair that this can't be a happy time for all of us!" María Isabel said out loud. She sighed. Then she turned off the light, snuggled under her blanket, and fell asleep trying to figure out a way to save Wilbur from becoming Christmas dinner.

Two days were left until the pageant. The morning was cloudy and gray. On the way to school, María Isabel wondered if it was going to snow. Maybe she would be able to make that snowman. But shortly after she got to school, it started to drizzle.

Since they couldn't go outside, the students spent their time rehearsing. No one made a mistake. Melchior didn't forget what he had to say to Amahl's mother. Amahl dropped his crutch only once. Best of all, though, the shepherds remembered when they were supposed to enter, without bumping into the Three Kings.

Even Tony and Jonathan seemed interested in the play. They volunteered to help carry the manger and the shepherds' baskets on- and offstage.

Satisfied with the final rehearsal, the teacher decided there was time for one last class exercise before vacation. "It's been a couple of days since we've done some writing," she said when the students returned to class. "The new year is a time for wishes. Sometimes wishes come true; sometimes they don't. But it's important to have wishes and, most of all, to know what you really want. I'd like you all to take out some paper and write an essay titled 'My Greatest Wish.'"

María Isabel sighed and put away *Charlotte's Web*. Charlotte had just died, and María Isabel wondered what was going to happen to the sack of eggs that Wilbur had saved, and when Charlotte's babies would be born. But María Isabel would have to wait to find out. She bit down on her pencil and wrote: "My greatest wish . . ."

This shouldn't be so hard, María Isabel thought. If I finish writing early, I can probably finish my book. She started to write: "My greatest wish is to make a snowman. . . ."

María Isabel read over what she had just written, and realized that it wasn't what she really wanted. She put the paper aside, took out a new sheet, and wrote down the title again. "My greatest wish is to have a part in *Amahl*. . . ."

María Isabel stopped writing again. She thought, Would Charlotte have said that her greatest wish was to save Wilbur? Or would she have wished for something impossible, like living until the next spring and getting to know her children? The teacher just said that wishes don't always come true. If I'm going to wish for something, it should be something really worth wishing for.

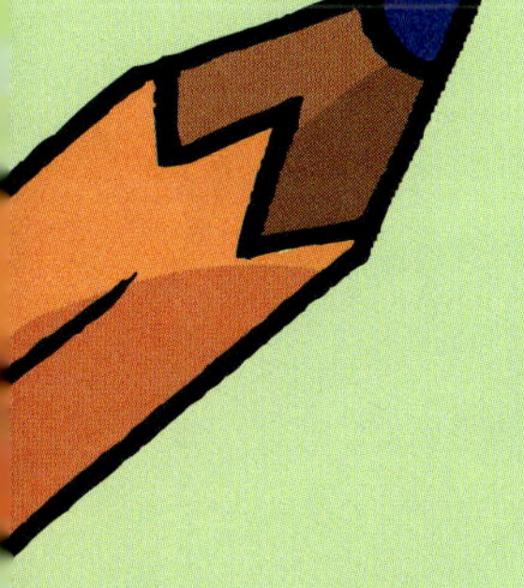

María Isabel took out a third sheet of paper and wrote down the title again. This time, she didn't stop writing until she got to the bottom of the page.

My Greatest Wish

When I started to write I thought my greatest wish was to make a snowman. Then I thought my greatest wish was to have a part in the Winter Pageant. But I think my greatest wish is to be called María Isabel Salazar López. When that was my name, I felt proud of being named María like my papá's mother, and Isabel, like my grandmother Chabela. She is saving money so that I can study and not have to spend my whole life in a kitchen like her. I was Salazar like my papá and my grandpa Antonio, and López, like my grandfather Manuel. I never knew him but he could really tell stories. I know because my mother told me.

If I was called María Isabel Salazar López, I could listen better in class because it's easier to hear than Mary López. Then I could have said that I wanted a part in the play. And when the rest of the kids sing, my mother and father wouldn't have to ask me why I didn't sing, even though I like the song about the Hanukkah candles so much.

The rest of the class had already handed in their essays and were cleaning out their desks to go home when María Isabel got up. She quietly went to the front of the room and put her essay on the teacher's desk. María Isabel didn't look up at the teacher, so she didn't see the woman smiling at her. She hurried back to her desk to get her things and leave.

Holiday spirit was everywhere at school the next day. The paper wreaths and lanterns the class had made were hung up all over the room. The teacher had put the "greatest wish" essays up on the bulletin board, next to the cutouts of Santa Claus, the Three Kings, and a menorah.

All the students were restless. Marta Pérez smiled when María Isabel sat down next to her. "Look at the pretty Christmas card I got from my cousin in Santo Domingo," she said excitedly. María Isabel looked at the tropical Christmas scene, all trimmed in flowers. But she couldn't answer Marta because the teacher had started to speak.

"We're going to do one last rehearsal because there's a small change in the program."

The rest of the kids listened attentively, but María Isabel just kept looking down at her desk. After all, she had nothing to do with the pageant.

Then she heard the teacher say, “María Isabel, María Isabel Salazar López . . .” María Isabel looked up in amazement.

“Wouldn’t you like to lead the song about the Hanukkah candles?” the teacher said with a wide grin. “Why don’t you start by yourself, and then everyone else can join in. Go ahead and start when you’re ready.”

María Isabel walked nervously up to the front of the room and stood next to the teacher, who was strumming her guitar. Then she took a deep breath and began to sing her favorite holiday song.

While her mother was getting the rice and beans ready that night, Mr. Salazar called María Isabel over to him. “Since you can’t wear makeup yet, Chabelita, I’ve brought you something else that I think you’ll like.” In the palm of his hand were two barrettes for her hair. They were shaped like butterflies and gleamed with tiny stones.

“Oh, Papá. They’re so pretty! Thank you!” María Isabel exclaimed. She hugged her father and ran to her room to put them on.

At school the next day, María Isabel stood in the center of the stage. She was wearing her special yellow dress, a pair of new shoes, and the shining butterflies. She spoke clearly to the audience. “My name is María Isabel Salazar López. I’m going to sing a song about the Jewish feast of Hanukkah, that celebrates the rededication of the Temple in Jerusalem.” The music started, and María Isabel began to sing.

The Candles of Hanukkah

One little candle,
Two little candles,
Three little candles,
Let us celebrate.
Four little candles,
Five little candles,
Six little candles,
Let us celebrate.
Hanukkah, Hanukkah,
Let us celebrate.
Seven little candles,
Eight little candles,
Nine little candles,
Let us celebrate.
Hanukkah, Hanukkah,
Let us celebrate.
With our menorah,
Fine potato latkes,
Our clay trumpets,
Let us celebrate.
With our family,
With our friends,
With our presents,
Let us celebrate.

And the butterflies in María Isabel's hair sparkled under the stage lights so much that it seemed that they might just take off and fly.

Think and Respond

1. What two things does María Isabel want? How does she get them?
2. How do you know that the teacher does not mean to hurt María Isabel's feelings and is sorry for her mistake?
3. How does reading *Charlotte's Web* help María Isabel with her problems?
4. Do you think a **pageant** is a good way to celebrate holidays of different cultures? Explain you answer.
5. How did using a reading strategy help you as you read this story?

Meet the Author

Alma Flor Ada

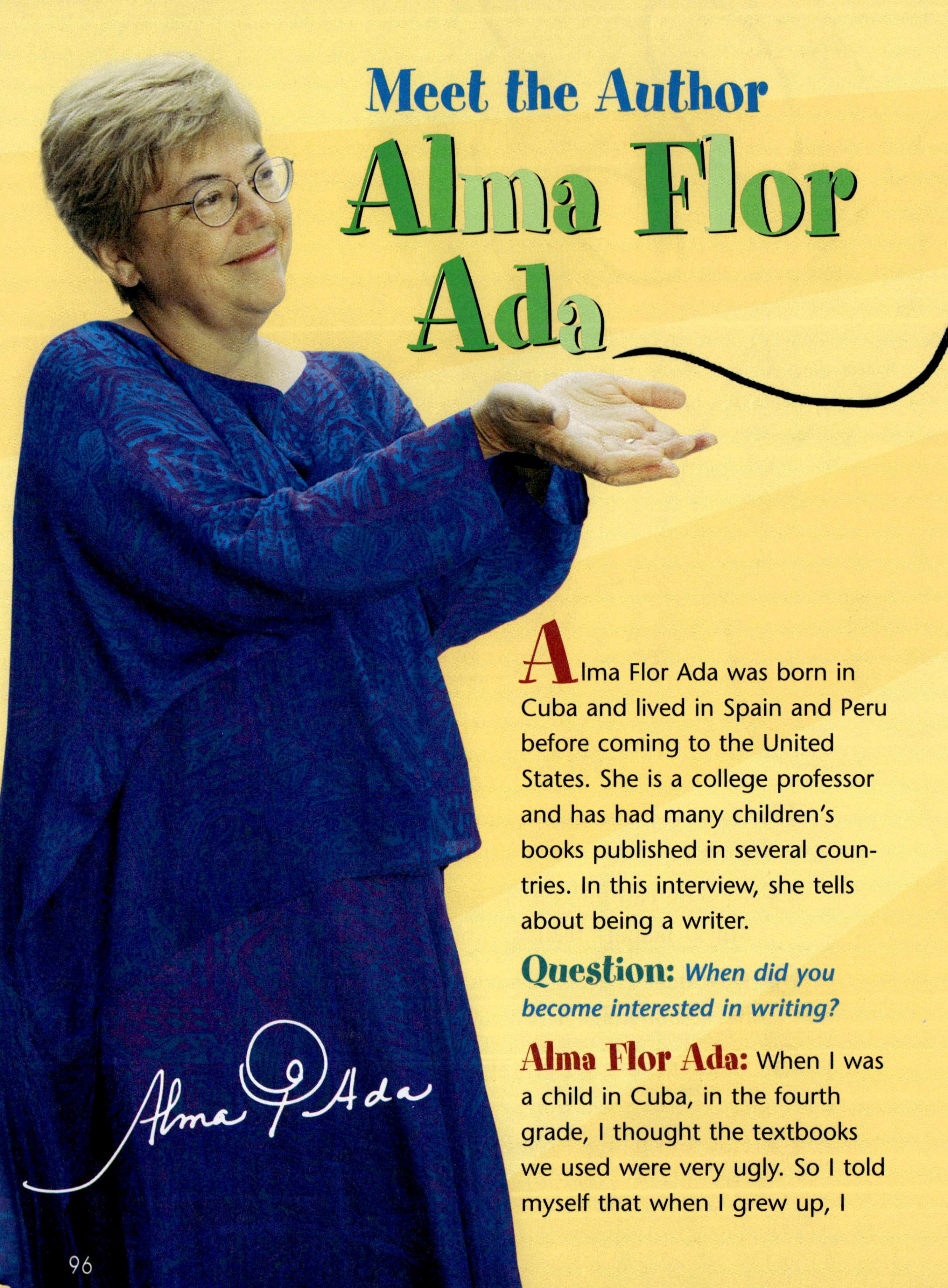

Alma Flor Ada was born in Cuba and lived in Spain and Peru before coming to the United States. She is a college professor and has had many children's books published in several countries. In this interview, she tells about being a writer.

Question: ***When did you become interested in writing?***

Alma Flor Ada: When I was a child in Cuba, in the fourth grade, I thought the textbooks we used were very ugly. So I told myself that when I grew up, I would write books that were fun to look at. Then, as an adult, I went to college and graduate school and did scholarly writing.

One day when my daughter was about five, she said, "I am making a book. Do you know why?" I replied, "No, why?" And she said, "Because the books you make are so ugly!" That brought everything back to me. I decided to collect the poems and stories of my childhood, and that was my first project. When I began, I thought of myself as a collector of stories. I didn't know that I was also a writer, but that is what I became.

Question: ***Was there anything about your childhood that prepared you to become a writer?***

Ada: My grandmother was a wonderful storyteller. She could make her stories so real that I felt I was actually there. My father loved to tell stories, too. Every night he invented a new story to explain something, such as how fire was used for the first time or how someone thought of making shoes. My father was a professor and my mother was a teacher, so we always had books in our home. I liked poetry and fairy-tale books when I was very young. Later I liked to read about real people just like me.

Question: ***How did you get the idea for* My Name Is María Isabel*?***

Ada: I wrote the story about María Isabel because I observed a teacher who kept saying a child's name wrong. The child would not correct the teacher out of courtesy and respect, but I knew it hurt. Our name is important to all of us.

Question: ***Do you write in both Spanish and English?***

Ada: Yes, I do. Most of my early books were in Spanish. I wrote *My Name Is María Isabel* in Spanish first. I am happy that most of my books are published both in English and in Spanish.

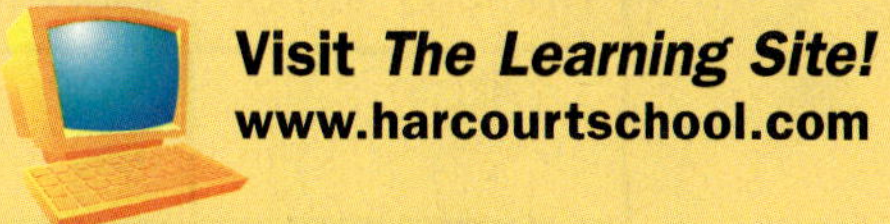

▲ My Name Is María Isabel

Making Connections

Text to Self • Text to Text • Text To World

Compare Texts

NC STANDARDS: ELA 2.02e interact with text/connect text to own experiences, 2.04b identify theme, 3.02 analyze/compare texts, 3.03 examine effects of language/visuals

1. Why do you think the story "My Name Is María Isabel" is in the theme You Can Do It? INTERPRETATION / EVALUATING
2. Why does page 90 look different from the other pages of the story? COGNITION / EVALUATING
3. Think of another story in which a character writes something. Is what that character writes as important to the story as María Isabel's essay? Explain. CONNECTIONS / ANALYZING
4. What else have you read that deals with the importance of your feelings? How is it similar to "My Name Is María Isabel"? How is it different? CONNECTIONS / ANALYZING
5. "My Name Is María Isabel" mentions holiday traditions. Which one are you interested in learning more about? Why? INTERPRETATION / EVALUATING

Write a Book Review

Writing CONNECTION

In the weeks before the Winter Pageant, María Isabel reads and enjoys *Charlotte's Web*. Write a review of a book you have read and enjoyed. Give the title and author of the book. Briefly tell what the book is about. Then tell why you liked it. Use a chart like the one below to plan your review.

Title and Author	Important Events	Why I Liked the Book

NC STANDARDS: ELA 3.06 conduct research using a variety of tools, 4.02b use oral language to communicate with others, 4.05 use planning strategies to organize ideas; Social Studies 3.05 describe political/social history of North Carolina and analyze its influence today

Research Your State's Name

Social Studies CONNECTION

María Isabel writes an essay explaining how her parents named her. Find out how your state got its name. You might use an encyclopedia, a social studies book, or a nonfiction book about your state. Use a web to organize your information. Then prepare and present a brief oral report.

How My State Got Its Name

NC STANDARDS: ELA 3.05 use graphs/charts/maps to expand understanding, 3.06 conduct research using a variety of tools

Explain How Snow Forms

Science CONNECTION

In the story, María Isabel wants to make a snowman. Look in an encyclopedia or a science book to find out how snow forms. Then make a sequence diagram like the one below, and fill it in with the information you find. Use your sequence diagram to help you write a paragraph explaining how snow forms or to help you create a graphic aid showing this.

Making Connections

▲ **My Name Is María Isabel**

Narrative elements include the characters, setting, and plot of a story. To understand the plot of a story, you need to identify the **problem**, or **conflict**, and the **resolution**. Ask yourself what problem the main character faces and how the problem gets solved. Paying attention to the order of events can help you understand the steps a character takes to solve his or her problem.

Look at this problem-and-resolution chart for "My Name Is María Isabel." You can use a similar chart to help you figure out the problem and resolution in other fictional stories.

Problem
María Isabel wants to take part in the Winter Pageant at school.

↓

Problem-Solving Steps

1. María Isabel writes an essay that explains why she wants a part.
2. Her teacher reads the essay and gives her a part in the pageant.

↓

Resolution
María Isabel sings her favorite song in the school pageant.

Visit *The Learning Site!*
www.harcourtschool.com

See *Skills and Activities*

Test Prep

Narrative Elements

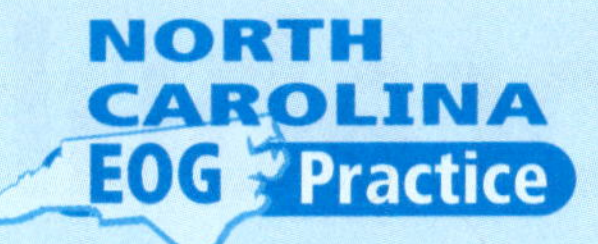

NC STANDARDS: ELA 2.04c
identify main idea/details

▶ **Read the story. Then answer the questions.**

"Are you going to try out for the school play?" asked Dwight.

"No," Steve replied.

Eddie laughed. "Plays are silly," he said.

Dwight had been looking forward to the play. Now he had his doubts. Maybe others would feel the same way Steve and Eddie did. Dwight was new in the school and wanted to be liked.

When the teacher asked who wanted to try out, Dwight didn't raise his hand. He was surprised to see so many hands raised. Slowly, Dwight raised his hand. Maybe Steve and Eddie would think he was silly, but he thought the play would be fun.

CRITICAL STANCE / INTEGRATING

1. Who is the main character in this story?

A Steve

B Eddie

C Dwight

D the teacher

To identify the main character, ask yourself, "Who is the story mostly about?"

CRITICAL STANCE / INTEGRATING

2. What problem does the main character face?

F He isn't sure whether or not to try out for the play.

G He thinks plays are silly.

H He doesn't have any friends.

J He wants to do whatever Steve and Eddie do.

Ask yourself what is causing the main character to feel unhappy or unsure of what to do.

▲ Lou Gehrig: The Luckiest Man

Vocabulary Power

- **immigrants**
- **courageous**
- **salary**
- **valuable**
- **tremendous**
- **appreciation**
- **sportsmanship**
- **modest**

The selection "Lou Gehrig: The Luckiest Man" tells about a famous baseball player whose family came to the United States from Germany. Many people feel lucky to live in the United States of America.

The United States is sometimes called a nation of **immigrants** because everyone but Native Americans came here from other lands. Some people came in recent times. Others are here because members of their families were immigrants long ago.

Immigrants have to be **courageous** because it takes bravery to leave your home and travel to a new land. Some came here hoping for a better **salary**, more pay for their work. Others came for the freedom to share their ideas. The laws of our country say that everyone's ideas are **valuable**, or important.

Tremendous numbers of immigrants, millions and millions, have come to the United States from all over the world. It is important to show our **appreciation** for each other's customs, to show that we recognize their value.

Sportsmanship is important when we play games, but showing respect for others should go far beyond sports. We can show respect by treating each other fairly and by acting in a **modest**, not boastful, way. We are lucky to live in this great country built by immigrants from so many lands!

Vocabulary–Writing CONNECTION

Think about someone or something that is important to you. Write a paragraph explaining why this person or thing is **valuable**.

Genre

Biography

A biography is a story about a person's life written by another person.

In this selection, look for

- Information about why the person is important
- Opinions and personal judgments based on facts

LOU GEHRIG

THE LUCKIEST MAN

by
David A. Adler

illustrated by
Terry Widener

NY

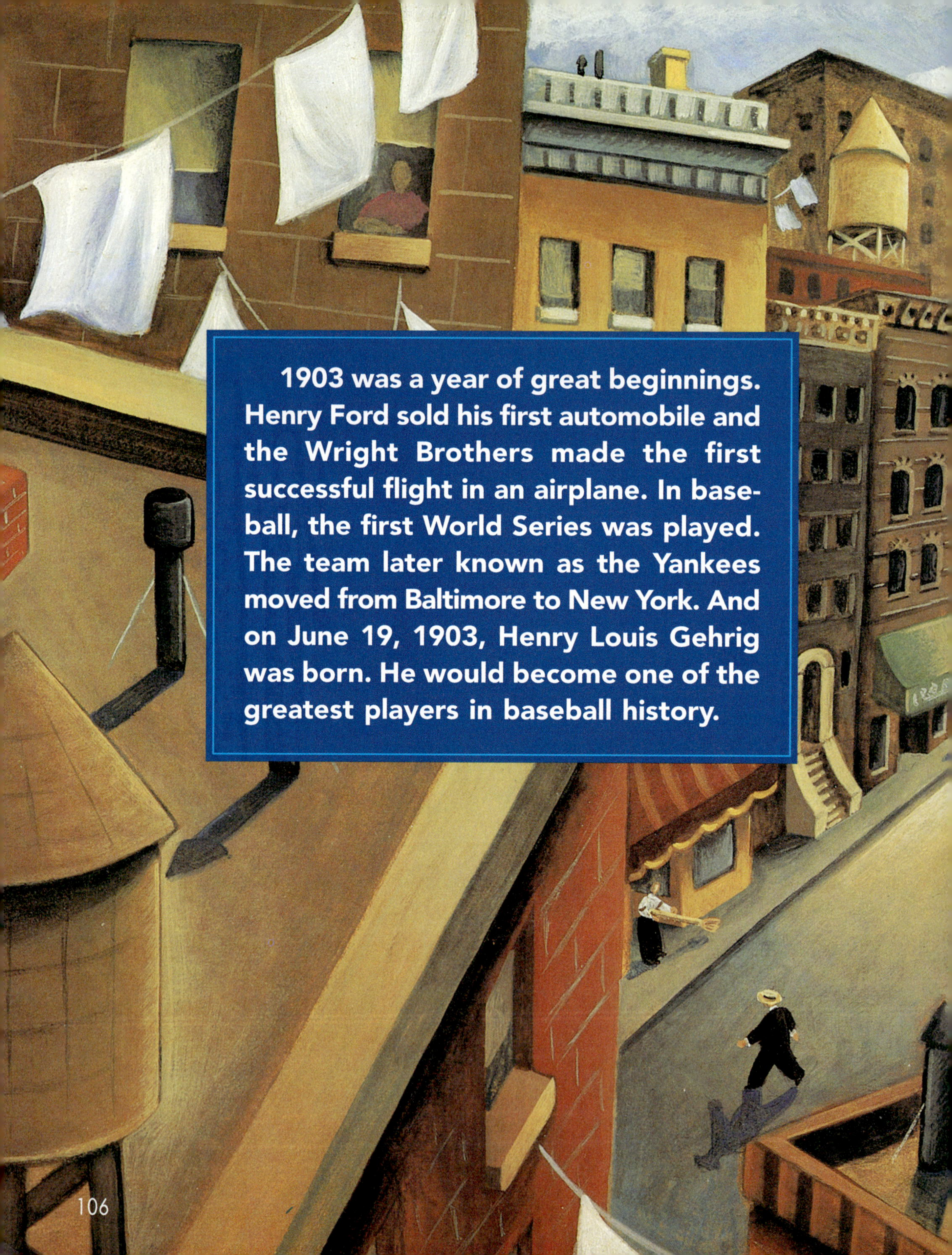

1903 was a year of great beginnings. Henry Ford sold his first automobile and the Wright Brothers made the first successful flight in an airplane. In baseball, the first World Series was played. The team later known as the Yankees moved from Baltimore to New York. And on June 19, 1903, Henry Louis Gehrig was born. He would become one of the greatest players in baseball history.

Lou Gehrig was born in the Yorkville section of New York City. It was an area populated with poor immigrants like his parents, Heinrich and Christina Gehrig, who had come to the United States from Germany.

Christina Gehrig had great hopes for her son Lou. She dreamed that he would attend college and become an accountant or an engineer. She insisted that he study hard. Through eight years of grade school, Lou didn't miss a single day.

Lou's mother thought games and sports were a waste of time. But Lou loved sports. He got up early to play the games he loved—baseball, soccer, and football. He

played until it was time to go to school. In high school Lou was a star on his school's baseball team.

After high school Lou Gehrig went to Columbia University. He was on the baseball team there, too, and on April 26, 1923, a scout for the New York Yankees watched him play. Lou hit two long home runs in that game. Soon after that he was signed to play for the Yankees.

The Yankees offered Lou a $1,500 bonus to sign plus a good salary. His family needed the money. Lou quit college and joined the Yankees. Lou's mother was furious. She was convinced that he was ruining his life.

On June 1, 1925, the Yankee manager sent Lou to bat for the shortstop. The next day Lou played in place of first baseman Wally Pipp. Those were the first two games in what would become an amazing record: For the next fourteen years Lou Gehrig played in 2,130 consecutive Yankee games. The boy who never missed a day of grade school became a man who never missed a game.

Lou Gehrig played despite stomachaches, fevers, a sore arm, back pains, and broken fingers. Lou's constant play earned him the nickname Iron Horse. All he would say about his amazing record was, "That's the way I am."

Lou was shy and modest, but people who watched him knew just how good he was.

In 1927 Lou's teammate Babe Ruth hit sixty home runs, the most hit up to that time in one season. But it was Lou Gehrig who was selected that year by the baseball writers as the American League's Most Valuable Player. He was selected again as the league's MVP in 1936.

Then, during the 1938 baseball season—and for no apparent reason—Lou Gehrig stopped hitting. One newspaper reported that Lou was swinging as hard as he could, but when he hit the ball it didn't go anywhere.

Lou exercised. He took extra batting practice. He even tried changing the way he stood and held his bat. He worked hard during the winter of 1938 and watched his diet.

But the following spring Lou's playing was worse. Time after time he swung at the ball and missed. He had trouble fielding. And he even had problems off the field. In the clubhouse he fell down while he was getting dressed.

Some people said Yankee manager Joe McCarthy should take Lou out of the lineup. But McCarthy refused. He had great respect for Lou and said, "Gehrig plays as long as he wants to play." But Lou wasn't selfish. On May 2, 1939, he told Joe McCarthy, "I'm benching myself . . . for the good of the team."

When reporters asked why he took himself out, Lou didn't say he felt weak or how hard it was for him to run. Lou made no excuses. He just said that he couldn't hit and he couldn't field.

On June 13, 1939, Lou went to the Mayo Clinic in Rochester, Minnesota, to be examined by specialists. On June 19, his thirty-sixth birthday, they told Lou's wife, Eleanor, what was wrong. He was suffering from amyotrophic lateral sclerosis, a deadly disease that affects the central nervous system.

Lou stayed with the team, but he didn't play. He was losing weight. His hair was turning gray. He didn't have to

be told he was dying. He knew it. "I don't have long to go," he told a teammate.

Lou loved going to the games, being in the clubhouse, and sitting with his teammates. Before each game Lou brought the Yankee lineup card to the umpire at home plate. A teammate or coach walked with him, to make sure he didn't fall. Whenever Lou came onto the field, the fans stood up and cheered for brave Lou Gehrig.

But Yankee fans and the team wanted to do more. They wanted Lou to know how deeply they felt about him. So they made July 4, 1939, Lou Gehrig Appreciation Day at Yankee Stadium.

Many of the players from the 1927 Yankees—perhaps the best baseball team ever—came to honor their former teammate. There was a marching band and gifts. Many people spoke, too. Fiorello La Guardia, the mayor of New York City, told

Lou, "You are the greatest prototype of good sportsmanship and citizenship."

When the time came for Lou to thank everyone, he was too moved to speak. But the fans wanted to hear him and chanted, "We want Gehrig! We want Gehrig!"

Dressed in his Yankee uniform, Lou Gehrig walked slowly to the array of microphones. He wiped his eyes, and with his baseball cap in his hands, his head down, he slowly spoke.

"Fans," he said, "for the past two weeks you have been reading about a bad break I got. Yet today I consider myself the luckiest man on the face of the earth."

It was a courageous speech. Lou didn't complain about his terrible illness. Instead he spoke of his many blessings and of the future. "Sure, I'm lucky," he said when he spoke of his years in baseball. "Sure, I'm lucky," he said again when he spoke of his fans and family.

Lou spoke about how good people had been to him. He praised his teammates. He thanked his parents and his wife, whom he called a tower of strength.

The more than sixty thousand fans in Yankee Stadium stood to honor Lou Gehrig. His last words to them—and to the many thousands more sitting by their radios and listening—were, "So I close in saying that I might have had a bad break, but I have an awful lot to live for. Thank you."

Lou stepped back from the microphones and wiped his eyes. The stadium crowd let out a tremendous roar, and Babe Ruth did what many people must have wanted to do that day. He threw his arms around Lou Gehrig and gave him a great warm hug.

The band played the song "I Love You Truly," and the fans chanted, "We love you, Lou."

When Lou Gehrig left the stadium later that afternoon, he told a teammate, "I'm going to remember this day for a long time."

In December 1939 Lou Gehrig was voted into the Baseball Hall of Fame. And the Yankees retired his uniform. No one else on the team would ever wear the number four. It was the first time a major-league baseball team did that to honor one of its players.

Mayor Fiorello La Guardia thought Lou's courage might inspire some of the city's troubled youths to be courageous, too. He offered Lou a job

working with former prisoners as a member of the New York City Parole Commission. Lou had many opportunities to earn more money, but he believed this job would enable him to do something for the city that had given him so much.

Within little more than a year, Lou had to leave his job. He was too weak to keep working. He stayed at home, unable to do the simplest task.

Lou had many visitors. He didn't speak to them of his illness or of dying. When he saw one friend visibly upset by the way he looked, Lou told him not to worry. "I'll gradually get better," he said. In cards to his friends Lou wrote, "We have much to be thankful for."

By the middle of May 1941, Lou hardly left his bed. Then on Monday, June 2, 1941, just after ten o'clock at night, Lou Gehrig died. He was thirty-seven years old.

On June 4 the Yankee game was canceled because of rain. Some people thought it was fitting that the Yankees did not play; this was the day of Lou Gehrig's funeral.

At the funeral the minister announced that there would be no speeches. "We need none," he said, "because you all knew him." That seemed fitting, too, for modest Lou Gehrig.

Think and Respond

1. Why did so many people love and respect Lou Gehrig?
2. Why do you think the author includes quotations in this biography?
3. What examples does the author give that show Lou Gehrig's **sportsmanship**?
4. Do you think athletes should boast about their ability or be **modest** like Lou Gehrig? Explain your answer.
5. How did using a reading strategy help you better understand what you read?

Meet the Author
David A. Adler

Team: New York Writers
Position: Third base and right (write) field

Bats right-handed. Throws right-handed. Writes right-handed.

Hits (books published): 142

David A. Adler loves baseball, and he loves to write. He is married and has three sons. One son loves baseball. Two sons love to write. All three sons love to read.

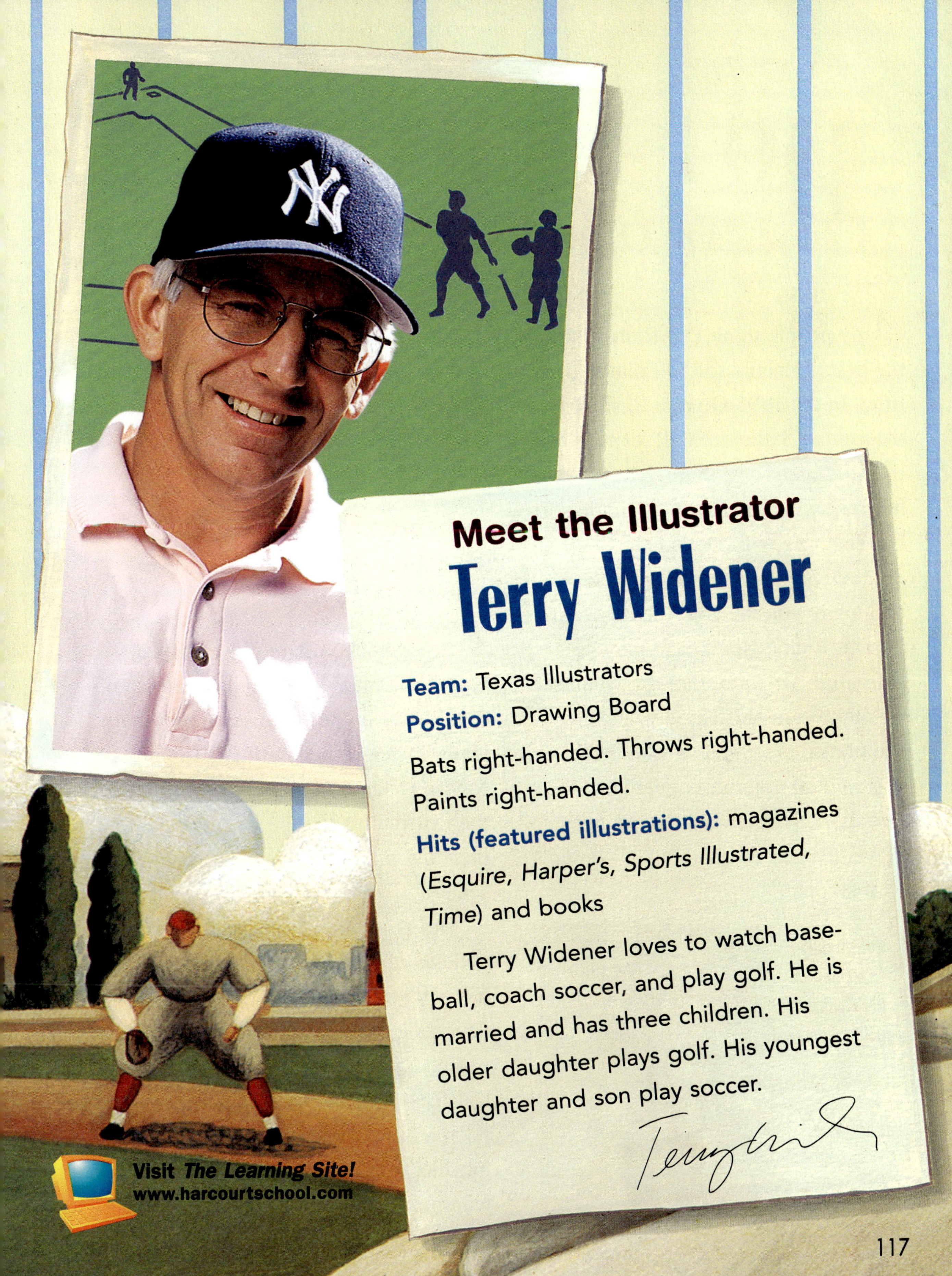

Meet the Illustrator

Terry Widener

Team: Texas Illustrators

Position: Drawing Board

Bats right-handed. Throws right-handed. Paints right-handed.

Hits (featured illustrations): magazines (*Esquire, Harper's, Sports Illustrated, Time*) and books

Terry Widener loves to watch baseball, coach soccer, and play golf. He is married and has three children. His older daughter plays golf. His youngest daughter and son play soccer.

Visit *The Learning Site!*
www.harcourtschool.com

Genre
Magazine Article

DOT RICHARDSON:

An Olympic Champion

Many people think Dot Richardson is the best women's softball player of all time. In the 1996 Olympics, she led the United States softball team to win the gold medal. At that Olympics, she hit the first home run in Olympic softball history! With Dot's help in the 2000 Olympics, the United States softball team won the gold medal again.

Dot Richardson began playing softball in Orlando, Florida, when she was ten years old. Three years later she played the game so well that she was invited to join the Orlando Rebels. This made her the youngest player ever to be on a major women's softball team.

Dot proudly holds one of her Olympic gold medals.

Dot is sure to voice her opinion when a game is at stake.

In high school Dot played volleyball, basketball, and tennis — but she didn't play on her high school softball team. Instead, she continued to play for the Orlando Rebels. She preferred the fast-pitch style the Rebels used to the slow-pitch style used at her high school.

Dot continued to play softball in college while studying medicine. She had always known she wanted to be a doctor. Today she works as an orthopedic surgeon in Los Angeles, California, taking care of problems people have with their bones, joints, muscles, and nerves. Her softball teammates call her "Doctor Dot."

The U.S. softball team listens to "The Star-Spangled Banner" after winning the Olympic gold medal.

There are many things Dot still wants to do. She is thinking about coaching the United States softball team in the 2004 Olympics, if she doesn't play on the team herself. She is also thinking about being the orthopedic surgeon for the team in the 2008 and 2012 Olympic Games.

Dot Richardson loves her busy life. She says, "Every minute that goes by is a minute that's lost if we don't enjoy it." Maybe that's why she is always willing to sign her name on a glove, ball, or bat. No wonder her fans love her!

Dot's mighty swing scores a home run for her team.

Think and Respond

What do you admire about Dot Richardson?

▲ Lou Gehrig

Making Connections

Text to Self • Text to Text • Text To World

Compare Texts

NC STANDARDS: ELA 2.04d identify word choice, 2.05 support inferences/conclusions, 3.06 conduct research using a variety of tools

1. What can people learn from Lou Gehrig's life that may help them in their own lives? COGNITION / INTEGRATING
2. How does the author's word choice change after Lou is selected as American League Most Valuable Player in 1936? CRITICAL STANCE / EVALUATING
3. Compare the way the authors of the biography and the article feel about their subjects, Lou Gehrig and Dot Richardson. CONNECTIONS / ANALYZING
4. Think of a biography you have read about a person who was not an athlete. What qualities or characteristics did that person have in common with Lou Gehrig? CONNECTIONS / ANALYZING
5. What resources could you use to learn more about the history of baseball? INTERPRETATION / EVALUATING

Write a Newspaper Article

Writing CONNECTION

Write a news story about the day Lou Gehrig was honored. Tell when, where, and why the event took place, what happened, and who took part in it. Use a graphic organizer like this one to plan. Then use your completed chart to help you write your article.

When?	
Where?	
Why?	
What?	
Who?	

NC STANDARDS: ELA 3.06 conduct research using a variety of tools, 4.02a use writing to communicate with others, 4.10 use technology as a tool; Social Studies 4.05 assess role of prominent persons in North Carolina

Design a Trading Card

Social Studies CONNECTION

Choose an athlete who was born in your state, who lived and played in your state at one time, or who lives and plays there now. Use the Internet or other resources to find information about him or her. Then design a trading card to honor this athlete. Draw or paste a picture of the athlete on one side of an index card. On the other side, write some information about the person.

NC STANDARD: ELA 3.06 conduct research using a variety of tools

Give an Oral Report

Science CONNECTION

The disease that struck Lou Gehrig affects the nervous system. Find information about the nervous system on the Internet, in a science text or nonfiction book, or in an encyclopedia. Prepare an oral report on what you find out. Include one or more diagrams that show how the nervous system works.

▲ Lou Gehrig

Prefixes, Suffixes, and Roots

When you come upon long or unfamiliar words in your reading, look to see if they have familiar prefixes, suffixes, roots, or root words.

Henry Ford sold his first automobile.

Here is how you might figure out the underlined word:

root	+	root word	=	new word
auto ("self")		**mobile** ("able to move")		**automobile** ("a vehicle able to move by itself")

Now look at some other words from "Lou Gehrig." How does using prefixes, suffixes, roots and root words help you figure out the meaning of these words?

Word	Prefix	Root Word	Meaning
unable	un ("not")	able	"not able"

Word	Root	Suffix	Meaning
visibly	vis ("see")	-ible ("able") -ly ("characteristic of")	"characteristic of being able to be seen"

Visit *The Learning Site!*
www.harcourtschool.com

See *Skills* and *Activities*

Test Prep

Prefixes, Suffixes, and Roots

NORTH CAROLINA EOG Practice

NC STANDARD: ELA 1.02 use roots/prefixes/suffixes to decode meanings

▶ **Read the passage. Then answer the questions.**

Jackie Robinson was the first African American to play major-league baseball and to be elected to the Baseball Hall of Fame. He played with the Brooklyn Dodgers from 1947 to 1956. A great hitter, Robinson was also known as a fearless base runner. In later years, he made an undeniable contribution to society by serving as special assistant for civil rights to the governor of New York.

COGNITION / KNOWLEDGE

1. Fearless means—

   A timid

   B frightening

   C terrible

   D daring

Tip

Identify the root word and the suffix. Think about the meaning of the suffix and how it changes the meaning of the root word.

COGNITION / KNOWLEDGE

2. Undeniable means—

   F not able to be denied

   G very important

   H not able to be believed

   J filled with honor

Tip

Identify the prefix, the root word, and the suffix. Combine the meanings of the word parts to figure out the meaning of the new word.

▲ Amelia and Eleanor Go for a Ride

Vocabulary Power

- **outspoken**
- **practical**
- **elegant**
- **elevations**
- **brisk**
- **starstruck**
- **miniatures**
- **marveled**

"Amelia and Eleanor Go for a Ride" tells about two famous women who share an experience worth remembering. You can have an experience worth remembering, too. Here are some tips for having a memory-filled family vacation.

Plan your trip together. Don't be too **outspoken**. It's okay to say what is on your mind, but remember that everyone's opinion counts.

Take **practical** clothes that suit your planned activities. Your favorite outfit might be **elegant**, but you wouldn't want to ruin your beautiful clothes. If you are going to the mountains, take a jacket. The air at the higher **elevations** will probably be **brisk**—chillier and breezier than it is lower down.

Enjoy even the smallest details of your trip. Take time to look up at a **starstruck** sky, full of twinkling stars. Notice how tiny the people and cars below look from high on a mountain—like **miniatures**! These things may amaze you, and you will be glad you **marveled** at them. Details like these will help you remember your trip long after you've returned home.

Vocabulary-Writing CONNECTION

Think of a time when you **marveled** at something in nature. Write a paragraph describing how you felt and what caused you to feel that way.

Genre

Historical Fiction

Historical fiction is a story that is set in the past and portrays people, places, and events that did happen or could have happened.

In this selection, look for

- **A real time and place in the past**
- **Some made-up events**

Amelia and Eleanor Go for a Ride

BASED ON A TRUE STORY

BY PAM MUÑOZ RYAN
ILLUSTRATED BY BRIAN SELZNICK

AMELIA AND ELEANOR were birds of a feather.

Eleanor was outspoken and determined.

So was Amelia.

Amelia was daring and liked to try things other women wouldn't even consider.

Eleanor was the very same.

So when Eleanor discovered that her friend Amelia was coming to town to give a speech, she naturally said, "Bring your husband and come to dinner at my house! You can even sleep over."

It wasn't unusual for two friends to get together. But Eleanor was Eleanor Roosevelt, the First Lady of the United States, who lived in the White House with her husband, President Franklin Roosevelt.

Amelia was Amelia Earhart, the celebrated aviator who had been the first female pilot to fly solo across the Atlantic Ocean. And when two of the most famous and adventurous women in the world got together, something exciting was bound to happen.

In a guest room at the White House, Amelia and her husband, G.P., dressed for dinner. Amelia pulled on the long white evening gloves that were so different from the ones she sometimes wore while flying.

Many people didn't understand why a woman would want to risk her life in a plane. But Amelia had said it more than once: "It's for the fun of it." Besides, she loved the feeling of independence she had when she was in the cockpit.

She carefully folded a gift for Eleanor—a silk scarf that matched her own. The powder blue with streaks of indigo reminded Amelia of morning sky.

Meanwhile, Eleanor dressed for dinner, too. Her brother, Hall, would be escorting her this evening because the President had a meeting to attend. But Eleanor was used to that.

She pulled on the long white evening gloves that were so different from the ones she sometimes wore while driving. Then she peeked out the window at the brand-new car that had just been delivered that afternoon. She couldn't wait to drive it.

Many people thought it was too bold and dangerous for a woman to drive a car, especially the First Lady of the United States. But Eleanor always gave the same answer: "It's practical, that's all." Besides, she loved the feeling of independence she had when she was behind the wheel.

It was a brisk and cloudless April evening. The guests had gathered in the Red Room, and the table looked elegant, as even small dinner parties at the White House can be.

Eleanor and Hall greeted Amelia and G.P., as well as several reporters and a photographer.

Amelia gave Eleanor the scarf.

"I love it!" Eleanor exclaimed. "It's just like yours."

Dinner started with George Washington's crab chowder.

"This is delicious," said Amelia. "But if soup at the White House has such a fancy name, what will dessert be called?"

Perhaps Abraham Lincoln's peach cobbler? Or maybe

Thomas Jefferson's custard? They laughed as everyone took turns guessing.

By the time they got to the roast duck, the conversation had turned to flying.

"Mrs. Roosevelt just received her student pilot's license," said one of the reporters.

Amelia wasn't surprised. She had been the one to encourage Eleanor. She knew her friend could do anything she set her mind to.

"I'll teach you myself," offered Amelia.

"I accept! Tell us, Amelia, what's it like to fly at night in the dark?"

Everyone at the table leaned closer to hear. Very few people in the whole world had ever flown at night, and Amelia was one of them. Amelia's eyes sparkled. "The stars glitter all about and seem close enough to touch.

"At higher elevations, the clouds below shine white with dark islands where the night sea shows through. I've seen the planet Venus setting on the horizon, and I've circled cities of twinkling lights."

"And the capital city at night?" asked Eleanor.

"There's no describing it," said Amelia. "You just have to experience it on a clear night, when you can see forever. Why,

we should go tonight! We could fly the loop to Baltimore and back in no time!"

The Secret Service men protested. "This hasn't been approved!"

"Nonsense!" said Eleanor. "If Amelia Earhart can fly solo across the Atlantic Ocean, I can certainly take a short flight to Baltimore and back!"

Before dessert could be served, Amelia had called Eastern Air Transport and arranged a flight.

Within the hour, Amelia and Eleanor boarded the Curtis Condor twin-motor airplane. For a moment, both women looked up at the mysterious night sky. Then, without changing her gloves, Amelia slipped into the cockpit and took the wheel.

The plane rolled down the runway, faster and faster. Lights from the airstrip flashed in front of them. And they lifted into the dark.

"How amusing it is to see a girl in a white evening dress and high-heeled shoes flying a plane!" Eleanor said.

Amelia laughed as she made a wide sweep over Washington, D.C., and turned off all the lights in the plane.

Out the window, the Potomac River glistened with moonshine. The capitol dome reflected a soft golden halo. And the enormous, light-drenched monuments looked like tiny miniatures.

Soon the peaceful countryside gave way to shadowy woodlands. The Chesapeake Bay became a meandering outline on the horizon. And even though they knew it wasn't so, it seemed as if the plane crawled slowly through starstruck space.

Eleanor marveled, "It's like sitting on top of the world!"

When it was time to land, Amelia carefully took the plane down. A group of reporters had gathered, anxious to ask questions.

"Mrs. Roosevelt, did you feel safe knowing a girl was flying that ship?"

"Just as safe!" said Eleanor.

"Did you fly the plane, Mrs. Roosevelt?" asked one reporter.

"What part did you like best?" said another.

"I enjoyed it so much, and no, I didn't actually fly the plane. Not yet. But someday I intend to. I was thrilled by the city lights, the brilliance of the blinking pinpoints below."

Amelia smiled. She knew just how Eleanor felt.

As the Secret Service agents drove them slowly back to the White House, Amelia and Eleanor agreed that there was nothing quite as exciting as flying. What could compare? Well, they admitted, maybe the closest thing would be driving in a fast car on a straightaway road with a stiff breeze blowing against your face.

Arms linked, they walked up the steps to the White House. Eleanor whispered something to Amelia, and then they hesitated, letting the rest of the group walk ahead of them.

"Are you coming inside, Mrs. Roosevelt?" someone asked.

But by then, they had wrapped their silk scarves around their necks and were hurrying toward Eleanor's new car.

Without changing her gloves, Eleanor quickly slipped into the driver's seat and took her turn at the wheel. With the wind in their hair and the brisk air stinging their cheeks, they flew down the road.

And after they had taken a ride about the city streets of Washington, D.C., they finally headed back to the White House . . . for dessert! Eleanor Roosevelt's pink clouds on angel food cake.

Think and Respond

1. What was unusual about what Amelia and Eleanor did?
2. When did the events in the story take place, and why is it important to know this?
3. How does the author show that Eleanor was **outspoken** and determined?
4. If Amelia and Eleanor had invited you to go flying with them that night, would you have gone? Why or why not?
5. What strategy did you use as you read this selection? Explain how it helped you understand what was happening.

Meet the Author

Pam Muñoz Ryan

Pam Muñoz Ryan grew up in California's San Joaquin Valley. Like many Americans, she has a diverse cultural background. She is Spanish, Mexican, Basque, and Italian.

After college, Mrs. Ryan knew she wanted a career that had to do with books. She was a teacher before a friend encouraged her to write her first books. She has been writing ever since! She was inspired to write *Amelia and Eleanor Go for a Ride* because, she says, "I'm drawn to stories which might be fresh for readers. I also come from a family with a lot of strong, determined women, so those types of stories just naturally appeal to me."

Pam Muñoz Ryan lives north of San Diego, California, with her husband, four children, and two dogs, Sami and Buster. She enjoys visiting schools to speak about writing and to answer questions from her readers. She wants young writers to know that writing is "like anything else in life, the harder you work the more lucky you get. The more you practice, the better you get."

Meet the Illustrator

Brian Selznick

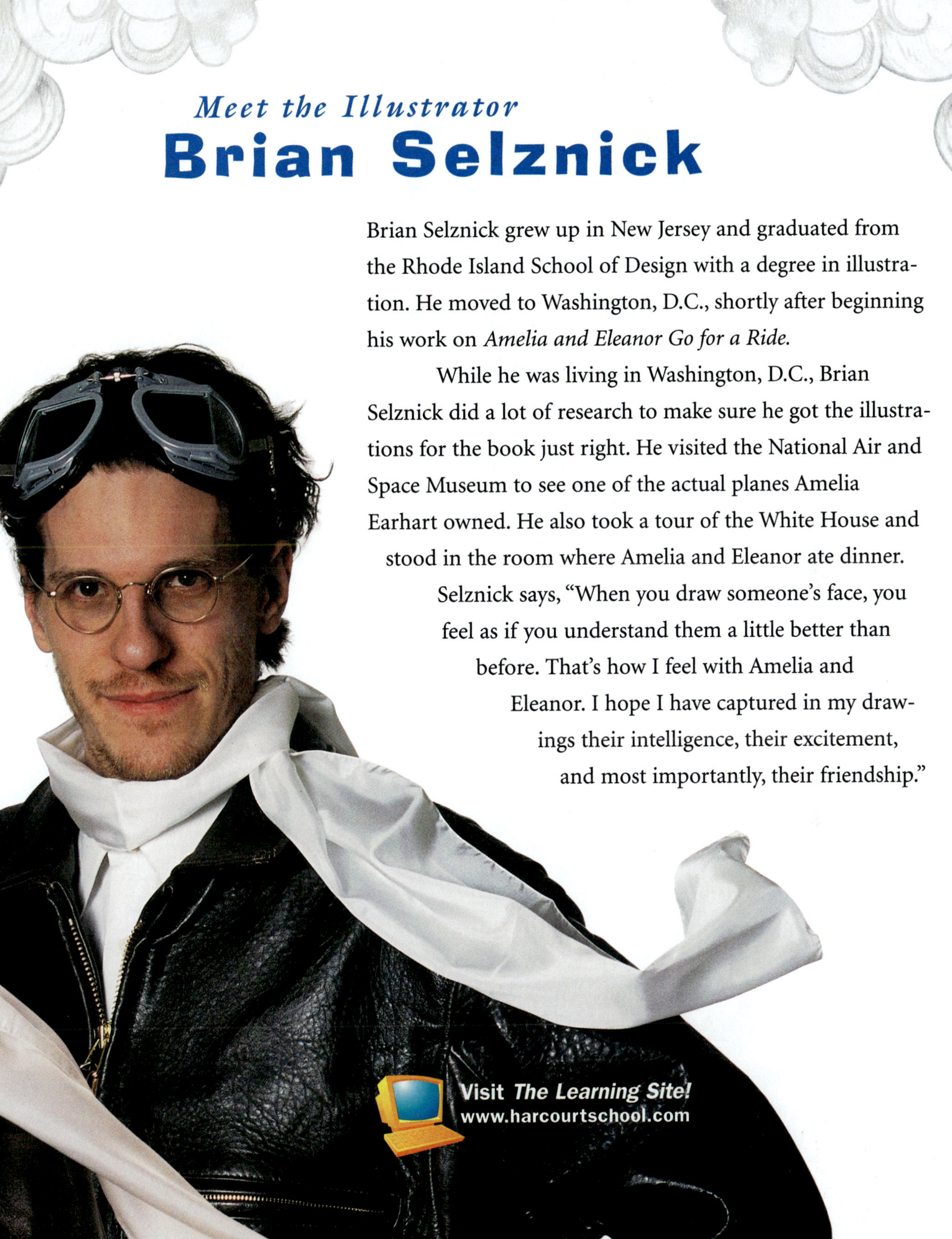

Brian Selznick grew up in New Jersey and graduated from the Rhode Island School of Design with a degree in illustration. He moved to Washington, D.C., shortly after beginning his work on *Amelia and Eleanor Go for a Ride.*

While he was living in Washington, D.C., Brian Selznick did a lot of research to make sure he got the illustrations for the book just right. He visited the National Air and Space Museum to see one of the actual planes Amelia Earhart owned. He also took a tour of the White House and stood in the room where Amelia and Eleanor ate dinner.

Selznick says, "When you draw someone's face, you feel as if you understand them a little better than before. That's how I feel with Amelia and Eleanor. I hope I have captured in my drawings their intelligence, their excitement, and most importantly, their friendship."

Visit *The Learning Site!*
www.harcourtschool.com

Wings of Hope

by Marianne J. Dyson

Eleven-year-old Kimberly Renaud was a little scared. She was about to take her very first flight—not in a big jet, but in a plane so small that passengers seated inside could touch both sides with arms outstretched. But what was really different about this flight was that both the pilot and the passenger rode to the plane in wheelchairs.

The pilot was Theron Wright. An accident left Theron paralyzed from the waist down. He was in college at the time, and had just received his pilot's license. After the accident, Theron thought he'd never fly again. That all changed when he met Rick Amber.

Rick had been a fighter pilot for the U.S. Navy during the Vietnam War. In 1971, his jet crashed, and Lieutenant Amber lost the use of his legs.

In 1993, he founded Challenge Air. This nonprofit group offers free flights to disabled and seriously ill children. The pilots (who call themselves "disAbled pilots") want kids to know that anyone can overcome a physical or mental obstacle. The group's motto is, "All it takes is desire, and truly the sky is the limit." The pilots have flown more than 6,000 children and their friends in seventeen states across the country.

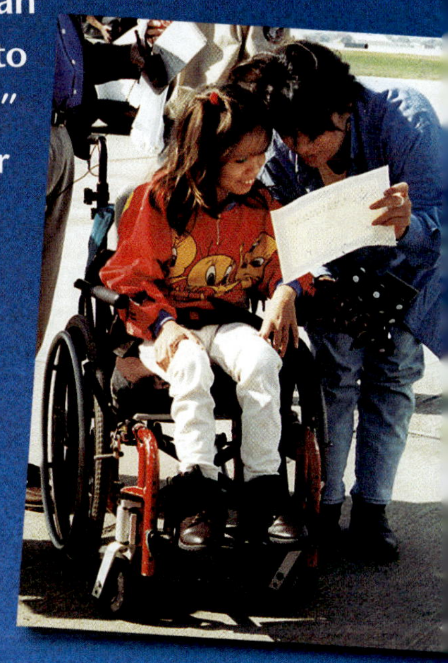

Theron Wright learned to fly again using Rick Amber's plane. It had been set up to be flown using hand controls alone. "Rick taught me not to quit and to continue striving to achieve my goals in aviation," says Theron.

Kimberly Renaud smiled as Challenge Air volunteers helped her into the back seat of Theron's plane. To protect her ears from engine noise, she was given a headset to wear. A pillow served as a booster to help her see out of the window. With safety belts snug, Theron taxied the plane down the runway at Houston's Hobby Airport, then roared off into a blue sky.

From high above the city, Kimberly saw downtown skyscrapers and the hospital where she goes for treatment. "We saw houses, and I saw the city and little cars. Everything looked small from up there," she remarked. After landing, Kimberly received her gold aviator's wings (a special Challenge Air pin).

Kimberly loves math and wants to work with computers when she grows up. Challenge Air has shown her that there really is no limit—not even the sky—to what you can achieve when you believe in yourself.

Think and Respond

How do Challenge Air volunteers teach children about meeting challenges?

▲ Amelia and Eleanor Go for a Ride

Making Connections

Text to Self • Text to Text • Text To World

Compare Texts

NC STANDARDS: ELA 2.04c identify main idea/details, 3.01b interpret/evaluate text/examine characters' actions/motives, 3.06 conduct research using a variety of tools

1. What qualities did Amelia Earhart and Eleanor Roosevelt have that enabled them to achieve their goals? INTERPRETATION / ANALYZING
2. How is the author's description of what Amelia and Eleanor saw during their flight different from her description of what happened before and after? CRITICAL STANCE / EVALUATING
3. What are some similarities between "Amelia and Eleanor Go for a Ride" and "Wings of Hope"? CRITICAL STANCE / ANALYZING
4. Compare "Amelia and Eleanor Go for a Ride" with another historical fiction story. Which of the two did you find more interesting? Explain. CONNECTIONS / ANALYZING
5. What questions do you still have about Amelia Earhart or Eleanor Roosevelt? How could you find the answers? INTERPRETATION / EVALUATING

Write an Interview

Writing CONNECTION

Imagine you are a reporter who will interview Amelia Earhart. Write three or four questions that you might ask her. Then answer your questions as if you were Amelia Earhart. Use information from the story, an encyclopedia, or a biography to help you. You can make a graphic organizer like this one to plan your interview.

What I Know	What I Want to Find Out	What I Learned

NC STANDARDS: ELA 3.06 conduct research using a variety of tools, 4.02a use writing to communicate with others, 4.05 use planning strategies to organize ideas

Make a Time Line

Social Studies CONNECTION

Airplanes have changed a great deal since they were invented by Orville and Wilbur Wright. Research the history of the airplane from its invention to the present. You may find information on the Internet, in an encyclopedia, or in a nonfiction book about airplanes. Set up a time line like the one below, and use your information to complete it.

1903–The Wright brothers made the first successful powered flight in a heavier-than-air machine.

Present

NC STANDARD: ELA 3.06 conduct research using a variety of tools

Construct Models

Science CONNECTION

Design and construct your own model planes of different shapes and sizes. You might create airplanes from different weights and sizes of paper or cardboard. Try different ideas and materials. Then set up and conduct experiments to see which of your planes flies best. Record your results and the conclusions you draw.

▲ Amelia and Eleanor Go for a Ride

Locate Information

After reading "Amelia and Eleanor Go for a Ride," you might be interested in finding more information on a topic such as Amelia Earhart or the history of aviation.

Possible sources of information on topics such as these include textbooks and other nonfiction books. This chart shows book parts that can help you locate information in these kinds of books.

Book Part	Description	Location in Book
title	name of a book	on the cover and the title page
table of contents	a list of chapters with the page number where each can be found	near the front
preface	a brief introduction to a book	near the front
headings	names of sections within a unit or chapter	within the text to show how it is organized
glossary	dictionary of terms used in a book	at the back
appendix	a section that gives additional information	at the back
index	alphabetical list of topics with pages where they can be found	at the back

Where would you look if you wanted to read an introduction to the book?

Visit *The Learning Site!*
www.harcourtschool.com

See *Skills and Activities*

Test Prep
Locate Information

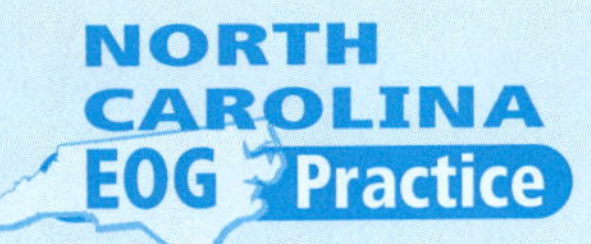

▶ **Look at the sample table of contents. Then answer the questions.**

Mae Jemison, Astronaut

COGNITION / ORGANIZING

1. You could use this table of contents to find out—

A detailed information about the Peace Corps

B what chapters tell about Mae Jemison's training as an astronaut

C what *astronaut* means

D what astronauts learn from space travel

Read each answer choice. Look carefully at the table of contents to determine whether or not you can find that information.

COGNITION / ORGANIZING

2. Where would you look to locate the meaning of a word used in *Mae Jemison, Astronaut*?

F table of contents

G appendix

H index

J glossary

You can eliminate one answer choice because the sample table of contents does not provide definitions.

THEME 2

SIDE BY SIDE

CONTENTS

▲ The Baker's Neighbor

Vocabulary Power

- shiftless
- indignantly
- ad lib
- shamefacedly
- luxury
- assent
- privilege
- elated

The next selection you will read is written in the form of a play. Here are some descriptions of other plays put on by fourth-grade classes.

This play is about a farmer who believes that his donkey is lazy and **shiftless**. In this scene, the farmer speaks **indignantly** to the donkey. He speaks angrily because the donkey won't carry the sack for him. The other actors **ad lib**, or make up lines on the spot, telling the farmer they think the sack is too heavy for the little donkey.

In this play, a boy has taken a hat that doesn't belong to him. He stands **shamefacedly** before the queen, showing by the expression on his face how ashamed he is for what he has done. The queen tells him he must return the hat to its owner. Such a wonderful hat is a **luxury** because it is costly and gives pleasure but isn't really necessary. The queen says she will give the boy a plain wool cap to keep him warm. Her advisors agree and nod in **assent**.

The main character in this play is a boy who longs for the **privilege**, or special favor, of carrying the American flag in a parade for the very first Independence Day celebration. In this scene, the boy has just found out that he may carry the flag and lead the parade. He is **elated**, filled with joy.

Vocabulary-Writing CONNECTION

Do you think television is a **luxury** or a necessity in our modern world? Write a sentence expressing your opinion. Then give three reasons to explain why you feel as you do.

The Baker's

Genre

Play

A play is a story that can be performed for an audience.

In this selection, look for

- **Acts that are divided into scenes**
- **Text telling the reader where the characters are positioned on stage**

Neighbor

adapted by Adele Thane
illustrated by Mary GrandPré

Characters

Manuel Gonzales, *a baker*
Pablo Perez, *his neighbor*
Carlos, *a boy*
Ramona, Inez, Isabel — *his sisters*

Judge
Three Women
Villagers

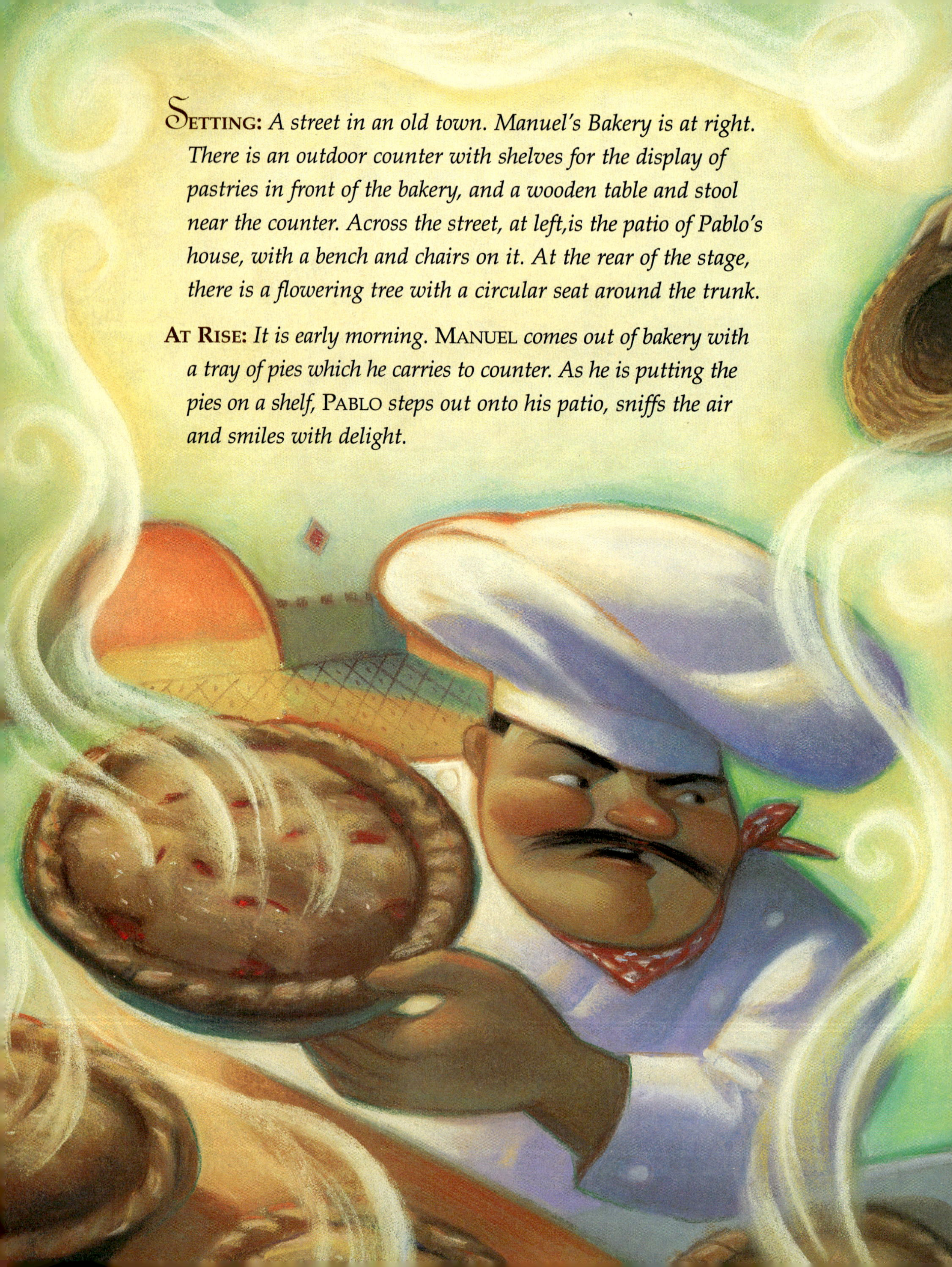

Setting: *A street in an old town. Manuel's Bakery is at right. There is an outdoor counter with shelves for the display of pastries in front of the bakery, and a wooden table and stool near the counter. Across the street, at left,is the patio of Pablo's house, with a bench and chairs on it. At the rear of the stage, there is a flowering tree with a circular seat around the trunk.*

At Rise: *It is early morning.* Manuel *comes out of bakery with a tray of pies which he carries to counter. As he is putting the pies on a shelf,* Pablo *steps out onto his patio, sniffs the air and smiles with delight.*

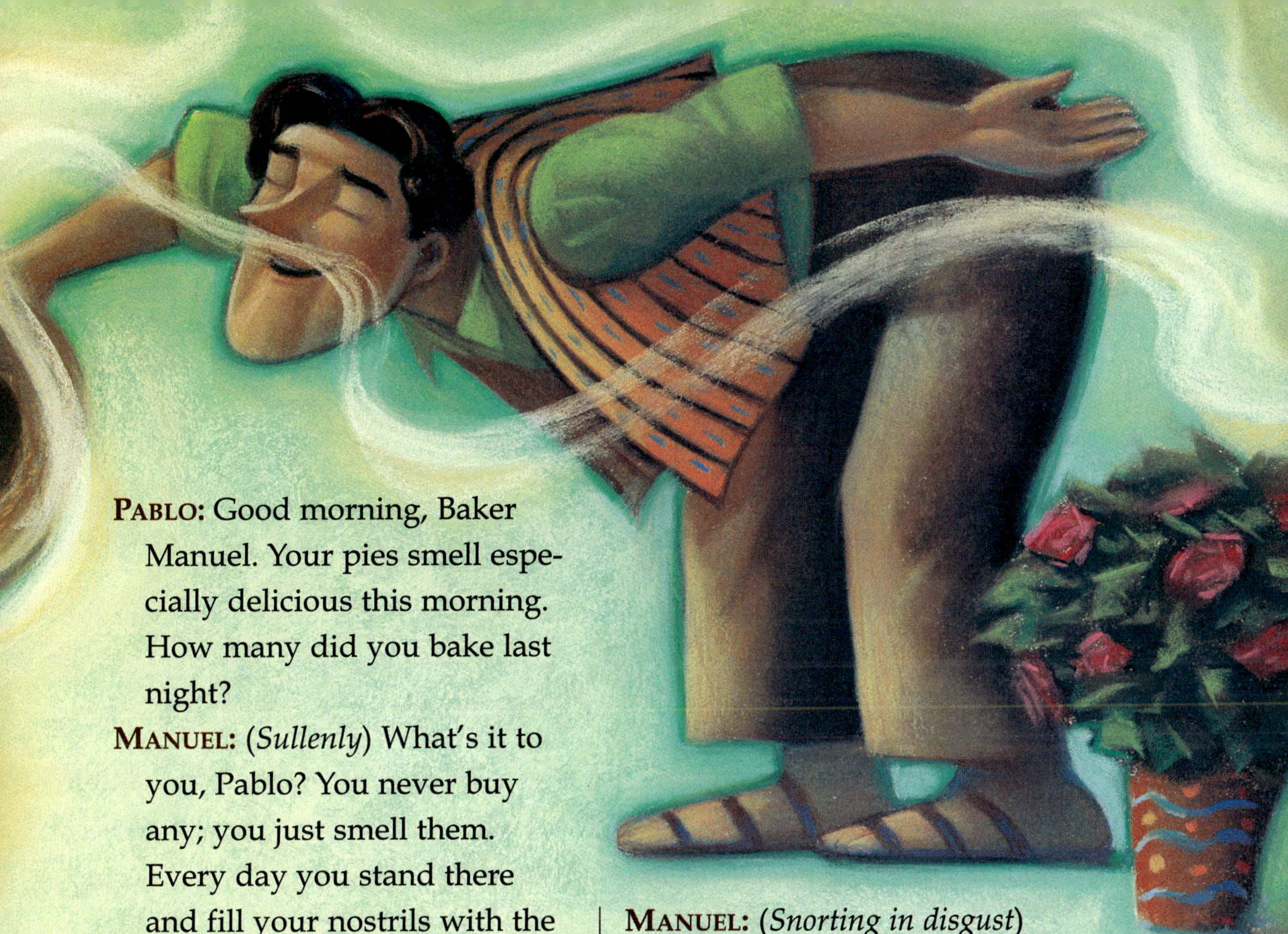

PABLO: Good morning, Baker Manuel. Your pies smell especially delicious this morning. How many did you bake last night?

MANUEL: (*Sullenly*) What's it to you, Pablo? You never buy any; you just smell them. Every day you stand there and fill your nostrils with the fragrance of my pastries. It's amazing there's any flavor left in them when my customers come to buy.

PABLO: But it makes me happy to smell your pastries. You are the best baker in town. Everyone says so.

MANUEL: Well, why don't you buy a pie or a cake and take it home? Then you could smell it all you want.

PABLO: Oh, but if I bought it and ate it, I couldn't smell it any more.

MANUEL: (*Snorting in disgust*) Bah! (*When he finishes setting out the pies he goes into the bakery with the empty tray.* PABLO *crosses to the counter and inhales deeply, closing his eyes in delight.* MANUEL *returns with tray of cakes and cash box. He pushes* PABLO *away from counter.*) Hey! Take your nose away from there! I can't sell those pies if you sniff them all over! (PABLO *saunters back to his patio.* MANUEL *places tray of cakes on counter, then carries cash box to table and sits down.*)

PABLO: Are you going to count your money, Manuel? (MANUEL *ignores* PABLO *but empties coins from cash box onto table.* PABLO *then sits in a chair and watches* MANUEL *with an amused smile.*) How much did you take in yesterday?

MANUEL: None of your business! (*He inspects each coin carefully, then writes in a small notebook, adds figures, scowling and mumbling to himself.* CARLOS *and his sisters enter left. They stop when they see* MANUEL *counting his money and talk quietly together.*)

RAMONA: Gracious, what a lot of money!

CARLOS: Papa says the bakery has made Manuel the richest man in town.

INEZ: If he's that rich, why doesn't he smile? He looks so cross and unfriendly.

CARLOS: That's because he's a miser. A miser doesn't like people—only money. The more money he has, the more he wants. And he keeps it all to himself—he never shares it with anyone.

ISABEL: (*Catching sight of* PABLO) There's Pablo!

CARLOS AND GIRLS: (*Enthusiastically; ad lib*) Hello, Pablo! How are you? Good to see you! (*Etc.*)

Pablo: (*Beaming at them as he gets up*) Hello, my young friends, hello! You're up bright and early.

Isabel: We're going to the bakery.

Ramona: Carlos is going to treat us.

Carlos: I helped Papa pick beans and he gave me this. (*He holds up a silver coin.*)

Pablo: You're a good boy, Carlos.

Inez: (*Starting across to the bakery*) Come on! Let's see what there is. (*Children crowd around the counter.*)

Ramona: Look at those coconut patties!

Isabel: And the jelly roll! Yummy!

Inez: Carlos, why don't you buy a pie and cut it into quarters? Then we'd each have a piece.

Carlos: I don't know. I'd sort of like a cake.

Manuel: (*Impatiently*) Well, young fellow, what do you want? (*To* Inez) Keep your fingers off that pie!

Inez: (*Indignantly*) I didn't touch it!

MANUEL: Come now, hurry up and decide. This isn't a waiting room. I have to make a living. What with rent and taxes, it's as much as I can do.

CARLOS: How much is that cake with the pink frosting?

MANUEL: You can't afford that. How much money do you have? (CARLOS *holds out his hand to show him.*) Not enough. That cake costs three times what you can pay.

CARLOS: What *can* I buy with my money? I want something for all of us.

MANUEL: You can have four tapioca tarts—and I'm giving them away at that price. (*He hands tarts to* CARLOS.) Here you are. Now take your tarts over to Pablo and let him smell them. (*He puts* CARLOS'S *coin with others on table, sits down and makes entry in his notebook.* CARLOS *passes out tarts to his sisters as they cross to the patio*).

CARLOS: (*Offering tart to* PABLO) Have a bite?

PABLO: No, thank you, Carlos. You earned it—you eat it.

ISABEL: Pablo, why did Manuel say we should let you smell our tarts?

PABLO: Oh, he's annoyed, because every morning I stand here and enjoy the smell of his freshly-baked pies and cakes when they are right out of the oven. Ah, what fragrance! It's as if the bakery has burst into bloom.

RAMONA: If you could be a beautiful smell, Pablo, instead of a man—would you like to be a beautiful bakery smell?

PABLO: (*Laughing*) Well, that's a new one on me! If I were a *smell* instead of a man? Of all the comical ideas!

INEZ: (*Explaining*) It's a game we play among ourselves. We ask each other what thing we'd like to be if we weren't a person—what color, what sight, what sound?

RAMONA: What sound would *you* like to be, Pablo, if you weren't a person?

PABLO: This minute?

RAMONA: Any minute.

PABLO: Let me think. (*Suddenly he slaps his knee.*) I have it! If I were a sound instead of a man, I'd choose to be a song! A happy little song in children's hearts. Or turning up in a boy's whistle—like this! (*He whistles a merry tune.*)

ISABEL: What sound do you think Manuel would like to be?

CARLOS: That's easy. He'd be the sound of gold pieces jingling in his own pocket.

ISABEL: I'm going to ask him. (*She goes to the table where* MANUEL *is putting his money back into cash box.*) Manuel, may I ask you a question?

MANUEL: (*Scowling*) What is it?

ISABEL: If you were a sound instead of a baker, what sound in the whole wide world would you choose to be?

MANUEL: Well, of all the idiotic nonsense! Clear out of here and stop bothering me! I have better things to do than to answer stupid questions. (ISABEL *returns to patio, and* PABLO *goes center.*)

PABLO: It has taken you a long time to count your money, Manuel.

Manuel: (*Sneering*) It wouldn't take *you* long to count yours.

Pablo: That's right. I don't care much for money.

Manuel: You're too lazy to earn it.

Pablo: (*Good-naturedly*) Oh, I work. But I'd rather sit in the sun and take advantage of all the small, everyday pleasures that life has to offer.

Manuel: Like smelling my pastries, I suppose—without charge?

Pablo: (*Shrugging*) The air is free.

Manuel: It's not as free as you think.

Pablo: What do you mean?

Manuel: I'm going to make you pay for all the pastry smells I've supplied you with for many years.

Pablo: (*Smiling in disbelief*) You can't mean that!

Manuel: But I do! You stand outside my bakery every day and smell my pies and cakes. To my mind, that is the same as taking them without paying for them. You are no better than a thief, Pablo Perez!

Pablo: (*Mildly*) I never took anything that didn't belong to me, and you know it. What's more, I haven't done your business any harm. Why, I've even helped it. People often stop when they see me standing here and go in to buy something. (*Children giggle, then begin to taunt* Manuel *and run around him, sniffing.*)

Isabel: I smell raisins!

Ramona: I smell spice!

Inez: How much does it cost to smell the flour on your apron?

Carlos: May I smell your cap for a penny? (*He snatches baker's cap from* Manuel's *head and sniffs it, laughing.*)

Manuel: (*Angrily, snatching it back*) You'll laugh on the other side of your face when I get the Judge!

PABLO: When you get *who*?

MANUEL: The Judge. I'm going to tell him the whole story. I'll show you I'm not joking. The Judge will make you pay me. (*He grabs his cash box from table and exits left as* THREE WOMEN *enter right. They come downstage and question the children.*)

1ST WOMAN: What's the matter with Manuel?

2ND WOMAN: Will he be back soon? I want to buy a cake.

3RD WOMAN: So do I. What happened?

1ST WOMAN: He looked so angry. Where's he gone?

GIRLS: (*Excitedly, ad lib*) He's gone to get the Judge! He is angry! He is furious! (*Etc.*)

1ST WOMAN: The Judge! What for?

CARLOS: He says Pablo will have to pay for smelling his cakes and pies.

2ND WOMAN: (*To* PABLO) He wants you to pay him for doing that?

3RD WOMAN: He can't be serious!

PABLO: Oh, yes, he is! But I think it's very funny. (*He laughs, and the* WOMEN *join in.*)

1ST WOMAN: It's ridiculous! Everyone who goes by the shop smells his pastry.

2ND WOMAN: Is he going to take everyone in town to court? (*They are all in gales of laughter when* MANUEL *returns with* JUDGE, *followed by several* VILLAGERS.)

MANUEL: (*To* JUDGE) There he is! (*Points to* PABLO) There's the thief!

JUDGE: Calm yourself, Manuel. It has not yet been proved that Pablo is a thief. First he must have a fair trial. (*He sits down at table and motions for two chairs to be placed facing him.* VILLAGERS *and* THREE WOMEN *gather under tree and on patio with children. They whisper and talk together as they seat themselves.*)

1ST VILLAGER: In all my days, I've never heard of a case like this before.

2ND VILLAGER: How can a man steal the *smell* of anything?

3RD VILLAGER: I'm surprised the Judge would even listen to the baker's story. Money for smelling his cakes! How absurd!

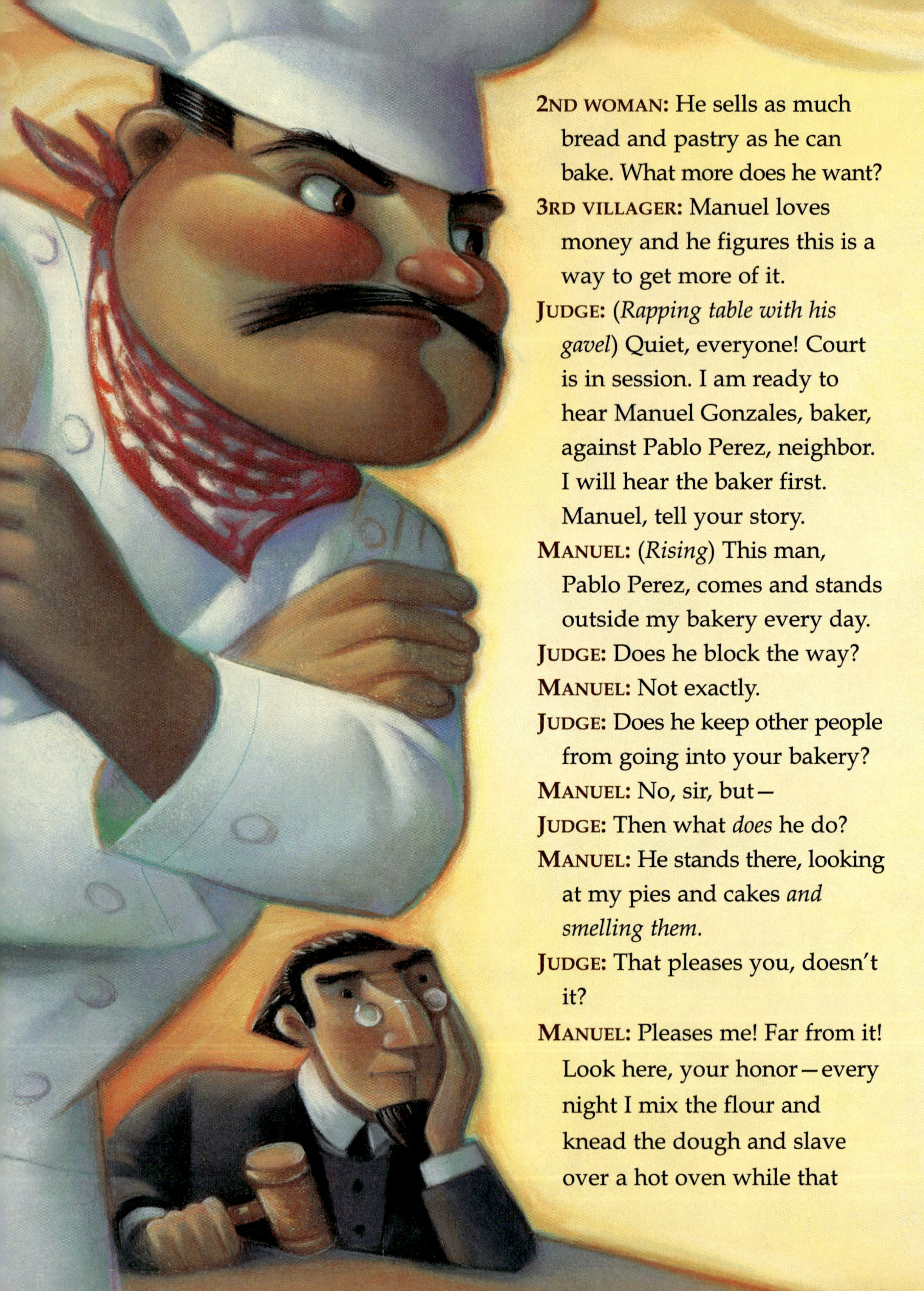

2ND WOMAN: He sells as much bread and pastry as he can bake. What more does he want?

3RD VILLAGER: Manuel loves money and he figures this is a way to get more of it.

JUDGE: (*Rapping table with his gavel*) Quiet, everyone! Court is in session. I am ready to hear Manuel Gonzales, baker, against Pablo Perez, neighbor. I will hear the baker first. Manuel, tell your story.

MANUEL: (*Rising*) This man, Pablo Perez, comes and stands outside my bakery every day.

JUDGE: Does he block the way?

MANUEL: Not exactly.

JUDGE: Does he keep other people from going into your bakery?

MANUEL: No, sir, but—

JUDGE: Then what *does* he do?

MANUEL: He stands there, looking at my pies and cakes *and smelling them.*

JUDGE: That pleases you, doesn't it?

MANUEL: Pleases me! Far from it! Look here, your honor—every night I mix the flour and knead the dough and slave over a hot oven while that shiftless, good-for-nothing Pablo sleeps. Then he gets up in the morning, fresh as a daisy, and comes out here to smell the fine sweet pastry I've baked. He takes full value of this free, daily luxury. He acts as if it's his privilege. Now I ask you, Judge—is it right that I should work so hard to provide him with this luxury, without charge? No! He should pay for it!

JUDGE: I see. You may sit down, Manuel. Now, Pablo Perez, it is your turn. (PABLO *stands.*) Is it true that you stand in front of Manuel's bakery and smell his cakes and pies?

PABLO: I can't help smelling them, your honor. Their spicy fragrance fills the air.

JUDGE: Would you say you *enjoy* it?

PABLO: Oh, yes, sir. I am a man of simple pleasures. Just the smell of a bakery makes me happy.

JUDGE: But did you ever pay the baker for this pleasure?

PABLO: Well, no, sir. It never occurred to me that I had to pay him.

JUDGE: Pablo Perez, you will now put ten gold pieces on this table—for Manuel Gonzales. (VILLAGERS *gasp.* MANUEL *looks surprised and delighted.*)

PABLO: (*Stunned*) Ten gold pieces! For smelling the air near my own house?

JUDGE: Do you have that amount?

PABLO: I—I guess so, but it's my life's savings.

JUDGE: Where is it?

PABLO: In my house.

JUDGE: Get it and bring it here. (*Slowly* PABLO *crosses patio and exits left. Villagers talk to each other disapprovingly.*)

1ST VILLAGER: The Judge shouldn't make Pablo pay.

1st woman: Pablo is an honest man.

2nd villager: I don't see how the Judge could rule in the baker's favor.

3rd villager: Why, he's richer than the Judge himself.

2nd woman: And now he's going to get poor Pablo's savings.

3rd woman: It's not fair!

Judge: (*Rapping with his gavel*) Silence in the court! (Pablo *returns sadly with purse, puts it on table before* Judge. Manuel, *elated, rubs his hands together greedily.*)

Manuel: (*To* Judge) I knew your honor would do the right thing by me. Thank you, Judge. (*He picks up purse and starts to put it into his cash box.*)

Judge: (*Rising*) Not so fast, Manuel! Empty that purse on the table and count the gold pieces, one by one.

Manuel: (*Grinning craftily*) Ah, yes, your honor. I must make sure I haven't been cheated. How kind of you to remind me! (*He empties purse and begins to count, excitedly.* Judge *watches* Manuel *as he lovingly fingers each coin.*)

Judge: It gives you great pleasure to touch that gold, doesn't it, Manuel? You *enjoy* it.

Manuel: Oh, I do, I do! . . . Eight . . . nine . . . ten. It's all here, your honor, and none of it false.

Judge: Please put it back in the purse. (*Manuel does so.*) Now return it to Pablo.

Manuel: (*In disbelief*) *Return* it! But—but you just told Pablo to pay it to me.

Judge: No, I did not tell him to pay it to you. I told him to put it on this table. Then I instructed you to count the money, which you did. In doing so, you enjoyed Pablo's money the way he has enjoyed your cakes and pies. In other words, he has smelled your pastry and you have touched his gold. Therefore, I hereby declare that the case is now settled. (*He raps twice with his gavel.* Manuel *shamefacedly shoves purse across table to* Pablo *and turns to leave.* Judge *stops him.*)

Just a moment, Manuel! I hope this has been a lesson to you. In the future, think less about making money and more about making friends. Good friends and neighbors are better than gold. And now, if you please—my fee!

MANUEL: Yes, your honor. (*He opens his cash box willingly but* JUDGE *closes the lid.*)

JUDGE: Put away your money. There's been enough fuss over money already today. The fee I am asking is this—pies and cakes for everyone here—free of charge! (MANUEL *nods his head vigorously in assent.* VILLAGERS *and children cheer, then they rush to pastry counter and help themselves.* MANUEL *goes into bakery and reappears with more pastry piled high on tray.* PABLO *and* JUDGE *hold a whole pie between them and start to eat from opposite edges toward the center of pie, as the curtain closes.*)

THE END

Think and Respond

1. What is the problem between Manuel the baker and his neighbor Pablo? How does the judge solve it?
2. How would this story be different if the author had not told it in the form of a play?
3. Why does the author have Manuel nod in **assent** at the end of the play?
4. Do you think the judge's solution is fair? Explain your answer.
5. When did you use a reading strategy as you read this play? Tell how the strategy helped you.

Meet the Illustrator

Mary GrandPré

Mary GrandPré is well known for her lively, colorful illustrations. She has received awards from The Society of Children's Book Illustrators, and the magazines *Communication Arts* and *Art Direction*. She now is thinking about writing her own books. "I already have lots of ideas written down for stories," she said.

Mary GrandPré grew up in Minnesota, where she still lives with her two dogs and one cat. In her spare time she likes to cook and to remodel houses. She loves her illustrating work and said she likes to create books that people of all ages can enjoy.

Visit *The Learning Site!*
www.harcourtschool.com

▲ The Baker's Neighbor

Making Connections

Text to Self • Text to Text • Text To World

NC STANDARDS: ELA 1.04g increase vocabulary/use discussion, 2.04b identify theme, 3.01b interpret/evaluate text/examine characters' actions/motives, 3.01d interpret/evaluate text/ analyze differences among genres, 3.06 conduct research using a variety of tools

Compare Texts

1. Why does "The Baker's Neighbor" belong in a theme about working with others? INTERPRETATION / EVALUATING
2. How does the author use stage directions to show a change in Manuel from the beginning of the play to the end? COGNITION / KNOWLEDGE
3. How and why do Pablo's feelings change during the play? INTERPRETATION / EVALUATING
4. How would "The Baker's Neighbor" be different if it were written as a story instead of a play? COGNITION / EVALUATING
5. In the play, Manuel owns a bakery. How could you find out more about what it takes to start a business? INTERPRETATION / EVALUATING

Write an Ad

Suppose Manuel the baker asked you to write an ad to persuade people to go to his bakery. Use information from the play to write your ad. Include words and phrases that appeal to the senses. Organize your ideas in a web like this one.

Writing CONNECTION

NC STANDARDS: ELA 2.02b interact with text/make predictions, 2.05 support inferences/conclusions, 3.05 use graphs/charts/maps to expand understanding, 3.06 conduct research using a variety of tools

Conduct Experiments

Science CONNECTION

Manuel bakes pies and cakes in his bakery. The ingredients he uses probably include flour, sugar, and salt. Find out which of these substances dissolve in water. Conduct an experiment in which you stir 1 teaspoon of each substance into 1 cup of water. Write a prediction about the outcome of each experiment, keep a record of what happens, and then draw a conclusion.

Substance	Prediction	Results When Stirred	Results After One Hour	Conclusion
salt				
sugar				
flour				

NC STANDARDS: ELA 3.06 conduct research using a variety of tools, 4.02a use writing to communicate with others

Create a Pamphlet

Social Studies CONNECTION

The neighbors in "The Baker's Neighbor" ask the Judge to settle a disagreement. Research your state's court system. Create a pamphlet about the court system in your state. Include written information and illustrations.

▲ The Baker's Neighbor

A cause is an action or event that makes something happen. An **effect** is what happens as a result of an action or event.

Sometimes authors use signal words such as *because* or *so* to help readers identify a cause and an effect. Other times, readers must figure out causes and effects on their own.

INEZ: If Manuel is that rich, why doesn't he smile?
CARLOS: That's because he's a miser. A miser doesn't like people—only money.

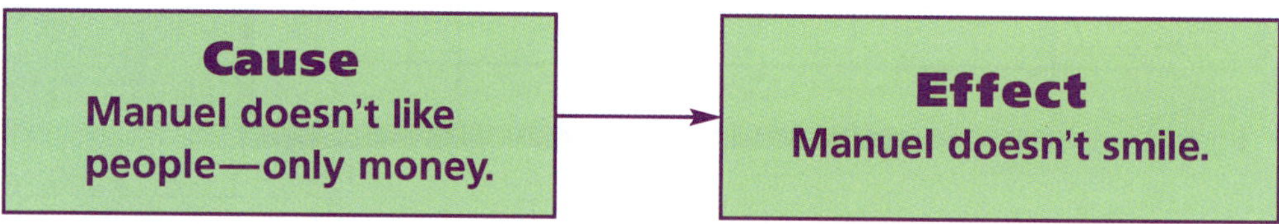

Understanding causes and effects can help you better understand the plot of a story. Sometimes an effect has more than one cause. A cause can also have more than one effect.

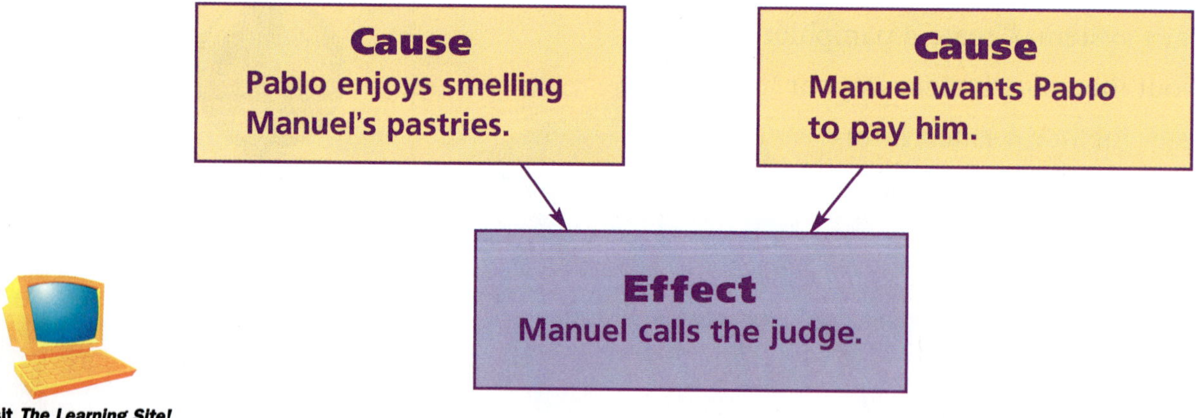

Visit *The Learning Site!*
www.harcourtschool.com
See *Skills* and *Activities*

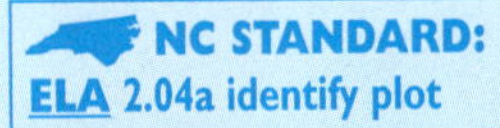

Test Prep
Cause and Effect

▶ **Read the passage. Then answer the questions.**

Kevin decided to bake his dad a cake for his birthday. He took out the recipe book and gathered the ingredients. He did not understand the part of the recipe that told him to sift the flour, so he dumped the flour into the bowl. When he went to add the sugar, he realized that he didn't have enough, so he added extra salt. Then he poured the batter into the pan and called his mom to turn on the oven. After the cake was in the oven, he realized that he had forgotten to grease the pan. He hoped the cake would turn out.

CRITICAL STANCE / ANALYZING

1. What causes Kevin to decide to bake a cake?

A He has never baked a cake before.

B He wants dessert.

C The recipe looks easy.

D It is his father's birthday.

Tip

The question gives the effect and asks you to find the cause. To find a cause, ask yourself, *Why did this happen?*

CRITICAL STANCE / ANALYZING

2. If the cake turns out poorly, which of these actions will *not* be a cause?

F following the recipe

G not sifting the flour

H adding more salt instead of sugar

J forgetting to grease the pan

Tip

Read the question carefully. Remember that you are looking for the one action that will *not* cause the cake to turn out poorly.

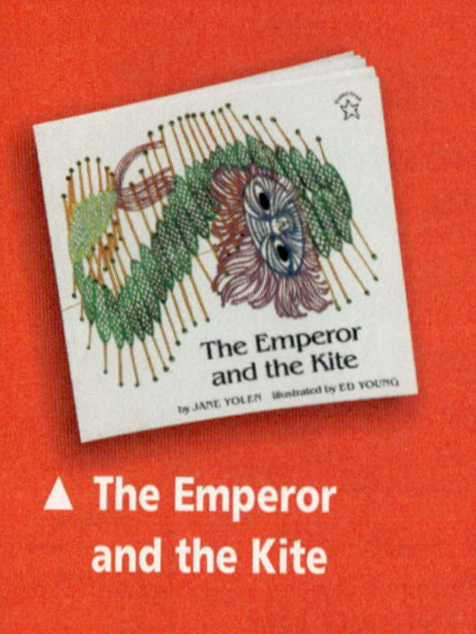

▲ The Emperor and the Kite

Vocabulary Power

- insignificant
- steely
- unyielding
- twined
- neglected
- loyal
- plotting
- encircling

The main character in "The Emperor and the Kite" is very small. It is sometimes surprising what someone or something small is able to do.

Spiders Although most spiders are less than a half inch long, it would be a mistake to think of these tiny creatures as **insignificant**, or unimportant. Many thousands of types of spiders are found all over the world.

Spiders produce silk threads from their bodies. They use the silk to make webs for catching their food. The silk threads of a spiderweb may look delicate, but they are **steely** strands. Some people say that spider threads, if twisted into a string as thick as a pencil, could stop a jet plane in the sky! What other material is so **unyielding** that it would not give way under that kind of force?

In a spiderweb, the silk threads are not **twined**, or twisted together. Instead, they are held together by tiny drops of glue. When the glue begins to loosen, the spider eats its old web and makes a new one. If the spider **neglected** this task, or ignored it, the spider would soon go hungry.

Some stories picture spiders as **loyal** friends. However, many stories picture evil spiders **plotting**, or secretly planning, to capture things in their webs. In fact, spiders make webs just to catch insects for food. Some spiders also use their silk to wrap up their food for later. They move around and around an insect's body, **encircling** it in silk.

Vocabulary–Writing CONNECTION

Think about what makes someone a **loyal** friend. Then write to describe someone you think of as a loyal friend.

Genre

Folktale

Folktales are stories that were first told orally. They reflect the customs and beliefs of a culture.

In this selection, look for

- A plot that teaches a lesson
- A main character who reflects the values of a culture

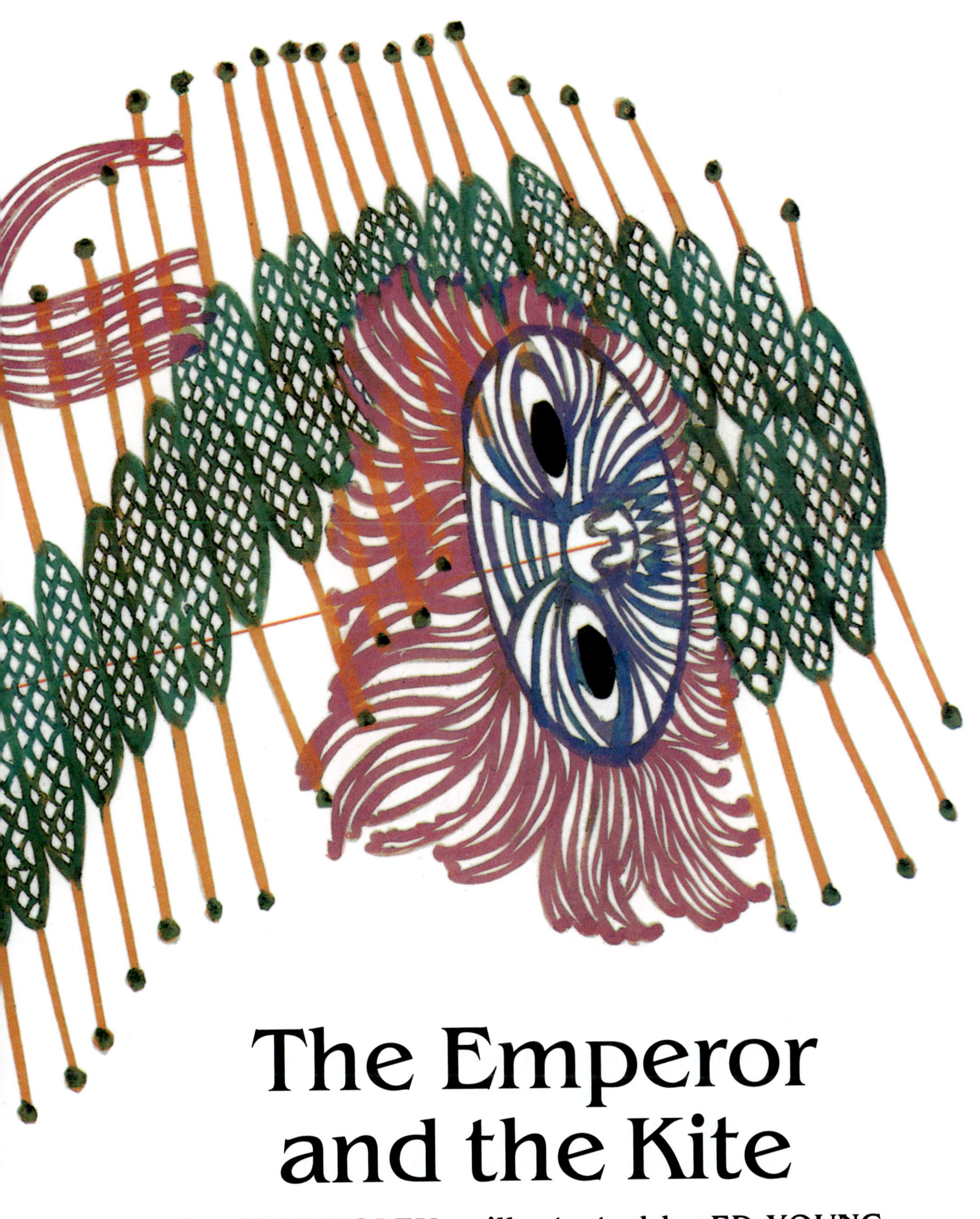

The Emperor and the Kite

by JANE YOLEN illustrated by ED YOUNG

Once in ancient China there lived a princess who was the fourth daughter of the emperor. She was very tiny. In fact she was so tiny her name was Djeow Seow, which means "the smallest one." And, because she was so tiny, she was not thought very much of—when she was thought of at all.

Her brothers, who were all older and bigger and stronger than she, were thought of all the time. And they were like four rising suns in the eyes of their father. They helped the emperor rule the kingdom and teach the people the ways of peace.

Even her three sisters were all older and bigger and stronger than she. They were like three midnight moons in the eyes of their father. They were the ones who brought food to his table.

But Djeow Seow was like a tiny star in the emperor's sight. She was not even allowed to bring a grain of rice to the meal, so little was she thought of. In fact she was so insignificant, the emperor often forgot he had a fourth daughter at all.

And so, Djeow Seow ate by herself. And she talked to herself.

And she played by herself, which was the loneliest thing of all. Her favorite toy was a kite of paper and sticks.

Every morning, when the wind came from the east past the rising sun, she flew her kite. And every evening, when the wind went to the west past the setting sun, she flew her kite. Her toy was like a flower in the sky. And it was like a prayer in the wind.

In fact a monk who passed the palace daily made up a poem about her kite.

My kite sails upward,
Mounting to the high heavens.
My soul goes on wings.

But then he was a monk, and given to such thoughts. As for Princess Djeow Seow, she thanked him each day for his prayer. Then she went back to flying her toy.

But all was not peaceful in the kingdom, just as the wind is not always peaceful. For the wind can trouble the waters of a still pond. And there were evil men plotting against the emperor.

They crept up on him one day when he was alone, when his four sons were away ruling in the furthermost parts of the kingdom and his three daughters were down in the garden. And only Princess Djeow Seow, so tiny she seemed part of the corner where she sat, saw what happened.

The evil men took the emperor to a tower in the middle of a wide, treeless plain. The tower had only a single window, with an iron bar across the center. The plotters sealed the door with bricks and mortar once the emperor was inside.

Then they rode back to the palace and declared that the emperor was dead.

When his sons and daughters heard this, they all fled to a neighboring kingdom where they spent their time sobbing and sighing. But they did nothing else all day long.

All except Djeow Seow. She was so tiny, the evil men did not notice her at all. And so, she crept to the edge of the wide, treeless plain. And there she built a hut of twigs and branches.

Every day at dawn and again at dark, she would walk across the plain to the tower. And there she would sail her stick-and-paper kite. To the kite string she tied a tiny basket filled with rice and poppyseed cakes, water chestnuts and green tea. The kite pulled the basket high, high in the air, up as high as the window in the tower. And, in this way, she kept her father alive.

So they lived for many days: the emperor in his tower and the princess in a hut near the edge of the plain. The evil men ruled with their cruel, harsh ways, and the people of the country were very sad.

One day as the princess prepared a basket of food for her father, the old monk passed by her hut. She smiled at him, but he seemed not to see her. Yet as he passed, he repeated his prayer in a loud voice. He said:

My kite sails upward,
Mounting to the high heavens.
My emperor goes on wings.

The princess started to thank him. But then she stopped. Something was different. The words were not quite right. "Stop," she called to the monk. But he had already passed by. He was a monk, after all, and did not take part in things of this world.

And then Djeow Seow understood. The monk was telling her something important. And she understood.

Each day after that, when she was not bringing food to her father, Djeow Seow was busy. She twined a string of grass and vines, and wove in strands of her own long black hair. When her rope was as thick as her waist and as high as the tower, she was ready. She attached the rope to the string of the stick-and-paper kite, and made her way across the treeless plain. When she reached the tower, she called to her father. But her voice was as tiny as she, and her words were lost in the wind.

At last, though, the emperor looked out and saw his daughter flying her kite. He expected the tiny basket of food to sail up to his window as it had done each day. But what should he see but the strand of vines and grass and long black hair. The wind was raging above, holding the kite in its steely grip.

And the princess was below, holding tight to the end of the rope.

Although the emperor had never really understood the worth of his tiniest daughter before, he did now. And he promised himself that if her plan worked she would never again want for anything, though all she had ever wanted was love. Then he leaned farther out of the tower window and grasped the heavy strand. He brought it into his tower room and loosened the string of the kite. He set the kite free, saying, "Go to thy home in the sky, great kite." And the kite flew off toward the heavens.

Then the emperor tied one end of the thick strand to the heavy iron bar across the window and the other end stretched all the way down to Djeow Seow's tiny hands.

The emperor stepped to the window sill, slipped under the iron bar, saluted the gods, and slid down the rope. His robes billowed out around him like the wings of a bright kite.

When his feet reached the ground, he knelt before his tiny daughter. And he touched the ground before her with his lips. Then he rose and embraced her, and she almost disappeared in his arms.

With his arm encircling her, the emperor said, "Come to thy home with me, loyal child." He lifted the tiny princess to his shoulders and carried her all the way back to the palace.

At the palace, the emperor was greeted by wild and cheering crowds. The people were tired of the evil men, but they had been afraid to act. With the emperor once again to guide them, they threw the plotters into prison.

And when the other sons and daughters of the emperor heard of his return, they left off their sobbing and sighing, and they hurried home to welcome their father. But when they arrived, they were surprised to find Djeow Seow on a tiny throne by their father's side.

To the end of his day, the emperor ruled with Princess Djeow Seow close by. She never wanted for anything, especially love. And the emperor never again neglected a person—whether great or small. And, too, it is said that Djeow Seow ruled after him, as gentle as the wind and, in her loyalty, as unyielding.

Think and Respond

1. How does Djeow Seow save her father, the emperor?
2. Why is the character of the monk important to the story?
3. Why did people think of Djeow Seow as **insignificant**?
4. Do you think people can learn something important from this folktale? Explain your answer.
5. How did using a reading strategy help you as you read this selection?

Meet the Author

Jane Yolen

Jane Yolen began her writing career as a journalist and poet before turning to children's literature. She has written over 150 children's books, including the Piggins mystery series, and has won many literary awards. She says she comes from a family of storytellers, so writing children's tales continues the family tradition. Family is very important to Jane Yolen. She often includes family in her stories, having fashioned several characters after her husband and children.

Meet the Illustrator

Ed Young

Ed Young has been illustrating children's books for more than 20 years. He says that when he worked as an advertising designer, he used to spend his lunch breaks at the zoo sketching the animals.

Young uses different techniques in the books he illustrates. For *The Emperor and the Kite,* he used an Oriental paper cutting technique. Besides being a gifted illustrator, he is also a talented writer. In fact, his book *Lon Po Po* won the Caldecott Medal.

Ed Young was born in Tientsin, China, and grew up in Shanghai. He now lives in Hastings-on-Hudson, New York, with his wife, Filomena.

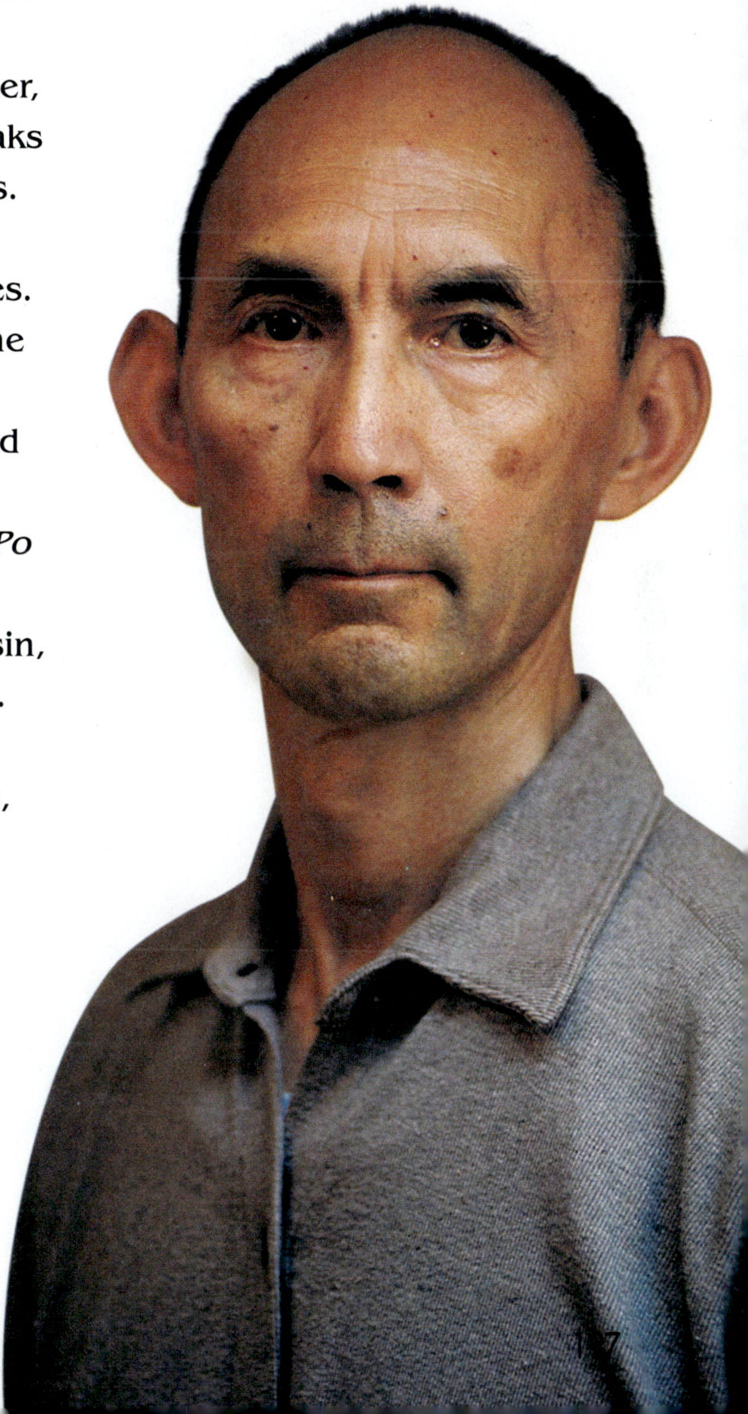

Genre Magazine Article

KITE FESTIVALS

All around the world, people get together to have fun with their kites at festivals. One is held every spring at the Washington Monument in Washington, D.C. People enter their special kites in flying competitions. You can see breathtaking flights of animal kites like the ones shown here. There are kite festivals year round, but most happen in spring.

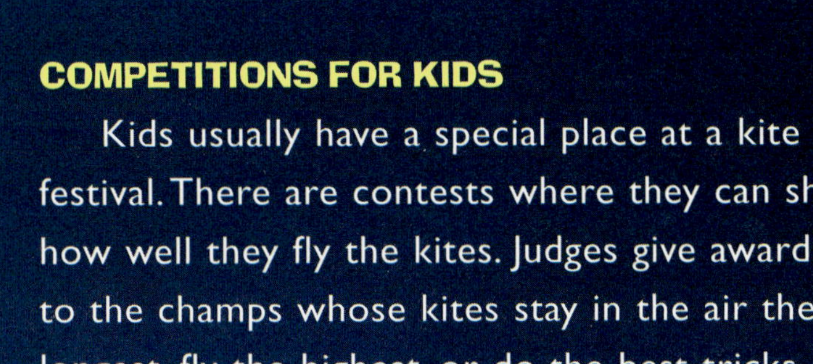

COMPETITIONS FOR KIDS

Kids usually have a special place at a kite festival. There are contests where they can show how well they fly the kites. Judges give awards to the champs whose kites stay in the air the longest, fly the highest, or do the best tricks.

PRETTY TRICKY

At a festival, you might see someone flying a kite with more than one line. A stunt kite like that can do all kinds of tricks in the air.

Some stunt kites can fly in "figure eights" and dive at 60 miles (96 km) per hour! You might also see teams of people flying kites that "dance" to music.

FIGHTER KITES

To see some really skillful flying, look for kite battles at a festival. Each fighter kite is flown on a strong line. Two people fly their kites so that their lines cross. Then each person tries to use the wind to saw through the other one's line. The person with the last kite in the air wins!

KITE TALES

SO LONG AGO

The Chinese invented kites about 3,000 years ago. People living in Hamamatsu, Japan, have been flying kites at festivals for at least 400 years—long before the United States became a country.

RECORD-SETTING KITES

In 1919, some people in Germany flew a train of kites more than five miles (8 km) above the Earth. A group in Japan flew more than 11,000 kites on a single line in 1990. A bunch of college students in Long Beach, Washington, kept a kite in the air for more than a week!

NOT JUST A TOY

Did you know that the Wright brothers' first airplane was a lot like a kind of kite called a box kite? Imagine how brave they were to fly off in a kite with a motor and a propeller.

WHOA, KITES, WHOA!

About 150 years ago, a teacher in England built a carriage that was pulled by a train of kites. With a good wind, it could go about as fast as a carriage pulled by horses, and the teacher didn't have to feed his kites anything!

HELP-ME KITES

People sometimes carry a small kite on wilderness hikes. Then, if they need to be rescued, they can fly the kite to help show rescuers where they are.

THE BEST KITE OF ALL?

The very best kite is one you make and fly yourself. Many kinds of kites can be made with materials found around your house. Libraries have books on making and flying kites.

PAPER FOLD KITE

This kite can be flown in light winds or indoors in a large space.

What you need:

- Typing, copier, or computer paper (8 by 11 inches)
- Clear tape
- Drinking straw
- Sewing thread or light string for the flying line
- Crepe paper for the tail

What you do:

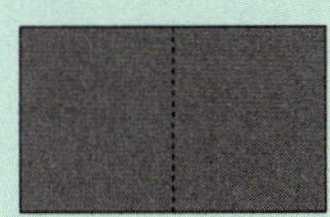

1. Fold sheet of paper in half, top to bottom.

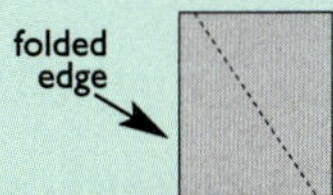

2. Mark a diagonal on the folded paper. Offset the diagonal by 3/8 of an inch.

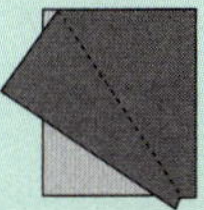

3. Fold the top leaf forward along the diagonal line and the bottom leaf backward.

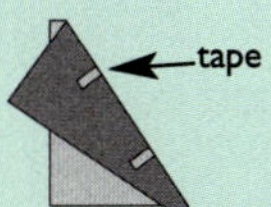

4. Tape the keel together (see diagram 4) by putting tape across the wings.

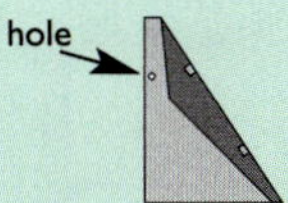

5. Make a hole 3 inches from the top of the keel.

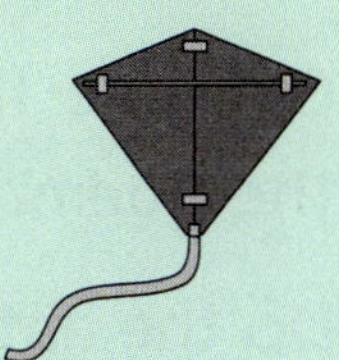

6. Tape the drinking straw from wingtip to wingtip.

7. Make a tail the length of the kite. Tape the tail at bottom of kite point.

8. Attach the flying line through the hole (see diagram 5).

9. To fly indoors: Use a three-foot flying line attached to a ruler or a balloon stick.

Happy Flying!

SAFETY TIP:

Fly your kite in an open area at a park, field, or beach. Never use wire for your line. Stay away from electrical wires, and don't fly a kite during a thunderstorm. Also, if you fly a big kite, be sure to wear gloves. That will keep your hands from getting burned by a fast-moving line.

▲ The Emperor and the Kite

Making Connections

Text to Self • Text to Text • Text To World

Compare Texts

NC STANDARDS: ELA 2.02e interact with text/connect text to own experiences, 3.06 conduct research using a variety of tools, 5.02 use correct grammar in speaking/writing

1. How does "The Emperor and the Kite" fit into the theme Side by Side? INTERPRETATION / EVALUATING
2. On page 184, what small change does the monk make to the poem? What is he trying to tell Djeow Seow? INTERPRETATION / APPLYING
3. Do the author of "The Emperor and the Kite" and the author of "Kite Festivals" have the same viewpoint about kites? Explain. COGNITION / EVALUATING
4. Think about another folktale you have read. In what ways is it like "The Emperor and the Kite"? CONNECTIONS / ANALYZING
5. If you wanted to read more folktales from Asia, where might you look for them? INTERPRETATION / EVALUATING

Write to Explain

Suppose the emperor decides to put Djeow Seow's kite on display. Write a paragraph to be displayed with the kite. Explain how Djeow Seow used the kite to rescue her father. Make a chart like this one to organize your ideas.

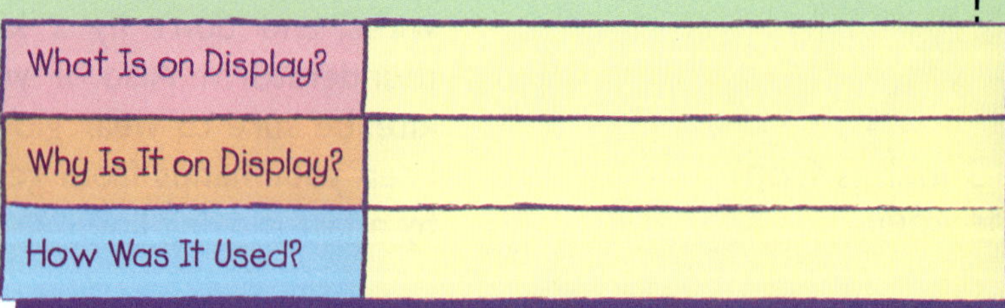

What Is on Display?	
Why Is It on Display?	
How Was It Used?	

Create a Display

NC STANDARD: ELA 3.06 conduct research using a variety of tools

Social Studies CONNECTION

Kites were invented in China about 3,000 years ago. Research a more recent invention, such as the electric light or the automobile. Make or use drawings, diagrams, or other graphic aids to create a visual display about this invention. Write captions for each graphic you include.

NC STANDARD: Math 2.02 solve problems using area/perimeter

Measure Perimeter and Area

Math CONNECTION

Kites are made in many different shapes and sizes, including squares and rectangles. Cut several square and rectangular miniature kites of different sizes from construction paper. Then find the perimeter and area of each shape, and write the measurements on it.

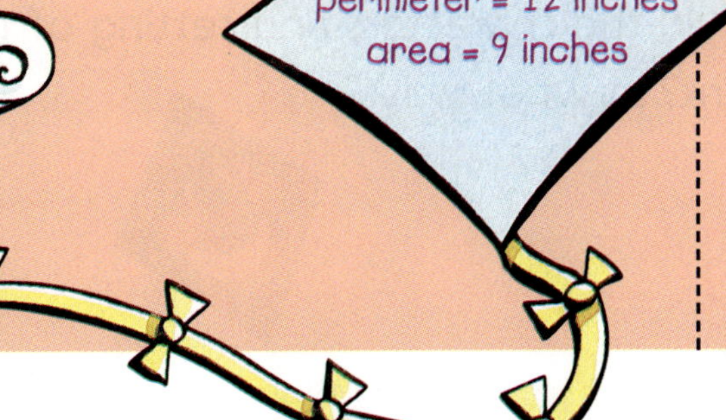

▲ The Emperor and the Kite

NC STANDARDS: ELA 2.04a identify plot, 5.08a demonstrate language cohesion/use logical sequence in retells

Narrative Elements

Remember that narrative elements of a story include **characters**, **setting**, and **plot**. These elements combine to create a particular story. Changing any one of the elements would cause changes in the others as well, resulting in a different story.

The diagram shows how all of the elements are related.

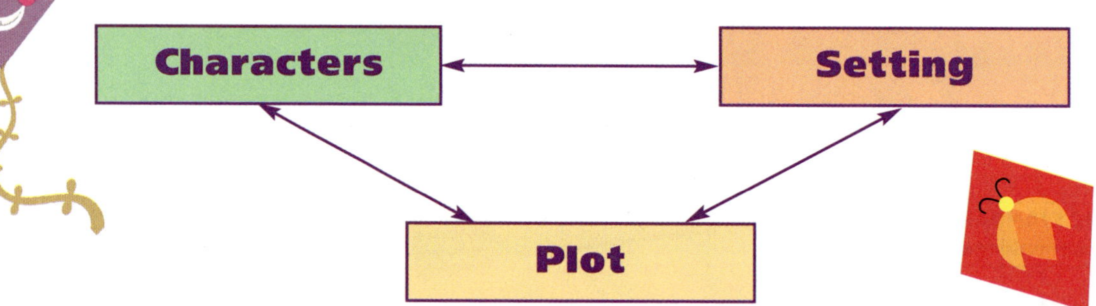

For example, if "The Emperor and the Kite" was set in the United States in the present, there would be no emperor. As a result, the plot of the story would also change.

Think about these questions:

- If the character Djeow Seow was not so tiny and insignificant, how might that change the plot of the story?
- If the rescue in the plot was by a helicopter rather than by a kite, would the characters and setting of the story also be different? In what ways?

Visit *The Learning Site!*
www.harcourtschool.com
See *Skills* and *Activities*

Test Prep
Narrative Elements

NC STANDARDS: ELA
2.04a identify plot, 2.04c identify main idea/details

Focus Skill

▶ **Read the passage. Then answer the questions.**

Harlan was the biggest boy in town. Some people said he was the biggest, strongest boy on the whole western frontier.

One day Harlan's father was plowing the fields when his ox Bessie fell into a ditch and hurt her leg. Poor Bessie couldn't get up. Harlan's father ran to fetch him from the schoolhouse.

Harlan lifted Bessie out of the ditch. Bessie's leg was sore, so Harlan carried her up and down the fields while his father steered the plow.

CRITICAL STANCE / INTEGRATING

1. How would the plot change if the character of Harlan was not so big and strong?

- **A** Bessie would have to be rescued a different way.
- **B** There would be a different plow.
- **C** Bessie would not have fallen in the ditch.
- **D** There would be no change.

Identify an event that could not take place if the character was not so big and strong.

CRITICAL STANCE / INTEGRATING

2. If the plot changed so that Harlan's father needed help reeling in a huge fish, how else would the story change?

- **F** It would be set in a different place.
- **G** It would be set in a different time.
- **H** Harlan would not have to be so big and strong.
- **J** There would be no change.

Think about how the characters and the setting would have to change for this story to be about fishing.

▲ Nights of the Pufflings

Vocabulary Power

It's interesting to read about different kinds of animals. Jack read an article about prairie dogs. Read his notebook to find out what he learned.

- **uninhabited**
- **burrows**
- **stranded**
- **venture**
- **instinctively**
- **nestles**

I just finished reading an article about prairie dogs. They live on plains and prairies. They aren't really dogs, but their cries sound like dogs barking.

Prairie dogs live mostly in **uninhabited** areas, where there are no people to bother them. They dig deep holes, or **burrows**, in the earth. During the day they come out of their burrows to find food and to spend time with other prairie dogs.

It would be unusual to find a prairie dog **stranded**, alone and helpless. Prairie dogs stay close to their burrows and don't **venture** out into dangerous places. They **instinctively** live together in large groups called towns. They don't think about it or plan to stay together. They do it because this kind of life is natural for them.

I like to imagine a little prairie dog deep down in its burrow at night. First it **nestles** close to its brothers and sisters. Then, when it is all snug and cozy, it closes its eyes and goes to sleep.

Vocabulary–Writing
CONNECTION

Birds **instinctively** build nests. What kinds of things do you do instinctively? Write a few sentences about each thing.

Nights of the Pufflings

WRITTEN AND PHOTO-ILLUSTRATED BY BRUCE MCMILLAN

Genre

Nonfiction

Nonfiction tells about people, things, events, or places that are real.

In this selection, look for

- **Characters who help out**
- **Information about a topic**

Halla *(HATTL•lah)* searches the sky every day. As she watches from high on a cliff overlooking the sea, she spots her first puffin of the season. She whispers to herself, "Lundi" *(LOON•dah)*, which means "puffin" in Icelandic.

Soon the sky is speckled with them—puffins, puffins everywhere. Millions of these birds are returning from their winter at sea. They are coming back to Halla's island and the nearby uninhabited islands to lay eggs and raise puffin chicks. It's the only time they come ashore.

While Halla and her friends are at school in the village beneath the cliffs, the puffins continue to land. These "clowns of the sea" return to the same burrows year after year. Once back, they busy themselves getting their underground nests ready. Halla and all the children of Heimaey *(HAY•mah•ay)* can only wait and dream of the nights of the pufflings yet to come.

On the weekends, Halla and her friends climb over the cliffs to watch the birds. They see puffin pairs *tap-tap-tap* their beaks together. Each pair they see will soon tend an egg. Deep inside the cliffs that egg will hatch a chick. That chick will grow into a young puffling. That puffling will take its first flight. The nights of the pufflings will come.

In the summer, while Halla splashes in the cold ocean water, the puffins also splash. The sea below the cliffs is dotted with puffins bobbing on the waves. Like Halla, many puffins that ride the waves close to shore are young. The older birds usually fly further out to sea where the fishing is better. The grown-up puffins have to catch lots of fish, because now that it's summer they are feeding more than just themselves.

Halla's friend, Arnar Ingi *(ATT•nar ING•ee)*, spies a puffin overhead. "Fisk" *(FIHSK)*, he whispers as he gazes at the returning puffin's bill full of fish. The puffin eggs have hatched, and the parents are bringing home fish to feed their chicks.

The nights of the pufflings are still long weeks away, but Arnar Ingi thinks about getting some cardboard boxes ready.

Halla and her friends never see the chicks—only the chicks' parents see them. The baby puffins never come out. They stay safely hidden in the long dark tunnels of their burrows. But Halla and her friends hear them calling out for food. "*Peep-peep-peep.*" The growing chicks are hungry. Their parents have to feed them—sometimes ten times a day—and carry many fish in their bills.

All summer long the adult puffins fish and tend to their feathers. By August, flowering baldusbrá *(BAL•durs•broh)* blanket the burrows. With the baldusbrá in full bloom, Halla knows that the wait is over. The hidden chicks have grown into young pufflings. The pufflings are ready to fly and will at last venture out into the night. Now it's time.

It's time for Halla and her friends to get out their boxes and flashlights for the nights of the pufflings. Starting tonight, and for the next two weeks, the pufflings will be leaving for their winter at sea. Halla and her friends will spend each night searching for stranded pufflings that don't make it to the water. But the village cats and dogs will be searching, too. It will be a race to see who finds the stray pufflings first. By ten o'clock the streets of Heimaey are alive with roaming children.

In the darkness of night, the pufflings leave their burrows for their first flight. It's a short, wing-flapping trip from the high cliffs. Most of the birds splash-land safely in the sea below. But some get confused by the village lights—perhaps they think the lights are moonbeams reflecting on the water. Hundreds of the pufflings crash-land in the village every night. Unable to take off from flat ground, they run around and try to hide.

Dangers await. Even if the cats and dogs don't get them, the pufflings might get run over by cars or trucks.

Halla and her friends race to the rescue. Armed with their flashlights, they wander through the village. They search dark places. Halla yells out "puffling" in Icelandic. "Lundi pysja!" *(LOON•dah PEESH•yar)*. She has spotted one. When the puffling runs down the street, she races after it, grabs it, and nestles it in her arms. Arnar Ingi catches one, too. No sooner are the pufflings safe in the cardboard boxes than more of them land nearby. "Lundi pysja! Lundi pysja!"

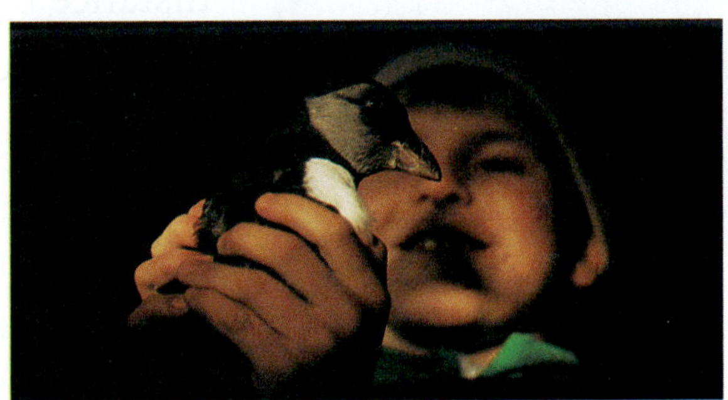

For two weeks all the children of Heimaey sleep late in the day so they can stay out at night. They rescue thousands of pufflings. There are pufflings, pufflings everywhere, and helping hands too—even though the pufflings instinctively nip at helping fingers. Every night Halla and her friends take the rescued pufflings home. The next day they send their guests on their way. Halla meets her friends and, with the boxes full of pufflings, they hike down to the beach.

It's time to set the pufflings free. Halla releases one first. She holds it up so that it will get used to flapping its wings. Then, with the puffling held snugly in her hands, she counts "Einn–tveir–ÞRÍR!" *(EYN • TVAIR • THEER)* as she swings the puffling three times between her legs. The last swing is the highest, launching the bird up in the air and out over the water beyond the surf. It's only the second time this puffling has flown, so it flutters just a short distance before safely splash-landing.

Day after day Halla's pufflings paddle away, until the nights of the pufflings are over for the year. As she watches the last of the pufflings and adult puffins leave for their winter at sea, Halla bids them farewell until next spring. She wishes them a safe journey as she calls out "goodbye, goodbye" in Icelandic. "Bless, bless!"

Think and Respond

1. What do Halla and the other children do to help the **stranded** pufflings?
2. How does the author help readers understand what the children do and how they feel?
3. What do you think happens to the pufflings that hatch on the **uninhabited** islands nearby?
4. Would you like to help Halla and her friends rescue the **stranded** pufflings? What do you think you would like or dislike about the experience?
5. What reading strategy did you use as you read "Nights of the Pufflings"? How was the strategy helpful to you?

TRAVEL

Photo-illustrator Highlights Iceland

Bruce McMillan

Author and photographer Bruce McMillan says he loves happy endings.

NEWS

Meet the Author

REYKJAVIK, ICELAND — Children's book author Bruce McMillan has traveled all over, from Alaska to the Caribbean, to create his popular books. Three of his recent works, *Nights of the Pufflings, Gletta the Foal,* and *My Horse of the North,* are set in Iceland.

McMillan has been taking photographs all his life, but he did not start writing until he spent two years living on an island off the coast of Maine. While he was there, he wrote a book about lobstering and took photographs for it. He decided to make it a children's book because he noticed not many children's books had photographs.

McMillan gets most of his ideas from his own interesting experiences and from things happening around him. For example, he tells about growing apples and making sneakers. He does more than just give information, though. He likes to tell a story with his books. "I love a happy ending," he says.

Bruce McMillan likes speaking to groups about his work—and they can tell that he likes being an author. His readers hope he will create many more colorful books for them to enjoy.

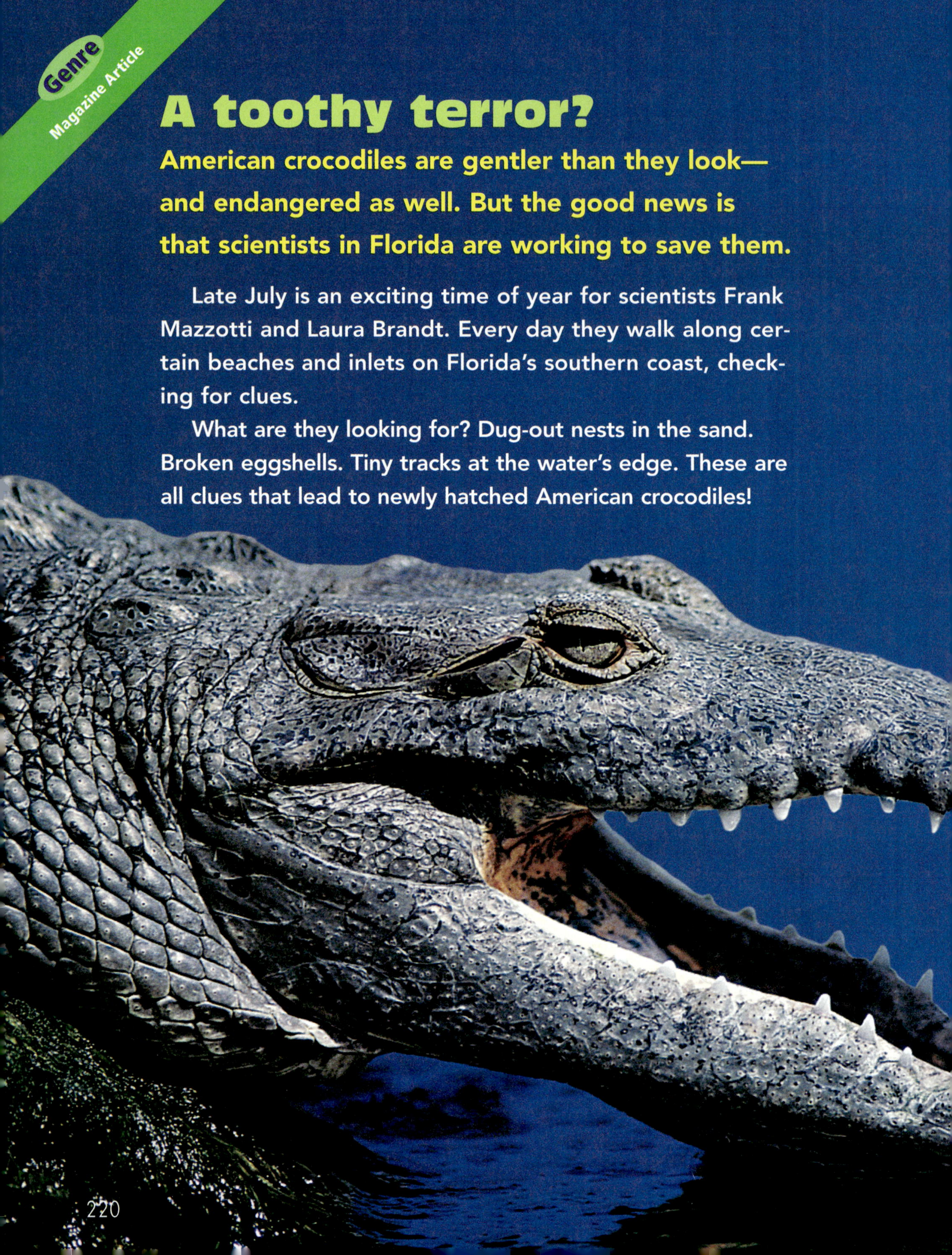

A toothy terror?

American crocodiles are gentler than they look—and endangered as well. But the good news is that scientists in Florida are working to save them.

Late July is an exciting time of year for scientists Frank Mazzotti and Laura Brandt. Every day they walk along certain beaches and inlets on Florida's southern coast, checking for clues.

What are they looking for? Dug-out nests in the sand. Broken eggshells. Tiny tracks at the water's edge. These are all clues that lead to newly hatched American crocodiles!

Frank and Laura have been studying this endangered species since 1977. At that time, the number of crocodiles in southern Florida had dropped to about 300. One reason was that too much of the crocs' natural home area had been bulldozed to make way for houses. (Crocs like to live around beaches, lagoons, and bays—just as people do.)

Luckily, by the early 1980s, the U.S. government started to help. It began to protect a big chunk of what remained of the crocs' natural area. And since then, the number of crocs in southern Florida has grown to almost 500.

This pop-up croc is a Nile crocodile. It's half-way hatched from its leathery egg.

But these huge reptiles are still endangered. To help save them, Frank and Laura have been studying the animals. Where do crocs go after they hatch? How

CARING for CROCS

BY LYLE PRESCOTT

Scientists Laura Brandt and Frank Mazzotti cruise up a Florida waterway in search of American crocodiles. They've studied these crocs for many years. And there's still a lot to learn.

much living space do they need? The two scientists have been trying to answer questions like these.

One thing they've learned is that these crocs aren't so scary. "American crocodiles are more scared of people than you need to be of them," says Laura.

NESTING SEASON

The two scientists study the crocs year round. But the most important time is nesting season. It begins in late April when female crocs trudge ashore to make nests in the sand or soil. (A nest can be a hole a female digs in the ground or a mound of leaves and dirt she pushes together above the ground.) When a female has laid about 40 eggs in her nest, she kicks sand, dirt, or leaves over the eggs to bury them.

The female comes back often to check on her nest. After about 90 days, she hears little chirps coming out of it. She lays her head on the nest to listen closely. Her babies are finally hatching! She helps them dig their way out of the nest. Then she starts carrying them one by one in her mouth down to the water's edge.

The babies will hang out near the water's edge for a few weeks. While they're there, Frank and Laura get busy catching the little creatures to weigh and measure them. They also clip a few scales off each baby's tail (see photo at right).

Later, by looking at the different patterns of clipped scales, the scientists can tell the crocs apart. This helps them keep track of where each croc goes and what it does—even when it's grown up. For example, they've found that a female croc often makes her nest in the exact same spot each year.

HOME, SWEET HOME

The scientists have also learned that each crocodile roams an area about the size of 250 football fields. A croc may share most of this area with other crocs. But each croc needs this much space to find enough crabs, birds, fish, turtles, snakes, and other favorite prey.

The scientists mark each croc by clipping different scales off its tail (above). That way they can recognize it if they catch it later.

They also measure the length of each baby. This newly hatched croc is about 10 inches (25 cm) long.

No, this is not a game of hang-croc. The rope is attached to a scale, which Frank is using to weigh a baby croc. By catching and weighing crocodiles often, the scientists keep track of how fast they grow.

Some people think that the way to save these endangered animals is to dig up their eggs and raise the babies in labs. But Frank says he has learned that's not the best idea. "The most important way we can help these animals is to make sure their habitat is protected," he explains. "If we protect their natural areas and then leave them alone, they do just fine."

Right now the two scientists are getting ready to weigh and mark a whole new batch of hatchlings. Keep up the good work, Frank and Laura!

Think and Respond

Why is it important for the scientists to study American crocodiles?

These baby crocs just hatched from a nest under a pile of leaves. Only a couple of the hatchlings in each nest will live to become adults. Big birds and fish will snatch up most of them before they're a year old.

▲ Nights of the Pufflings

Making Connections

Text to Self • Text to Text • Text To World

Compare Texts

NC STANDARDS: ELA 2.04b identify theme, 3.03 examine effect of language/visuals, 4.04 share texts from different genres

1. What does "Nights of the Pufflings" show about working together? INTERPRETATION / EVALUATING
2. How do the photographs help you understand Halla's emotions at the beginning and the end of the selection? CRITICAL STANCE / ANALYZING
3. How are the children in "Nights of the Pufflings" and the scientists in "Caring for Crocs" alike? How are they different? CRITICAL STANCE / ANALYZING
4. Would you find the story of the pufflings as interesting to read if it were written as fiction instead of nonfiction? Why or why not? COGNITION / EVALUATING
5. What questions about puffins do you still have? INTERPRETATION / EVALUATING

Write a Project Description

Saving pufflings is an exciting project for the children of Heimaey. Think of an activity that would make a good project for a group of student volunteers where you live. Write a short description of the project. You may want to use a chart like the one below to help you organize your ideas.

Why Would This Be a Good Project?	How Many People Would Be Needed?	What Supplies Might Be Needed?	What Are the Main Steps of the Project?

Make a Map

NC STANDARDS: ELA 3.05 use graphs/charts/maps to expand understanding, 3.06 conduct research using a variety of tools

Social Studies CONNECTION

The people in Iceland use their land to raise livestock, and they catch fish in the water off their coast. Find out how people in your state use their land and water. Then create a product map of your state to show how its land and water are used. You may want to look at an example of a product map in your social studies book before you draw your map.

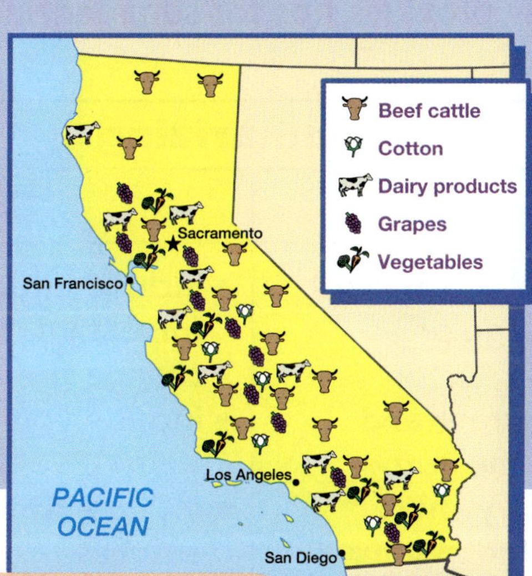

Make a Scientific Drawing

Science CONNECTION

All birds have adaptations that help them live in their environments. Choose a bird to research. Draw a picture of the bird and its environment. Add captions that describe how this bird's wings, beak, feet, and other body parts are suited to where and how it lives.

NC STANDARDS: ELA 3.05 use graphs/charts/maps to expand understanding, 3.06 conduct research using a variety of tools

▲ Nights of the Pufflings

NC STANDARDS: ELA 2.06 summarize major points, 4.02a use writing to communicate with others

Summarize

When you **summarize** a passage or selection, you tell about the most important parts in a few words.

The chart below provides tips for summarizing.

Summarizing	
Do	**Do Not**
• tell about the most important ideas in the passage or selection • follow the same order and pattern used by the author • keep your summary short • tell the information in your own words • summarize to help you understand and remember what you read	• include information that is not important • change the author's meaning • include your own ideas or opinions • include information from other sources

If a friend asked you what "Nights of the Pufflings" is about, what information would you include? What would you leave out?

Visit *The Learning Site!*
www.harcourtschool.com
See *Skills* and *Activities*

Test Prep
Summarize

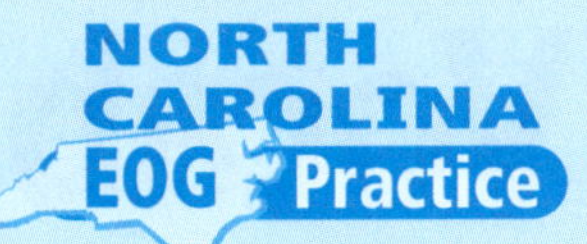

NC STANDARD: ELA 2.06 summarize major points

Focus Skill

▶ **Read the passage. Then answer the questions.**

Children who live in parts of Florida or the Caribbean, along the Amazon River system in South America, or near the rivers and coasts of West Africa may have manatees for neighbors. Manatees are large water mammals, also called sea cows. Three different species live in these three different parts of the world. They all have skin that is light to dark gray in color, eat large amounts of water plants, have front legs shaped like paddles, and have no hind legs.

All three species are threatened or endangered, but efforts are being made to protect them. The United States government is among those that have taken steps to save the manatees. One reason for protecting them is their usefulness in eating weeds that might otherwise block waterways.

COGNITION / INTEGRATING

1. **What is the most important information to include in a summary of this article?**

   A Manatees have no hind legs.

   B Manatees are threatened or endangered.

   C Manatees are found along the Amazon River system.

   D Manatees' front legs are shaped like paddles.

Decide which of the sentences states the most important idea. Which of these sentences is the subject of a paragraph?

COGNITION / INTEGRATING

2. **On another sheet of paper, write a brief summary of the article.**

Express the most important ideas from the article in your own words.

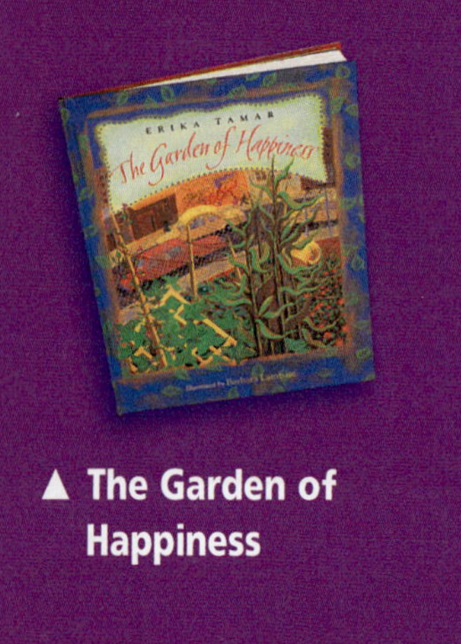

▲ The Garden of Happiness

Vocabulary Power

- **mural**
- **lavender**
- **inhaled**
- **haze**
- **skidded**

You can plant many things in a garden. Herbs, flowers, and vegetables are just a few of the possibilities. These students are painting a picture of a flower garden.

The students' picture is a **mural** on a wall. Their mural shows a flower garden in bloom.

One part of the mural shows a girl smelling some flowers. The flowers are **lavender**, or light purple, in color. The girl has **inhaled**, or breathed in, to enjoy their sweet scent.

The flowers at the right side of the mural are partly hidden by **haze**, or fog. The students want to show that it is early morning and the sun hasn't reached that part of the garden yet.

Do you see the paintbrush on the floor? Maggie gave it a push, and it **skidded**, or slid, across the floor to Anthony.

Vocabulary–Writing CONNECTION

Think about a **mural** you would like to paint. Write a paragraph describing what it would look like.

Notable Social Studies Trade Book

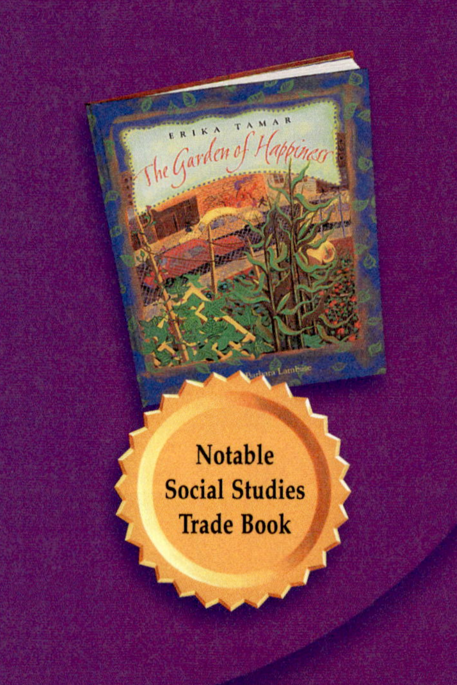

Genre

Realistic Fiction

Realistic fiction has characters and events that are like people and events in real life.

In this selection, look for

- **A setting that could be a real place**
- **Realistic characters and events**

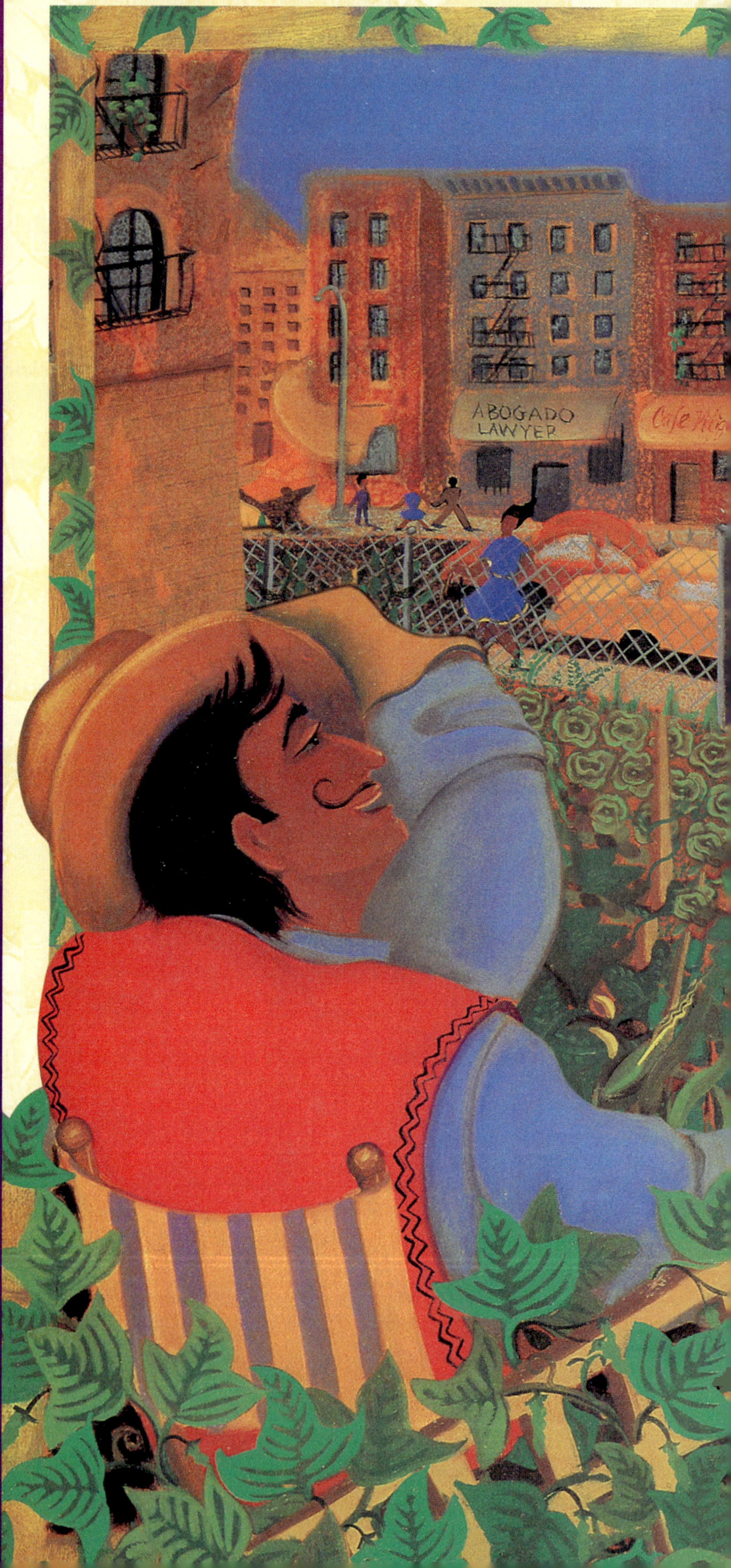

The Garden of Happiness

by Erika Tamar
illustrated by Barbara Lambase

On Marisol's block near East Houston Street, there was an empty lot that was filled with garbage and broken, tired things. It had a funky smell that made Marisol wrinkle her nose whenever she passed by.

One April morning, Marisol was surprised to see many grown-ups busy in the lot. Mr. Ortiz carried a rusty refrigerator door. Mrs. Willie Mae Washington picked up newspapers. Mr. Singh rolled a tire away.

The next afternoon, Marisol saw people digging up stones. Mr. Ortiz worked with a pickax.

"*¿Qué pasa?*" Marisol asked.

Mrs. Willie Mae Washington leaned on her shovel and wiped her forehead. "I'm gonna grow black-eyed peas and greens and sweet potatoes, too," she said. "Like on my daddy's farm in Alabama. No more store-bought collard greens for me."

"We will call it The Garden of Happiness," Mr. Singh said. "I am planting *valore*—such a beautiful vine of lavender and red. Yes, everyone is happy when they see this bean from Bangladesh."

On another day, Marisol watched Mr. Castro preparing the ground. Mrs. Rodriguez rolled a wheelbarrow full of peat moss. Marisol inhaled the fresh-soil smell of spring.

"Oh, I want to plant something in The Garden of Happiness!" Marisol said.

"Too late, *niña*," Mr. Ortiz said. "All the plots are already taken."

Marisol looked everywhere for a leftover spot, but the ground was crisscrossed by markers of sticks and string. She looked and looked. Just outside the chain-link fence, she found a bit of earth where the sidewalk had cracked.

"*¡Mira!* Here's my patch!" Marisol called. It was no bigger than her hand, but it was her very own. She picked out the pebbles and scraped the soil with a stick.

Marisol noticed a crowd of teenagers across the street from the lot. They were staring at a brick wall. It was sad and closed

up, without windows for eyes. Marisol crossed over to ask what they were doing.

"City Arts is giving us paint to make a mural on the wall," a girl told her.

"What will it be?" Marisol asked.

"Don't know yet," one of the big boys said. "We haven't decided."

"I'm making a garden," Marisol said. "I haven't decided, either, about what to plant."

In The Garden of Happiness, the ground had become soft and dark. Mr. Castro talked to his seedlings as he placed them in straight rows. "Come on now, little baby things, grow nice and big for me."

Marisol had no seedlings or even small cuttings or roots. *What can I do,* she thought, *where can I find something to plant?*

She went to the corner where old Mrs. Garcia was feeding the pigeons. Marisol helped herself to a big flat seed. The birds fluttered about angrily. "Only one," she told them, "for my garden."

Marisol skipped back to her patch. She poked a hole with her finger, dropped in the seed, and patted the soil all around. And every single day that spring, Marisol carried a watering can to the lot and gave her seed a cool drink.

Before long, a green shoot broke through in Marisol's patch. Even on rainy days, she hurried to the lot to see. Soon there were two leaves on a strong, straight stalk, and then there were four. It became as high as Marisol's knee!

Green things were growing all around in The Garden of Happiness. Mr. Castro's tiny seedlings became big bushy things with ripe tomatoes shining like rubies.

"What's *my* plant?" Marisol asked. Now it reached to her shoulder. "What's it going to be?"

"Dunno," Mrs. Willie Mae Washington answered. "But it sure is *somethin'!*"

Marisol pulled out the weeds in the late afternoons, when it wasn't so summer-hot.

Sometimes she watched the teenagers across the street. They measured the wall. They talked and argued about what they would paint.

Often Marisol saw Mr. Ortiz in his plot, resting in a chair.

"I come back from the factory and breathe the fresh air," he said. "And I sit among my *habichuelas*, my little piece of Puerto Rico."

"Is *my* plant from Puerto Rico? Do you know what it is?" Marisol asked.

Mr. Ortiz shook his head and laughed. "*¡Muy grande!* Maybe it's Jack's beanstalk from the fairy tale."

By the end of July, Marisol's plant had grown way over her head. And then, at the very top, Marisol saw a bud! It became fatter every day. She couldn't wait for it to open.

"Now don't be lookin' so hard," Mrs. Willie Mae Washington chuckled. "It's gonna open up behind your back, just when you're thinkin' about somethin' else."

One morning, Marisol saw an amazing sight from halfway down the block. She ran the rest of the way. Standing higher than all the plants and vines in the garden was a flower as big as a plate! Her bud had turned into petals of yellow and gold.

"A sunflower!" Mrs. Anderson exclaimed as she pushed her shopping cart by. "Reminds me of when I was a girl in Kansas."

Mrs. Majewska was rushing on her way to the subway, but she skidded to a stop. "Ah, *słoneczniki!* So pretty in the fields of Poland!"

Old Mrs. Garcia shook her head. "No, no, *los girasoles* from Mexico, where they bring joy to the roadside."

"I guess sunflowers make themselves right at home in every sun-kissed place on earth," Mrs. Willie Mae Washington said.

"Even right here in New York City," Marisol said proudly.

The flower was a glowing circle, brighter than a yellow taxi. *A flower of sunshine*, Marisol thought, *the happiest plant in The Garden of Happiness*.

All summer long, it made the people on the street stop and smile.

Soon the air became cool and crisp with autumn. Mr. Castro picked the last of his tomatoes. Mr. Singh carried away a basket full of beans. Mrs. Rodriguez picked her *tomatillos*. "To dry and cut up for *salsa*," she said.

Mrs. Willie Mae Washington dug up orange potatoes. "I can almost smell my sweet potato pie." She winked at Marisol. "I'm gonna save an extra big slice for a good little gardener I know."

But something terrible was happening to Marisol's flower. Its leaves were turning brown and dry.

Marisol watered and watered until a stream ran down the sidewalk. But her flower's leaves began to fall.

"Please get well again," Marisol whispered.

Every day, more golden petals curled and faded.

"My flower of sunshine is sick," Marisol cried. "What should I do?"

"Oh, child," Mrs. Willie Mae Washington said. "Its season is over. There's a time to bloom and a time to die."

"No! I don't want my flower to die!"

"*Mi cariño,* don't cry," Mrs. Rodriguez said. "That's the way of a garden. You must save the seeds and plant again next spring."

Marisol's flower drooped to the ground. The Garden of Happiness wasn't happy for her anymore. The vines had tumbled down. The bushy green plants were gone. She collected the seeds and put them in her pocket, but spring was much too far away.

Marisol was too sad to go to the empty lot anymore. For a whole week, she couldn't even look down the block where her beautiful flower used to be.

Then one day she heard people calling her name.

"Marisol! Come quick!"

"Marisol! *¡Apúrate!* Hurry!"

A golden haze shone on the street. There was a big crowd, like on a holiday. Music from the *bodega* was loud and bright. And what she saw made Marisol laugh and dance and clap her hands.

Think and Respond

1. How do Marisol's feelings about the garden change from the spring to the end of summer?
2. At the end of the story, what information do you get from a picture rather than from words? Why do you think the author chose to end the story this way?
3. Why does the **mural** make Marisol so happy?
4. Do you think Marisol's neighborhood is a good example of how people should get along? Explain your answer.
5. What reading strategies did you use as you read this story? How were they helpful?

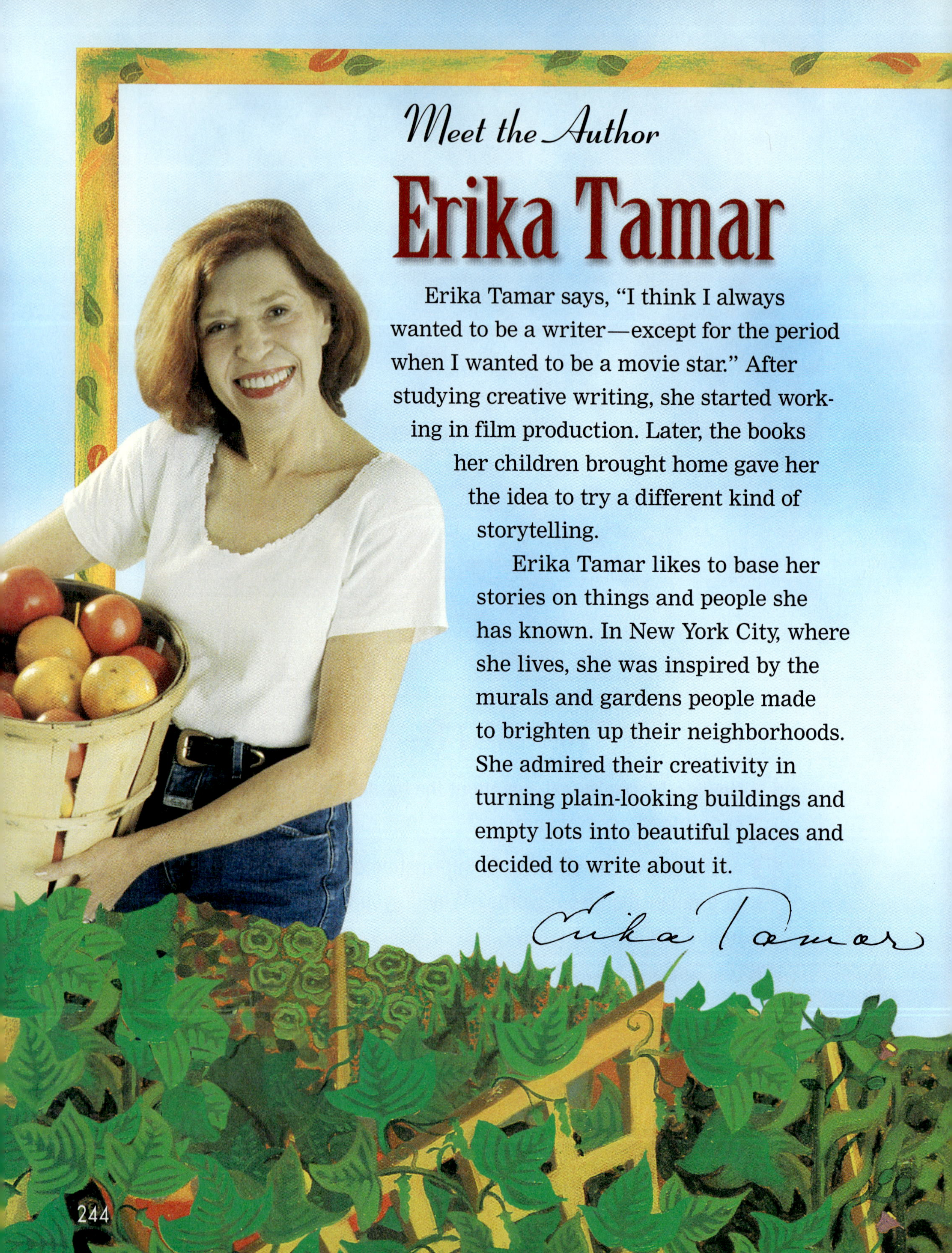

Meet the Author

Erika Tamar

Erika Tamar says, "I think I always wanted to be a writer—except for the period when I wanted to be a movie star." After studying creative writing, she started working in film production. Later, the books her children brought home gave her the idea to try a different kind of storytelling.

Erika Tamar likes to base her stories on things and people she has known. In New York City, where she lives, she was inspired by the murals and gardens people made to brighten up their neighborhoods. She admired their creativity in turning plain-looking buildings and empty lots into beautiful places and decided to write about it.

Erika Tamar

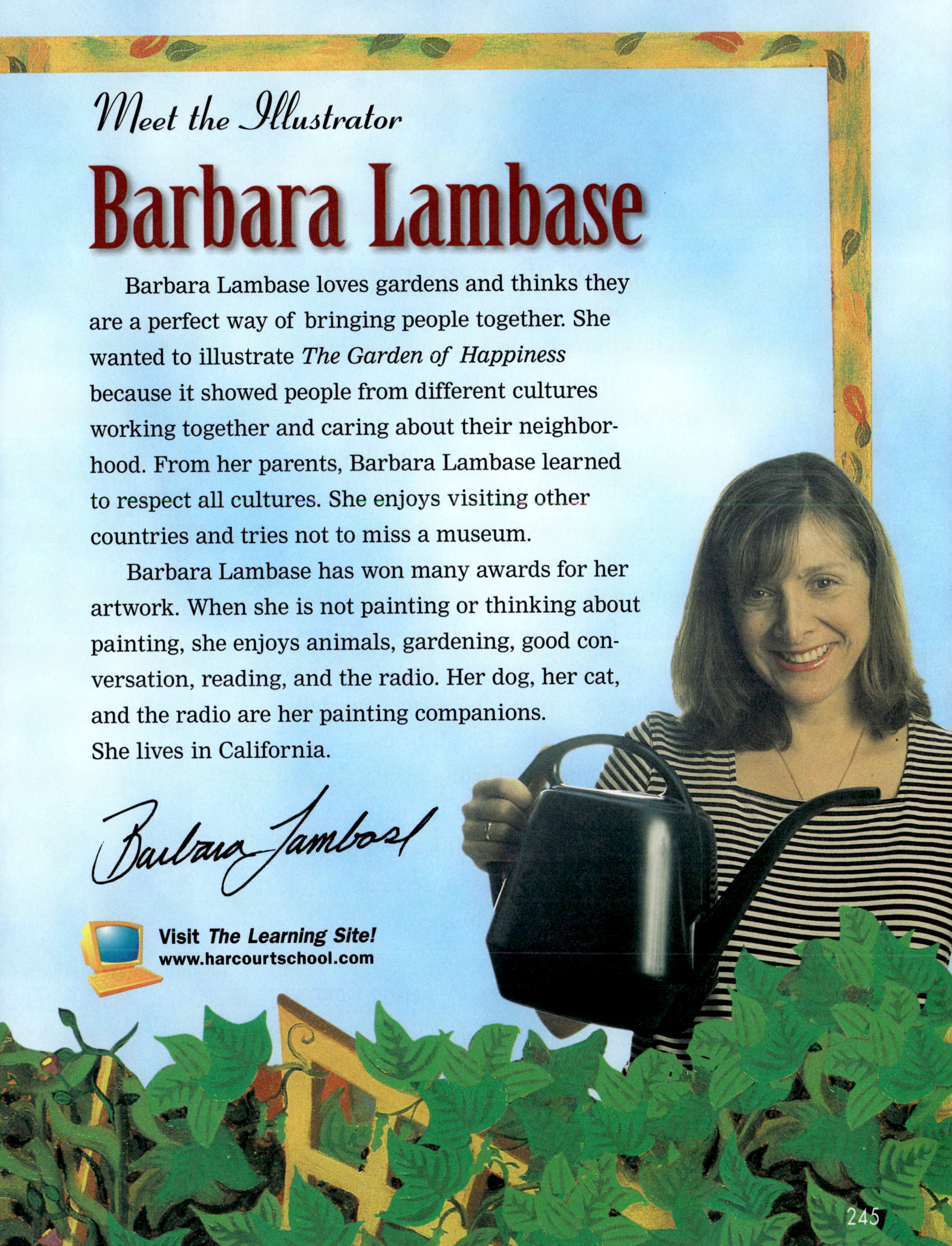

Meet the Illustrator

Barbara Lambase

Barbara Lambase loves gardens and thinks they are a perfect way of bringing people together. She wanted to illustrate *The Garden of Happiness* because it showed people from different cultures working together and caring about their neighborhood. From her parents, Barbara Lambase learned to respect all cultures. She enjoys visiting other countries and tries not to miss a museum.

Barbara Lambase has won many awards for her artwork. When she is not painting or thinking about painting, she enjoys animals, gardening, good conversation, reading, and the radio. Her dog, her cat, and the radio are her painting companions. She lives in California.

Barbara Lambase

Visit *The Learning Site!*
www.harcourtschool.com

I do not plant my garden,
but every year it appears.
On summer days I go out hunting
for those ripe wild raspberries
that glow so red against the leafy green
along the forest's edge. And then I watch as
catbirds! thrushes! bluebirds!
gobble berries, too.
On summer days I go out
hunting the tart and sweet blueberries
that lie hidden under clusters of leaves
down low, or high, in trees. And then I watch
as cedar waxwings eat the ones I've left.
This garden is for all of us—
for me and for the birds,
for all the hunters and the gatherers,
for the turtles, the chipmunks, and the slugs,
for the bees, the butterflies,
and the bugs.

written and illustrated by Lynne Cherry

The City

If flowers want to grow
right out of the concrete sidewalk cracks
I'm going to bend down to smell them.

written by David Ignatow
illustrated by Erika LeBarre

▲ The Garden of Happiness

Making Connections

Text to Self • Text to Text • Text To World

Compare Texts

NC STANDARDS: ELA 2.02e interact with text/connect text to own experiences, 2.04b identify theme, 2.04c identify main idea/details, 3.01b interpret/evaluate text/examine characters' actions/motives

1. How do the characters in "The Garden of Happiness" work together? INTERPRETATION / EVALUATING
2. How are the neighbors who plant the garden different from each other? How are they alike? CRITICAL STANCE / ANALYZING
3. How is the garden in the poem "I do not plant my garden" different from the garden in the story? CRITICAL STANCE / ANALYZING
4. Think of another realistic fiction story that has a surprise ending. Which ending did you like better, and why? COGNITION / EVALUATING
5. How could you find out more about community projects where you live? INTERPRETATION / EVALUATING

Write to Explain

Marisol's fellow gardeners talk about the special dishes they plan to make. Think about something you know how to make, such as a favorite sandwich. Write a paragraph that explains the steps involved. Use a graphic organizer like this to organize your steps.

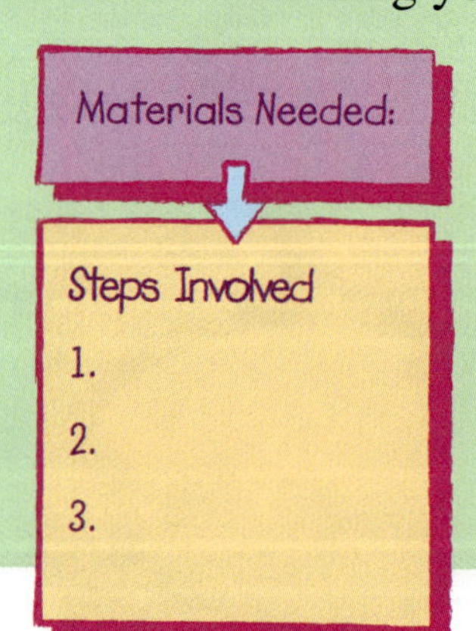

Writing CONNECTION

Make a Booklet

NC STANDARD: ELA 3.06 conduct research using a variety of tools

Science CONNECTION

Did you know that sunflowers are also an important farm crop? Research where and how sunflowers are grown and how they are used for foods and other products. Look for information in an encyclopedia or in nonfiction books on farm crops and gardening. Create a booklet of information about sunflowers.

Paint a Mural

NC STANDARD: ELA 4.05 use planning strategies to organize ideas

Art CONNECTION

Work with a group to create a mural to display on a wall in your classroom or school. Brainstorm ideas for an interesting mural. Choose the idea you like best, or combine several ideas that work well together. Sketch the mural lightly in pencil on a long strip of paper. Use markers or paints and brushes to complete it.

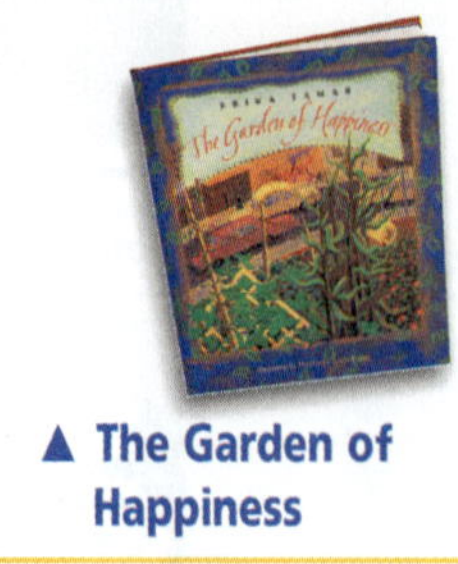

▲ The Garden of Happiness

NC STANDARD: ELA 2.04a identify plot

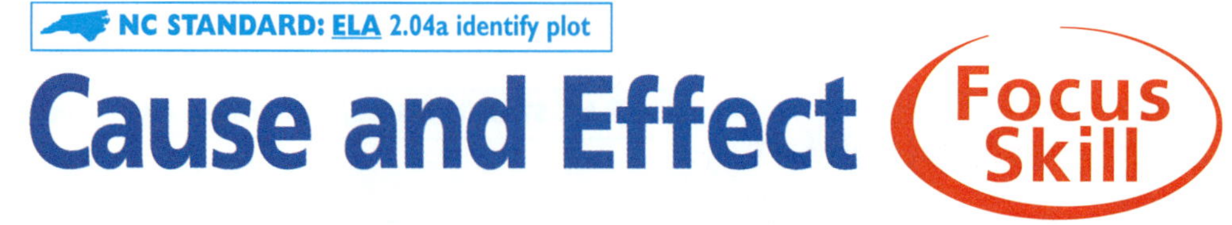

Cause and Effect

Focus Skill

Remember that a **cause** is an action or event that makes something happen. An **effect** is what happens as a result of an action or event. An event may have more than one cause or effect. Understanding causes and effects can help you understand why characters in a story feel or act as they do. Look at this chart, which shows causes and effects in "The Garden of Happiness."

Cause		Effect or Effects
A green shoot breaks through in Marisol's patch.	→	Even on rainy days, Marisol hurries to the garden.
Marisol's sunflower blooms.	→	1. Marisol is happy. 2. Neighbors recall sunflowers in places they once lived. 3. All summer long, people stop and smile.

What causes Marisol to feel happy? What effect does her plant's sprouting have on Marisol?

Visit *The Learning Site!*
www.harcourtschool.com

See *Skills and Activities*

Test Prep
Cause and Effect

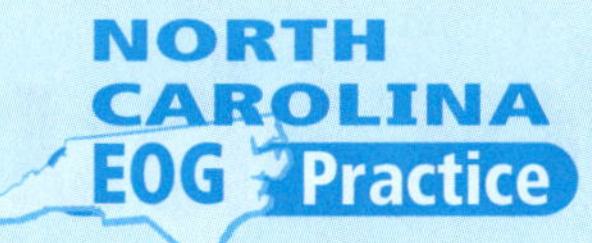

NC STANDARDS: ELA
2.04a identify plot, 2.04c identify main idea/details

▶ **Read the passage. Then answer the questions.**

Juan liked his new home, but he missed the flower garden he had at his house in Puerto Rico. One day, Juan found an old bucket with a small hole in it. Juan had an idea. He filled the bucket with soil, planted some seeds, and set it by the front steps of his apartment house. No one passing in the street noticed the old bucket until at last the flowers bloomed. Then Juan saw people pointing to the bright red and yellow flowers. Their frowns turned to smiles at the beautiful sight.

CRITICAL STANCE / ANALYZING

1. Why does Juan plant seeds in the bucket?

A to make people smile

B so people will point at his flowers

C so people will bring him more containers

D because he misses his flower garden

Two of the choices tell what happens after Juan plants his garden. Only one answer tells why he planted it.

CRITICAL STANCE / ANALYZING

2. What happens as a result of the flowers' blooming?

F People frown.

G People smile.

H People start buying old buckets.

J No one notices the flowers.

The words *as a result* in the question tell you that you need to identify the effect of the event described in the question.

▲ How to Babysit an Orangutan

Vocabulary Power

endangered

jealous

smuggled

displeasure

facial

coordination

In "How to Babysit an Orangutan," you will read about a woman who learns how to care for orphaned orangutans. People who own a pet must also learn how to care for their animal friends.

For my tenth birthday, I asked my parents if I could have a chimpanzee. I had seen a television show about a scientist who worked with one, and it looked like so much fun. My parents explained that chimpanzees are **endangered**. Animals that are in danger of dying out cannot be kept as pets. Instead, I got Bronco, my border collie puppy.

My friends were all **jealous** that I had my own dog, but they weren't filled with envy for long. They soon saw that caring for a puppy is a big responsibility.

I trained Bronco myself. Every time he did something good, I smiled and scratched behind his ears. I taught him that some things were wrong, such as stealing food from the table. When he **smuggled** my socks, I showed my **displeasure** by putting on a big frown. Using **facial** expressions works well because Bronco really understands smiles and frowns!

Bronco needs a lot of exercise. He loves to run, and he can jump and catch at the same time, because of his good **coordination**. Plenty of activity outdoors makes him more manageable in the house. He is easy to control after a lot of exercise because he is usually ready for a nap!

Vocabulary-Writing
CONNECTION

Think of two games or other activities you enjoy. One should require your eyes and hands to work in **coordination**. The other should not. Write a paragraph to compare and contrast the two games or activities.

Genre

Nonfiction

Nonfiction tells about people, things, events, or places that are real.

In this selection, look for

- **Facts and details about orangutans**
- **Text features such as photographs and captions**

How to Babysit an Orangutan

story and photographs by

Tara Darling and Kathy Darling

How do you babysit an orangutan? Well, first you have to find an orangutan that needs babysitting.

That's easy here at Camp Leakey. Located in the middle of a rain forest on the island of Borneo, Camp Leakey is not your average camp. It's really an orangutan orphanage.

Ordinarily, orangutan babies don't need human babysitters, but the mothers of these little red apes have been killed and the orphans are too young to survive alone in the jungle. Without babysitters, all the babies would die from disease, starvation, or injuries.

My friend Birute Galdikas is teaching me how to be an orangutan sitter. For more than twenty years she has been taking care of orangutan babies and training babysitters at Camp Leakey.

The first thing she told me was that babysitting an orangutan is not a "forever" job. A good babysitter's job is done when the baby grows up and can go off into the rain forest and live as a wild ape.

Our job is to teach the orphans the skills they need to get along on their own. That usually takes until they are seven or eight years old, the age when they would leave their natural mother. Then we must say good-bye.

Orangutans at Camp Leakey like to hug.

Study time in the rain forest

This is not easy. Orangutan babies are cute and cuddly and especially loving. These are the qualities that landed them in the orphanage in the first place. A lot of people think the adorable apes would be good pets, so greedy animal dealers can get a lot of money for one of the endangered babies. But mother orangutans will not give up their babies without a fight and they are usually killed by the baby snatchers. Then the little orphans are smuggled out of Borneo and Sumatra, the only place the remaining 5,000 wild orangs live. For every baby that reaches a circus, private zoo, or movie trainer, eight orangutans don't survive the trip.

Only a few of the babies are lucky enough to be rescued and brought back to the rain forest. They need tropical forests to find food, and the forests are disappearing as fast as the orangutans, which once numbered in the millions.

Five-year-old Nanang is my special favorite, but I am also helping with other orphans. Those under two years old take a lot of time, so all the babysitters help with them. The infants are pretty helpless for the first couple of years, much like human children.

Wild orangutan mothers nurse their babies for five or six years. So, if babies under this age come to camp, we must give them milk. Twice a day we mix up a big bucket of powdered cow's milk. Infants get the milk in a bottle. Three- and four-year-olds prefer to drink from a cup, and the wise-guy five- and six-year-olds think it is cool to slurp right from the bucket.

Milk is good for orangutan babies.

The babies depend on us for all their food. Like most children, baby orangutans are messy eaters. Babysitters must be prepared to have some food spit at them. Although we feed the babies a lot of bananas, we try to get our charges to eat foods that wild orangutans eat. Fruit is the main part of an orangutan's diet, but they also dine on nuts, flowers, leaves, and many plants that grow in the jungle. The only animals they eat regularly are termites and ants.

I want little Nanang to grow up strong. I'm willing to take a sip of milk to show him that milk tastes good. I enjoy eating bananas with him. I'll even nibble on some leaves once in a while to encourage him to try them. But I absolutely, positively refuse to eat either termites or ants. Surely, insect eating goes beyond a babysitter's duty!

Tom loves to slurp soap lather.

Bananas are the babies' favorite food.

This baby is jealous that Nanang has my hat and has made himself a hat out of a leaf.

In the rain forest it rains a lot. (I am sure this does not come as much of a surprise to you.) To make sure a downpour doesn't take me by surprise, I wear a rain hat. Nanang is very jealous. He snatches my hat and plops it onto his own head whenever he can. He loves wearing it even though it is so big he can't see anything with it on.

In a heavy rain, wild orangutans often hold leaf umbrellas over their heads. Orangutans don't like to get wet. That's why bath time is not fun for a babysitter. The littlest orangs get skin diseases and lose their hair in the hot months. It is the babysitter's unlucky chore to give medicine baths. There is a lot of screaming and biting during the bath.

Orangutans don't like baths, but they do love soap. When I do my wash, Tom always begs for a bar. He has rather unusual ideas about what to do with soap. He thinks of it as food, soaping his arm and sucking the lather off with great slurps of delight. I guess he never heard that washing your mouth out with soap was supposed to be a punishment.

Orangutan games almost always include biting. Not only do the apes nip each other as they play, but they will bite the babysitter if they can.

A playful orangutan shows its bottom teeth. It looks like an angry face, but it isn't. Angry orangutans stick out their lips and make kissing noises to show their displeasure. They burp a lot too. A babysitter has to be able to read the facial expressions of the orangutans. If you mistake the really angry face, with both sets of teeth showing, for a grin, you will surely feel those teeth.

Most of the time, little orangutans have a happy face. They are very playful. "Best friends" form play groups with three or four members. Sometimes we are assigned to watch one baby and other times we get a whole play group.

Best friends do everything together. The little orphans are lonesome, and it seems almost like they adopt each other and form a family. They hang around together every day. Hanging around means something

Tara is teaching Nanang to feel at home in the trees.

different to an orangutan. Any game that is fun on the ground is more fun when hanging in the trees.

One of the most important lessons we teach to the orphan orangutans is that they belong in the trees. Every day we go to the forest so they can build muscles, practice balancing, and get the judgment and coordination necessary for life in the rain forest canopy. Thank goodness the babysitter is not required to climb into the trees with her charges. I couldn't begin to go where Nanang goes with ease. He can hang on with his feet as well as his hands. His wrists allow him to swivel around without changing grip. Even so, he falls once in a while. It takes a few years to get the hang of hanging around.

Nanang knows I can't climb very well. When it is bedtime, he climbs right to the very top of a tree. He hangs up there sucking his thumb till I lure him down with a banana snack.

Nanang isn't old enough to sleep alone in the forest. A wild orangutan would sleep in its mother's nest for five or six years. Peter, for instance, still sleeps with Princess. There are some big snakes that could kill a sleeping baby.

Nanang has his own way to play hide-and-seek.

Orangutans like a nice, soft place to sleep. Every night they make a new nest from leaves and branches. It takes about five or ten minutes to build one. The other great apes—gorillas and chimpanzees—also build tree nests, but only the orangutans put a roof on the top to keep out the rain. We can't show our charges how to build a nest in the trees. The best we can do is let them practice on the ground. The babies try to build a nest out of any materials they can find.

Nest building is much easier to learn if the babies have an older ape to watch. When Camp Leakey was first built, there were only human babysitters. The little orangutans they raised grew

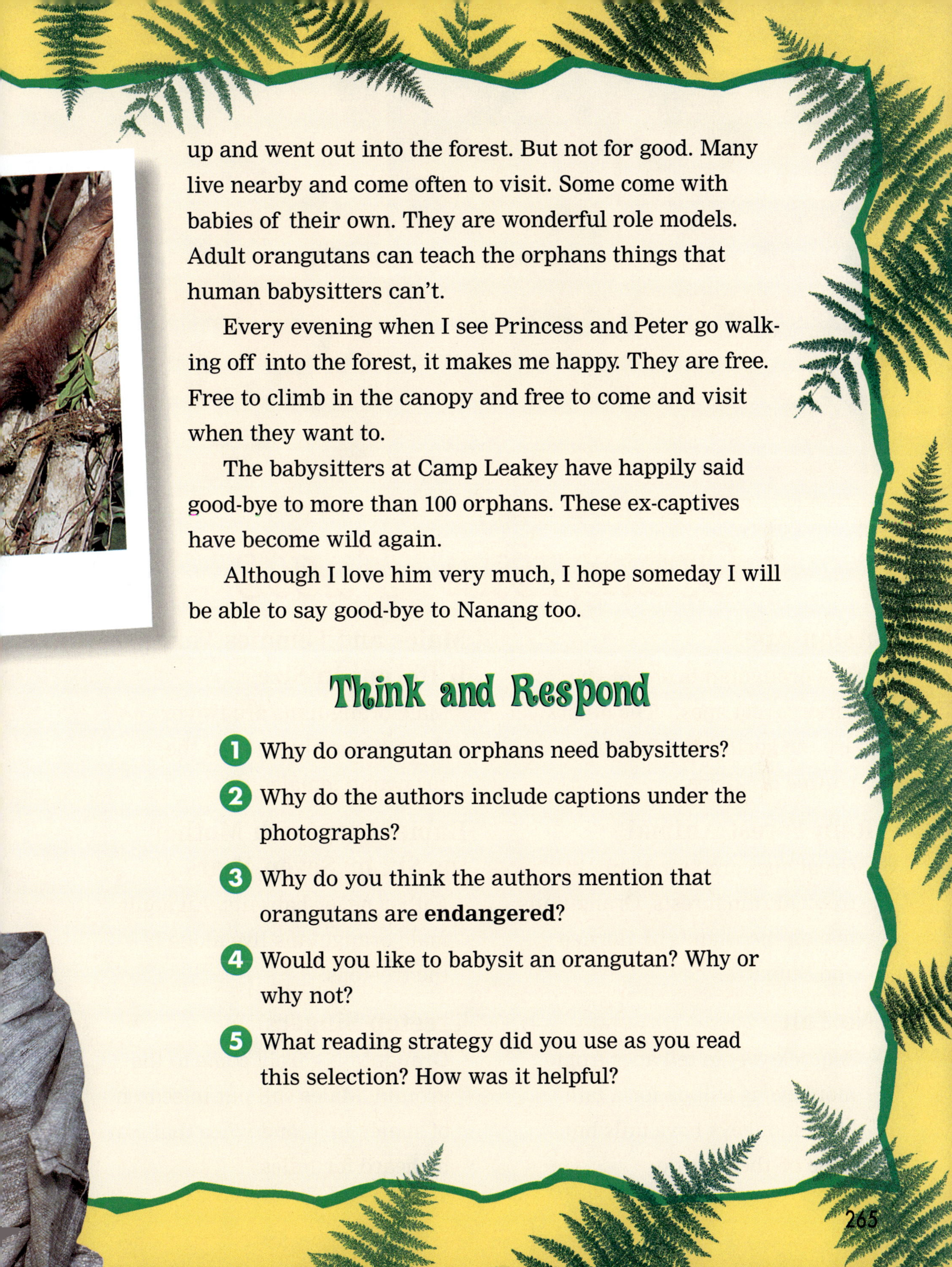

up and went out into the forest. But not for good. Many live nearby and come often to visit. Some come with babies of their own. They are wonderful role models. Adult orangutans can teach the orphans things that human babysitters can't.

Every evening when I see Princess and Peter go walking off into the forest, it makes me happy. They are free. Free to climb in the canopy and free to come and visit when they want to.

The babysitters at Camp Leakey have happily said good-bye to more than 100 orphans. These ex-captives have become wild again.

Although I love him very much, I hope someday I will be able to say good-bye to Nanang too.

Think and Respond

1. Why do orangutan orphans need babysitters?
2. Why do the authors include captions under the photographs?
3. Why do you think the authors mention that orangutans are **endangered**?
4. Would you like to babysit an orangutan? Why or why not?
5. What reading strategy did you use as you read this selection? How was it helpful?

Orangutan Facts

Asian Ape

The orangutan is one of the three "great apes." The others are the gorilla and the chimpanzee of Africa.

Rain Forest Animal

Great apes are found only in tropical rain forests. Orangutans live on the islands of Borneo and Sumatra.

No Tail

A quick way to tell apes from monkeys is to look for a tail. Most monkeys have tails but none of the apes do.

Males and Females Very Different in Size

Male orangutans are two or three times bigger than the 100-pound females.

Babies Stay with Mother for Six or Seven Years

Father never babysits. All adult male orangutans live alone in the treetops.

Treetop Singers

Orangutans rarely come to the ground. Males call out in search of mates in a loud voice that can be heard for miles.

Meet the Authors

Tara and Kathy Darling

Kathy Darling edited children's books for several years before she started writing them herself. For more than twenty-five years, she has been writing books that are fun and interesting. Much of her writing is about science subjects. For example, she has written many books about animals. She raises dogs as a hobby and also writes articles for magazines about dogs.

Tara Darling, Kathy's daughter, is a photographer. This family team has traveled all over the world to study animals. The Darlings have made books about other animal babies besides the little orangutans you just met.

Visit ***The Learning Site!***
www.harcourtschool.com

▲ How to Babysit an Orangutan

Making Connections

Text to Self • Text to Text • Text To World

Compare Texts

NC STANDARDS: ELA 2.02c interact with text/formulate questions, 2.02e interact with text/connect text to own experiences, 2.04b identify theme, 3.01a interpret/evaluate text/see characters' points of view, 3.03 examine effect of language/visuals

1. What can readers learn about working together from "How to Babysit an Orangutan"? INTERPRETATION / EVALUATING
2. How do the photos and captions help you better understand the selection? COGNITION / KNOWLEDGE
3. Why do you think the authors make frequent comparisons between young orangutans and human children? CRITICAL STANCE / EVALUATING
4. Think of another nonfiction selection or article you have read about an animal. How is it similar to this selection? How is it different? CONNECTIONS / APPLYING
5. What questions would you like to ask the authors about orangutans? INTERPRETATION / EVALUATING

Write Instructions

Writing CONNECTION

Nanang's babysitter has a day off. Write instructions to help the new sitter know what to do for the day. Use details from the selection to describe daily activities. Clearly explain each part of the day. Use a sequence chart like this one to organize your ideas.

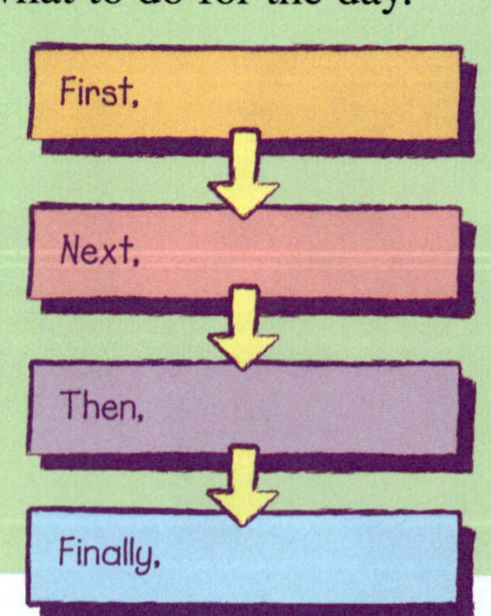

NC STANDARDS: ELA 3.06 conduct research using a variety of tools, 4.02a use writing to communicate with others, 4.05 use planning strategies to organize ideas, 4.10 use technology as a tool

Give an Oral Report

Social Studies CONNECTION

Find out about a group of people who help animals. Many organizations have websites. You might do a telephone interview with someone in your community who works for this kind of organization. Take notes, and report on your findings.

Make a Diagram

Science CONNECTION

Camp Leakey is located on the island of Borneo. Use the Internet, encyclopedia articles, and nonfiction books to learn about rain forests in Borneo or another part of the world. Use your information to create a diagram that shows how some of the plants and animals are connected.

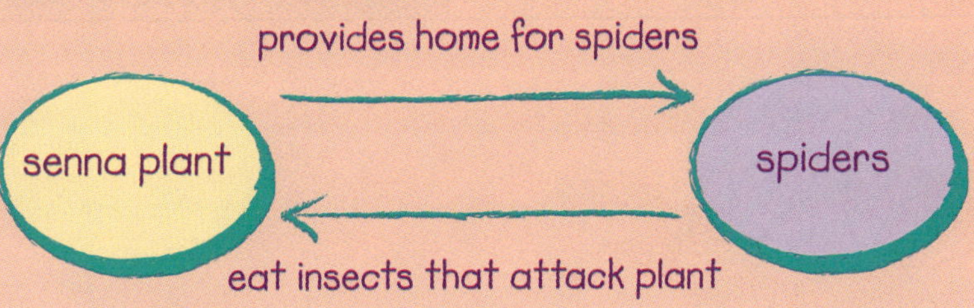

NC STANDARDS: ELA 3.05 use graphs/charts/maps to expand understanding; Science 1.01 observe/describe how an animal is affected by living/nonliving things, 1.03 observe/discuss how an animal's body/behavior aids survival

▲ How to Babysit an Orangutan

Summarize

To **summarize** a passage or a selection, you should briefly retell the most important information.

Turn back to page 260 of "How to Babysit an Orangutan" and reread the information on that page. How would you summarize it? What would you include or not include?

Now look at the chart for some ideas about summarizing this information.

Include in Summary		Do Not Include in Summary
The Most Important Idea	Other Important Information That Supports the Most Important Idea	Information That Is Not as Important
Babysitters feed the baby orangutans.	• The babysitters encourage the orangutans to eat the same foods as wild orangutans. • Orangutans mainly eat fruit, but they also need to learn to eat other foods.	• Orangutans are messy eaters who spit food. • The author drinks milk and eats bananas with Nanang, but she does not eat termites or ants.

Visit *The Learning Site!*
www.harcourtschool.com

See *Skills and Activities*

Test Prep

Summarize

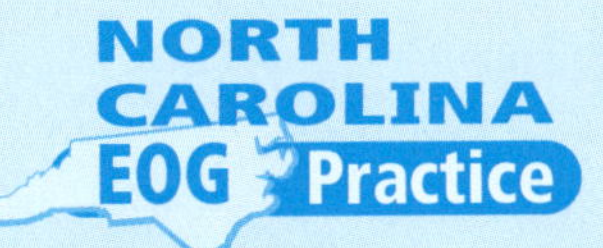

NC STANDARD: ELA 2.06 summarize major points

▶ **Read the passage. Then answer the questions.**

Monkey Tails

Monkeys, lively and playful, are a favorite attraction in zoos. Many people think that orangutans and other apes are types of monkeys, but monkeys and apes are actually different kinds of animals.

There are more than 200 species of monkeys in the world, ranging in size from about 6 inches to about 32 inches long, not including the length of the tail. A monkey's tail is very useful. Monkeys use their tails to help them balance as they run or jump, or to slow them down as they soar from branch to branch. Some monkeys can swing by their tails and hold objects with them.

COGNITION / INTEGRATING

1. Which of these ideas is most important to include in a summary of this passage?

A Some monkeys are only 6 inches long.

B An orangutan is a kind of ape.

C Monkeys are favorite attractions in zoos.

D Monkeys' tails are very useful.

Choose the sentence that states the most important idea. The title of the passage provides a clue.

COGNITION / INTEGRATING

2. On a separate sheet of paper, write a brief summary of the passage.

State the most important ideas from the passage in your own words.

THEME
3

Make Yourself at Home

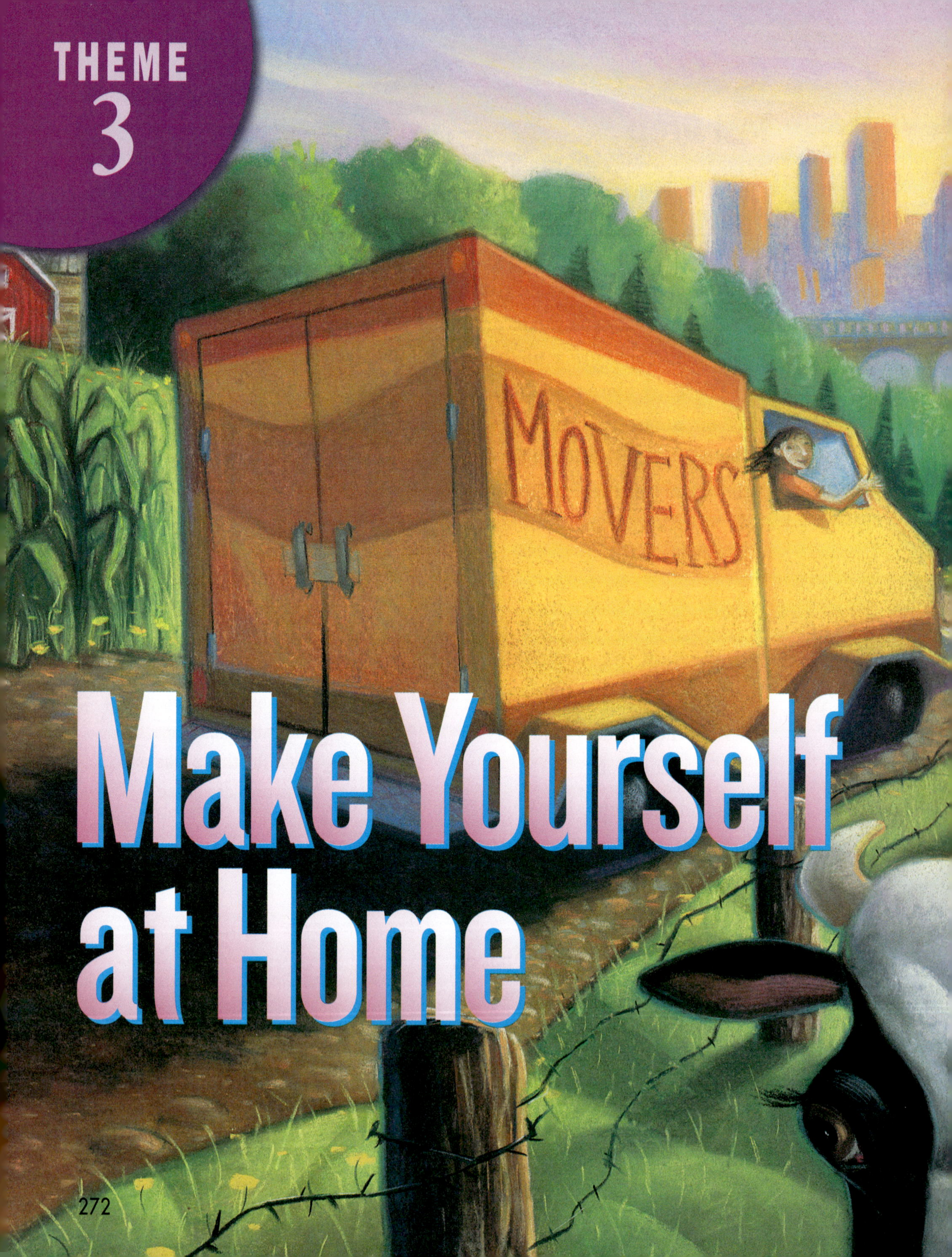

CONTENTS

▲ Sarah, Plain and Tall

paddock

alarmed

windbreak

rustle

conch

Vocabulary Power

In "Sarah, Plain and Tall" the main character moves to a farm on the prairie. Have you ever lived on a farm or visited one? Join Jonathan on a tour of his family's farm on the prairie.

One of my favorite parts of farm life is taking care of the horses. During the day, they like to graze in a fenced-in area called a **paddock**. The horses are safe in the paddock because if they become **alarmed**, or frightened, the fence keeps them from running away.

Another one of my favorite things to do is to sit under the trees that form our windbreak. The **windbreak** was planted to protect the barn from the wind. I like to sit in the shade and listen to the **rustle** of the leaves as they rub together.

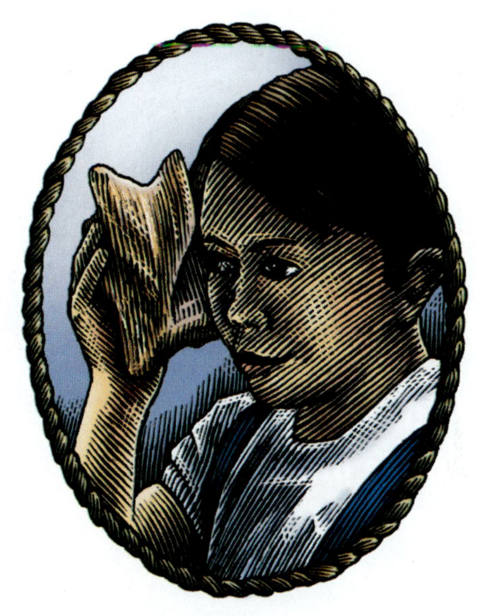

The last thing I want to show you is my **conch** shell. I found it on a trip to the beach. I love its spiral shape and creamy pink color. After a day of chores, it helps me to remember my visit to the beach.

Vocabulary-Writing
CONNECTION

Compare a place where you might find a **conch** with a place where you might find a **paddock**.

SARAH,

Genre

Historical Fiction

Historical fiction is a story that is set in the past and portrays people, places, and events that did happen or could have happened.

In this selection, look for

- **A real time and place in the past**
- **A main character who adjusts to a new place**

PLAIN and TALL

by Patricia MacLachlan
illustrated by Craig Spearing

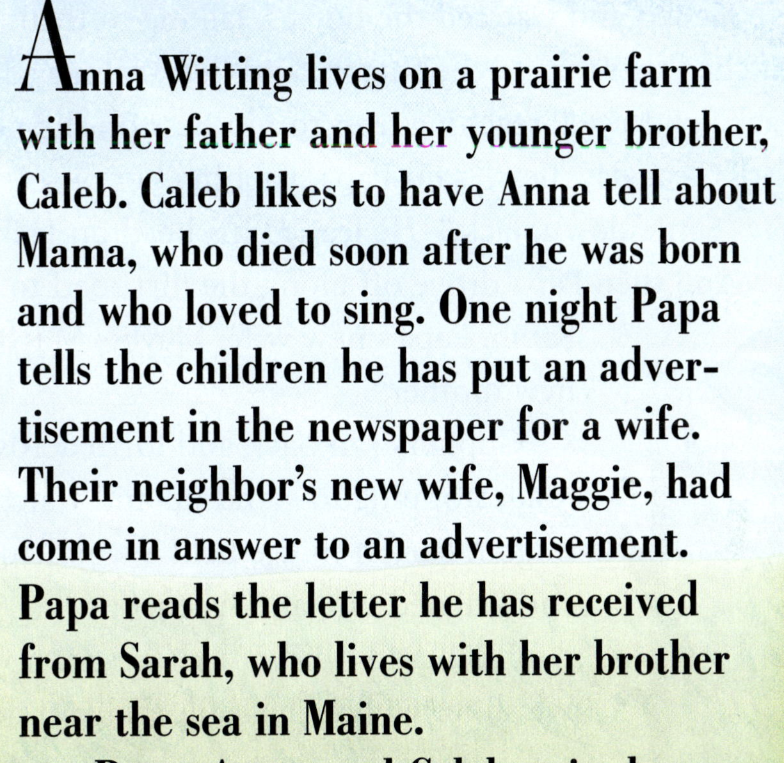

Anna Witting lives on a prairie farm with her father and her younger brother, Caleb. Caleb likes to have Anna tell about Mama, who died soon after he was born and who loved to sing. One night Papa tells the children he has put an advertisement in the newspaper for a wife. Their neighbor's new wife, Maggie, had come in answer to an advertisement. Papa reads the letter he has received from Sarah, who lives with her brother near the sea in Maine.

Papa, Anna, and Caleb write letters to Sarah. They find out that she has a cat named Seal and that she sings. Now Sarah is coming for a month's visit, "to see how it is."

Sarah came in the spring. She came through green grass fields that bloomed with Indian paintbrush, red and orange, and blue-eyed grass.

Papa got up early for the long day's trip to the train and back. He brushed his hair so slick and shiny that Caleb laughed. He wore a clean blue shirt, and a belt instead of suspenders.

He fed and watered the horses, talking to them as he hitched them up to the wagon. Old Bess, calm and kind; Jack, wild-eyed, reaching over to nip Bess on the neck.

"Clear day, Bess," said Papa, rubbing her nose.

"Settle down, Jack." He leaned his head on Jack.

And then Papa drove off along the dirt road to fetch Sarah. Papa's new wife. Maybe. Maybe our new mother.

Gophers ran back and forth across the road, stopping to stand up and watch the wagon. Far off in the field a woodchuck ate and listened. Ate and listened.

Caleb and I did our chores without talking. We shoveled out the stalls and laid down new hay. We fed the sheep. We swept and straightened and carried wood and water. And then our chores were done.

Caleb pulled on my shirt.

"Is my face clean?" he asked. "Can my face be *too* clean?" He looked alarmed.

"No, your face is clean but not too clean," I said.

Caleb slipped his hand into mine as we stood on the porch, watching the road. He was afraid.

"Will she be nice?" he asked. "Like Maggie?"

"Sarah will be nice," I told him.

"How far away is Maine?" he asked.

"You know how far. Far away, by the sea."

"Will Sarah bring some sea?" he asked.

"No, you cannot bring the sea."

The sheep ran in the field, and far off the cows moved slowly to the pond, like turtles.

"Will she like us?" asked Caleb very softly.

I watched a marsh hawk wheel down behind the barn.

He looked up at me.

"Of course she will like us." He answered his own question. "We are nice," he added, making me smile.

We waited and watched. I rocked on the porch and Caleb rolled a marble on the wood floor. Back and forth. Back and forth. The marble was blue.

We saw the dust from the wagon first, rising above the road, above the heads of Jack and Old Bess. Caleb climbed up onto the porch roof and shaded his eyes.

"A bonnet!" he cried. "I see a yellow bonnet!"

The dogs came out from under the porch, ears up, their eyes on the cloud of dust bringing Sarah. The wagon passed the fenced field, and the cows and sheep looked up, too. It rounded the windmill and the barn and the windbreak of Russian olive that Mama had planted long ago. Nick began to bark, then Lottie, and the wagon clattered into the yard and stopped by the steps.

"Hush," said Papa to the dogs.

And it was quiet.

Sarah stepped down from the wagon, a cloth bag in her hand. She reached up and took off her yellow bonnet, smoothing back her brown hair into a bun. She was plain and tall.

"Did you bring some sea?" cried Caleb beside me.

"Something from the sea," said Sarah, smiling. "And me." She turned and lifted a black case from the wagon. "And Seal, too."

Carefully she opened the case, and Seal, gray with white feet, stepped out. Lottie lay down, her head on her paws, staring. Nick leaned down to sniff. Then he lay down, too.

"The cat will be good in the barn," said Papa. "For mice."

Sarah smiled. "She will be good in the house, too."

Sarah took Caleb's hand, then mine. Her hands were large and rough. She gave Caleb a shell—a moon snail, she called it—that was curled and smelled of salt.

"The gulls fly high and drop the shells on the rocks below," she told Caleb. "When the shell is broken, they eat what is inside."

"That is very smart," said Caleb.

"For you, Anna," said Sarah, "a sea stone."

And she gave me the smoothest and whitest stone I had ever seen.

"The sea washes over and over and around the stone, rolling it until it is round and perfect."

"That is very smart, too," said Caleb. He looked up at Sarah. "We do not have the sea here."

Sarah turned and looked out over the plains.

"No," she said. "There is no sea here. But the land rolls a little like the sea."

My father did not see her look, but I did. And I knew that Caleb had seen it, too. Sarah was not smiling. Sarah was already lonely. In a month's time the preacher might come to marry Sarah and Papa. And a month was a long time. Time enough for her to change her mind and leave us.

Papa took Sarah's bags inside, where her room was ready with a quilt on the bed and blue flax dried in a vase on the night table.

Seal stretched and made a small cat sound. I watched her circle the dogs and sniff the air. Caleb came out and stood beside me.

"When will we sing?" he whispered.

I shook my head, turning the white stone over and over in my hand. I wished everything was as perfect as the stone. I wished that Papa and Caleb and I were perfect for Sarah. I wished we had a sea of our own.

The dogs loved Sarah first. Lottie slept beside her bed, curled in a soft circle, and Nick leaned his face on the covers in the morning, watching for the first sign that Sarah was awake. No one knew where Seal slept. Seal was a roamer.

Sarah's collection of shells sat on the windowsill.

"A scallop," she told us, picking up the shells one by one, "a sea clam, an oyster, a razor clam. And a conch shell. If you put it to your ear you can hear the sea." She put it to Caleb's ear, then mine. Papa listened, too. Then Sarah listened once more, with a look so sad and far away that Caleb leaned against me.

"At least Sarah can hear the sea," he whispered.

Papa was quiet and shy with Sarah, and so was I. But Caleb talked to Sarah from morning until the light left the sky.

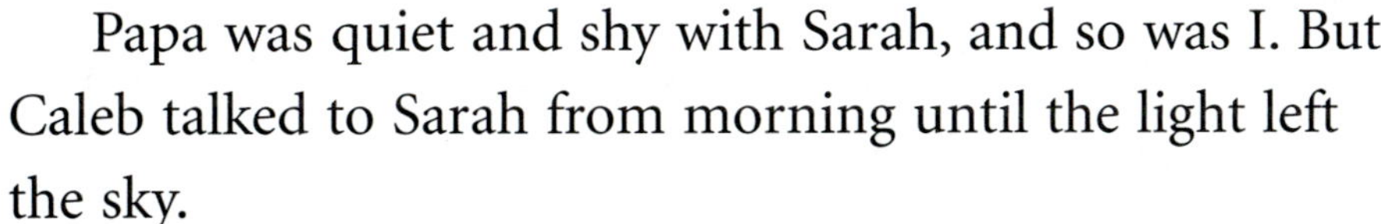

"Where are you going?" he asked. "To do what?"

"To pick flowers," said Sarah. "I'll hang some of them upside down and dry them so they'll keep some color. And we can have flowers all winter long."

"I'll come, too!" cried Caleb. "Sarah said winter," he said to me. "That means Sarah will stay."

Together we picked flowers, paintbrush and clover and prairie violets. There were buds on the wild roses that climbed up the paddock fence.

"The roses will bloom in early summer," I told Sarah. I looked to see if she knew what I was thinking. Summer was when the wedding would be. *Might* be. Sarah and Papa's wedding.

We hung the flowers from the ceiling in little bunches. "I've never seen this before," said Sarah. "What is it called?"

"Bride's bonnet," I told her.

Caleb smiled at the name.

"We don't have this by the sea," she said. "We have seaside goldenrod and wild asters and woolly ragwort."

"Woolly ragwort!" Caleb whooped. He made up a song.

"Woolly ragwort all around.
Woolly ragwort on the ground.
Woolly ragwort grows and grows,
Woolly ragwort in your nose."

Sarah and Papa laughed, and the dogs lifted their heads and thumped their tails against the wood floor. Seal sat on a kitchen chair and watched us with yellow eyes.

We ate Sarah's stew, the late light coming through the windows. Papa had baked bread that was still warm from the fire.

"The stew is fine," said Papa.

"Ayuh." Sarah nodded. "The bread, too."

"What does 'ayuh' mean?" asked Caleb.

"In Maine it means yes," said Sarah. "Do you want more stew?"

"Ayuh," said Caleb.

"Ayuh," echoed my father.

After dinner Sarah told us about William. "He has a gray-and-white boat named *Kittiwake*." She looked out the window. "That is a small gull found way off the shore where William fishes. There are three aunts who live near us. They wear silk dresses and no shoes. You would love them."

"Ayuh," said Caleb.

"Does your brother look like you?" I asked.

"Yes," said Sarah. "He is plain and tall."

At dusk Sarah cut Caleb's hair on the front steps, gathering his curls and scattering them on the fence and ground. Seal batted some hair around the porch as the dogs watched.

"Why?" asked Caleb.

"For the birds," said Sarah. "They will use it for their nests. Later we can look for nests of curls."

"Sarah said 'later,'" Caleb whispered to me as we spread his hair about. "Sarah will stay."

Sarah cut Papa's hair, too. No one else saw, but I found him behind the barn, tossing the pieces of hair into the wind for the birds.

Sarah brushed my hair and tied it up in back with a rose velvet ribbon she had brought from Maine. She brushed hers long and free and tied it back, too, and we stood side by side looking into the mirror. I looked taller, like Sarah, and fair and thin. And with my hair pulled back I looked a little like her daughter. Sarah's daughter.

And then it was time for singing.

Sarah sang us a song we had never heard before as we sat on the porch, insects buzzing in the dark, the rustle of cows in the grasses. It was called "Sumer Is Icumen in," and she taught it to us all, even Papa, who sang as if he had never stopped singing.

"Sumer is icumen in,
Lhude sing cuccu!"

"What is sumer?" asked Caleb. He said it "soomer," the way Sarah had said it.

"Summer," said Papa and Sarah at the same time. Caleb and I looked at each other. Summer was coming.

Think and Respond

1. When do Anna and Caleb worry that Sarah will go back to Maine? When do they think she will stay?
2. How does the author show that Papa and the children are nervous about meeting Sarah?
3. Why did Sarah bring the **conch** shell and other shells all the way from Maine?
4. What do you like most about Sarah?
5. When did you use a reading strategy? Tell how using a reading strategy helped you.

Meet the Author Patricia MacLachlan

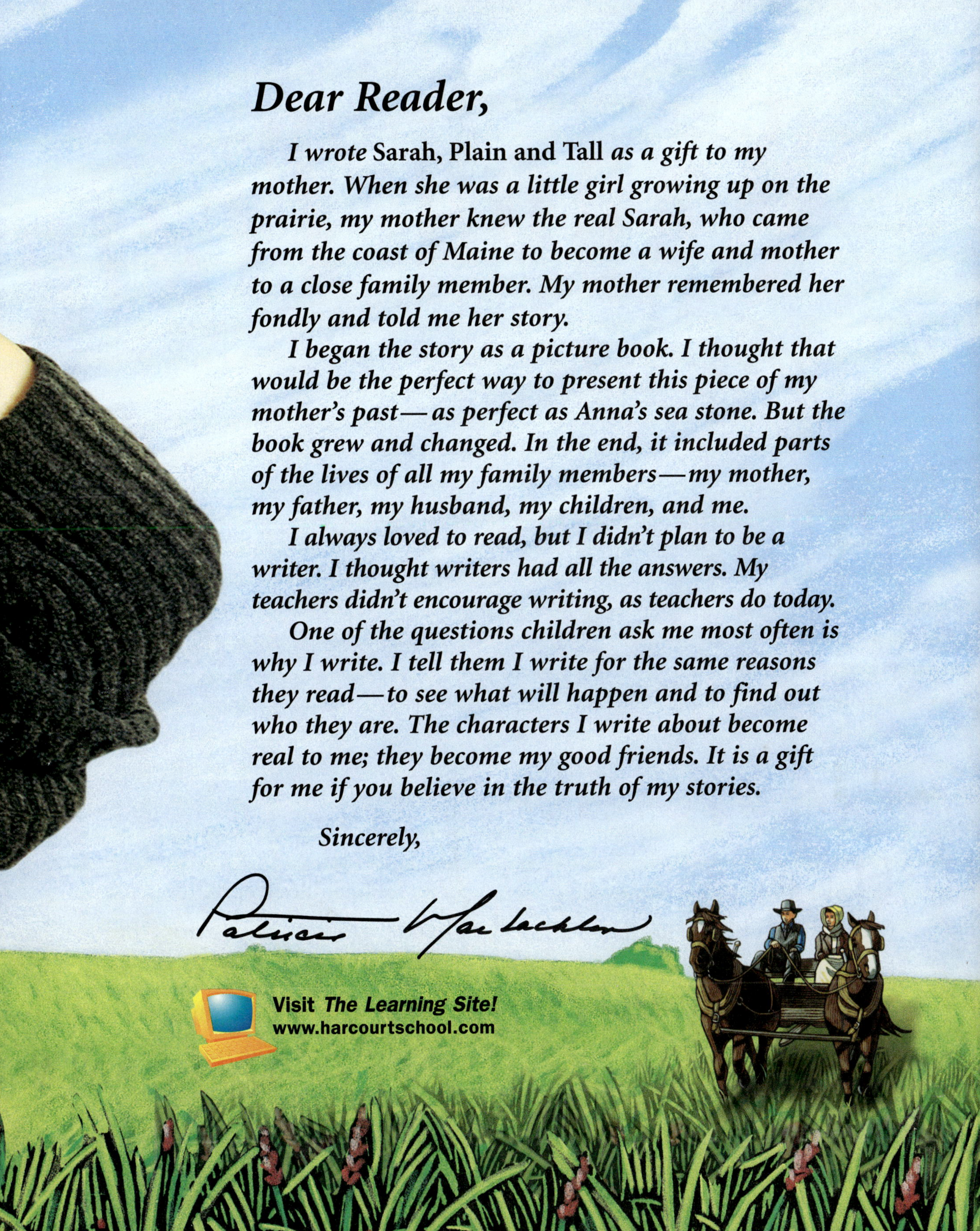

Dear Reader,

I wrote Sarah, Plain and Tall *as a gift to my mother. When she was a little girl growing up on the prairie, my mother knew the real Sarah, who came from the coast of Maine to become a wife and mother to a close family member. My mother remembered her fondly and told me her story.*

I began the story as a picture book. I thought that would be the perfect way to present this piece of my mother's past—as perfect as Anna's sea stone. But the book grew and changed. In the end, it included parts of the lives of all my family members—my mother, my father, my husband, my children, and me.

I always loved to read, but I didn't plan to be a writer. I thought writers had all the answers. My teachers didn't encourage writing, as teachers do today.

One of the questions children ask me most often is why I write. I tell them I write for the same reasons they read—to see what will happen and to find out who they are. The characters I write about become real to me; they become my good friends. It is a gift for me if you believe in the truth of my stories.

Sincerely,

Patricia MacLachlan

Visit *The Learning Site!*
www.harcourtschool.com

Wagon Train

HAVE YOU EVER wondered what it might be like to ride in a covered wagon? I've tried it—it's very bumpy! Some people today have built covered wagons just like those the pioneers used. These people, like the Pat Miller family of Ronan, Montana, use big draft horses or mules to pull their covered wagons on trips across the grasslands. They get together with friends and family, camping overnight along the trail.

Vacationing in a covered wagon is fun for a weekend adventure. But for the pioneers,

Adventure

by Dorothy Hinshaw Patent   photos by William Muñoz

traveling across the plains and mountains to Utah, Oregon, and California was dangerous, hard work. Even so, tens of thousands of people left their homes east of the Missouri River between 1840 and 1880 and headed west in hopes of finding a better life.

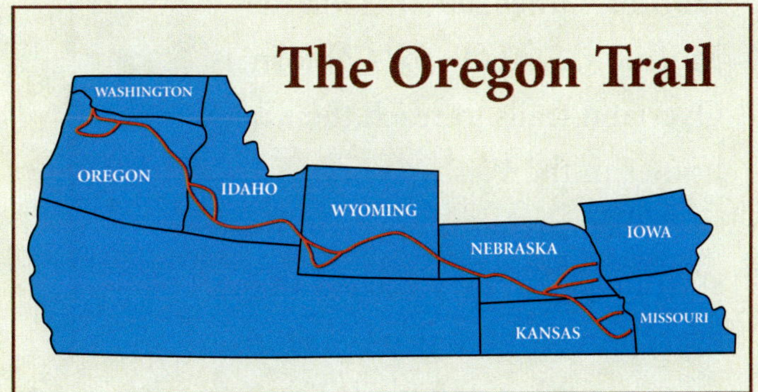

Covered wagons, built high off the ground for riding over rough trails, are sturdy and practical.

Most of these travelers used the Oregon Trail. They left from Independence or Saint Joseph, Missouri, for the Willamette Valley in Oregon. The journey covered 2,000 miles and took more than four months. Other settlers took the Mormon, Santa Fe, or California Overland trails to reach their new homes in the West.

When the pioneers arrived at the starting point, they needed to buy everything for the trip—wagons, oxen or mules, and food. There was little room in the wagons for more than supplies, so families could take along only their most prized possessions. Before setting out, the travelers organized into groups of wagons, called wagon trains. Sometimes families and friends got together for the journey, but often the fellow travelers were strangers. A wagon train needed about fifty to seventy men, enough to hunt, protect the group, and help care for the animals. Each wagon train chose a captain, who decided when and where to stop and who should take on which jobs during the trip.

The pioneers began their journey

in the spring. They needed to cross the prairie while the grass was green so their animals could graze. If they left too late, they might face blistering heat on the plains or blinding blizzards by the time they reached the Rocky Mountains.

Each day on the wagon train began before dawn. The people ate breakfast, harnessed the animals, packed up, and headed out. Riding in the back of a wagon was so uncomfortable that most people walked. Only the seat in front, where the driver and one or two other people could sit, had springs to make the ride less jolting. The older boys kept an eye on livestock such as cattle, extra mules or oxen, and horses.

Routes were planned so that the wagons reached water around midday. Once the animals were watered and the people had eaten lunch and rested, the wagons headed out again. The wagon train traveled fifteen to twenty miles each day, ending up before sunset at another watering place. At the end of the day, the men and older boys brought the wagons into a tight circle for the night. The

In the old days, draft animals had to graze along the trail. Today, wagoners bring in hay.

circle provided a corral for animals that might wander.

While the older boys and men unhitched the animals, took them to water, and put them out to graze, the youngest children gathered buffalo chips for the fires, since there was little or no wood on the prairies. The women and older girls prepared the evening meal. They usually had only beans, rice, bacon, dried fruit, and basic ingredients such as sugar, flour, and cornmeal to work with. Sometimes the men were able to hunt or trade with the Indians for fresh meat. After a few weeks, everyone complained about the boring food.

Modern-day wagoners head out for a weekend adventure.

Often, people were so exhausted from the trail that they went to bed right after supper. But someone might take out a guitar or accordion, and the travelers would sing around the campfire. Now and then, the group would stop for a day or two to rest the animals and do chores like laundry. Such stops gave the children a chance to explore close to camp and play games.

At first, the trails west were only faint marks across the prairies. The earliest pioneers needed guides to show them the way. As time went on, guidebooks set down standard routes showing campsites and dangers to watch out for. The trails became wide, dusty paths or deep ruts that anyone could follow.

The pioneers faced many hazards during their journey. Crossing rivers often meant removing wheels, sealing the bodies of the wagons with pitch or buffalo skins, and then floating the wagons through swift currents. People and animals alike drowned during river crossings, and wagons were lost. Climbing up to mountain passes was difficult, too. Extra animals were sometimes hitched up, and rocks were placed behind the wheels, step by step, as the wagons inched up steep slopes. Cholera and other diseases were also dangers, killing many pioneers before they could reach their destinations.

The trip is much easier for today's wagoners. They only go out for a few days at a time and they can bring coolers full of fresh food and cold soft drinks. Even so, their trips can remind us of the long, difficult journey pioneer families made, hoping to find happiness at the other end of the trail.

Think and Respond

What are some words that describe the pioneers who were part of the wagon trains?

▲ Sarah, Plain and Tall

Making Connections

Text to Self • Text to Text • Text to World

Compare Texts

NC STANDARDS: ELA 2.02e interact with text/connect text to own experiences, 2.04c identify main idea/details, 3.01b examine characters' actions/motives, 3.01d analyze differences among genres

1. How do the members of the Witting family grow and change? INTERPRETATION / EVALUATING
2. How does the author show the change in Papa's behavior toward Sarah as he gets to know her? INTERPRETATION / EVALUATING CRITICAL STANCE / EVALUATING
3. What differences are there in the way the authors of "Sarah, Plain and Tall" and "Wagon Train Adventure" tell about pioneer life on the prairie? CONNECTIONS / ANALYZING
4. Think of another historical fiction story you have read. Which of the two stories seems more historically correct to you? Explain. CONNECTIONS / ANALYZING
5. What questions do you have about pioneer life? INTERPRETATION / EVALUATING

Write to Explain

Writing CONNECTION

Sarah brings gifts from the sea. Suppose you were going to visit someone. What gift could you take that would tell something about your home? Write a paragraph to explain what gift you chose and why you chose it. Collect your ideas in a graphic organizer.

What is the Gift?	Why Did I Choose This Gift?

NC STANDARDS: ELA 3.06 conduct research using a variety of tools, 4.05 use planning strategies to organize ideas; Social Studies 3.04 compare movement of people/goods/ideas in the past and now

Compare and Contrast

Social Studies CONNECTION

In the days when "Sarah, Plain and Tall" is set, there were no airplanes or cars. Brainstorm ways of traveling long ago and in modern times. You can use an encyclopedia or nonfiction books about transportation. Compare and contrast transportation in the past with transportation in the present. Organize your information in a Venn diagram like this one.

Transportation in the Past | Both | Transportation in the Present

Draw a Habitat

Science CONNECTION

"Sarah, Plain and Tall" mentions some plants and animals that live on the prairie. Choose a type of environment in one part of the country, and use magazines, nonfiction books, and field guides to find out what plants and animals live there. Draw a picture of the environment or habitat. Label each plant and animal.

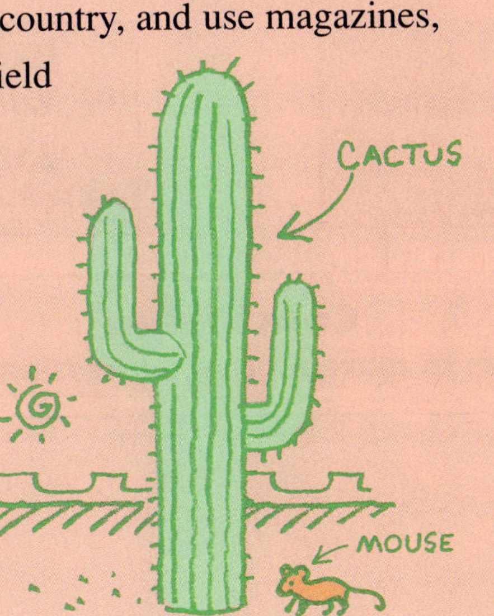

NC STANDARD: Science 1.04 explain/discuss how humans/animals adapt behavior to habitats

▲ Sarah, Plain and Tall

Draw Conclusions

Focus Skill

NC STANDARD: ELA 2.05 support inferences/conclusions

In "Sarah, Plain and Tall," these phrases tell what Papa's horses are like: "Old Bess, calm and kind; Jack, wild-eyed." Sometimes an author tells something in a direct way. At other times, readers must use story information and their own knowledge to help them understand the story. This is called **drawing conclusions.**

Think about the conclusion you drew from this passage at the beginning of the selection:

> **Papa got up early for the long day's trip to the train and back. He brushed his hair so slick and shiny that Caleb laughed. He wore a clean blue shirt, and a belt instead of suspenders.**

From the story details and your own knowledge, you could draw the conclusion that Papa wants to make a good impression on Sarah.

Story Details
brushed hair slick and shiny
clean blue shirt, belt

Own Knowledge
People try to look nice when they want to make a good impression.

Conclusion
Papa wants to make a good impression on Sarah.

Visit *The Learning Site!*
www.harcourtschool.com

See *Skills* and *Activities*

Test Prep

Draw Conclusions

NC STANDARD: ELA 2.05 support inferences/conclusions

NORTH CAROLINA EOG Practice

▶ **Read the passage. Then answer the questions.**

> **Ricky stood at the window, his eyes glued to the road. Each time there was a glare of approaching headlights, he leaned forward eagerly. Each time the headlights passed by, his shoulders slumped. Michelle looked at the clock. It was getting late. Dad should have been home by now, even if traffic was heavy. She watched Ricky lean forward again. Then he turned to grin at her and ran to the door.**

INTERPRETATION / ANALYZING

1. What conclusion can you draw about Ricky?

A He enjoys watching cars go by.

B He is anxious for his father to get home.

C He is angry that his father is late.

D He likes to tease Michelle.

Think about why you would act like Ricky. Use story details and your own knowledge to draw a conclusion about Ricky.

INTERPRETATION / ANALYZING

2. What conclusion can you draw about the outcome of the story?

F Ricky goes out to try to find his father.

G Michelle sends Ricky to bed because it's late.

H Ricky gets tired of waiting and goes to his room.

J Ricky and Michelle's father arrives home.

Look for clues about the outcome of the story, at the end of the passage. The conclusion you drew should make sense.

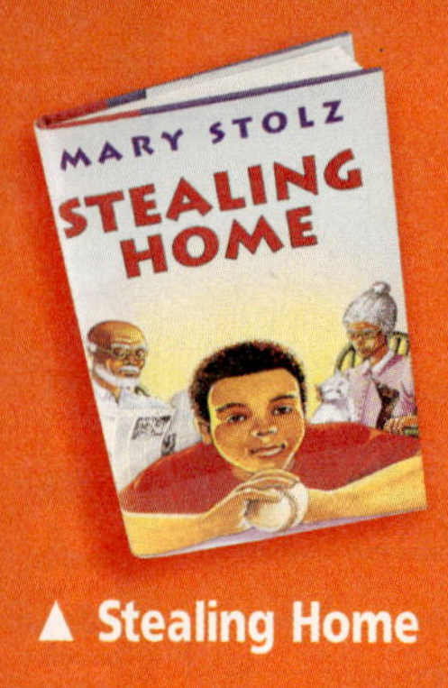

▲ Stealing Home

Vocabulary Power

In the selection "Stealing Home," the people in the family stop getting along with each other. How can that be prevented? What are some tips to help people get along and to keep a home peaceful?

- pastimes
- bicker
- grudge
- irritably
- tutor
- impose
- glumly
- disposition

Enjoy **pastimes** together, such as playing games, listening to music, and watching movies. Don't **bicker**, or quarrel, over what game to play or what movie to watch. Take turns choosing. That way, no one will feel left out and hold a **grudge**, an angry feeling, against the others.

Do some people answer **irritably**, or grumpily, when you suggest an activity? It could just be that they do not know how to do it. Why not offer to **tutor** them so that they will know how? Teaching others can be very rewarding. It does not take long. It will not **impose** a burden on you.

Don't spend time sitting **glumly** in a chair, with your face set in a frown. Try as much as possible to have a sunny **disposition** around others. Soon you won't have to try very hard. Your usual way of acting will become sunnier and brighter.

Vocabulary–Writing
CONNECTION

Think about some **pastimes** you enjoy. Choose one, and write a paragraph telling about it.

Realistic Fiction

Realistic fiction has characters and events that are like people and events in real life.

In this selection, look for

- A setting that could be a real place
- Realistic characters and events

BY
MARY STOLZ

ILLUSTRATED BY
CEDRIC LUCAS

Stealing Home

Thomas likes his life with Grandfather in their small house near the beach in Florida. They enjoy gardening, playing games, collecting "treasures," and listening to baseball on the radio. Ringo, Thomas's cat, and Ivan the Terrible, a bad-tempered duck, live with them.

One day Thomas's great-aunt Linzy, with whom Grandfather does not get along, writes that she plans to come and stay for a while. When Aunt Linzy arrives, she takes Thomas's room. Thomas turns to his friend Donny for comfort.

Next morning, Aunt Linzy came into the kitchen smiling. "I slept like a baby. In spite of this awful heat, and your ceiling fans are of little help, Joseph. They just move the hot air in a circle. Nevertheless—like a *baby*. I wouldn't have believed it possible. Of course, I was desperately tired, which probably accounts for it. Thomas! Your cat is delightful! He spent the entire night at the foot of my bed. I am flattered!"

Grandfather, with a quick glance at Thomas, said, "It's the room he's used to, of course."

Thomas, with an ache in his throat, turned away. "I'm going over to Donny's."

"You haven't had breakfast—"

"I don't want any. I'll—I'll be back—sometime."

A week later, Thomas and Donny were eating cones in a yogurt shop.

"It's not going so good, huh?" said Donny.

Thomas shrugged.

"Did you get all her boxes unpacked?"

"Some of them. Grandfather told her we'd have to put the rest in a storage place. There isn't enough *room* for it all."

"Did Grandfather get a cot for you in his room, like he said?"

"Yes."

"Don't you want to talk?"

"Yes."

"So?"

Thomas burst out, "She's cleaning the whole place. I mean, the cards and checkers and dominoes and we had a Scrabble game halfway done and she just swept all the tiles into the bag, and *everything's* in drawers now, she says we can get them out when we play but isn't it tidier to tidy them away when we aren't. And Grandfather caught her just in time before she cleared all our shells and bottle glass and even the fossil into a box. . . ."

A day or two after her arrival, Grandfather and Thomas had come in from a morning on the beach to find Aunt Linzy sitting near the bookshelves with one of her boxes on the floor beside her. She was wrapping in tissue paper, then putting in the box, all their shells, bottle glass, beachstone figures, the smaller pieces of sculpture. She was clearing from their shelves years and years of treasures.

"Linzy!" Grandfather shouted. "What the deuce are you doing?"

"As you see, Joseph. I am carefully packing your collection of—" She picked up the fossil. "Goodness, I remember this. You've had it for ages, haven't you. I think I remember Marta showing it to—"

"Why are you packing our things?"

"For safekeeping, of course. And to make room."

"They've been safe enough where they are all these years. I do not think they'll be safer in a—Room for what?"

"There is, Joseph, the matter of *my* possessions. I've only been able to empty this one box, and there are all the others on the porch. I don't think I'll be able to get much more in my room—"

Thomas swallowed hard to keep himself from saying, "*Whose* room?" He didn't dare look at Grandfather.

"So? What happened?" Donny asked.

"Grandfather made her—I mean, asked her—to put our stuff back, and they had a—a talk—about her boxes on the porch. She got a lot of the stuff out, and the rest we've put in a U-Store U-Lock over on Cortez. She says she's going to buy another dresser to put in my room. Except she calls it her room. She says she's going to tutor me in arithmetic, when school starts. So she's going to be here then. When it starts. I think she'll still be here when I get to high school. I think she's moved *in*. Period."

"Gee. It sounds—" Donny finished his cone, wiped his mouth, and asked gently, like a doctor touching a sore spot, "What about Ringo—I mean, is he—"

"She's taken him over, too. Her room, her cat. It'll be her house, probably, pretty soon."

"Oh, that's not so, Thomas. I mean, Ringo. He's *always* been your cat."

"Not anymore. Grandfather says I must make allowances for feline vagaries."

"What're they?"

"Dumb stupid ideas."

"Really?"

"No, not really."

"Grandfather knows lots of fancy words."

"He reads lots of books. You know what else he says? He says I should be *glad* that Ringo has made another friend. That's supposed to make me feel better. If you ask *me*," Thomas continued bitterly, "he's a traitor. That's what he is."

"*Grandfather*?"

"Don't be dumb. Ringo. He's turned against me."

"Gosh, Thomas—that's awful. How are you going to stand it, having her there, I mean—living with you?"

Thomas lifted his shoulders. "She's gotta live somewhere, I suppose."

"You know something?"

"Probably not."

"That's what you said about Ivan one time. You said he's gotta live somewhere."

"So—they both gotta, and we're stuck with them. And that fool Ivan is as bad as Ringo. Follows her around like she was the rainbow the pot of gold is at the end of."

"Funny."

"What's *funny*?"

"How animals like her. Maybe it makes up to her for you and Grandfather not liking her."

"What's that supposed to mean?"

"I don't know," Donny said in confusion. "I guess it doesn't mean anything."

"Nothing means anything. Let's get our bikes and go for a long ride."

"Okay."

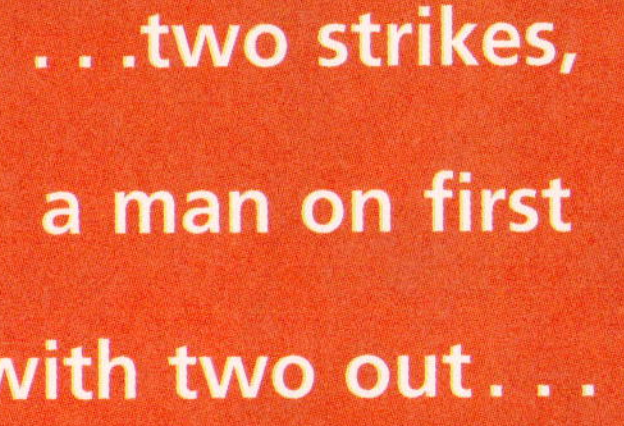

"Goodness," said Aunt Linzy, coming into the living room on an afternoon in late August. "Is that game still going on?" Grandfather held up a shushing hand. The score was tied in the bottom of the tenth, game at Wrigley Field, Cubs batter up, count no balls, two strikes, a man on first with two out. . . .

"Well, really! I was only going to say—"

Andre Dawson, with a line single to left, drove in the winning run and Grandfather turned the radio off.

"If their pitching doesn't fall apart," he said, "Chicago might actually win the division. Who'd have thought it, in spring training?"

"In spring training," Thomas said glumly, "I was *sure* the Pirates would."

Aunt Linzy said brightly, "I looked in the paper this morning, to see the boxing scores—"

"Box scores," Grandfather muttered.

"Oh really, Joseph. I am trying to take an interest."

"It is not necessary, Linzy. Really. Thomas and I understand that baseball isn't your sport."

Jigsaw puzzles, thought Thomas. That's her sport. She finished puzzles he and Grandfather had started, without asking if they minded. Thomas minded. By herself, she did the three hard ones a lot faster than he and Grandfather, together, could do the kind that had scenery.

"I believe," she was saying, "that family members should have interests in common. That's why I'm trying to understand the fascination of baseball even if it seems to me shocking that men get such ridiculous salaries for playing what is a—"

"Child's game. Yes, Linzy. That's been said many times. But believe me, we don't in the *least* wish to impose our pastimes on you."

We don't, Thomas thought, want to share baseball with you. Or fishing—which anyway Aunt Linzy wouldn't dream of sharing. Or our house. Or Ringo.

Ringo came in from the kitchen, briefly brushed along Thomas's leg, sprang to Aunt Linzy's lap. For Thomas, after all these weeks it still felt like a punch in the heart when Ringo, his own cat that had been his from a kitten he'd rescued from the rain, showed that he preferred somebody else. Ringo didn't absolutely ignore him, but if Aunt Linzy was in the room, to her he went. Every time.

"According to the boxing—I mean, *box* scores—your team, the Philadelphia Pirates, is sixteen games out of first place."

"Pittsburgh."

"What?"

"Pittsburgh Pirates."

"Of course. I mix them up."

Grandfather muttered, close to Thomas's ear, "She only does it to annoy, because she knows it teases."

Thomas was sure of that. Aunt Linzy was a lot of things, only dumb wasn't one of them. She knew baseball terms by now, but mixed them up on purpose. To show she was too good for it? To make him and Grandfather look silly, being crazy about a kid's game? Who knew why she did it, or why she did any of the other things that she'd been doing since she got here.

Like ironing sheets and underwear.

One day, shortly after she'd moved in, Aunt Linzy said, "I can't find your ironing board, Joseph."

"We don't have one."

"How do you iron things?"

"When we do—which is practically never—we put a blanket and a sheet on the kitchen table. Works fine."

"For my part, I think beautifully pressed clothes and bed linen are very important."

"I see. All right, I'll get an ironing board."

"Good. From now on, you can leave the laundering to me. It's the least I can do."

"That is not necess—"

"Nonsense. It will be my pleasure."

Thomas and Grandfather found their shirts, trousers, underwear, and sheets pressed and neatly stacked on their beds each week.

"Do you suppose she'd iron my sneakers if I asked?" Thomas said.

"Please. Spare me." Later Grandfather said to Aunt Linzy, "The sheets are supposed to be no-iron."

"There's no such thing. You must admit that unwrinkled bed linen is much pleasanter to sleep on."

Grandfather admitted nothing of the kind, but didn't protest. Nor did he say much when Aunt Linzy, using the sewing machine she'd brought with her, made curtains, and then slipcovers to match.

"There!" she exclaimed, when the job was finished. "Doesn't that look much nicer than blank windows and that tattered old upholstery?"

"It's pretty," Grandfather said, and added, "Thank you, Linzy."

"My pleasure."

Aunt Linzy always said, "My pleasure," when she made improvements that Thomas didn't always think improved things. Like the vacuum cleaner she bought. He and Grandfather had never had one, because they had no rugs. But Aunt Linzy found ways to use it every few days. She was bothered at how sand got tracked into the house, so she put sisal mats just inside the kitchen and front doors. They already had them on the outside. She asked, once, if it wouldn't be a good idea for them to remove their shoes before coming in the house, but Grandfather said they weren't living in Japan, and that was that.

Aunt Linzy was a good cook, and made dinner two or three times a week, using lots of vegetables and pasta. She made soup with things from the stir-fry garden, or even fruit, that Grandfather said was as good as any he made with soup bones.

She had made, in the time she'd been with them, lots of changes in their house, in their lives. Grandfather, trying to look on the sunny side, said it wasn't all bad, now was it, Thomas?

They were sitting on the front-porch swing, Ringo on his railing perch, listening to the evening choir of birds. Aunt Linzy had gone to visit Mrs. Price. They'd become vegetarian friends and exchanged recipes about how to make turnips exciting and amaze people with tofu. Or make soup from plums.

"Plum soup," Thomas said irritably. "That's crazy."

"Tasted pretty good, didn't it?"

Thomas wriggled. "I suppose."

"Do you want to talk about it, Thomas?"

"About what?"

"Now, now. You know about what."

"What's to say?"

"I know how difficult this is being for you. But don't you think it *could* be worse?"

"How?"

"Well—Ivan doesn't bite us anymore. There's that."

"Hah-hah."

After a short silence, Grandfather said, "Your aunt Linzy has a good disposition, which is nothing to hah-hah about. Too many people are constantly whining and

complaining about their lot in life. You must admit your aunt is usually pretty cheerful."

"And I think it's funny."

"What do you mean?"

"Grandfather. If you lived someplace where people were wondering how much longer you were going to stay, would you be cheerful? I wouldn't be. I'd be—" He hesitated.

"What would you be?"

Grumpy, Thomas started to say, but changed his mind. "Sad, I guess."

"Thomas, tell me. Have you once tried to look at this situation from your aunt's point of view instead of your own?"

"No. Have you?"

"Yes. Could you try?"

"No."

Grandfather continued to have the waiting look he got when he expected something more from Thomas.

"She took my room away from me."

"We're making out all right in mine, aren't we?"

"It isn't that, Grandfather—"

"I know." He held up one hand. "You needn't say what you're thinking. But *I* am thinking of what people all over the world have to endure that you and I do not. Millions of human beings hungry, hopeless, frightened. *Homeless*, Thomas. Nowhere to *live*. You and I just have to put up for a while with one lonely old lady."

"What does 'for a while' mean? I don't think it's for a while. I think she's *living* with us."

"Thomas, Thomas. You don't often disappoint me. But sometimes you do, really you do. If that should be the case — what do you suggest? Tell her to pack up and get out?"

"She stole my cat."

Thomas looked at Ringo, beautiful and composed on the railing. It made his throat, and his heart, really ache—the way Ringo had left him for Aunt Linzy.

Grandfather put an arm over Thomas's shoulders and pulled him close.

"Things never can remain the same, Thomas. It's the way life is. . . . Everything changes, and we can't stop that."

Thomas sighed. Grandfather always knew what he was thinking. "You don't bicker with her anymore, do you?"

"No. It would make things worse."

"I'm not being a good sport, am I?"

"Not especially."

"I don't want to disappoint you, Grandfather."

"I know that."

"I'll try to be better."

"Good. How about a game of Scrabble before we go to bed?"

"Okay. I mean, I'd like that."

They went into the living room, to the games table, got the Scrabble set from the drawer where Aunt Linzy had stored it, and set up.

Ringo followed, leaping to Thomas's lap. He settled down and began to run his motor. Thomas, one hand on the large silky head, thought how impossible it was to hold a grudge against a cat. The same as they didn't hold grudges against people.

Think and Respond

1. How does Aunt Linzy try to show her interest in Grandfather's and Thomas's **pastimes**?
2. Why does Aunt Linzy say she is flattered when Ringo, the cat, sleeps at the foot of her bed?
3. How does the author use Ringo the cat to help show the problem in the story?
4. Think about Thomas's games and other interests. What are some pastimes that you enjoy?
5. What reading strategies did you use to help you understand "Stealing Home"? When did you use them?

Mary Stolz

Besides liking cats and cooking, Mary Stolz loves reading. When she was a child, she wanted to be like characters in books she read. Mary Stolz finds that the things she learns in books, about people and life in general, help her write interesting stories. For her, the most important goal is to capture the reader's imagination. She must be doing a good job because her books have been published in thirty languages.

"In writing, I want to entertain. Failing that, you might as well forget it."

Visit *The Learning Site!*
www.harcourtschool.com

Genre
Poem

from

Grandfather Is a Chinese Pine

Grandfather is a Chinese pine
Standing firm on the sloping hillside.
From his bright, piercing eyes
All can see the evergreen spirit
That pushed its way up from poor, stony soil.

I love, honor and revere him,
Our sturdy tree of shade and support.
From the tall height of his example
I can see my way straight and far.

—Zheng Xu, age 18
New York, New York

▲ Stealing Home

Making Connections

Text to Self • Text to Text • Text to World

Compare Texts

NC STANDARDS: ELA 2.04b identify narrative elements/theme, 3.01d analyze differences among genres, 3.02 analyze/compare texts, 3.03 examine effects of language/visuals, 3.06 conduct research using a variety of tools

1. How does the selection "Stealing Home" express the theme that we need to understand each other's points of view? INTERPRETATION / EVALUATING
2. Look at the illustrations on pages 305 and 311. How do they help you understand how Thomas is feeling? INTERPRETATION / GENERATING
3. Think about the poem "Grandfather Is a Chinese Pine" and the selection "Stealing Home." Compare Thomas's and Zheng Xu's relationships with their grandfathers. CONNECTIONS / ANALYZING
4. What makes the selection "Stealing Home" realistic fiction? Explain your answer. COGNITION / EVALUATING
5. Thomas and Grandfather live in Florida. How could you find out more about what it is like to live in Florida? INTERPRETATION / EVALUATING

Explain How to Be a Good Listener

Writing CONNECTION

Reread Thomas's conversation with his friend Donny. What makes Donny such a good listener? Write a paragraph explaining how to be a good listener. Use a graphic organizer like this one to plan your paragraph.

Listening Tips

Make a Chart

NC STANDARDS: ELA 3.06 conduct research using a variety of tools, 4.05 use planning strategies to organize ideas

Science CONNECTION

Ringo is Thomas's pet cat. Many types of cats also live in the wild. Do research to find out about one cat in the wild, such as a lion, tiger, or panther. Make a chart like this one and fill it in with the information you find.

Type of Cat	
Where It Lives	
What It Eats	
Special Adaptations	

Write a Biographical Sketch

Social Studies CONNECTION

"Stealing Home" is set in the state of Florida. Many men and women have made contributions to the development of Florida over the years. Choose a person who has made an important contribution to your state. Research that person. Write a brief "sketch" of the person, explaining his or her contribution to the history and development of your state.

NC STANDARDS: ELA 3.06 conduct research using a variety of tools, 4.02a use writing to communicate with others; Social Studies 3.02 identify people/symbols/events/documents key to North Carolina's history

▲ Stealing Home

Compare and Contrast

NC STANDARDS: ELA 2.01e use metacognitive strategies to clarify text/vocabulary/ask questions, 4.05 use planning strategies to organize ideas

When you think about how things are alike, you **compare**. When you think about how things are different, you **contrast**. Comparing and contrasting can help you better understand the characters and events in a story.

In "Stealing Home," Thomas's life changes when Aunt Linzy comes to stay. However, many important things stay the same. You can use a chart like the one below to compare and contrast Thomas's life before and after Aunt Linzy comes for an extended visit.

Before Aunt Linzy Visits	After Aunt Linzy Visits
Thomas and Grandfather play games together.	Aunt Linzy puts unfinished games away.
Thomas and Grandfather listen to baseball on the radio.	Thomas has to give his bedroom to Aunt Linzy.
Thomas has a cat named Ringo.	Ringo prefers Aunt Linzy to Thomas.

In addition to comparing settings, characters, and plot events within a story, you can also compare and contrast different stories. How is "Stealing Home" like another story you have read? How is it different?

Visit *The Learning Site!*
www.harcourtschool.com

See *Skills* and *Activities*

Test Prep

Compare and Contrast

NORTH CAROLINA EOG Practice

NC STANDARD: ELA 3.02 analyze/compare texts

▶ **Read the passage. Then answer the questions.**

Annie was almost out the door when Grandma stopped her. "You're not going out in this cold weather without a hat and scarf," she insisted. "Believe me, I know what's best."

Annie sighed. There was no use arguing with Grandma. She was too stubborn. Besides, she would tell Annie's parents that Annie had been disrespectful, and then they would lecture her again about getting along with Grandma. "I wish it was just Mom and Dad and me, the way it used to be," she thought. Since Grandma came to live with them, it was three adults against one Annie.

CRITICAL STANCE / ANALYZING

1. How is Annie in this story different from Thomas in "Stealing Home"?

A She has difficulty getting along with an older relative.

B Her home life has changed.

C She feels that all the adults are against her.

D She knows she must be respectful.

Eliminate answer choices that are true for Thomas as well as for Annie. The correct answer is true for Annie but not for Thomas.

CRITICAL STANCE / ANALYZING

2. Compare and contrast the plot of this story with the plot of "Stealing Home." Write your answer on a separate sheet of paper.

Tip

Before writing, draw a Venn diagram to compare and contrast the plot of this story with the plot of "Stealing Home."

▲ The Cricket in Times Square

Vocabulary Power

Meeting new friends can be an adventure. Read what Jenna wrote about getting to know people in her new neighborhood.

- **acquaintance**
- **scrounging**
- **eavesdropping**
- **wistfully**
- **sympathetically**
- **logical**
- **excitable**

Today I made the **acquaintance** of two of my neighbors. I'm glad I finally met somebody, but it happened in a funny way.

I was walking my dog, Flip. He was **scrounging** around near a trash basket, looking for scraps of food. Then I heard two people talking nearby. I didn't mean to be **eavesdropping**, or secretly listening to what they were saying. I just couldn't help overhearing them.

"I wish Rosita hadn't moved away," a girl's voice said. She spoke **wistfully**, as if she was sadly remembering something nice.

"I know you miss her very much," a deep voice answered. The man spoke **sympathetically**, in a way that showed he understood and cared about her feelings. It seemed **logical**, or reasonable, that he must be the girl's father.

Just at that moment, a squirrel ran across the path. Flip began barking and running after the squirrel, tugging me along with him. He can be very **excitable** sometimes!

I got tangled in Flip's leash and fell down right in front of the girl and the man. That's how I met Tanya and her father. She and I are the same age. I hope we'll be friends!

Vocabulary-Writing CONNECTION

Good friends show that they care about each other's feelings. Write about a time when you acted **sympathetically** toward a friend.

Genre

Fantasy

A fantasy is an imaginative story that may have unrealistic characters and events.

In this selection, look for

- **Story events that could not happen in real life**
- **Characters that may behave in an unrealistic way**

Tucker Mouse lives in the Times Square subway station in New York City, where he scrounges for food and watches the world go by. He has just overheard a boy named Mario Bellini begging his parents, who run the station newsstand, to let him keep a cricket he has found and put in a matchbox. Tucker had heard a chirping sound, and now that he knows its source, he hurries to find out more.

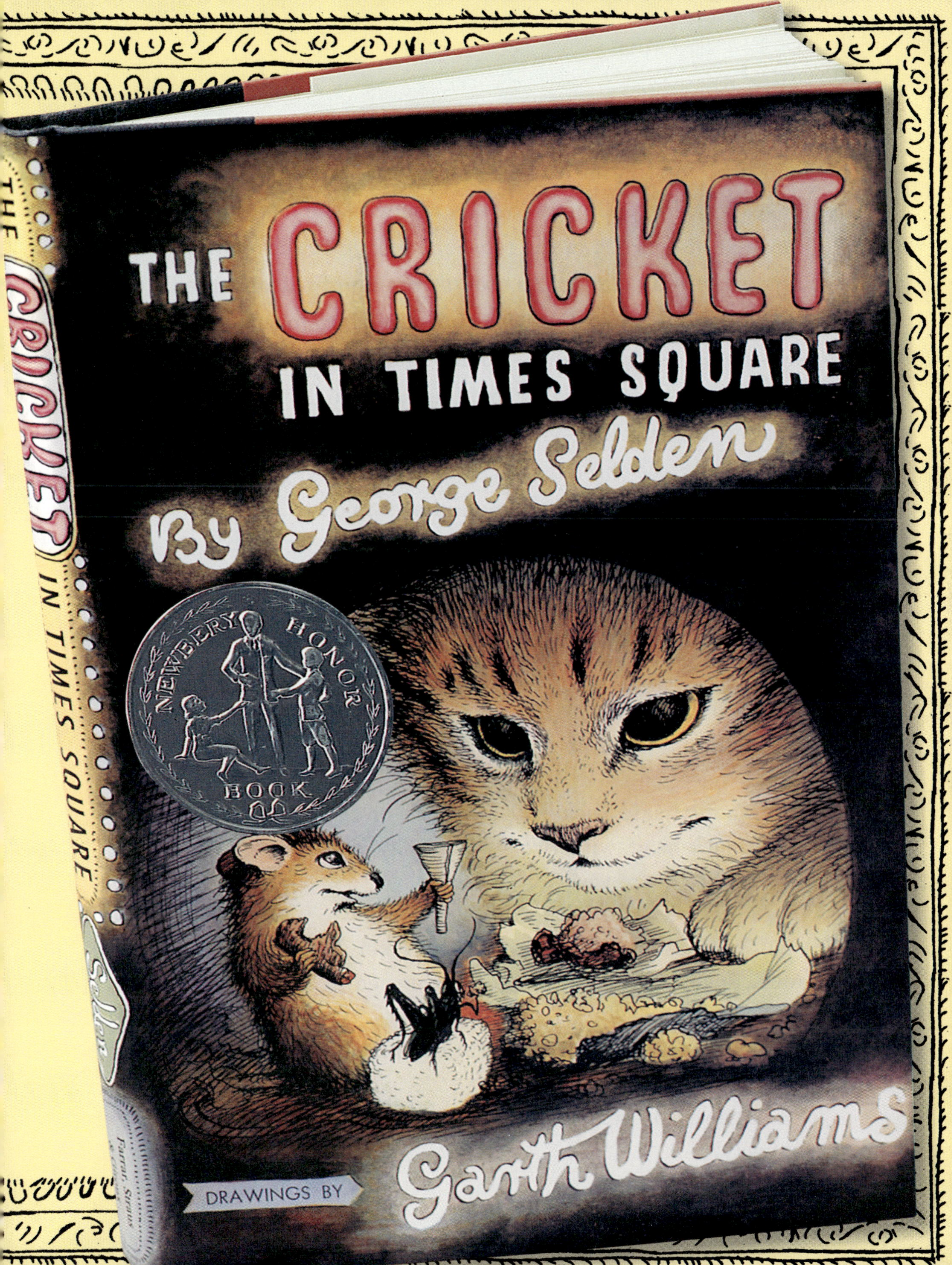
THE CRICKET
IN TIMES SQUARE
By George Selden
NEWBERY HONOR BOOK
DRAWINGS BY
Garth Williams
THE CRICKET IN TIMES SQUARE
Selden

Tucker Mouse had been watching the Bellinis and listening to what they said. Next to scrounging, eavesdropping on human beings was what he enjoyed most. That was one of the reasons he lived in the Times Square subway station. As soon as the family disappeared, he darted out across the floor and scooted up to the newsstand. At one side the boards had separated and there was a wide space he could jump through. He'd been in a few times before—just exploring. For a moment he stood under the three-legged stool, letting his eyes get used to the darkness. Then he jumped up on it.

"Psst!" he whispered. "Hey you up there—are you awake?"

There was no answer.

"Psst! Psst! Hey!" Tucker whispered again, louder this time.

From the shelf above came a scuffling, like little feet feeling their way to the edge. "Who is that going 'psst'?" said a voice.

"It's me," said Tucker. "Down here on the stool."

A black head, with two shiny black eyes, peered down at him. "Who are you?"

"A mouse," said Tucker. "Who are *you*?"

"I'm Chester Cricket," said the cricket. He had a high, musical voice. Everything he said seemed to be spoken to an unheard melody.

"My name's Tucker," said Tucker Mouse. "Can I come up?"

"I guess so," said Chester Cricket. "This isn't my house anyway."

A black head, with two shiny eyes, peered down at him.

Tucker jumped up beside the cricket and looked him all over. “A cricket,” he said admiringly. “So you’re a cricket. I never saw one before.”

“I’ve seen mice before,” the cricket said. “I knew quite a few back in Connecticut.”

“Is that where you’re from?” asked Tucker.

“Yes,” said Chester. “I guess I’ll never see it again,” he added wistfully.

“How did you get to New York?” asked Tucker Mouse.

“It’s a long story,” sighed the cricket.

“Tell me,” said Tucker, settling back on his haunches. He loved to hear stories. It was almost as much fun as eavesdropping—if the story was true.

“Well it must have been two—no, three days ago,” Chester Cricket began. “I was sitting on top of my stump, just enjoying the weather and thinking how nice it was that summer had started. I live inside an old tree stump, next to a willow tree, and I often go up to the roof to look around. And I’d been practicing jumping that day too. On the other side of the stump from the willow tree there’s a brook that runs past, and I’d been jumping back and forth across it to get my legs in condition for the summer. I do a lot of jumping, you know.”

“Me too,” said Tucker Mouse. “Especially around the rush hour.”

“And I had just finished jumping when I smelled something,” Chester went on, “liverwurst, which I love.”

“You like liverwurst?” Tucker broke in. “Wait! Wait! Just wait!”

In one leap, he sprang down all the way from the shelf to the floor and dashed over to his drain pipe. Chester shook his head as he watched him go. He thought Tucker was a very excitable person—even for a mouse.

Inside the drain pipe, Tucker's nest was a jumble of papers, scraps of cloth, buttons, lost jewelry, small change, and everything else that can be picked up in a subway station. Tucker tossed things left and right in a wild search. Neatness was not one of the things he aimed at in life. At last he discovered what he was looking for: a big piece of liverwurst he had found earlier that evening. It was meant to be for breakfast tomorrow, but he decided that meeting his first cricket was a special occasion. Holding the liverwurst between his teeth, he whisked back to the newsstand.

"Look!" he said proudly, dropping the meat in front of Chester Cricket. "Liverwurst! You continue the story—we'll enjoy a snack too."

"That's very nice of you," said Chester. He was touched that a mouse he had known only a few minutes would share his food with him. "I had a little chocolate before, but besides that, nothing for three days."

"Eat! Eat!" said Tucker. He bit the liverwurst into two pieces and gave Chester the bigger one. "So you smelled the liverwurst—then what happened?"

"I hopped down from the stump and went off toward the smell," said Chester.

"Very logical," said Tucker Mouse, munching with his cheeks full. "Exactly what I would have done."

"It was coming from a picnic basket," said Chester.

"A couple of tuffets away from my stump the meadow begins, and there was a whole bunch of people having a picnic. They had hard-boiled eggs, and cold roast chicken, and roast beef, and a whole lot of other things besides the liverwurst sandwiches which I smelled."

Tucker Mouse moaned with pleasure at the thought of all that food.

"They were having such a good time laughing and singing songs that they didn't notice me when I jumped into the picnic basket," continued Chester. "I was sure they wouldn't mind if I had just a taste."

"Naturally not," said Tucker Mouse sympathetically. "Why mind? Plenty for all. Who could blame you?"

"Now, I have to admit," Chester went on, "I had more than a taste. As a matter of fact, I ate so much that I couldn't keep my eyes open—what with being tired from the jumping and everything. And I fell asleep right there in the picnic basket. The first thing I knew, somebody had put a bag on top of me that had the last of the roast beef sandwiches in it. I couldn't move!"

"Imagine!" Tucker exclaimed. "Trapped under roast beef sandwiches! Well, there are worse fates."

"At first I wasn't too frightened," said Chester. "After all, I thought, they probably come from New Canaan or some other nearby town. They'll have to unpack the basket sooner or later. Little did I know!" He shook his head and sighed. "I could feel the basket being carried into a car and riding somewhere and then being lifted down. That must have been the railroad station. Then I went up again and there was a rattling and roaring sound, the way a train makes. By this time I was pretty scared. I knew every minute was taking me farther away from my stump, but

there wasn't anything I could do. I was getting awfully cramped too, under those roast beef sandwiches."

"Didn't you try to eat your way out?" asked Tucker.

"I didn't have any room," said Chester. "But every now and then the train would give a lurch and I managed to free myself a little. We traveled on and on, and then the train stopped. I didn't have any idea where we were, but as soon as the basket was carried off, I could tell from the noise it must be New York."

"You never were here before?" Tucker asked.

"Goodness no!" said Chester. "But I've heard about it. There was a swallow I used to know who told about flying over New York every spring and fall on her way to the North and back. But what would I be doing here?" He shifted uneasily from one set of legs to another. "I'm a country cricket."

"Don't worry," said Tucker Mouse. "I'll feed you liverwurst. You'll be all right. Go on with the story."

"It's almost over," said Chester. "The people got off one train and walked a ways and got on another—even noisier than the first."

"Must have been the subway," said Tucker.

"I guess so," Chester Cricket said. "You can imagine how scared I was. I didn't know *where* I was going! For all I knew they could have been heading for Texas, although I don't guess many people from Texas come all the way to Connecticut for a picnic."

"It could happen," said Tucker, nodding his head.

"Usually I don't chirp until later on in the summer—

"Anyway I worked furiously to get loose. And finally I made it. When they got off the second train, I took a flying leap and landed in a pile of dirt over in the corner of this place where we are."

"Such an introduction to New York," said Tucker, "to land in a pile of dirt in the Times Square subway station. Tsk, tsk, tsk."

"And here I am," Chester concluded forlornly. "I've been lying over there for three days not knowing what to do. At last I got so nervous I began to chirp."

"That was the sound!" interrupted Tucker Mouse. "I heard it, but I didn't know what it was."

"Yes, that was me," said Chester. "Usually I don't chirp until later on in the summer—but my goodness, I had to do *something*!"

The cricket had been sitting next to the edge of the shelf. For some reason—perhaps it was a faint noise, like padded feet tiptoeing across the floor—he happened to look down. A shadowy form that had been crouching silently below in the darkness made a spring and landed right next to Tucker and Chester.

"Watch out!" Chester shouted. "A cat!" He dove head-first into the matchbox.

Chester buried his head in the Kleenex. He didn't want to see his new friend, Tucker Mouse, get killed. Back in Connecticut he had sometimes watched the one-sided

but my goodness, I had to do *something*!"

Chester crept out, looking first at one, then the other.

fights of cats and mice in the meadow, and unless the mice were near their holes, the fights always ended in the same way. But this cat had been upon them too quickly: Tucker couldn't have escaped.

There wasn't a sound. Chester lifted his head and very cautiously looked behind him. The cat—a huge tiger cat with gray-green eyes and black stripes along his body—was sitting on his hind legs, switching his tail around his forepaws. And directly between those forepaws, in the very jaws of his enemy, sat Tucker Mouse. He was watching Chester curiously. The cricket began to make frantic signs that the mouse should look up and see what was looming over him.

Very casually Tucker raised his head. The cat looked straight down on him. "Oh him," said Tucker, chucking the cat under the chin with his right front paw, "he's my best friend. Come out from the matchbox."

Chester crept out, looking first at one, then the other.

"Chester, meet Harry Cat," said Tucker. "Harry, this is Chester. He's a cricket."

"I'm very pleased to make your acquaintance," said Harry Cat in a silky voice.

"Hello," said Chester. He was sort of ashamed because of all the fuss he'd made. "I wasn't scared for myself. But I thought cats and mice were enemies."

"In the country, maybe," said Tucker. "But in New York we gave up those old habits long ago. Harry is my oldest friend. He lives with me over in the drain pipe. So how was scrounging tonight, Harry?"

"Not so good," said Harry Cat. "I was over in the ash cans on the East Side, but those rich people don't throw out as much garbage as they should."

"Chester, make that noise again for Harry," said Tucker Mouse.

Chester lifted the black wings that were carefully folded across his back and with a quick, expert stroke drew the top one over the bottom. A *thrumm* echoed through the station.

"Lovely—very lovely," said the cat. "This cricket has talent."

"I thought it was singing," said Tucker. "But you do it like playing a violin, with one wing on the other?"

"Yes," said Chester. "These wings aren't much good for flying, but I prefer music anyhow." He made three rapid chirps.

Tucker Mouse and Harry Cat smiled at each other. "It makes me want to purr to hear it," said Harry.

"Some people say a cricket goes 'chee chee chee,'" explained Chester. "And others say, 'treet treet treet,' but we crickets don't think it sounds like either one of those."

"It sounds to me as if you are going 'crik crik crik,'" said Harry.

"Maybe that's why they call him a 'cricket,'" said Tucker.

They all laughed. Tucker had a squeaky laugh that sounded as if he were hiccupping. Chester was feeling much happier now. The future did not seem nearly as gloomy as it had over in the pile of dirt in the corner.

"Are you going to stay a while in New York?" asked Tucker.

"I guess I'll have to," said Chester. "I don't know how to get home."

"Well, we could always take you to Grand Central Station and put you on a train going back to Connecticut," said Tucker. "But why don't you give the city a try. Meet new people—see new things. Mario likes you very much."

"Yes, but his mother doesn't," said Chester. "She thinks I carry germs."

"Germs!" said Tucker scornfully. "She wouldn't know a germ if one gave her a black eye. Pay no attention."

"Too bad you couldn't have found more successful friends," said Harry Cat. "I fear for the future of this newsstand."

"It's true," echoed Tucker sadly. "They're going broke fast." He jumped up on a pile of magazines and read off the names in the half-light that slanted through the cracks in the wooden cover: *"Art News—Musical America.* Who would read them but a few long-hairs?"

"I don't understand the way you talk," said Chester. Back in the meadow he had listened to bullfrogs, and woodchucks, and rabbits, even a few snakes, but he had never heard anyone speak like Tucker Mouse. "What is a long-hair?"

Tucker scratched his head and thought a moment. "A long-hair is an extra-refined person," he said. "You take an Afghan hound—that's a long-hair."

"Do Afghan hounds read *Musical America*?" asked the cricket.

"They would if they could," said Tucker.

Chester shook his head. "I'm afraid I won't get along in New York," he said.

"Oh, sure you will!" squeaked Tucker Mouse. "Harry, suppose we take Chester up and show him Times Square. Would you like that, Chester?"

"I guess so," said Chester, although he was really a little leery of venturing out into New York City.

The three of them jumped down to the floor. The crack in the side of the newsstand was just wide enough for Harry to get through. As they crossed the station floor, Tucker pointed out the local sights of interest, such as the Nedick's lunch counter—Tucker spent a lot of time around there—and the Loft's candy store. Then they came to the drain pipe. Chester had to make short little hops to keep from hitting his head as they went up. There seemed to be hundreds of twistings and turnings, and many other pipes that opened off the main route, but Tucker Mouse knew his way perfectly—even in the dark. At last Chester saw light above them. One more hop brought him out onto the sidewalk. And there he gasped, holding his breath and crouching against the cement.

They were standing at one corner of the Times building, which is at the south end of Times Square. Above the cricket, towers that seemed like mountains of light rose up into the night sky. Even this late the neon signs were still blazing. Reds, blues, greens, and yellows flashed down on

HOTEL
ASTOR
CHEVROLET
8 8
KINSEY
BO
CRITE

him. And the air was full of the roar of traffic and the hum of human beings. It was as if Times Square were a kind of shell, with colors and noises breaking in great waves inside it. Chester's heart hurt him and he closed his eyes. The sight was too terrible and beautiful for a cricket who up to now had measured high things by the height of his willow tree and sounds by the burble of a running brook.

"How do you like it?" asked Tucker Mouse.

"Well—it's—it's quite something," Chester stuttered.

"You should see it New Year's Eve," said Harry Cat.

Gradually Chester's eyes got used to the lights. He looked up. And way far above them, above New York, and above the whole world, he made out a star that he knew was a star he used to look at back in Connecticut. When they had gone down to the station and Chester was in the matchbox again, he thought about that star. It made him feel better to think that there was one familiar thing, twinkling above him, amid so much that was new and strange.

Think and Respond

1. Why is being in a new place hard for Chester? What helps him feel better?
2. How does the setting affect the lives of the animals in the story?
3. How can you tell that Tucker is happy to make Chester's **acquaintance**?
4. Which character do you like best? Why?
5. How did using reading strategies help you understand the story?

About the Author

George Selden

George Selden started out as a playwright. A friend suggested that he try writing children's books. Selden became famous for writing stories about animals who act like humans. His characters show the importance of friends.

The Cricket in Times Square was an unusual story because of its city setting. Like Chester Cricket, George Selden was from Connecticut. He really heard a cricket chirp in the subway, and it made him homesick for the country. When he was asked to write a sequel, he waited ten years for an idea he thought was good enough. In the end, he wrote six more books about Chester and his friends.

Visit *The Learning Site!*
www.harcourtschool.com

▲ The Cricket in Times Square

Making Connections

Text to Self • Text to Text • Text to World

Compare Texts

NC STANDARDS: ELA 2.02d interact with text/locate information, 2.04a identify narrative elements/plot, 2.04b identify narrative elements/theme, 3.01d analyze differences among genres, 3.03 examine effects of language/visuals

1. Why is "The Cricket in Times Square" in the theme titled Make Yourself at Home? INTERPRETATION / EVALUATING
2. Why do you think the author chose three such different animals as a cricket, a mouse, and a cat as characters? CRITICAL STANCE / EVALUATING
3. Why does the illustrator show the scene on page 343 from an unusual point of view? INTERPRETATION / GENERATING
4. Do the characters in this story seem more like or less like real animals than the animal characters in other fantasy stories you have read? Explain. CONNECTIONS / ANALYZING
5. What did you learn about New York City from reading this selection? What else would you like to learn about it? INTERPRETATION / EVALUATING

Write a Postcard

Writing CONNECTION

If Chester sent a postcard to a friend back home in Connecticut, what would he write? Create a postcard that Chester might send. On one side, draw a city scene. On the other side, write Chester's message. Use an organizer like this one to plan your writing.

Experiences and Feelings	Comparing City Life to Country Life	Getting Used to a New Place

NC STANDARDS: ELA 3.06 conduct research using a variety of tools, 4.02b use oral language to communicate with others; Science 1.03 observe/discuss how an animal's behavior/body aids survival

Present an Oral Report

Science–Music CONNECTION

Crickets are one of a number of creatures that produce musical sounds. Many kinds of birds sing beautiful songs. Humpback whales sing, too. Research the sounds made by one kind of animal to learn what its "music" sounds like. Find out how and why it produces this music. Present your information to classmates.

Estimate Temperatures

Math CONNECTION

Crickets are nature's thermometers. One method for estimating the temperature is to count the number of cricket chirps in 13 seconds and add that number to 40. Make a temperature chart on a separate sheet of paper. Use the method from above to complete the chart.

Chirps in 13 seconds	Temperature
25	
16	
	80°

NC Math 5.03 verify mathematical relationships

▲ The Cricket in Times Square

Draw Conclusions

NC STANDARD: ELA 2.05 support inferences/conclusions

Drawing conclusions helps you understand information the author does not state directly. You can **draw conclusions** using story information and your own knowledge. You might draw conclusions about the story setting, the traits and actions of the characters, and why the characters act as they do.

At the beginning of "The Cricket in Times Square," when you first meet Tucker Mouse, you probably drew conclusions about his traits and actions.

Story Information

Tucker Mouse introduces himself to Chester and asks to come up next to Chester.

Your Own Knowledge

Friendly people seek out new neighbors and introduce themselves.

Conclusions You Can Draw About What Tucker Mouse Is Like

He is friendly.

What other conclusions can you draw about Tucker Mouse, using story information and your own knowledge?

Visit *The Learning Site!*
www.harcourtschool.com

See *Skills and Activities*

Test Prep

Draw Conclusions

NC STANDARD: ELA 2.05 support inferences/conclusions

NORTH CAROLINA EOG Practice

Focus Skill

▶ **Read the passage. Then answer the questions.**

Selma and Fred

Selma Snail poked her head out and looked all around. The sun was shining brightly. She could hear birds chirping cheerily. "I guess it's safe to go out," Selma decided. She gathered up her purse and her umbrella. Selma always took her umbrella, just in case.

Suddenly Fred Frog came hopping toward her. "Come with me, Selma!" he cried. "Some folks from the city are having a picnic nearby. They've brought all kinds of good things to eat!"

"Human beings?" Selma asked. With a gasp, she hurried back into her house and locked the door.

INTERPRETATION / ANALYZING

1. You can draw the conclusion that Selma Snail is—

A cautious

B careless

C bad-tempered

D bold

Tip

Think about Selma Snail's actions. Then think about what you know about people or animals who behave in the same way.

INTERPRETATION / ANALYZING

2. Why does Selma run back inside and lock the door?

F She is afraid of Fred Frog.

G so she won't get wet when it rains

H She is afraid of human beings.

J She has forgotten something.

Tip

What happens right before Selma Snail runs inside? Use that information to help you draw a conclusion.

▲ Two Lands, One Heart

Vocabulary Power

Visiting a land far from home can be both interesting and exciting. Read Monica's journal entry about her family's trip to Italy.

interpreter

overwhelm

hysterically

equivalent

appetizing

occasionally

irrigation

Last summer my family and I took an exciting trip to Italy. I will never forget it. I thought we would need an **interpreter**, but our tour guide spoke English, so we didn't need anyone to help us understand what was being said.

Our tour guide didn't want to **overwhelm** our group with too many activities, so we had time to relax each day. My dad and I enjoyed watching the street performers in our free time. We laughed **hysterically** at some of their skits. It was fun to see my dad laughing uncontrollably.

One thing that was different about Italy was the pizza. I thought it would be **equivalent** to the pizza I eat at home, but it was much better! The food always looked and smelled **appetizing**. Luckily, it usually tasted as delicious as it smelled.

Occasionally, from time to time, my mom worried about things back home. She was especially worried that our lawn would not get watered because she had forgotten to turn on our **irrigation** system. Still, the pictures we took of everyone smiling in front of the different sights prove that we all had a great time.

Everyone has a favorite food. Write a few sentences describing a food that you think is very appetizing.

Award-Winning Illustrator

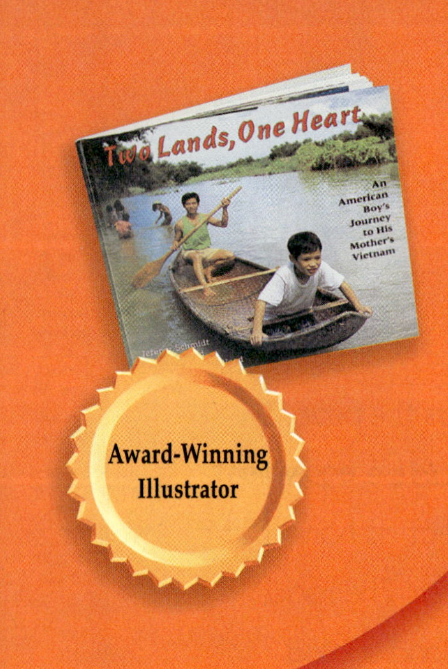

Genre

Nonfiction

Nonfiction tells about people, things, events, or places that are real.

In this selection, look for

- Characters, places, and events that are real
- Comparisons and contrasts between two places

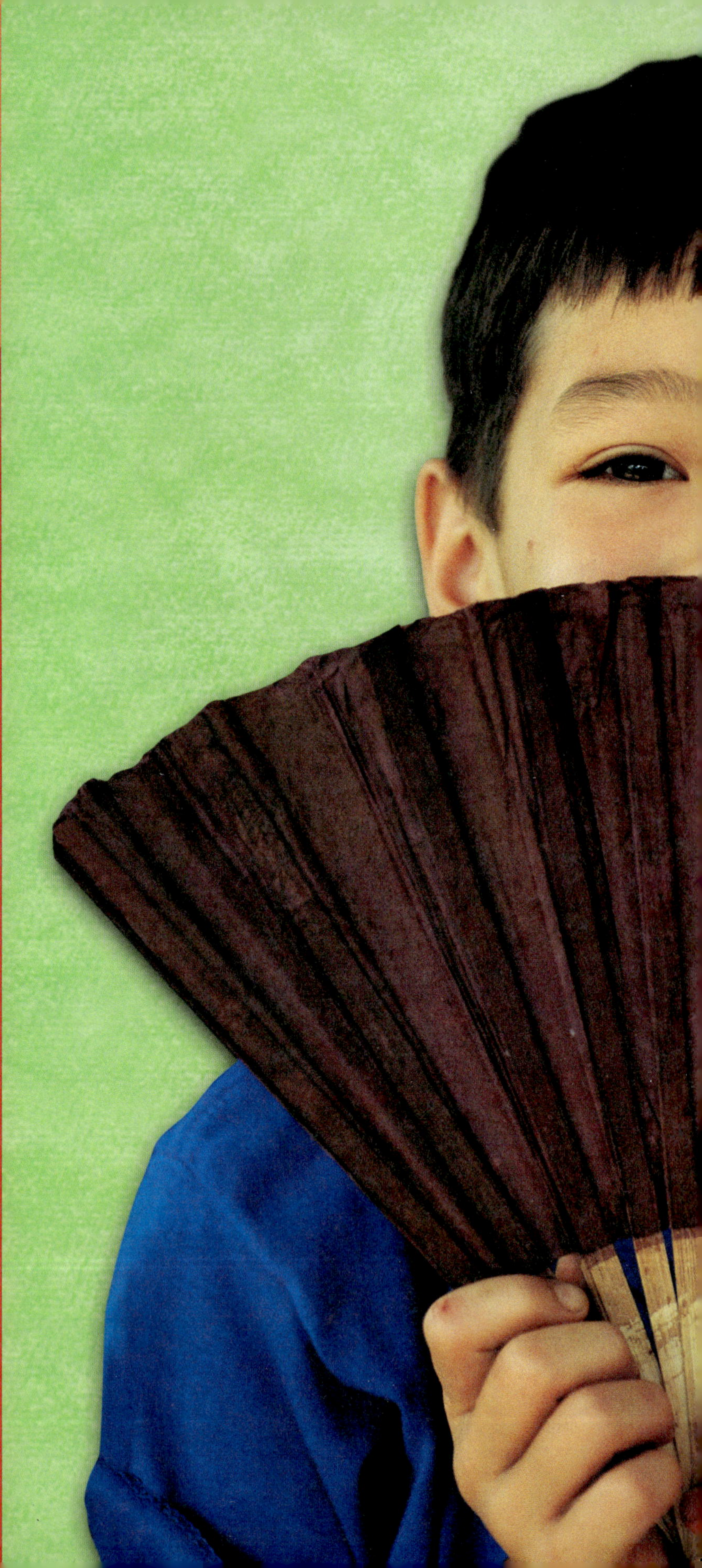

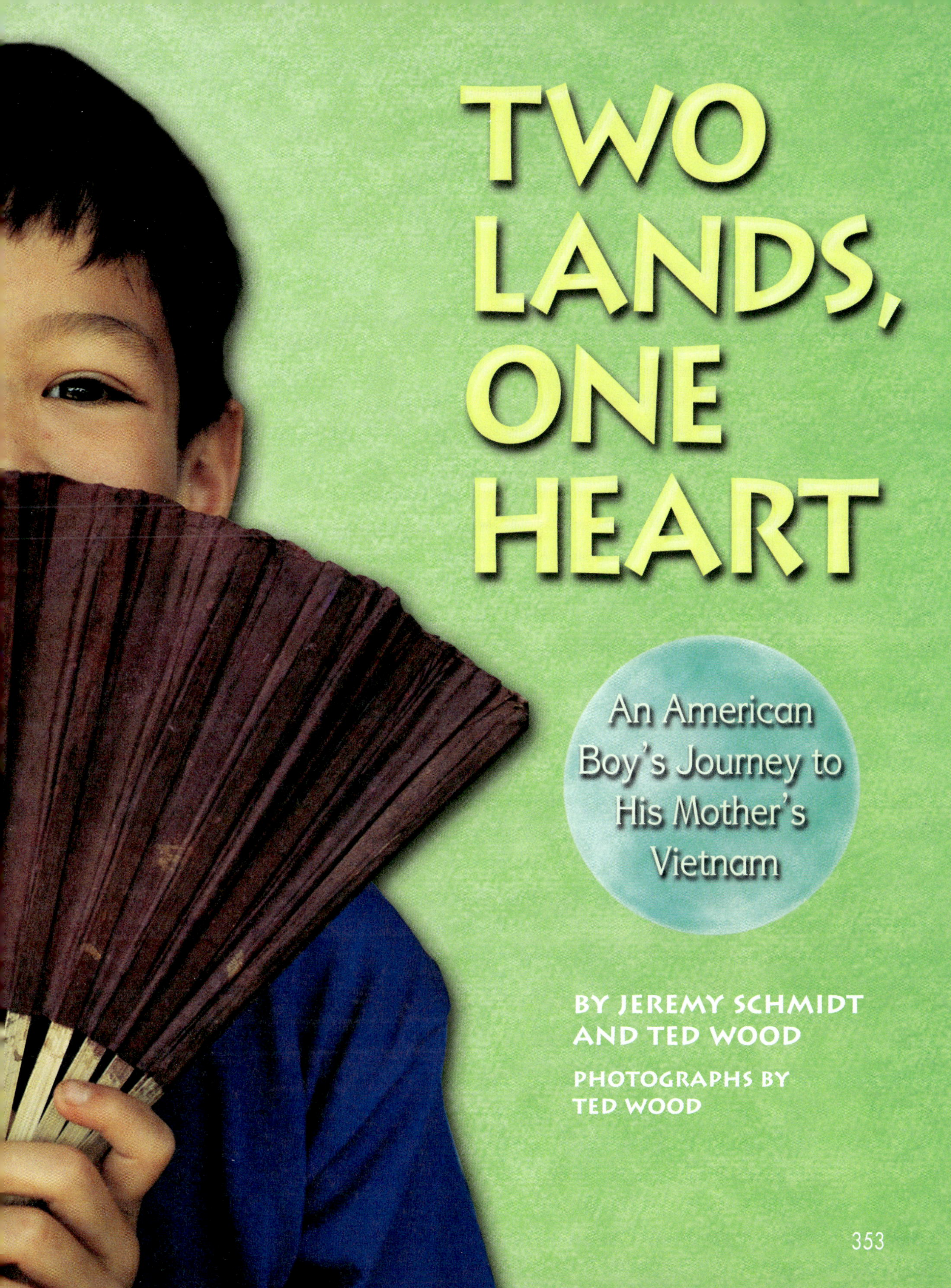

TWO LANDS, ONE HEART

An American Boy's Journey to His Mother's Vietnam

BY JEREMY SCHMIDT AND TED WOOD

PHOTOGRAPHS BY TED WOOD

TJ's mother, Heather, is from Vietnam. She and TJ's Uncle Jason and Aunt Jenny were separated from the rest of their family during the Vietnam War and grew up in an adoptive family in America. Many years later they have learned that their parents are alive and well.

TJ's mother and his Uncle Jason have already made one visit to Vietnam. This time TJ, his mother, his Aunt Jenny, and his American grandmother have made the long plane trip from Denver, Colorado, to Ho Chi Minh City. They still have two more days to travel before they reach TJ's grandparents' farm.

The countryside along the coast is bright green with rice fields that spread as far as the eye can see.

The flight to Vietnam, a country in Southeast Asia, is a long one.

After two days in Saigon[1], it's time for TJ and his family to journey to the family farm. At seven in the morning, a chartered van picks them up at the hotel, and an hour later the city lies behind them. The brilliant green landscape of rice paddies, coconut palms, and tall clumps of bamboo looks like the country TJ has seen in pictures. But even out here, the road is busy with bicycles, scooters, horse-wagons, cars, trucks, and heavy carts pulled by water buffalo—the traditional tractors of Vietnam. With over seventy million people in this small country, the roads are always crowded.

Around noon, they stop in a small town for lunch. This restaurant seems just like an American one with tables and waiters and glasses of water. But what a menu! Grilled

---

[1]Saigon was renamed Ho Chi Minh City [hoh chee mihn], but many people still call it Saigon.

TJ lives in the Rocky Mountains, and he has never seen the ocean before. Playing with his mother on the beach, TJ delights in his first feel of warm saltwater.

Small villages dot the Vietnam coast, and colorful fishing boats fill the calm bays.

sparrows, eel soup, fried frog legs, bird's nest soup. Maybe if his brother Bradley were here, TJ would order him an eel just to see if he would eat it. But for himself, he orders something familiar—fried chicken.

Then it's back on the road, which soon begins to climb into the mountains bordering the sea. TJ has never seen the ocean, and as the van tops the last ridge he spots the clear, blue South China Sea stretching forever before him. All he can think of is jumping into that big blue pool, but he has to wait until they stop in Nha Trang [nä dāng] that evening, where a sandy beach stretches for miles in front of their hotel. When he finally hits the beach, TJ can't believe his eyes. The beach is swarming with thousands of kids about his age. They try to play and talk with him, but TJ doesn't understand their language, and they walk away confused by his silence. Finally, he wades into the warm, gentle water and giggles as he bobs up and down. He wants to stay forever, but in the end, his mother drags him back to their hotel room.

The next day they start early. It's still a long drive to the farm. The mountains are steeper now, and looking down, TJ can see fishing villages in sandy coves hundreds of feet below. As the afternoon heats up and they leave the mountains, the landscape begins to blur into sameness until the driver slows and turns off the highway. Pavement is left behind as they enter a shady tunnel on a narrow red-dirt road that winds between rice fields. Suddenly everyone is awake, both eager and nervous. After six days of traveling, they are moments from the farm.

TJ can barely control his excitement as the van nears the family farm.

The house stands back from the road, barely visible behind a dense stand of trees and bamboo. The driver honks the horn. Led by TJ's grandparents, a crowd of people runs out to greet them. They are weeping hysterically as they overwhelm Jenny and Heather. TJ is swallowed by a mass of arms touching and pulling him close. He doesn't know what to do. The crying and commotion scare him, but he sees the love streaming from his grandparents' faces with their tears.

With his arms wrapped around Heather and Jenny, TJ's grandfather leads the way back to the house. Set beneath big shade trees, the house is made of brick with a tile roof. The family crowds into a small dining room to talk over some cool coconut juice.

TJ's grandparents throw a traditional feast to welcome them to Vietnam, with dozens of dishes TJ has never eaten before.

Although TJ already knows how to say "grandfather" (*ông*) in Vietnamese, all the talk is through an interpreter. After twenty years of living in America and speaking English, his mother has forgotten her Vietnamese. TJ would like to learn a few words, but it's a hard language to pronounce. For instance, the word *dau* [dou]: If you pronounce it with an upward tone, like asking a question (*dau?*), it means "headache." If you say it with a downward tone, it means "peanut." TJ might ask for a bowl of headaches, and what would that get him?

The next day relatives and friends come from miles around for a family feast. It's like a big Thanksgiving dinner with dozens of relatives crammed into one house. Even with tables in every room, people have to take turns eating. The American visitors are the main attraction. So many people are looking at them through the windows and doors that TJ can't see outside. From the kitchen comes an endless parade of dishes, some of them very weird to TJ. Who would think of putting spicy meat with fruit? Or of dipping sugary rice cakes in salty hot sauce? Or of frying a salad?

TJ likes some of the food, especially the fried rice. "*Ông!* Watch this," he says, and expertly lifts rice from his bowl with chopsticks. TJ wishes he could talk Vietnamese with his grandfather, but he's proud to show him that he can at least eat like a Vietnamese boy.

There are no microwaves or stoves in this house. TJ helps his aunts cook dinner over wood fires.

When he finishes, TJ wanders toward the kitchen. Of all the rooms, this one is the most different from houses in America. The only furniture is a table. TJ's aunts cook on the dirt floor in fireplaces with no chimneys, and the walls are black from the wood smoke that hangs in the air. Big kettles of soup bubble beside sizzling woks. There is no microwave oven, no electric stove, no blenders or mixers, not even a refrigerator. It's amazing to see a kitchen without any modern tools, but TJ loves it. It reminds him of his family camping trips in the Rockies. He takes charge of feeding sticks into the fireplace while the women of the family sit on the floor chopping and slicing.

Taking a shower on the farm means dumping a bucket of water over your head. TJ helps his younger cousin steady the bucket.

There is no running water in the house. TJ's grandfather shows him how to get water from the well.

Out the side door is the washing area. Instead of a sink there are several huge clay pots filled with water. The water comes from a well that his great-grandfather dug—a deep shaft about three feet across and lined with bricks. Leaning over the rim, TJ can make out a faint glimmer of water thirty feet below. His grandfather tells him how they used to pull water up with a bucket, but just this year they added an electric pump and a hose. *Ông* is proud of the pump. It's the only electric machine on the farm, and it makes life much easier. Nevertheless, he wants to show TJ how they drew water in the old days. He throws a bucket down; there is a deep splash; then he pulls it up by a rope, hand over hand. It seems like a lot of work for a bit of water to wash your hands in.

As the day ends, TJ spies the nose and warm brown eyes of an ox peering out of a small thatch barn. But it's time for his family to return to the hotel where they're staying, so he'll have to wait till tomorrow to discover the mysteries of the farm.

Although harmless, the big silkworms are a little too creepy for TJ.

The next morning, TJ can't wait to explore the farm and neighborhood. Only a few acres, the farm would be considered small in America. But not in Vietnam. It's the perfect size for TJ, and every few yards he discovers something new. In the fields grow rice, soybeans, corn, and mulberry leaves to feed silkworms. There is a vegetable garden in front of the house. Lining the footpaths, trees grow coconuts, guavas, papayas, avocados, bananas, and mangoes. Bamboo and eucalyptus provide wood and shade. The biggest trees have strange green fruits that grow right out of their trunks. Bigger than footballs and covered with spiny knobs, they are called jackfruit. They don't look very appetizing, but the insides are yellow and sweet. Now TJ knows why he hasn't seen any supermarkets; everyone has a supermarket right in their backyard.

One thing TJ is learning about Vietnam: It's a hot place, and May is the hottest time of year. Every day, the temperature rises to nearly 100 degrees. People work in the morning when it's cool and rest in the shade at midday. At home, TJ's mom would turn on the air conditioner. Here, people use old-fashioned ways to keep cool. His grandfather lies on a bamboo bed beneath a shady guava tree. The chickens climb into the rafters of the barn. TJ prefers the hammock. By pushing off the wall with one foot, he can keep the air circulating as if he's in a rocking bed under a fan.

TJ finds a jackfruit almost as big as he is, growing on a nearby tree.

When it cools in late afternoon, people start moving again. Women wearing straw hats work in the rice paddies, and Uncle Thao [tou] grabs TJ for a walk along the dirt road. TJ is eager to go. He likes Thao, maybe because his goofy joking reminds him of Uncle Jason, Thao's older brother. Thao looks like Jason and even laughs like Jason. At supper yesterday, Thao reached over to TJ's plate, snatched a whole rice cake, and ate it in one bite with a big grin—just like Jason showing off to TJ.

On the road, people pass them on bicycles carrying loads TJ would never see in Denver. One bicycle carries a pig as big as the bike in a basket. Another comes by with about 100 quacking ducks tied upside down by their feet to a big wooden frame. Down the road, a water buffalo has had the equivalent of a flat tire. One shoe has worn out, and three men are nailing on a new one. They are metal like horseshoes except that because a buffalo has split hooves he needs two shoes for each foot. When the men finish, the big animal lumbers into the irrigation ditch and lies in the water with only his head showing. Naturally, a water buffalo's favorite place is in the water.

Although his neighbors use buffalo instead of tractors, Thao is proud of his family's oxen, which are more valuable than buffalo and easier to command. TJ loves these gentle animals and is thrilled when Thao asks him to help plow a new cornfield. From the barn, Thao brings the oxen, the yoke, and the plow, and they head for the field. The oxen follow like dogs, as if they know what to do. At the field, they even stand together, making it easy for Thao to hitch up the plow.

Then, as simple as starting a car, Thao says one word and off they go around the edge of the field. It looks so easy, Thao just walking along, occasionally tapping one of the oxen with a bamboo switch to give directions, the plow digging straight, deep grooves. TJ wants to try but sees right away that even though the oxen are doing all the pulling, it's hard work at the back end, too. He tries to keep the plow upright, and angled so it cuts to the right depth. But it's heavy, and TJ falls sideways

The water buffalo is Vietnam's hardest-working farm animal.

Uncle Thao has a good laugh as TJ attempts to stay aboard one of the oxen.

TJ tries to tell the difference between a weed and a rice plant as he helps his aunt weed the rice field.

Getting coconuts from the palm tree is a tough job. TJ uses a long bamboo stick to shake the coconuts loose.

Uncle Thao and TJ explore the river that flows by the farm.

into the dirt while the oxen keep pulling. After making two passes, TJ turns around. His furrows look like snakes next to Thao's straight lines. He glances at Thao, and his uncle is laughing.

TJ tries another job with his aunt Phieu (pyo͞o), helping her in the rice paddy. At this time of year, the rice plants are only a foot high, and the main job is to pull weeds. Because rice needs lots of water, the paddy is flooded. TJ steps barefoot into squishy mud, careful to put his feet between the stalks so he won't crush any of the delicate plants. Phieu shows him how to tell weeds from rice, and once he starts pulling, weeds are everywhere. It's hard work, bending over in the hot sun with only a bamboo hat for shade. At home, TJ's main chore is to keep his room clean, a job that looks pretty good to him right now.

TJ is dying of thirst after all this hot work. At home he could open the refrigerator and grab a soda. But here you have to harvest your drink. *Ông* hands TJ a special stick and takes him to a coconut tree in the front yard. Using the stick, TJ knocks down one of the heavy green coconuts, ducking so it doesn't land on his head. Then Uncle Thao cuts it open with a big knife and pours the sweet, clear coconut milk into a glass. TJ's not used to seeing water come out of a fruit, and although it tastes pretty good, he'd really rather have a Coke.

Wandering back to the ox barn, TJ spots a bamboo canoe in the rafters. "Uncle Thao," he yells. "Can we take it to the river?" The canoe is not usually for fun. Its main purpose is to carry farm produce down the river to sell in town. But Thao can't pass up a chance to show off to TJ. With TJ's help, he carries the boat down to the water, where he drops it in with a splash.

The river is perfect for learning to canoe. Thao and TJ paddle past farm fields and under big over-hanging trees. A neighboring farmer walks along the bank with a herd of ducks. Around the bend they drift past two boys washing their oxen, and later a man crosses the river in a cart pulled by two water buffalo. The river hasn't changed since TJ's grandfather was a boy. It's a quiet place with no motors and nothing moving faster than a drifting canoe.

As they paddle back to the landing, TJ's four girl cousins are waiting with mischief written all over their faces. "Oh no!" he says, with a big smile. The water is so shallow the girls can walk out to the canoe, and without warning, they start a water fight. In seconds TJ is soaked. Thao jumps out laughing and leaves him to his cousins' mercy. Before long they are all in the river together, splashing and laughing. Cousins are the same everywhere.

Time to abandon ship as TJ's cousins playfully attack the canoe.

Think and Respond

1. Why does TJ travel to Vietnam, and what does he learn there?
2. Why are the photographs and captions an important part of this selection?
3. TJ's family members need an **interpreter** because they speak different languages. How else do they communicate?
4. Do you think "Two Lands, One Heart" is a good title for this story? Why or why not?
5. What reading strategies did you use as you read this selection? How did they help you understand the selection?

PAR AVION

CHỢ ĐƯỜNG 19599 70756

Bưu chính Việt Nam 1000đ

Meet the Authors

Jeremy Schmidt and Ted Wood

Dear Readers,

Hello from Vietnam — the mosquitoes send their greetings! It is hot and humid here. We are not used to this, because we are from the Mountain States, just like TJ. The scenery is beautiful, though.

Traveling to new places is one of the fun parts of our work. Jeremy has been to Asia many times before, and we went to India for the first book we did together. We have worked on magazines, books, travel guides, and photo essays. We think working on books like *Two Lands, One Heart* is the most fun — as long as you bring some insect repellent!

Happy trails,

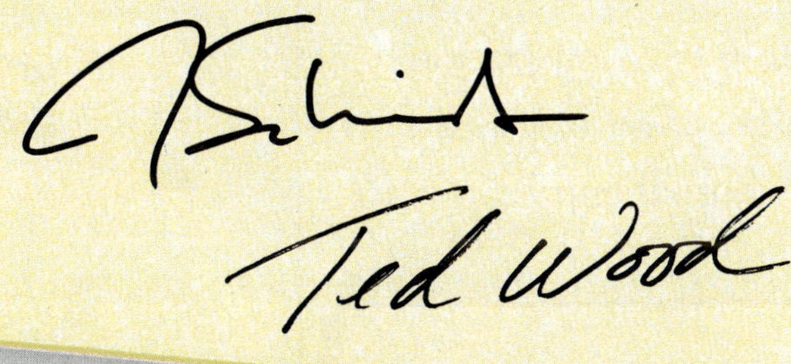

Visit *The Learning Site!*
www.harcourtschool.com

▲ Two Lands, One Heart

Making Connections

Text to Self • Text to Text • Text to World

Compare Texts

NC STANDARDS: ELA 2.04b identify narrative elements/theme, 2.04c identify main idea/details, 3.02 analyze/compare texts, 3.03 examine effects of language/visuals, 3.06 conduct research using a variety of tools

1. How does TJ grow and change as a result of his visit to Vietnam? INTERPRETATION / EVALUATING
2. Why does the author frequently mention events or items in TJ's life back home in America? CRITICAL STANCE / EVALUATING
3. How do the photographs on page 363 help you understand what water buffalo and oxen are like? INTERPRETATION / GENERATING
4. Think of another nonfiction selection you have read. How are the two selections similar to and different from each other? CONNECTIONS / ANALYZING
5. If you wanted to learn more about Vietnam, where might you look for information? INTERPRETATION / EVALUATING

Write a Journal Entry

Write a journal entry that TJ might have written at the end of one of his days in Vietnam. Since you will be writing as TJ, you will need to use first-person pronouns such as *I, me, my, mine,* and *we.* Use a graphic organizer to plan your journal entry.

Date	
What I Did Today	
How I Feel	

Writing CONNECTION

NC STANDARDS: ELA 3.06 conduct research using a variety of tools; Social Studies 6.04 assess use of North Carolina's natural resources

Create a Diagram

Social Studies CONNECTION

TJ's family in Vietnam gets water from a well that his great-grandfather dug. Where does the water come from that your family uses? Do research to trace back to the original source the water that comes from faucets in your home. Create a diagram that shows the steps by which your water gets to you.

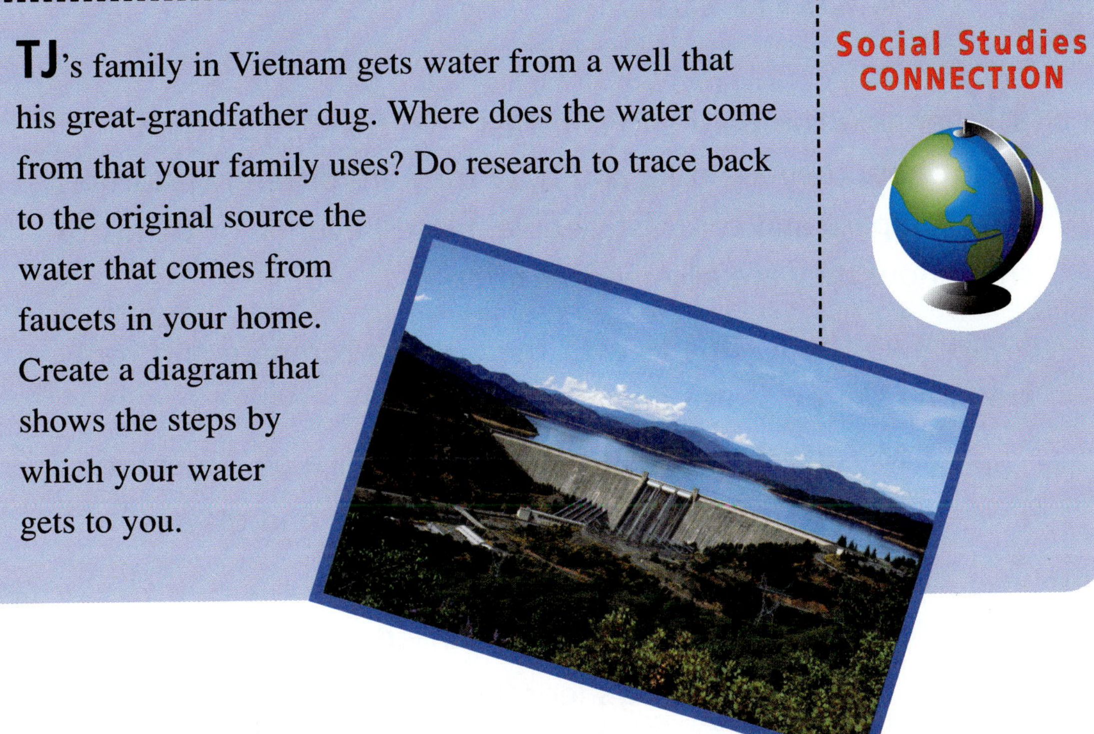

Make a Carbohydrate Collage

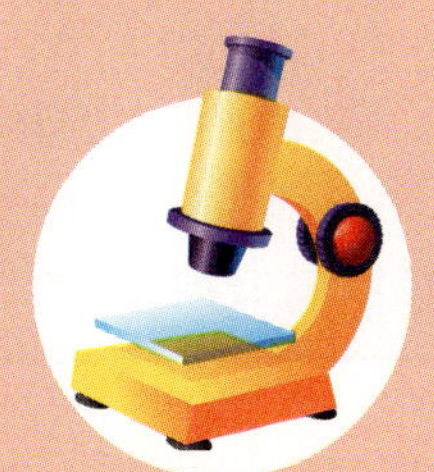

TJ learns that rice is an important part of people's diets in Vietnam. Rice contains mostly carbohydrates. Find out why people need to eat carbohydrates. Draw or cut out pictures of foods that are mostly carbohydrates, and use them to make a carbohydrate collage. Underneath your collage, write a paragraph explaining why carbohydrates are an important part of a healthful diet.

NC STANDARDS: ELA 3.06 conduct research using a variety of tools, 4.02a use writing to communicate with others; Science 4.03 discuss how foods provide energy/nutrients

▲ Two Lands, One Heart

Compare and Contrast

When you **compare** and **contrast** two things, you think about how they are alike and how they are different. Authors may compare and contrast people, places, events, or things to show how they are alike and different.

In "Two Lands, One Heart," the authors compare and contrast the United States and Vietnam.

COMPARE: This restaurant seems just like an American one with tables and waiters and glasses of water.

CONTRAST: But what a menu! Grilled sparrows, eel soup, fried frog's legs, bird's nest soup.

How else do the authors show how the two countries are alike and different? The chart shows some examples.

United States	Both Countries	Vietnam
Kitchen has microwave oven, electric stove, blenders and mixers, and refrigerator.	Relatives and friends get together for special meals.	Kitchen has no modern tools. Cooking is done on the dirt floor in fire-places.

Sometimes authors use words and phrases to signal likenesses or differences. Some words that signal likenesses, or comparisons, are ***all, also, and, both, in the same way,*** and ***too***. Words that signal differences, or contrasts, include ***although, different from, or, while, but***, and ***unlike***.

Visit *The Learning Site!*
www.harcourtschool.com
See *Skills and Activities*

Test Prep

Compare and Contrast

NC STANDARD: ELA 2.01e use metacognitive strategies to clarify text/vocabulary/ask questions

NORTH CAROLINA EOG Practice

▶ **Read the passage. Then answer the questions.**

Bamboo and coconut palms are two plants that grow in Vietnam. You might think they are both trees, but bamboo isn't a tree at all. It's a type of grass.

Both plants are sources of food. The meat of the coconut is an important food source. Bamboo provides grain.

These valuable plants have other uses as well. Various parts of bamboo are used for building houses, bridges, and rafts. Parts of the coconut palm are used for making soaps, candles, and rope.

CRITICAL STANCE / CONNECTIONS

1. **Which is an example of how the author compares the two plants?**

   A Bamboo isn't a tree at all.

   B Both plants are sources of food.

   C You might think they are both trees.

   D The meat of the coconut is a food source.

Tip

Look for signal words such as *all*, *also*, *as well*, and *both*. Remember that comparing means telling how things are alike.

CRITICAL STANCE / CONNECTIONS

2. **The author compares and contrasts to give information. How did this help you understand the information? Write your answer on a separate sheet of paper.**

Tip

Look for words and phrases that the author uses to signal comparisions and contrasts.

Focus Skill

▲ Look to the North

Vocabulary Power

abundant

tundra

piteously

surrender

ceases

bonding

Wolves! The word has sent fear into people's hearts for hundreds of years. Nowadays, people rarely even see wolves in the wild. Read on to find out where they have gone and what they are doing.

Wolves used to roam freely across much of the world. Now they live mostly in alpine, or mountainous, regions. Wolves have had to leave their fine hunting grounds where food was **abundant**. They now struggle to survive in places such as the Canadian **tundra**. Here, the ground remains frozen all year.

A wolf pup cries **piteously** for food, making the adults feel sorry for it. They try not to listen, but they finally **surrender** and bring it part of their own food to eat. The crying **ceases** right away, and the cave is quiet.

The wolf pups spend time together **bonding**. They will remain close to each other as they grow. After twelve months, they are no longer pups. Each is now a yearling and an important member of the wolf pack.

Vocabulary-Writing CONNECTION

Think about a plant or an animal that is **abundant** in the region where you live. Write a description of that plant or animal.

LOOK

BY JEAN CRAIGHEAD GEORGE
ILLUSTRATED BY LUCIA WASHBURN

Genre

Informational Narrative

An informational narrative is a story that presents information and facts.

In this selection, look for

- **Elements of nonfiction and fiction**
- **Information about a topic**

to the NORTH
A Wolf Pup Diary

1 Day Old

When you see dandelions turning silver, look to the north. Wolf pups are being born.

Boulder, Scree, and Talus arrive. They are blind and deaf. They can't even smell. Each weighs only one pound. They are curled against their warm mother in a nursery dug deep into a hillside.

Their father is standing in the snow by the den entrance.

The wind blows ice crystals across the cold mountaintop.

10 *Days Old*

When the yellow warblers return from the south, look to the north. The eyes of the wolf pups are opening.

Boulder sees his sister, Scree, and jumps on her. She knocks him off. He jumps on her again. She bites him with her sharp new baby teeth. He bites her back. They growl their first growls.

Talus nurses. He is the smallest pup.

2 Weeks Old

When the redwings are flashing their bright shoulder badges, look to the north. The mother wolf will take brief vacations.

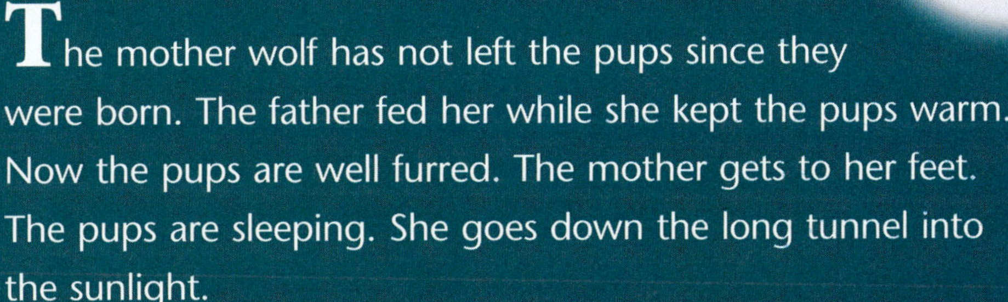

The mother wolf has not left the pups since they were born. The father fed her while she kept the pups warm. Now the pups are well furred. The mother gets to her feet. The pups are sleeping. She goes down the long tunnel into the sunlight.

She runs joyfully across the alpine tundra, then back to her pack. They run with her.

The pack is small—there are the mother and father, the alphas or leaders; an assistant, the beta; and a yearling male. They run close together like a flock of wheeling birds, never touching. Their ruffs ripple.

3 Weeks Old

When the spring azure blue butterflies are flitting, look to the north. The wolf pups can hear.

Boulder hears his pack howl. He stands up and listens. Scree hears the lambs of the mountain sheep bleating. Talus not only can hear all this, but can also smell it. Talus has a talent. He wobbles out of the den following the sweet scent of morning. Boulder and Scree follow him into the daylight.

The outdoors is bright and big. Boulder jumps on Scree and growls. She turns and bites his neck. He yelps. Talus follows the scent of a lemming and runs smack into his mother. With a low growl she turns him back and stops Scree from shaking Boulder by the neck. The pups scurry into the den.

4 Weeks Old

When you see baby robins, look to the north. Wolf pups are almost weaned.

The mother leaves the pups. The yearling is baby-sitter.

Boulder grabs Scree by the back of her neck and shakes hard. She yelps piteously, then grabs Boulder's neck. He breaks loose. Suddenly Scree rolls to her back, flashing her pale belly fur. This is the wolves' white flag of surrender. Boulder has won. He is alpha pup.

Scree, who is now his assistant, jumps on Talus and growls. Talus smells defeat and flashes his white flag. Scree stops biting.

Each pup has found his or her place in the pup society. They know who they are. All fighting ceases.

7 Weeks Old

On the longest day of the year, look to the north. Wolf pups are outdoors playing.

Boulder, Scree, and Talus are jumping on the babysitter. They chew his tail. They knock his feet out from under him. They play rough.

The wolf pack is returning, and Talus smells the scent of good food on their breaths.

He sticks his nose in the corner of his father's mouth, which says in wolf talk, "I'm a puppy—feed me." The father coughs up food for Talus. The wolves have brought food home for the pups in their belly baskets. The mother stops all milk snacks.

9 Weeks Old

When firecrackers shoot skyward, look to the north. Wolf pups are learning wolf talk.

Boulder, Scree, and Talus can lower their ears to say to their father and mother, "You are the beloved leaders of our pack." They can spank the ground with their front paws to say, "Come play with me," and they can scent mark bones and pretty stones to say, "This is mine."

The wolf den is swathed in blue harebell flowers. The wolves stop and look at them.

10 Weeks Old

*When you are eating July's **abundant** corn on the cob, look to the north. A change is coming to wolfdom.*

Talus smells excitement in his mother's sweet scent as she prances before the den. Boulder and Scree cock their heads. The mother suddenly dashes up the den mound and away. The adults trot after her. The pups follow. Not one adult wolf steps on a harebell.

The wolf family arrives at their summer den on a hill above a river. The den is a mere tunnel in which the pups can hide from the eagle, the grizzly bear, and the intense alpine-tundra sun.

The pups play king of the hill, tug-of-war, and football. When they are bored with these games, they play "jump on the baby-sitter."

They dig holes and chew bones, rocks, and puppy tails. Sometimes they chase mice and butterflies.

12 *Weeks Old*

When the crickets are chirping, look to the north. Wolf pups are learning adult wolf talk.

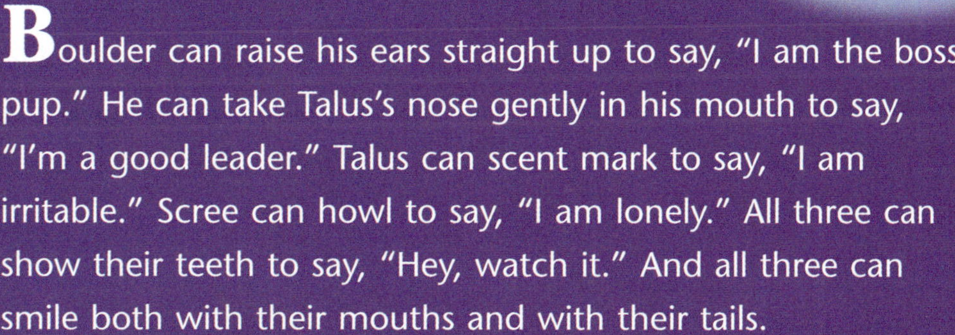

Boulder can raise his ears straight up to say, "I am the boss pup." He can take Talus's nose gently in his mouth to say, "I'm a good leader." Talus can scent mark to say, "I am irritable." Scree can howl to say, "I am lonely." All three can show their teeth to say, "Hey, watch it." And all three can smile both with their mouths and with their tails.

3 Months Old

When you see the early goldenrod blooming, look to the north. Wolf pups are ***bonding****.*

Scree and Talus follow Boulder around berries and over wildflower seeds. They run in a knot, never bumping. They leap as one. They chase birds in a posse. They move across the ridge — until Talus smells a distant grizzly and yips. Then they break ranks and speed home.

16 Weeks Old

When you are eating fresh blueberries, look to the north. Wolf pups are practicing their hunting skills.

Boulder nips Scree the way his father nips caribou. Scree trips Talus the way her mother trips moose. Talus shakes a piece of caribou fur so hard, he gets dizzy. All three can peel hide from the bone toys their parents bring them.

This day the beta does not come home.

The wolves are having trouble getting food without their assistant. It takes the cooperation of many to fell the big game needed to feed a wolf pack. The adults hunt night and day.

4 1/2 Months Old

When you are back in school, look to the north. Wolf pups are leaving their summer dens.

Boulder, Scree, and Talus follow their father and mother and the baby-sitter into the valley. They are gypsies. They sleep on open ridges by day and wander the river bottomlands to hunt at night.

Snow is falling in the mountains.

6 Months Old

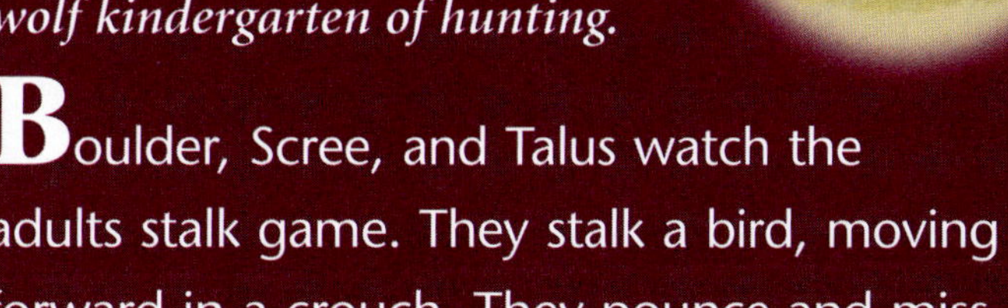

When you are out trick-or-treating, look to the north. Wolf pups are enrolled in the wolf kindergarten of hunting.

Boulder, Scree, and Talus watch the adults stalk game. They stalk a bird, moving forward in a crouch. They pounce and miss.

Talus hunts by sniffing the air. He picks up the scent of an injured animal and jogs a mile before he finds it. He howls for his pack. They join him and feast.

Talus is no longer the wolf on the bottom. His incredible nose moves him up into a place of high rank. The baby-sitter is now on the bottom.

7 Months Old

When you are eating turkey and watching football, look to the north. The wolf pups are full grown.

Talus smells another wounded animal. The pack follows him through snow and wind drift. They come to a twisted spruce tree. Beneath it lies the beta. He is injured and weak from eating only voles and birds.

The adults fell a caribou. The father brings food to his friend, then scratches a shallow saucer in the snow beside him. He curls up and goes to sleep. The rest of the pack make wolf beds, too. They will take care of the beta until he is well.

10 1/2 Months Old

When the day and night are of equal length, look to the north. New pups are on their way.

High up in the mountains, the young adult wolves are ready to help the pack raise their new brothers and sisters.

Think and Respond

1. Which pups show special talents, and what are their talents?
2. What do you think the author means when she says the pups can "smile with their mouths and with their tails"?
3. Why is it important that the pups learn how to hunt?
4. Did the selection change the way you feel about wolves? Why or why not?
5. How did using reading strategies help you as you read?

Meet the Author JEAN

Jean Craighead George loves animals. Her childhood home was full of pets—dogs, falcons, raccoons, owls, opossums, and insects. Her father, who worked for the U.S. Forest Service, took Jean and her brothers into wilderness areas to learn about plants and animals. At twenty-four, she wrote a book about a fox and discovered she was a children's book writer.

Jean Craighead George has studied wolves since 1971, when she learned to communicate with them at a research lab in Alaska. Her novel *Julie of the Wolves* won the Newbery Medal in 1973.

CRAIGHEAD GEORGE

Here, the author explains why she wrote *Look to the North.*

I love wolf pups. They have called me to Alaska's alpine tundras to lie on my stomach and watch them play. They have lured me west to my friend the wolf trainer's house, to hold them and feed them from bottles. They have included me in their pup games in Alaska and Montana. I have howled with them in Minnesota.

And I have kept notes on them.

Why do I love them so? In these nursing, tumbling, fighting, and growing children of the wild I see all children. And they are wonderful.

Jean Craighead George

Visit *The Learning Site!*
www.harcourtschool.com

Genre
Poem

MOON of Falling Leaves

Long ago, the trees were told
they must stay awake
seven days and nights,
but only the cedar,
the pine and the spruce
stayed awake until
that seventh night.
The reward they were given
was to always be green,
while all the other trees
must shed their leaves.

So, each autumn, the leaves
of the sleeping trees fall.
They cover the floor
of our woodlands with colors
as bright as the flowers
that come with the spring.
The leaves return the strength
of one more year's growth
to the earth.

This journey
the leaves are taking
is part of that great circle
which holds us all close to the earth.

by Joseph Bruchac
and Jonathan London

illustrated by Steve Johnson
and Lou Fancher

Thirteen Moons on Turtle's Back
A NATIVE AMERICAN YEAR OF MOONS
JOSEPH BRUCHAC and
JONATHAN LONDON
illustrated by
THOMAS LOCKER
Teachers' Choice
Outstanding
Science Trade Book

▲ Look to the North

Making Connections

Text to Self • Text to Text • Text to World

Compare Texts

NC STANDARDS: ELA 2.02d interact with text/locate information, 2.04b identify theme, 2.04f identify figurative language, 2.07 evaluate usefulness of content, 3.01d analyze differences among genres

1. How does "Look to the North" fit into this theme about growing and changing? INTERPRETATION / EVALUATING
2. How do the notes to the reader on each page of the selection relate to the text below them? INTERPRETATION / KNOWLEDGE
3. Compare and contrast the way the topic of life cycles is treated in the poem "Moon of Falling Leaves" and in the selection "Look to the North." CONNECTIONS / ANALYZING
4. How is this selection different from an encyclopedia article about wolves? CRITICAL STANCE / ANALYZING
5. What questions about wolves and cycles in nature do you still have after reading these selections? INTERPRETATION / EVALUATING

Write an Essay

Writing CONNECTION

In a wolf pack, there are leaders and there are followers who help them. Human communities also have leaders and followers. Write an essay explaining what qualities someone needs to be a good leader. Use a web like this one to organize your ideas.

Good Leaders

NC STANDARDS: ELA 3.06 conduct research using a variety of tools, 4.05 use planning strategies to organize ideas; Social Studies 4.04 understand how local/state governments work in North Carolina, 4.05 assess role of prominent persons in North Carolina

Make a Chart

Social Studies CONNECTION

You learned in "Look to the North" that individuals in a wolf pack have ranks. Many human organizations also have job ranks. Do research to learn the ranks of jobs in a branch of your local, state, or federal government. Create a chart that lists them in order and explains the responsibilities for each.

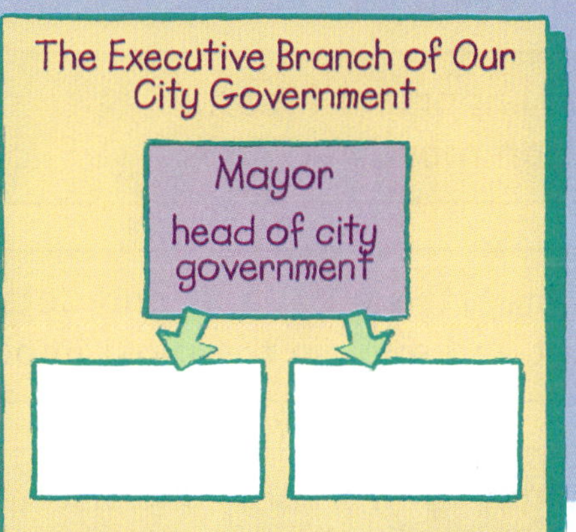

NC STANDARDS: ELA 3.06 conduct research using a variety of tools; Science 1.03 observe/discuss how an animal's behavior/body aids survival

Write an Animal Diary

Science CONNECTION

"Look to the North" is written like a diary of the first ten and a half months in the lives of three wolf pups. Choose another kind of animal to research. Find out about changes the animal goes through, especially when it is young. Then create an illustrated diary that describes these changes. Make a page for each important stage in the animal's life.

▲ Look to the North

Summarize

NC STANDARD: ELA 2.06 summarize major points

When you read a selection, you receive information in the form of ideas, facts, details, and examples. To **summarize** what you have read, follow these steps:

Select the most important ideas.
What is the selection mostly about?

↓

Evaluate the importance of facts and details.
What ones support and explain the most important ideas?

↓

Record your summary in a short and useful form.
This will help you understand and remember what you read.

You can use this process to summarize "Look to the North."

Most Important Idea: the daily lives of three wolf cubs for the first ten and one-half months of their lives

Important Facts to Include: how cubs grow and change; cubs are part of a pack; cubs are young adults at ten and one-half months
Do Not Include: facts and details about specific events in the lives of the cubs and the other wolves in the pack

Visit *The Learning Site!*
www.harcourtschool.com

See *Skills and Activities*

Test Prep

Summarize

NC STANDARD: ELA 2.04c interact with text/identify main idea/details

NORTH CAROLINA EOG Practice

▶ **Read the passage. Then complete the items.**

Arctic tundra is found in the cold northern regions of the world. A tundra is a cold, dry place where winters are long and summers are short and cool. No trees can grow there.

Many other plants do grow in the tundra, though. Mosses, grasses, and low shrubs grow rapidly in the spring. The plants provide food for animals such as caribou and reindeer. Other animals live in the tundra, too—wolves, arctic hares and foxes, grizzly bears, and polar bears. Some tundra animals, such as arctic hares, grow white coats in the winter. The coats make it more difficult for predators to see them in the snow.

COGNITION / INTEGRATING

1. Which is the most important idea to include in a summary?

A Tundra plants include mosses.

B Caribou and reindeer eat the plants.

C The tundra is home to many plants and animals.

D Arctic hares grow white coats in winter.

Tip

Think about which answer choices give details and which gives a more general, main idea.

COGNITION / INTEGRATING

2. On another sheet of paper, write a brief summary of the article.

Tip

Include only the most important ideas and details you want to remember.

THEME 4

CREATIVE MINDS

CONTENTS

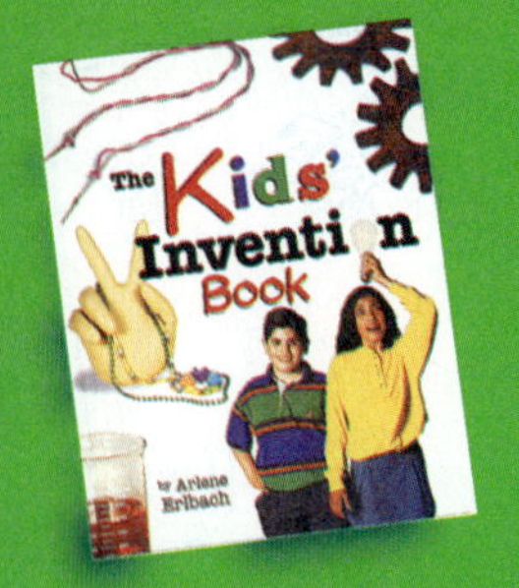

▲ The Kids' Invention Book

Vocabulary Power

In "The Kids' Invention Book" you will learn about useful items kids have made. Some of the inventions described below may surprise you.

- prosthetic
- disabilities
- modify
- device
- document
- circular
- scholarship

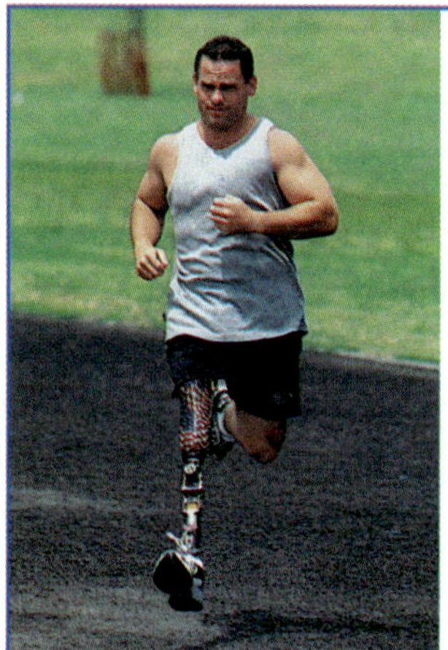

This runner is wearing a **prosthetic** leg. It replaces the runner's missing leg so that he can run and compete in races.

Many people have **disabilities**, conditions that make doing some things more difficult. Inventions can help people **modify**, or change, the way they do things. This **device** was built for a special purpose—it allows people with certain kinds of disabilities to ski.

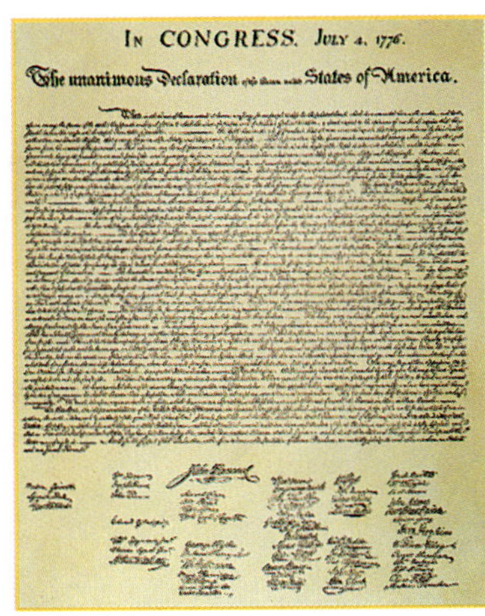

A **document** is a paper that contains important information. The document shown here is the Declaration of Independence. It was written in 1776. Inventors are always looking for better ways to preserve historical items like this one.

Inventors know that **circular** parts, such as wheels and gears, can make things easy to move. Using gears in big engines may take **scholarship**, or careful study.

Vocabulary-Writing CONNECTION

You read about inventions that help people with **disabilities** to run and to ski. Think of something you would like to invent, and write a description of it.

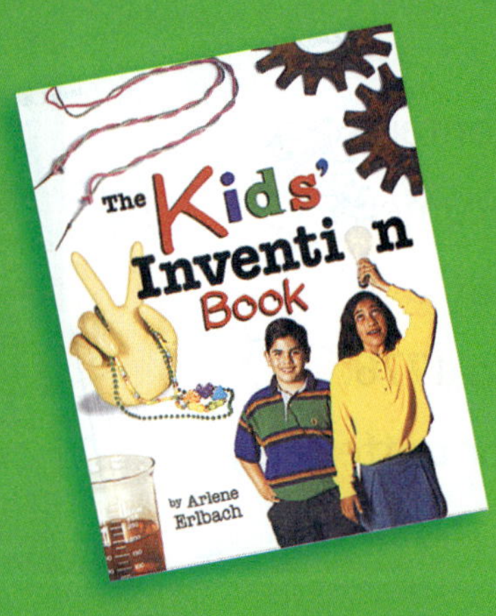

Genre

Expository Nonfiction

Expository nonfiction presents and explains information or ideas.

In this selection, look for

- Facts and details about a subject or topic
- Photographs and captions

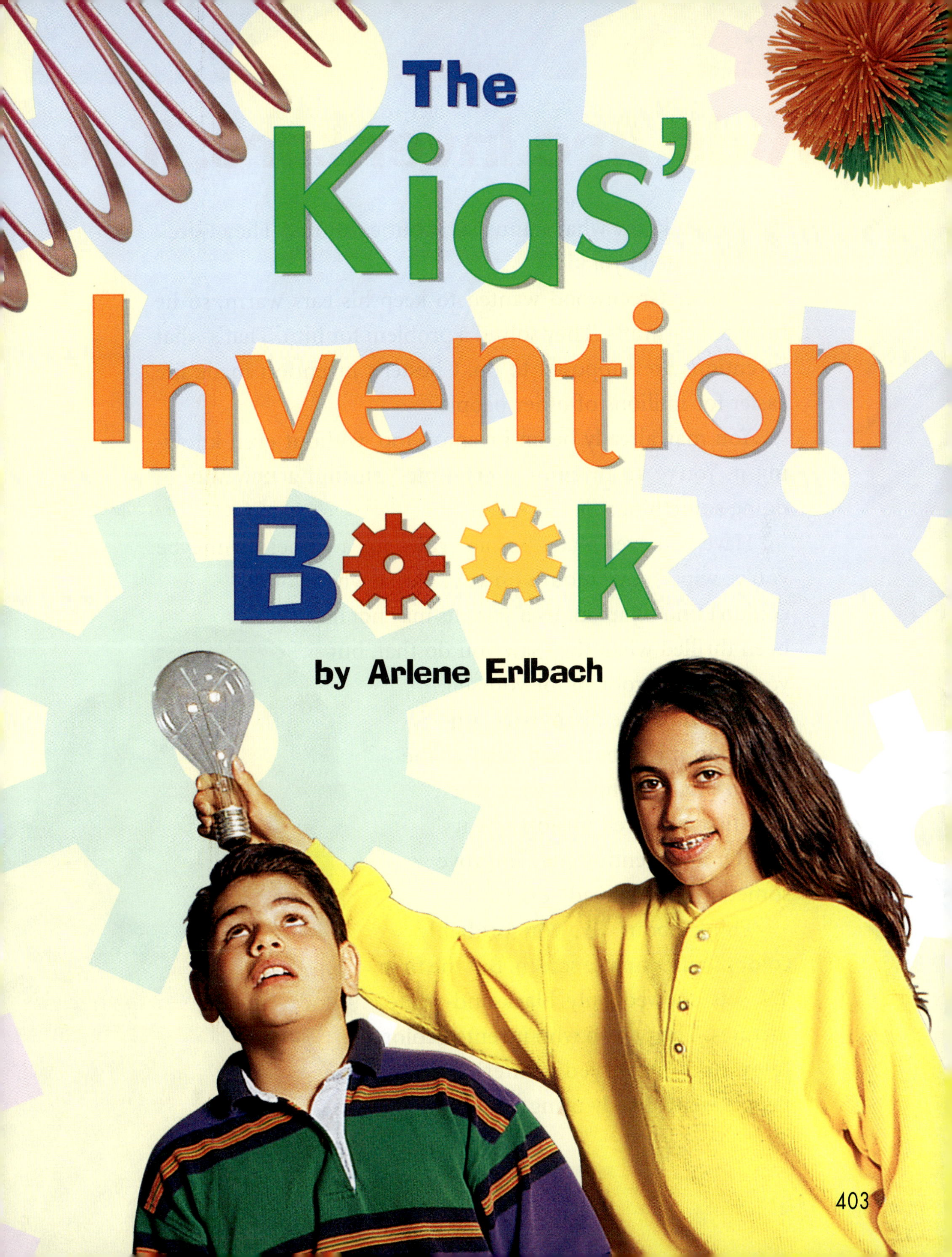

The Kids' Invention Book

by Arlene Erlbach

Kids Are Inventors, Too

Do you know what's unusual about earmuffs? They were invented by a kid!

Chester Greenwood wanted to keep his ears warm, so he invented earmuffs. They solved a problem for him. That's what inventions are supposed to do. Chester's invention made life easier for millions of other people.

You may already be an inventor, too, without even knowing it. You're an inventor every time you find a new way of doing something.

Have you ever made up new rules for a game? Or maybe you've wiped your mouth on your sleeve when you couldn't find a napkin. Your parents may not have been thrilled when they saw you do that, but you solved a problem for yourself.

Inventions are discoveries. An invention might be a new item, as the Koosh® Ball or Slinky® were when they first appeared in stores, years ago. Or an invention may improve something that already exists.

Think about TV. You probably see color pictures on the screen. But the first TV sets showed only black-and-white pictures. The person who invented color television improved something that people were already using.

Let's go back to earmuffs. They were invented in 1873, when Chester Greenwood was only 15 years old.

Chester lived in Farmington, Maine, and he loved to ice-skate. Anyone familiar with northeastern winters knows how hard they can be on your ears — even when you wear a hat. So Chester took a piece of wire and asked his grandmother to sew cloth pads on the ends.

At first Chester's friends thought his earmuffs looked weird, but they soon changed their minds. Chester could stay outside and skate longer than they did. His ears didn't get cold!

Soon Chester's friends wanted earmuffs, too. So he started making earmuffs and selling them. He also applied for a patent. A patent is a document issued by the U.S. government. It protects an inventor's idea so nobody else can make money from it.

Chester Greenwood, as an adult, still wearing his "Champion Ear Protectors"

Chester began manufacturing earmuffs and eventually became rich. He became famous, too. Farmington, Maine, celebrates Chester Greenwood Day each December.

Lots of kids—about 500,000 each year—invent things. Most kids don't sell their inventions or become rich. But they do have fun creating things and seeing them work.

The Prosthetic Catch & Throw Device

Inventor: Josh Parsons
Hometown: Houston, Texas

Josh Parsons wanted to help David Potter play baseball. Both of David's arms had been amputated below the elbows because of an accident he had had when he was two years old. Still, David wanted to be on a Little League team. Josh thought he could help David.

Josh's dad is the one who told Josh about David. Mr. Parsons is a Little League director. He judges kids' tryouts for teams. One evening, Mr. Parsons came home and told Josh about a kid without hands who had tried out for a baseball team.

Even without hands, David could catch and bat a ball! He caught the ball in a glove he wore at the end of his left arm. To bat, David held the bat between his left upper arm and chest. He used his right arm to push the bat. The only thing David couldn't do was throw a ball. Josh hoped he could change that.

First Josh thought about all the things David could already do. David was able to use a glove to catch. So maybe a special kind of glove could help him throw.

Josh decided to design a special glove that would replace David's lower right arm and hand. A device that replaces a missing body part is called a prosthesis (pross-THEE-sis).

Josh drew pictures of baseball gloves. Finally, he came up with a glove shaped like a scoop. Josh felt that this shape would allow David to both hold and then throw the ball.

Josh first made a model of the glove out of paper. Next, he sewed a glove from leather. The glove fit onto the end of David's right arm.

Josh hit a ball to David. David caught it in his left glove. Then he dumped the ball into the prosthetic glove and threw the ball into the air!

David started playing right field for the Spring Branch Mustangs. They won first place that season.

Josh's invention drew a lot of attention. He and David were interviewed on *Good Morning America* and the Cable News Network. Stories about the glove appeared in newspapers across the United States. Josh received an award from the Easter Seal Society, an organization that helps people with disabilities. He and David even threw out the first pitch at a Houston Astros game.

★★★ DAVID ★★★

Josh also received a prize from the Houston Inventors' Association—a 291-piece tool kit. He can make plenty of things with that. But, Josh says, "The most important part was that the glove helped David. That's why I invented it."

The All-in-One Washer/Dryer

Inventor: Reeba Daniel
Hometown: Palos Park, Illinois

"I wanted to design an automatic rabbit feeder for my school invention project," Reeba Daniel said. "But my teacher told me that automatic pet feeders had already been invented."

Then Reeba's mom gave her a suggestion. "Invent something everyone could use—something that saves time."

A few days later, Reeba was folding laundry. She thought about how doing laundry is a two-step job. First the clothes go into the washer. Then, when they're damp and heavy, somebody needs to lift them into the dryer. Reeba thought about inventing a machine that would wash and dry clothes in one step.

Reeba began drawing pictures. Her first idea involved placing the washer and dryer side by side. A conveyor belt would move the clothes from the washer to the dryer. The idea certainly seemed useful—but too complicated! It would also be very expensive to manufacture.

Reeba thought of a simpler way to make her idea work. The washer could be on top of the dryer. Her washer would have a trapdoor that would open following the drain cycle. The clothes would drop into the dryer, making it start. A computerized device could time each of the cycles.

Reeba didn't make a working model of her invention. It would have cost thousands of dollars to build. Instead, she did what many inventors do: Reeba drew a diagram of her invention. Then she made a model of it, from cardboard. From her diagram and model, people could see how her invention would look.

Reeba's invention won a prize at her school's invention fair. She also won a prize from a national organization that included a trip to Washington, D.C.

These aren't the first prizes Reeba has won. She has also won awards for acting and has received an American Legion award for courage, honor, patriotism, scholarship, and service. Reeba is also a straight "A" student.

Reeba hopes to become a doctor, engineer, or senator. She believes that the ability to keep trying is the key to anyone's success.

The Conserve Sprinkler

Inventor: Larry Villella
Hometown: Fargo, North Dakota

One of Larry Villella's chores was watering the lawn, which included watering eight trees and eight shrubs. He had to hose each tree and shrub separately or keep moving the sprinkler around.

Larry thought he was wasting a lot of water every time he would change the sprinkler or move the hose. He thought a sprinkler that actually fit around a tree or shrub would save water—and time. And the plant would get more water if the sprinkler had holes on the top *and* bottom.

Larry believed a circular sprinkler could do the trick. He'd just need to cut an opening in the sprinkler so it would fit around a tree or shrub. Then he'd need to seal the ends.

Larry and his dad cut a section from a sprinkler with a power saw. They sealed the ends by gluing on pieces of thin plastic. Then they drilled holes in the bottom of the sprinkler that were wider than the tiny holes on top. The bigger holes would allow water to seep into the ground and soak the plant's roots.

Larry's sprinkler won his school's invention contest. Then he and his dad showed it to Dr. Ron Smith, a professor of agriculture at North Dakota State University. Dr. Smith suggested a change. He thought the holes on the bottom should be even bigger, so more water would go into the ground and aerate (supply air to) the soil.

Larry began making Conserve Sprinklers by hand and selling them. They sold so well that Larry didn't have time to make them all. At first, he turned the manufacturing over to a training center for people who are handicapped. But sales grew even more, and Larry needed a place that could mass-produce the sprinklers. A company called Terhorst in Minot, North Dakota, began manufacturing them, and thousands of people have bought Larry's sprinklers.

You Can Do It

When you invent, you think up ideas. Then you make them work, step by step.

Steps to Creating an Invention

1. Think of ways to make life easier or better for you or people you know. Think of problems that need to be solved. Think about what goes on in your home or at school. Observe your friends, families, and pets. They may have problems you've never thought about before.
2. Make a list of these problems in a notebook. This notebook will be your invention journal. Whenever you think of another problem that needs solving, write about it in your journal. Some inventors take their journals with them wherever they go.

3. From your list of problems, choose one that you think you can solve. Make sure it's one you find important and interesting enough to keep working on.

4. Think about how to solve the problem. Lie down on your bed or sit in a comfortable chair. Think of lots of solutions to the problem. Some of them won't make any sense. Some will sound good. Some will seem absolutely terrific. This process is called *brainstorming*. It allows you to come up with many ideas, answers, and plans.

5. List the best solutions in your journal. Next, describe how the solutions might look if you turned them into something tangible—something you can see and touch.

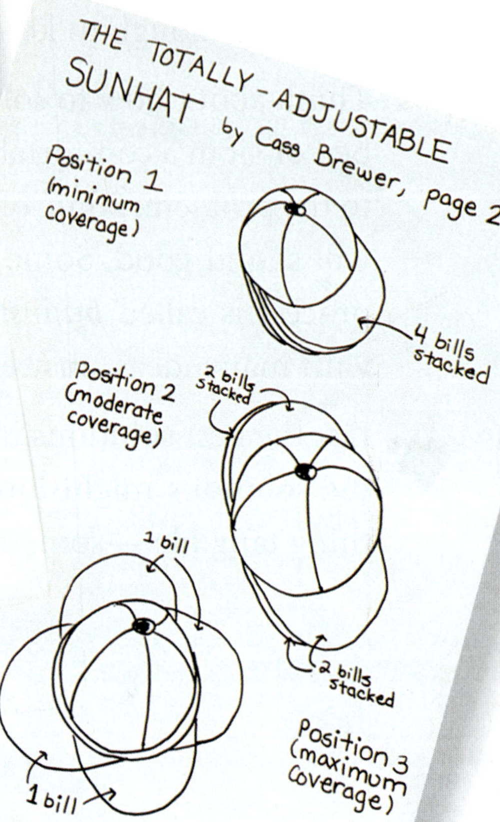

6. Look over your solutions. Which one can you actually make yourself—or with some adult help?

7. Once you've decided which solution you'll use, ask yourself these questions:

Is my invention really a new idea?
Is it useful?
Can it be made easily?
Does it use materials that are easily available?
Will it hold up after lots of use?
Will people really use it?

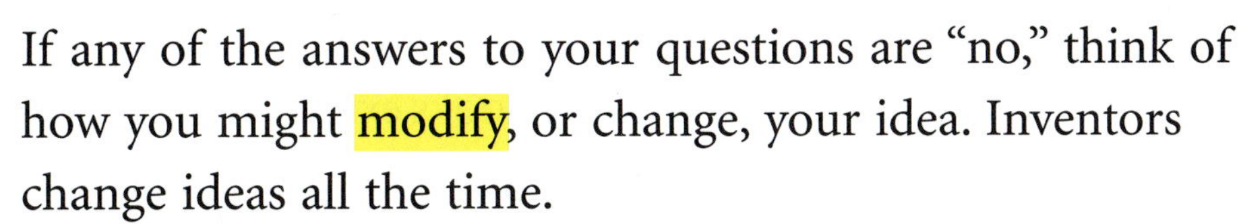

If any of the answers to your questions are "no," think of how you might modify, or change, your idea. Inventors change ideas all the time.

8. Once all the answers to your questions are "yes," draw pictures of how your invention should look. You don't need to be a great artist to do this. Simple line drawings will do. Your first drawing is a rough draft. It shows the basic idea of what the invention will look like. A rough draft is meant to be changed.

9. Next, you need to refine the drawing of your invention. This means redrawing until it looks exactly right. Sometimes this process takes lots of tries. On your final drawing, label all the parts. On the back of your paper, list the materials you'll need to make your invention.

10. Now comes a very important step — building the model. You might need an adult to help you. That's okay. Lots of adult inventors pay people to make models for them. You may need to build your model more than once. Sometimes inventions don't work as you had hoped.

11. Once your model is exactly the way you want it, have some of your friends and relatives use it. Use it a few times yourself. Does it hold up and work? Congratulations! You've just created a new invention!

Think and Respond

1. In this selection, the author gives steps for creating an invention. Which steps did the young inventors you read about follow?
2. How did the author organize this selection? How does the format help readers?
3. What qualities do the young inventors have in common? Why are these qualities important for an inventor?
4. Which **device** or invention in the selection do you find most interesting? Explain your answer.
5. How did using a reading strategy help you understand the information in this selection? Give an example.

Arlene Erlbach

To: students@anyschool.edu
From: editors@harcourt.com
Date: 09/12 01:04:36 PM
Subject: Arlene Erlbach

We are writing in response to your interest in the author of *The Kids' Invention Book.* Arlene Erlbach liked to make up stories when she was in elementary school, but she wasn't sure at first that she could be a writer. When teachers liked her writing, she decided to try.

Arlene Erlbach has written both fiction and nonfiction books. She gets ideas from her childhood, from her son, Matthew, and from the news. Since she is a school-teacher, she also gets ideas from experiences at school. She is in charge of the Young Authors' Program at her school in Illinois.

Arlene Erlbach

▲ The Kids' Invention Book

Making Connections

Text to Self • Text to Text • Text To World

Compare Texts

NC STANDARDS: ELA 2.02a interact with text/set purpose for reading, 2.02b interact with text/make predictions, 2.02e interact with text/connect text to own experiences

1. How might reading "The Kids' Invention Book" encourage students your age to have more confidence in their own creativity? INTERPRETATION / KNOWLEDGE
2. How are the first and last sections of the selection different from the other sections? CRITICAL STANCE / ANALYZING
3. Why do you think the author placed the section "You Can Do It" at the end of the book, instead of at the beginning? CRITICAL STANCE / EVALUATING
4. How would your response to this selection be different if the stories about young inventors were fictional? CRITICAL STANCE / EVALUATING
5. What questions would you like to ask the author of this selection? INTERPRETATION / EVALUATING

Write a Personal Narrative

Writing CONNECTION

The author says that "You're an inventor every time you find a new way of doing something." Think about an "invention" that you or someone you know created, such as a game or a creative way to solve a problem. Then write to tell about the experience. Use a graphic organizer like the one shown here to plan your narrative.

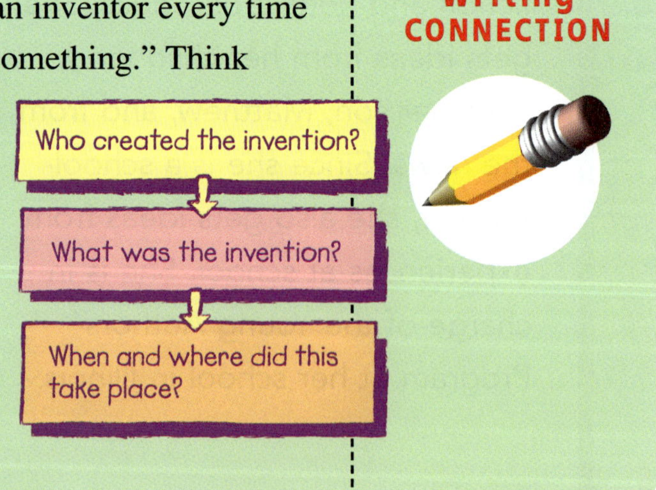

Design a Plaque

NC STANDARD: ELA 3.06 conduct research using a variety of tools

Social Studies CONNECTION

The inventions in "The Kids' Invention Book" were created for a variety of purposes. The motion picture industry is one area that has benefited from many inventions. Do research to learn about some of these. Then choose one and make a plaque honoring the inventor. Display your plaque in your classroom, and give a brief speech telling why this person deserves to be included in the Inventors' Hall of Fame.

Create an Invention

Science CONNECTION

Think of an invention you would like to create. It could be something that makes your life easier, or it could be something to conserve or recycle a natural resource. Follow the steps in the "You Can Do It" section of "The Kids' Invention Book." Write a plan for making and testing a model of your invention. Then make a diagram or construct a model to show how your invention works.

NC STANDARDS: ELA 3.01e interpret/evaluate text draw inferences/conclusions, 3.05 use graphs/charts/maps to expand understanding

▲ The Kids' Invention Book

NC STANDARD: ELA 2.04c identify main idea/details

Main Idea and Details

The **main idea** of a selection is what it is mostly about. The **details** give information to explain and support the main idea. Details usually answer questions about *who, what, where, when, why,* and *how*. This chart shows the main idea and some of the details in "The Kids' Invention Book."

Main Idea	Supporting Details
Kids can come up with inventions that will solve problems or make life easier.	Kids have created successful inventions that • keep people's ears warm • help a person without hands throw a ball

An author may organize a paragraph or passage by first stating the main idea and then giving supporting details. Sometimes the main idea is stated at the end instead, or it may not be stated at all. If it is not stated, the reader must use details as clues to figure it out.

Visit *The Learning Site!*
www.harcourtschool.com

See *Skills and Activities*

Test Prep

Main Idea and Details

NC STANDARD: ELA 2.04c identify main idea/details

Focus Skill

▶ **Read the passage. Then answer the questions.**

> **The bicycle is an invention that has been improved many times. The first bicycles had wooden wheels and no pedals. Riders moved by pushing their feet against the ground. An inventor added pedals in the 1830s. Early bikes had a huge front wheel and a tiny rear wheel. About 120 years ago, bikes with wheels the same size were built. These "safety bicycles" became very popular. By 1899, about one million bicycles a year were manufactured in the United States.**

COGNITION / KNOWLEDGE

1. The main idea of this paragraph is—

A Bicycles have been improved many times.

B Safety bicycles are very popular.

C Bicycles had wooden wheels.

D Early bikes had a huge front wheel.

Think about which answer choices give details and which give a more general, main idea.

COGNITION / KNOWLEDGE

2. How does the detail *An inventor added pedals in the 1830s* support the main idea?

F by explaining why bicycles became popular

G by giving an example of how bicycles have been improved

H by describing how bicycles looked years ago

J It does not support the main idea.

Think about how this detail might support or explain the main idea that you have identified.

▲ The Case of Pablo's Nose

Vocabulary Power

- straightaway
- alibi
- muttered
- retorted
- strengthening
- sculptor

In "The Case of Pablo's Nose," Encyclopedia Brown follows the clues to solve the mystery. Sometimes, though, it's not easy to prove who has done something wrong, as in the story below.

The trouble began when my sister Lisa came home. She went into her room and came out **straightaway**, not even a minute later, yelling my name.

"What's your **alibi** this time?" she asked. She knows I usually have an excuse to prove that I didn't do something wrong. Today, though, I didn't even know what she was talking about.

"Alibi for what?" I **muttered** quietly, with my lips partly closed. I was a bit angry because I don't like getting blamed for things I didn't do.

"You smashed my sculpture!" she **retorted**. She answered sharply because she was angry and upset. She also spoke loudly and strongly. Anger has a way of **strengthening** her voice.

"Your sculpture got smashed?" I asked. "Which one?" I felt bad, because Lisa is a good **sculptor**. I admired the statue she had made of Fifi, our cat.

I guess Lisa could tell from my questions that I was innocent. She calmed down and said, "It was the new one I was working on—the mouse." Just then Fifi ran by with something in her mouth. Sure enough, it turned out to be a piece of the mouse sculpture. Lisa is such a good sculptor that Fifi must have thought it was a real mouse!

Vocabulary-Writing CONNECTION

Imagine that you are a **sculptor**. Write a paragraph describing a statue you would like to make.

Genre

Mystery

A mystery is a story that focuses on questions such as these: *Who did it?*, *Where is it?*, or *What happened?* The action centers on finding the answer to the question.

In this selection, look for

- Realistic characters and events
- A problem that must be solved
- A solution to the problem

Encyclopedia Brown helps his father, the Idaville Chief of Police, solve cases. In the summer he runs a detective agency from the family's garage with the help of his friend Sally Kimball. True to his nickname, Encyclopedia has the answers, even to problems that stump everyone else.

THE CASE OF PABLO'S NOSE

by Donald J. Sobol

illustrated by Matthew Archambault

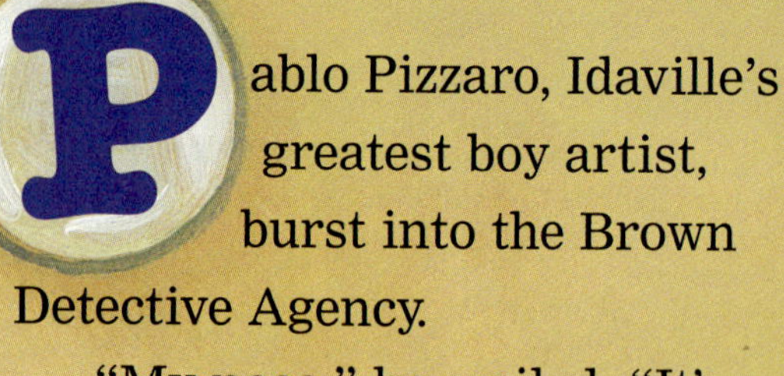

Pablo Pizzaro, Idaville's greatest boy artist, burst into the Brown Detective Agency.

"My nose," he wailed. "It's been stolen!"

"Whoever stole it returned it in very good shape," Sally observed.

"I don't mean *my* nose," Pablo said. "I mean Abraham Lincoln's."

He explained. Last month the nose on the statue of Abraham Lincoln in South Park had been smashed to pieces by a baseball. So the mayor had announced a New Nose Now contest. The winning nose would be put on the statue. The winning sculptor would get a cash prize.

"I thought I had a good chance of nosing out everyone else," Pablo said proudly, and told why.

First he had made a mold of the statue's face. Then, using photographs of Abraham Lincoln, he had built a nose in soft wax. Next he had ground down a piece of the same stone from which the statue had been carved to make sure he had the right texture and color. Then he had mixed that with his special glue. Finally he had shaped the mixture into a copy of the wax model.

"Golly, Pablo!" Sally exclaimed. "You're a regular plastic surgeon!"

Pablo smiled a weak smile. "The nose was my masterpiece," he said. "There isn't time to make another. The contest ends Thursday."

"Are you sure it was stolen?" Encyclopedia asked.

"Sure I'm sure," Pablo said. "I've been leaving the nose on the front lawn to weather so it would make an even better match with Lincoln's face."

Half an hour ago, he went on, he had discovered that the nose was gone. At the same time he'd noticed a girl biking away from his house like mad. She'd been holding something the size of the nose in her right hand.

"Did you see who she was?" Sally asked.

"I only saw her back," Pablo said sadly. "She wore a blue shirt and rode a purple bicycle."

He paused for a strengthening breath of air.

"I should have kept my nose a secret," he muttered. "Like a blockhead, I bragged all over the neighborhood."

He laid a quarter on the gas can beside Encyclopedia.

"Find my nose!" he pleaded.

"There are three purple bicycles in the neighborhood," Sally said. "Desmoana Lowry has one. So do Martha Katz and Joan Brand."

The detectives and Pablo started at Martha Katz's house. From Mrs. Katz they learned that Martha was spending the summer with her grandparents in Maine.

The news was no better at Joan Brand's house. Joan had gone off to Camp Winiwantoc in North Carolina a week ago.

"That leaves Desmoana Lowry," Sally said.

"She has to be the thief," Pablo said. "She's been jealous of me since I beat her in the tulip drawing contest last year."

"Being jealous isn't being a thief," Encyclopedia said quietly. "Let's pay her a visit."

Desmoana came to the front door herself. "What do you want?" she demanded, giving Pablo an unfriendly look.

Pablo accused her straightaway. "About an hour ago, you stole my nose, didn't you?"

"No, but I should have," Desmoana retorted. "I'd have improved your looks."

"He means Abraham Lincoln's nose," Sally said. "The thief wore a blue shirt and rode a purple bicycle."

"Does this look like a blue shirt?" Desmoana asked.

The shirt she had on looked very red to Encyclopedia.

"You could have changed your shirt," Sally said. "But you can't have repainted your purple bicycle in an hour."

"I didn't need to," Desmoana retorted. "I didn't steal anything."

She led the detectives and Pablo to the garage. A purple bicycle stood half hidden behind the water heater.

"When was the last time anyone saw me ride my bike?" she said. "Not for a long time, right? Fact is, it hasn't been ridden for nearly a year."

"That's the most unheard-of thing I ever heard of!" Pablo yelped.

Sally seemed uncertain. She glanced nervously at Encyclopedia.

Encyclopedia was uncertain, too. He tried to recall when he'd seen Desmoana on her bike last.

It was a bad moment.

Then a happy thought struck him.

"Why did you try to hide your bicycle?" he asked.

"I wasn't hiding it," Desmoana replied. "I put it out of the way. I'm into roller skating now. It's more fun."

"That's not the reason," Encyclopedia said. "Come on, tell the truth. You were never much good at riding a two-wheeler."

"Who says?" Desmoana snapped.

She rolled the purple bicycle out to the street.

"Slam your eyes on this," she invited, and forthwith did some trick riding.

She rode in a circle no-handed.

She sat on the handlebars and pedaled backward.

She lifted the front wheel off the ground and whipped through a figure eight.

"There!" she sneered. "I showed you how I can ride a two-wheeler."

"You showed me, all right," Encyclopedia agreed. "You showed me you're guilty!"

How did Encyclopedia know?

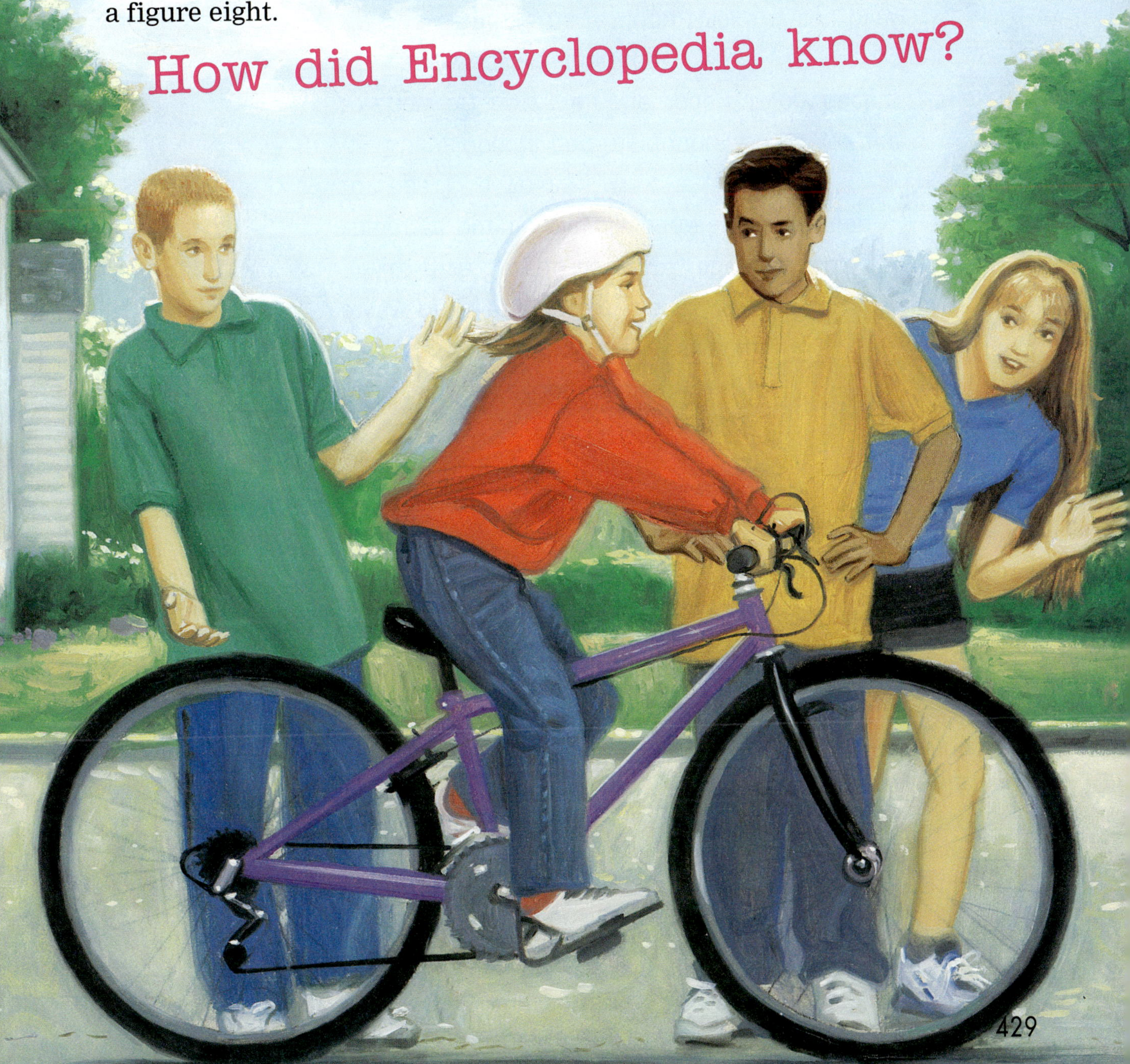

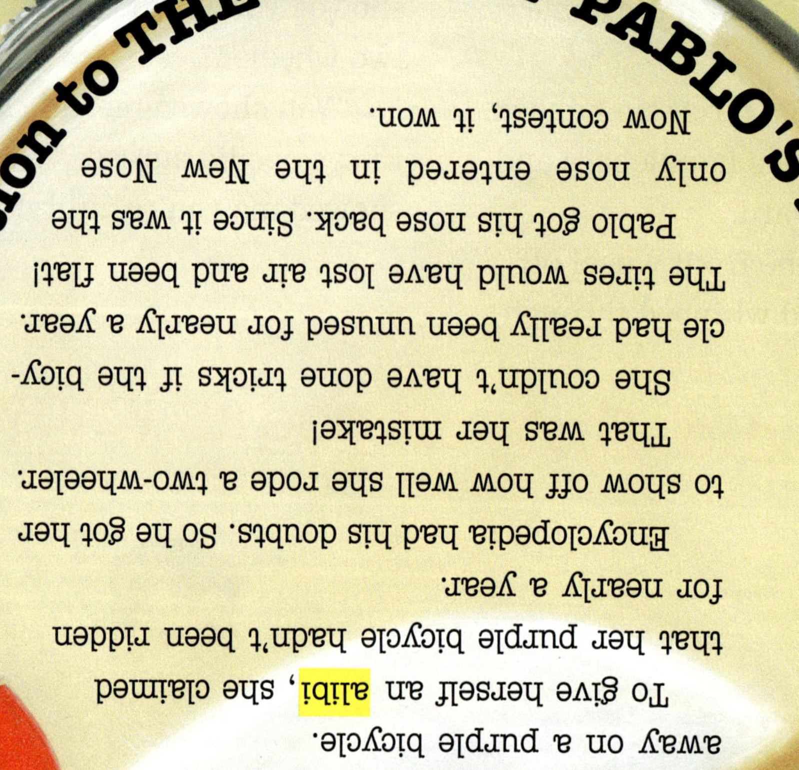

Solution to THE CASE OF PABLO'S NOSE

Desmoana denied being the girl who Pablo had seen riding away on a purple bicycle. To give herself an alibi, she claimed that her purple bicycle hadn't been ridden for nearly a year.

Encyclopedia had his doubts. So he got her to show off how well she rode a two-wheeler. That was her mistake! She couldn't have done tricks if the bicycle had really been unused for nearly a year. The tires would have lost air and been flat!

Pablo got his nose back. Since it was the only nose entered in the New Nose Now contest, it won.

Think and Respond

1. How does Encyclopedia Brown prove that Desmoana's **alibi** is false?
2. What kind of person is Pablo? How do you know?
3. What details does the author use to show you what Desmoana is like?
4. Before you read the solution, did you think Desmoana had taken Pablo's nose? Tell why or why not.
5. Where did you need to use a reading strategy?

MEET THE AUTHOR

Donald J. Sobol

When Donald Sobol was a boy, he read Sherlock Holmes mysteries and dreamed of becoming a detective. Now, for more than thirty years, he has been writing stories about boy detective Encyclopedia Brown. His books have been published in thirteen languages and in Braille.

When asked if Encyclopedia is a real boy, Donald Sobol says, "The answer is no. He is, perhaps, the boy I wanted to be—doing the things I wanted to read about but could not find in any book when I was ten."

Visit *The Learning Site!*
www.harcourtschool.com

The Hen and the Apple Tree

from *Fables*
by Arnold Lobel

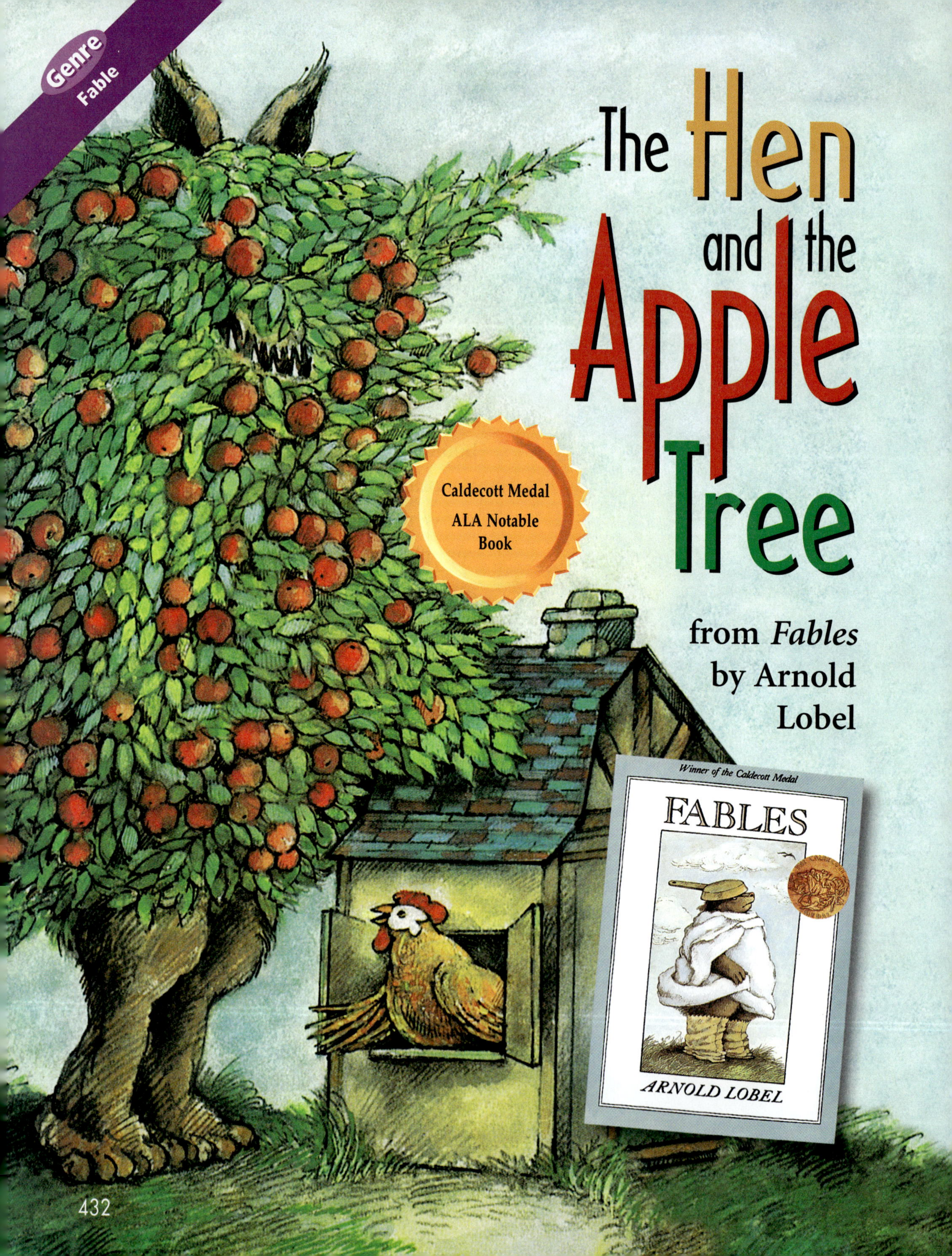

One October day, a Hen looked out her window. She saw an apple tree growing in her backyard.

"Now that is odd," said the Hen. "I am certain that there was no tree standing in that spot yesterday."

"There are some of us that grow fast," said the tree.

The Hen looked at the bottom of the tree.

"I have never seen a tree," she said, "that has ten furry toes."

"There are some of us that do," said the tree. "Hen, come outside and enjoy the cool shade of my leafy branches."

The Hen looked at the top of the tree.

"I have never seen a tree," she said, "that has two long, pointed ears."

"There are some of us that have," said the tree. "Hen, come outside and eat one of my delicious apples."

"Come to think of it," said the Hen, "I have never heard a tree speak from a mouth that is full of sharp teeth."

"There are some of us that can," said the tree. "Hen, come outside and rest your back against the bark of my trunk."

"I have heard," said the Hen, "that some of you trees lose all of your leaves at this time of the year."

"Oh, yes," said the tree, "there are some of us that will." The tree began to quiver and shake. All of its leaves quickly dropped off.

The Hen was not surprised to see a large Wolf in the place where an apple tree had been standing just a moment before. She locked her shutters and slammed her window closed.

The Wolf knew that he had been outsmarted. He stormed away in a hungry rage.

It is always difficult to pose as something that one is not.

Think and Respond

What is the hen's problem, and how does she solve it?

▲ The Case of Pablo's Nose

Making Connections

Text to Self • Text to Text • Text To World

Compare Texts

NC STANDARDS: ELA 1.04h increase vocabulary/examine author's craft, 2.04b identify theme, 3.01d interpret/evaluate text/ analyze differences among genres

1. How is "The Case of Pablo's Nose" related to the theme Creative Minds? INTERPRETATION / EVALUATING
2. How and why is the text on page 430 different from the rest of the story? INTERPRETATION / KNOWLEDGE
3. Compare and contrast "The Hen and the Apple Tree" with "The Case of Pablo's Nose." CRITICAL STANCE / ANALYZING
4. Think of another mystery story that you have read. How is it like "The Case of Pablo's Nose"? How is it different? CRITICAL STANCE / EVALUATING
5. After reading "The Case of Pablo's Nose," would you be more interested in learning about sculpture or about how police solve crimes? Where might you find out about this topic? INTERPRETATION / EVALUATING

Write a Persuasive Letter

Writing CONNECTION

Imagine that Desmoana writes Pablo a letter to persuade him to forgive her. Write the letter that you think Desmoana might write. Use a graphic organizer like the one shown here to plan your letter.

Audience:
Opinion:

Reason 1:
Examples/details:

Reason 2:
Examples/details:

Opinion restated/
action requested:

Make a Time Line

NC STANDARD: ELA 4.10 use technology as a tool

Social Studies CONNECTION

Pablo and Encyclopedia are good examples of artists and detectives using creativity to solve problems. To help them become creative problem solvers, all people can benefit from a good education. Research the history of your state's public education system. Make a time line to show the results of your research.

1849
California constitution calls for public school system

Sculpt a Coin

NC STANDARD: ELA 3.06 conduct research using a variety of tools

Art CONNECTION

Did you ever stop to think that people carry around tiny sculptures of Abraham Lincoln every day? These sculptures are on pennies! The style of sculpture used on coins is called relief, a technique in which a sculpture is partially raised from a flat surface. Use the Internet or online encyclopedias to find pictures of Presidents of the United States. Choose a President to show on a new coin that you will sculpt as a relief with clay.

▲ The Case of Pablo's Nose

Sequence

Sequence is the order in which events happen. In "The Case of Pablo's Nose," the author explains in sequence how Pablo made his nose.

First he had made a mold of the statue's face.

↓

Then, using photographs of Abraham Lincoln, he had built a nose in soft wax.

↓

Next he had ground down a piece of the same stone from which the statue had been carved to make sure he had the right texture and color.

↓

Then he had mixed that with his special glue.

↓

Finally he had shaped the mixture into a copy of the wax model.

The underlined words in the diagram are examples of time-order words. They help you follow the sequence of events in a story. Others include *last, before, after, earlier,* and *later*.

Sometimes the clues to a sequence of events are not stated, but you can use your own knowledge to identify the order.

Visit *The Learning Site!*
www.harcourtschool.com
See *Skills and Activities*

Test Prep

Sequence

NC STANDARD: ELA 2.04c identify main idea/details

Focus Skill

▶ **Read the story. Then answer the questions.**

> **Andrea announced, "I've solved the Case of the Teal Baseball Cap!" She held up her sister Lori's cap, which had been missing.**
>
> **"Where was it?" Lori asked, after she thanked Andrea.**
>
> **Andrea said she'd found it in their brother Teddy's toy box.**
>
> **"So why did Teddy tell me he hadn't seen it?" Lori asked.**
>
> **"You asked him if he'd seen your *teal* baseball cap," Andrea replied. "Teddy didn't know that teal is a color. When I asked if he'd seen your *blue* cap, he said he'd borrowed it for the dinosaur in his toy box."**

COGNITION / ORGANIZING

1. Which story event happens first?

- **A** Andrea tells Lori where she found the cap.
- **B** Lori asks where the cap was.
- **C** Lori thanks Andrea.
- **D** Andrea asks why Teddy didn't tell her.

Tip

Think about the time order of events in the story. Look for signal words that help make the sequence clear.

COGNITION / ORGANIZING

2. Why doesn't the author tell all of the events in this story in the order that they happened?

- **F** Andrea and Lori are talking about events that happened earlier
- **G** the order is not important
- **H** to keep readers in suspense
- **J** the mystery has not been solved

Tip

If you were telling a story about something that happened, in what order would you tell it?

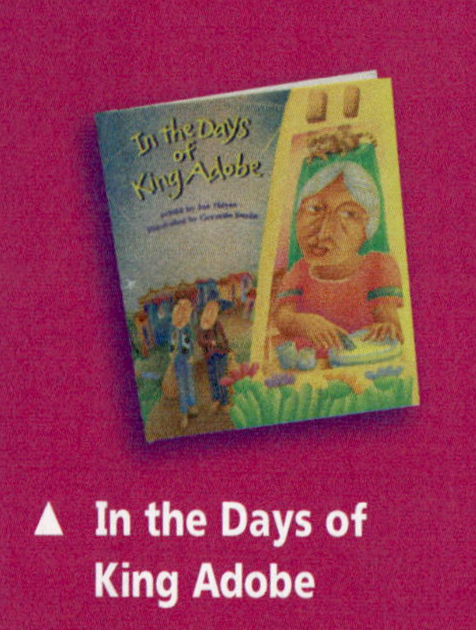

▲ **In the Days of King Adobe**

Vocabulary Power

fascinated

thrifty

generous

roguish

rascally

In the folktale "In the Days of King Adobe," a wise woman teaches two young men an important lesson. Fables, folktales, and familiar sayings often contain words of wisdom. Think about the meanings of these familiar sayings.

You may be **fascinated**, or filled with wonder, by the way someone or something looks. Remember, though, that what's inside is what really counts.

A **thrifty** person is careful about spending money. Thrifty people don't waste their money on foolish items or buy a lot of things they don't need.

No matter how good food may look, take only as much as you can eat. You can't eat a larger, or more **generous**, serving than your stomach can hold.

It is always better to be honest than to act in a **roguish**, **rascally**, dishonest way.

Vocabulary-Writing CONNECTION

Think about something you would like to buy. Write a list of ways you could be **thrifty** so you can save enough money to buy that item.

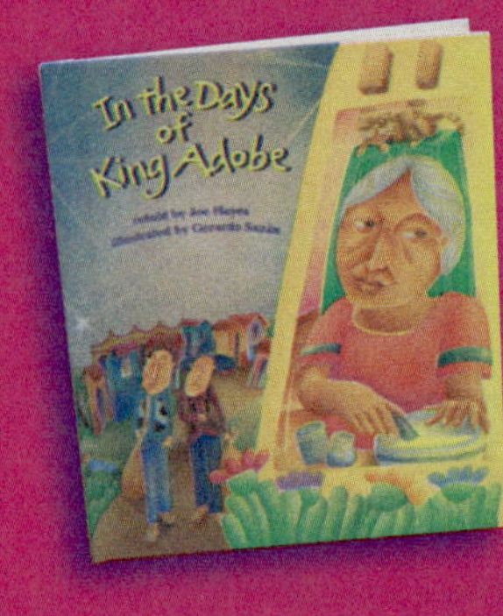

In the Days of King Adobe

retold by Joe Hayes
illustrated by Gerardo Suzán

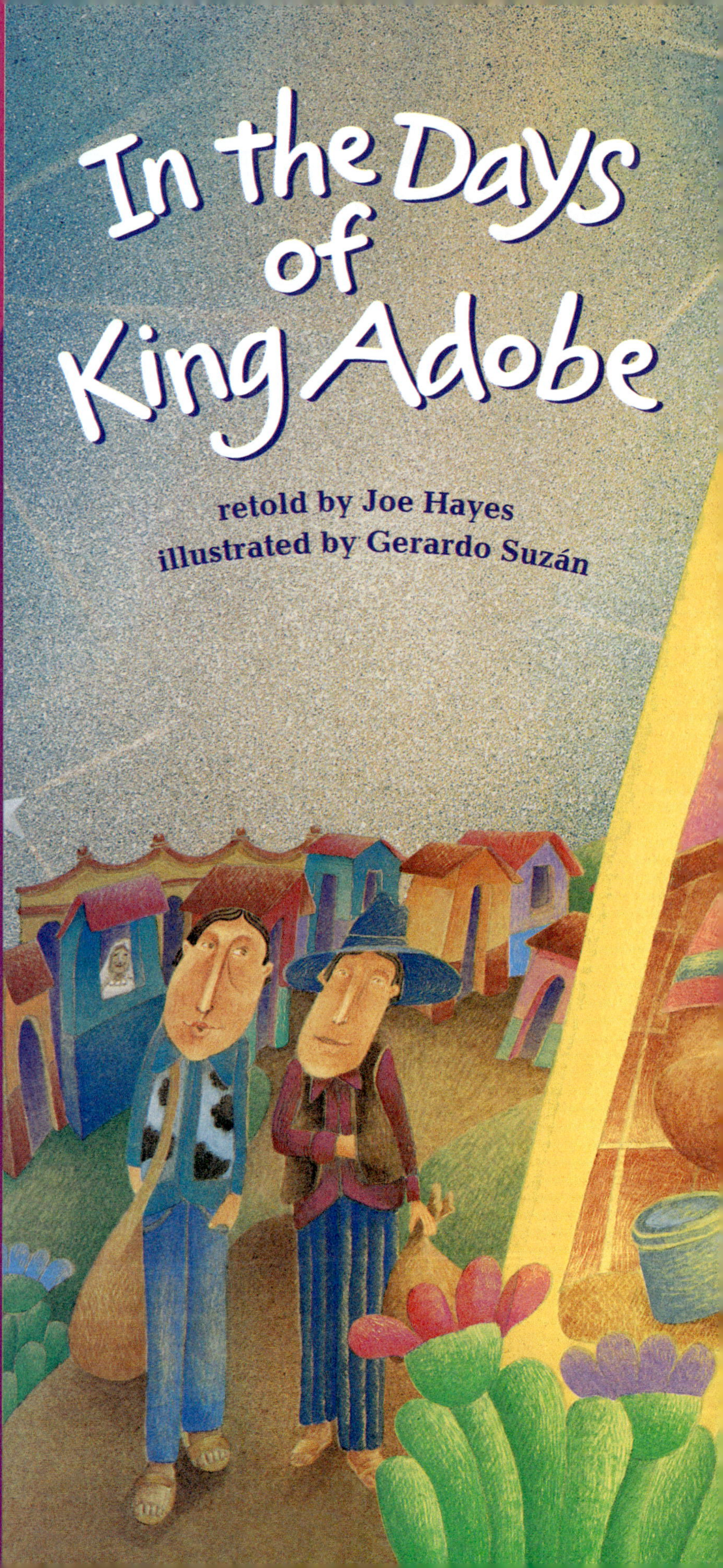

Genre

Folktale

Folktales are stories that were first told orally. They reflect the customs and beliefs of a culture.

In this selection, look for

- **A plot that teaches a lesson**
- **A main character who reflects the values of a culture**

THERE WAS ONCE AN OLD WOMAN who lived all alone in a tiny house at the edge of a village. She was very poor, and all she had to eat was beans and tortillas and thin cornmeal mush. Of course, she ate a few vegetables from her garden, but most of them she took into the village on market day to sell or trade for what little she needed for her simple life.

But the old woman was very thrifty, and by saving carefully—a penny a day, a penny a day—she was able to buy herself a big ham. She kept it hanging from a hook in a cool, dark closet behind the kitchen, and she only cut a thin slice from the ham on very special days—or if she was lucky enough to have company join her for a meal.

One evening a couple of young men who were traveling through the country stopped at the old woman's house and asked if they could have lodging for the night. The old woman had no extra beds, but she offered to spread a blanket on the floor for the young men to sleep on. They said that would be fine, and thanked the old woman for her kindness.

"It's nothing," the old woman told them. "I'm happy to have the company. I'll get busy and make us all a good supper."

She got out her pots and pans and then went to the closet and cut three slices from the ham—two thick, generous slices for the travelers and a thin one for herself.

The young men were delighted to see the old woman preparing ham for their supper. Seldom were they offered such good food in their travels. But those two young men were a couple of rascals, and right away a roguish idea came into their minds. They decided to steal the ham that night while the old woman was asleep.

After they had all eaten their fill, the old woman spread out a bed for the young men on the floor. She said good night and wished them good dreams and then went into her own room to sleep.

Of course, the young men didn't go to sleep. They lay on the floor joking and talking about how nice it was going to be to have a whole ham to eat. When they felt sure the

old woman was asleep, the young men got up and crept to the closet. They took the ham down from the hook and wrapped it in a shirt. One of the young men put the ham in his traveling bag. Then the two young men lay down to sleep with smiles on their faces. They had very good dreams indeed!

But the old woman hadn't gone to sleep either. In the many years of her life she had become a good judge of character, and she had noticed the rascally look in the young men's eyes. She knew she had better be on her guard. When she heard the young men getting up from their pad on the floor, she went to the door and peeked out. She saw everything the young men did.

Later that night, when the young men were sound asleep, the old woman crept from her room. She took the ham from the traveling bag and hid it under her bed. Then she wrapped an adobe brick in the shirt and put it in the traveling bag.

When the young men awoke in the morning, they were anxious to be on their way. But the old woman insisted they stay for a

bite of breakfast. "It will give you strength," she told them. "You have a long day of walking ahead of you. And you may not have anything else to eat all day."

One of the young men winked at the other as he sat down at the table and said, "You're probably right, *abuelita*, but who knows? Last night I dreamed that today my friend and I would be eating good food all day long."

"Is that right?" the old woman replied. "Tell me more about your dream. I'm fascinated by dreams. I believe they are sometimes true."

The young man thought he'd really make fun of the old woman. He smiled at his friend and then said, "I dreamed we were sitting under a tree eating. It was in a beautiful land. And the king of that country was named Hambone the First."

"Aha!" spoke up the second young man. "Now I remember that I had the same dream. And I remember that the land in which Hambone the First was king was named Travelibag."

The young men had to cover their mouths to keep from bursting out laughing. But the old woman didn't seem to notice. In fact, she seemed to be taking them very seriously.

"I had a similar dream last night myself!" she exclaimed. "I was in a land named Travelibag, and Hambone the First was king of that country. But then he was thrown out by the good people and replaced by a new king named Adobe the Great. And for some people, that meant a time of great hunger had begun."

"Isn't that interesting," the young men said, biting their lips to keep from laughing. "Oh, well, it was just a dream." They hurried to finish their breakfast and then went on their way, laughing at the old woman's foolishness.

All morning long the two rascals joked about the old woman as they traveled down the road. As midday approached, they began to grow tired. They sat down under a shady tree to rest.

"Well, now," said the first young man as he leaned back and closed his eyes. "Don't you think it's time

for dreams to come true? Here we are sitting under a tree, just as I dreamed. Open up the land of Travelibag. My stomach tells me I need to visit the king of that land."

"By all means," said the other. "Let's see how things are going with our old friend Hambone the First."

The young man opened his bag and pulled out the bundle wrapped in his shirt. Chuckling to himself he slowly unwrapped the shirt. Suddenly the smile disappeared from the young man's face. "Oh, no," he gasped. "The old woman knew more about dreams than we thought."

"What do you mean?" asked the other.

"Well," he said, "she told us Hambone the First had been thrown out, didn't she?"

"Yes."

"And do you remember who was put in his place?"

The young man laughed. "Adobe the Great! Where do you suppose she came up with a name like that?"

"Probably right here," said his friend. "Look."

The first young man opened his eyes. "I see what you mean," he groaned. "And I see what the old woman meant about the time of great hunger beginning. I'm starved!"

After several hungry days the two young men met another kind old woman who fed them a good meal. This time they didn't even think about trying to play any tricks.

Think and Respond

1. How does the old woman stop the **roguish** young men from stealing her ham? Why does she choose this method?
2. What character traits does the old woman have, and how does she show them?
3. Why is this story called "In the Days of King Adobe"?
4. What surprised you in this story? Why?
5. What reading strategy did you use as you read this selection? How did it help you understand the story?

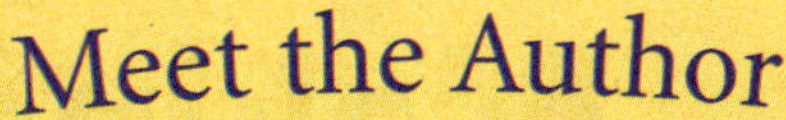

Meet the Author

Joe Hayes

"Kids will ask me, 'How long did it take you to write that book?' And I have to tell them, 'Well, I had been telling those stories for about four years before I wrote them down. So you could say it took four years. On the other hand, since I already had the stories in my head, it only took me about four hours to type them into my computer. So you could say it took four hours.'"

Joe Hayes has received several awards in the southwestern United States. He has written other stories based on Hispanic and Native American folk-tales told there.

Joe Hayes

Visit *The Learning Site!*
www.harcourtschool.com

▲ In the Days of King Adobe

Making Connections

Text to Self • Text to Text • Text To World

Compare Texts

NC STANDARDS: ELA 1.04h increase vocabulary/examine author's craft, 3.01b interpret/evaluate text/examine characters' actions/motives, 3.02 analyze/compare texts

1. How does the old woman in "In the Days of King Adobe" show creativity? INTERPRETATION / EVALUATING
2. How does the author describe the behavior of the two young men at breakfast and later, when they open the traveling bag? CRITICAL STANCE / EVALUATING
3. Why do the characters talk about their dreams? CRITICAL STANCE / EVALUATING
4. How is "In the Days of King Adobe" like other folktales you have read? How is it different? CRITICAL STANCE / ANALYZING
5. What topic or topics might you want to learn more about as a result of reading "In the Days of King Adobe"? CRITICAL STANCE / EVALUATING

Write a Character Sketch

Think about the actions of the old woman in the folktale. Then think about what these actions tell you about her character traits and personality. Write to describe the old woman's character traits and personality. Use a graphic like the one shown here to organize your character sketch.

CHARACTER TRAITS	SUPPORTING DETAILS AND QUOTATIONS

NC STANDARDS: ELA 2.01b use strategies to clarify text/vocabulary/ use other sources, 4.03a use visual aids, 4.03b be mindful of purpose/audience, 4.10 use technology as a tool; Social Studies 1.03 suggest influences of location on life in North Carolina

Make a Display

Adobe is a building material used in many areas where wood and other types of building materials are scarce. Find out about adobe dwellings or other types of dwellings used in the early United States. Choose one type of dwelling and create a display of it. You may draw a picture of the dwelling or make a model. Write about what the dwelling was made of, the people who built it, and its good and bad points.

A house where the Pueblo Indians lived. It was made of adobe clay bricks.

Research Microorganisms

Science CONNECTION

Meat, such as the old woman's ham, must be properly cooked to destroy any harmful microorganisms that might be present. However, many microorganisms are helpful to humans. Research microorganisms to find out some examples of helpful microorganisms and harmful microorganisms. Organize your information into a chart like the one below.

Helpful Microorganisms	Harmful Microorganisms

NC STANDARDS: ELA 2.01b use strategies to clarify text/vocabulary, use other sources, 4.10 use technology as a tool; Science 1.01 observe/describe how an animal is affected by living/nonliving things

▲ In the Days of King Adobe

Main Idea and Details

The **main idea** is what a selection is mostly about. The author may or may not state the main idea directly. Details provide information that supports the main idea.

In a work of fiction like "In the Days of King Adobe," the author is telling a story rather than giving information. The main idea is usually not stated in the story. Readers need to use details about the characters, setting, and events of the story to figure out the main idea.

Detail		Detail		Detail		Detail
An old woman is kind to two travelers.	+	During the night, they put her ham in their bag.	+	She replaces the ham with an adobe brick.	+	The rascals discover the old woman's trick.

Main Idea
Two rascals try to steal an old woman's ham, but she outsmarts them.

Knowing how to identify the main idea can help you understand and remember a story.

Visit *The Learning Site!*
www.harcourtschool.com

See *Skills and Activities*

Test Prep
Main Idea and Details

NC STANDARD: ELA 2.04c identify main idea/details

▶ **Read the passage. Then answer the questions.**

The Clever Fox

A hungry but crafty fox was trotting through a grove of trees when a sound made her look up at a branch above. There sat a blackbird holding a bunch of juicy grapes in his beak. "How can I get those grapes?" the fox asked herself. Then she had an idea.

"What beautiful feathers you have!" called the fox. The vain blackbird nodded. "But it's a shame," continued the fox, "that you can't sing." The blackbird, wanting to prove that his voice was as beautiful as his feathers, opened his mouth to sing. The bunch of grapes fell down and was snapped up by the fox.

COGNITION / KNOWLEDGE

1. **Which detail is least helpful in figuring out the main idea of this story?**

   A The fox heard a sound.

   B The fox wanted the grapes.

   C The fox tricked the blackbird.

   D The fox got the grapes.

Tip
Ask yourself which detail you would be least likely to include if you were retelling the story.

COGNITION / KNOWLEDGE

2. **How can you express the main idea of this story? On another sheet of paper, write a sentence that tells the main idea.**

Tip
Use the details from the story to figure out the main, or most important, idea.

▲ Red Writing Hood

Vocabulary Power

The selection "Red Writing Hood" is a story in the form of a play. A play that is presented in a theater may be reviewed in the newspaper. Read the following review of a new play.

- script
- repentant
- desperately
- discards
- acceptable
- injustice
- triumphantly
- circumstances

No Problems for *Problems*

BY PATRICIA KAHN

The play *Problems* is a huge success. The writer wrote a great **script**, and the actors do an outstanding job of acting out the written text. The play tells the story of a **repentant** young man who is sorry for what he did in the past. Now he **desperately** wants to make things right. He wants very badly to make up for the harm he has caused.

Kent DeLock stars in the play *Problems*, which opened last night at the Flagg Theater.

He comes up with several plans but **discards** each of them. He throws them out because they are not **acceptable**. For one reason or another, he does not find them good enough. He begins to feel that he can never make up for the **injustice**, or unfairness, of the things he's done.

Without giving away too much of the plot, I can tell you that the play ends **triumphantly**, with a joyful victory. You will have to see it for yourself to discover the **circumstances**, or events, that lead to the satisfying ending. Hurry down to the Flagg Theater for tickets today!

Vocabulary–Writing CONNECTION

Think of an idea for a play in which you would like a role. Write a brief **script** based on your idea. Include a part for yourself.

Genre

Play

A play is a story that can be performed for an audience.

In this selection, look for

- **Characters' actions and feelings shown through dialogue**
- **Stage directions**

Red Wri

by **Jane Tesh**
illustrated by
Bethann Thornburgh

CAST OF CHARACTERS
RED RIDING HOOD
WOLF
LITTLE MISS MUFFET
1ST PRINCE CHARMING
GOLDILOCKS
FATHER BEAR
MOTHER BEAR
BABY BEAR
BO PEEP
CINDERELLA
2ND PRINCE CHARMING
GOLDILOCKS' MOTHER
GOLDILOCKS' FATHER
AGENT GRIMM
AGENT ANDERSEN
AGENT RACKHAM

TIME: *Long ago.*

SETTING: *A forest. A few trees are scattered about.*

AT RISE: RED RIDING HOOD *skips on, whistling a happy tune, carrying a basket of goodies.* WOLF *comes out from behind a tree.*

WOLF: Hello there, little girl. What do you have in that basket?

RED RIDING HOOD: Oh, hello, Mr. Wolf. I have some treats for my dear grandma.

WOLF: Treats? That sounds nice. And where does your grandma live?

RED: In a little house at the edge of the forest.

WOLF (*Aside, to audience*): I'll just go along to grandma's and have a tasty treat of my own! (WOLF *starts to exit.*)

RED: Hold on! Wait a minute. (WOLF *halts. Aside*) I don't like the way this story's headed. I'm going to change a few things.

WOLF (*Puzzled*): What? (RED *takes a pencil and notepad out of her basket*). Hey, what are you doing?

RED: Changing the script.

WOLF (*Alarmed*): You can't do that! (RED *erases and scribbles.*)

RED: There! (*Reads*) "The wolf became a ballet dancer and never came near Red or her grandma again."

WOLF: What? A ballet dancer! (*Starts to dance*) Hey, this isn't the way the story goes! What about "What big ears you have"? "What big teeth you have"? (*Against his will, he pirouettes off, still protesting.*)

RED: This is great! I wonder what else I can do? (MISS MUFFET *enters, carrying tuffet and bowl.*)

MISS MUFFET: Oh, hi, Red. I was just about to have some curds and whey. Would you care to join me?

RED: No, thanks, Miss Muffet, but I may be able to help you out.

MISS MUFFET: Really? How?

RED: You do know a big ugly spider is going to sit down beside you and frighten you away.

MISS MUFFET (*Sighing*): That's usually how it goes.

RED (*Triumphantly*): Not any more! (*Takes pencil and notepad, erases, and writes*) Try this! (MISS MUFFET *sits on tuffet and starts to eat when* 1ST PRINCE CHARMING *enters, sits beside her, and smiles.*)

MISS MUFFET: My goodness! Prince Charming!

1ST PRINCE: That looks delicious! May I have some?

MISS MUFFET: Of course! But what in the world are you doing here? (RED *grins, taps pad with pencil.*)

RED: I decided a few things needed changing around here.

1ST PRINCE (*Taking* MISS MUFFET's *hand*): Miss Muffet, I would be honored if you'd share your curds and whey with me. Why don't we go to my palace?

MISS MUFFET: That sounds wonderful! (*To* RED) Thanks, Red! Goodbye! (MISS MUFFET *and* 1ST PRINCE *exit.*)

RED (*Smiling*): Now, who's next? (GOLDILOCKS *dashes onto stage.*)

GOLDILOCKS: Oh, Red Riding Hood! You have to help me! Those bears are after me again!

RED (*Scolding*): Did you break their furniture again?

GOLDILOCKS: I didn't mean to, but you know how it always is: too hard, too soft, too hot, too cold.

RED: Leave everything to me. (*Thinks a moment and then writes on her notepad. Growls are heard offstage.*)

GOLDILOCKS (*Looking off*): Oh, here they come! I'd better hide! (*She ducks behind tree as* FATHER BEAR, MOTHER BEAR, *and* BABY BEAR *enter.*)

RED (*Finishing writing*): That should do it. O.K., Goldie, you can come out now. (GOLDILOCKS *comes out from behind tree. She is now wearing bear ears.*)

FATHER BEAR: My goodness, what a cute little bear!

MOTHER BEAR: She's darling! Let's adopt her, Henry!

BABY BEAR: I've always wanted a sister!

GOLDILOCKS (*Patting ears and face*): Oh, wow! I'm a bear! This ought to be fun! (*To* RED) Thanks, Red! (GOLDILOCKS *and* BEARS *exit.*)

RED: This is neat! I wonder why I didn't think of it before? (BO PEEP *enters, sobbing.*)

BO PEEP: Oh, Red Riding Hood! Have you seen my sheep?

RED: Bo Peep, have you lost those sheep again?

BO PEEP: It does seem to be a habit, doesn't it?

RED (*Taking out pencil and paper*): I can find them for you. In fact, I can find as many as you want. Let's see, how about fifty to start?

BO PEEP: Fifty? That would be wonderful. (RED *writes. After a moment, loud baaing noises are heard off-stage.*)

RED: There they are! Go round 'em up! (BO PEEP *claps in delight.*)

BO PEEP: Thanks so much! (*She exits.* CINDERELLA *enters.*)

CINDERELLA: Red, have you seen Prince Charming? He's late for the ball.

RED (*Anxiously, to herself*): Gosh, it's Cinderella! The Prince went off with Miss Muffet. What can I do? (*Thinks a moment*) I know! I'll just bring in another prince! (*Writes hurriedly*) There! (2ND PRINCE CHARMING *enters.*)

2ND PRINCE: Cinderella, my dear!

CINDERELLA (*Hands on hips*): There you are! You're late for the ball. (1ST PRINCE *enters, followed by* MISS MUFFET.)

1ST PRINCE: Cinderella, my dear!

CINDERELLA (*Confused*): What's this? Are there two of you?

MISS MUFFET: I thought I was going to the ball with the prince! (*As* MISS MUFFET *and* CINDERELLA *stare from one prince to another,* GOLDILOCKS' MOTHER *and* FATHER *enter.*)

MOTHER: Red, have you seen Goldilocks?

RED (*To herself*): Oh, dear! Goldilocks' parents! I can't tell them I changed their daughter into a bear! (*To* MOTHER *and* FATHER) I think she went to visit the Three Bears.

FATHER: She does that every now and then, but she's usually home by now. We're getting a little worried. (GOLDILOCKS *enters, followed by* THREE BEARS.)

GOLDILOCKS: Red, I need to talk to you! (MOTHER *and* FATHER, *when they see* GOLDILOCKS, *react in horror to her appearance.*)

MOTHER and FATHER (*Ad lib*): Goldie! What's happened to you? What have they done? (*Etc.*)

GOLDILOCKS: You have to change me back! I don't like being a bear!

BABY BEAR: And she's eating us out of house and home!

RED: O.K., O.K., hang on! (*Gets out pencil and paper and starts to erase. Stops and stares at the end of pencil*) Oh, no! I've used up all my eraser!

GOLDILOCKS (*Alarmed*): What? You mean you can't change me back?

CINDERELLA: I don't need two Prince Charmings!

FATHER BEAR: We don't want to be the Four Bears!

MOTHER (*Desperately*): My baby! (BO PEEP *enters, frantic. Loud baaing is heard offstage.)*

BO PEEP: Red, you've given me too many sheep! I can't keep up with them! They're driving me crazy! (*Everyone begins to talk and complain.* WOLF *enters, dressed in tutu and ballet slippers, and begins to dance, getting in everyone's way.* BEARS *argue with* GOLDILOCKS *and her parents.* RED *stands in the middle of all the confusion, trying to scratch out words on her paper.*)

RED: If everyone could just be quiet a moment! (AGENTS GRIMM, ANDERSEN, *and* RACKHAM *come up aisle, dressed in dark suits, dark glasses, and carrying briefcases.*)

AGENTS (*Ad lib*): Wait! Stop! (*All stop talking and stare at* AGENTS. *Baaing stops.*) This has gone on long enough! (*Etc.* AGENTS *come up on stage.*)

RED: Who are you?

AGENTS (*Showing badges*): FBI.

RED: FBI?

AGENT GRIMM: Fairytale Believers, Incorporated. I'm Agent Grimm, this is Agent Andersen, Agent Rackham. (*Other agents nod.*)

RED: Fairytale Believers, Incorporated? I've never heard of you.

AGENT ANDERSEN: We believe fairy tales and nursery rhymes ought to be left alone.

AGENT RACKHAM (*To* RED): By changing the original stories, you're doing the world a terrible injustice.

RED (*Repentant*): I'm sorry! I only wanted to help. . . .

GRIMM (*Holding out hand*): The script, please. (RED *hands it over.* GRIMM *takes pencil from* ANDERSEN *and begins to write.*) Let's see now. Miss Muffet first. (*Writes. Large spider drops from trees.* MISS MUFFET *screams and runs off.*)

GRIMM: Cinderella needs only one Prince Charming. (2ND PRINCE *exits.*)

CINDERELLA: Thank you so much, sir. (*Exits with* 1ST PRINCE)

GRIMM: Goldilocks and the Four Bears would never be acceptable. (GOLDILOCKS *takes off bear ears and runs to her parents.*)

RACKHAM: I'll erase about forty sheep. That should do it. (BO PEEP *looks off and nods.*)

BO PEEP: Thank you so much!

GRIMM (*Starting to put pencil away*): There. All done.

WOLF: Hey, what about me?

GRIMM: Oh, right, sorry. (*Erases a little more.* WOLF *discards tutu and ballet slippers.*)

WOLF: Whew! My toes are killing me!

GRIMM: There! I think that takes care of everything.

ANDERSEN (*To* RED): I hope you've learned a lesson, Miss Riding Hood.

RED: I didn't mean for things to get so out of hand, but I didn't want to be eaten, and I didn't want my granny to be eaten, either.

ANDERSEN: But don't you remember?

RED: Remember what?

RACKHAM: The woodsman saves you and your grandmother.

GRIMM: He kills the wolf. (*All turn and look at* WOLF.)

WOLF: Give me that pencil! (*Snatches pencil and paper from* GRIMM)

AGENTS: Wait! (WOLF *writes something hurriedly*

and hands it back. AGENTS *read it, look at each other, and nod.*)

ANDERSEN: I think, under the circumstances, we can allow this.

WOLF (*To audience, reads*): "And they *all* lived happily ever after!"

ALL: The end! (*Curtain*)

THE END

Think and Respond

1. What is Red Riding Hood's goal in rewriting the **script**? Does she succeed?
2. How do the author's stage directions add humor to the play? Give examples, and explain why they are funny.
3. Why do you think the author chose stories and nursery rhymes that are familiar to most people?
4. Do you agree with the agents that fairy tales and nursery rhymes should be left alone? Explain.
5. How did using a reading strategy add to your understanding or enjoyment of the play?

▲ Red Writing Hood

Making Connections

Text to Self • Text to Text • Text To World

Compare Texts

NC STANDARDS: ELA 2.02e interact with text/connect text to own experiences, 2.04c identify main idea/details, 3.06 conduct research using a variety of tools

1. What lesson does Red learn about solving problems in a creative way? CRITICAL STANCE / APPLYING
2. How do Red's feelings change in the course of the play? INTERPRETATION / EVALUATING
3. How is reading this play different from reading the fairy tale "Little Red Riding Hood"? CONNECTIONS / ANALYZING
4. Name another play that you have read. Which play would you rather see performed, "Red Writing Hood" or the other? Explain. CRITICAL STANCE / EVALUATING
5. After reading "Red Writing Hood," you might be interested in learning about children's theater groups and performances in your own community. Where might you find out about them? INTERPRETATION / EVALUATING

Write a Revised Tale

In "Red Writing Hood," Red rewrites some old fairy tales. Think of another fairy tale that you could change in a humorous way. Then rewrite it to entertain. Use a graphic organizer like the one shown here to plan changes in the story events.

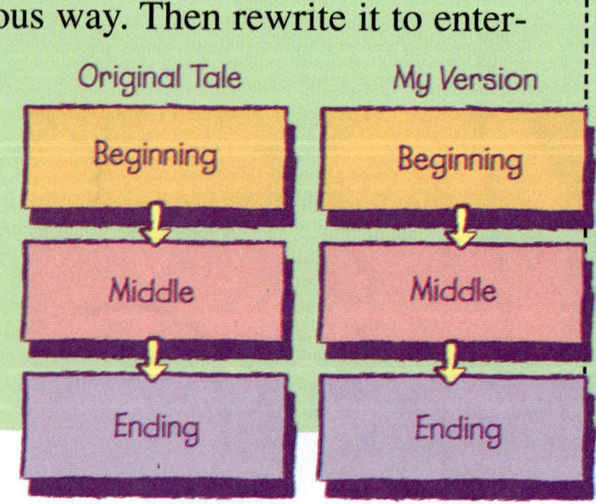

Writing CONNECTION

NC STANDARDS: ELA 3.06 conduct research using a variety of tools, 4.03a use visual aids; Science 1.04 explain/discuss how humans/animals adapt behavior to habitats

Make a Poster

Science CONNECTION

Think about what the wolf is like in "Red Writing Hood" and what you know about real wolves. Do research to find out about real wolves and fictional wolves. Begin by using a card catalog or computerized catalog. Look up *wolf* as a subject heading. Choose the most interesting facts to include on a poster. List them under the headings *Real Wolves* and *Fictional Wolves*. Draw pictures to illustrate your poster.

Research a Country

Social Studies CONNECTION

Folktales and fairy tales often reflect the values and beliefs of the culture from which they come. Find a folktale from a country you would like to learn more about. Read the folktale. Then research the culture of the country. How does the folktale reflect the values and beliefs of the country? Share with classmates the folktale you chose and some information about the culture of the country from which it came.

NC STANDARD: ELA 3.06 conduct research using a variety of tools; Social Studies 2.04 describe influence of different ethnic groups on North Carolina

▲ Red Writing Hood

NC STANDARDS: ELA 2.04a identify plot, 5.08b demonstrate language cohesion/use time order sequence of events

Sequence

Events in a story follow a **sequence**, or order, that makes sense. The sequence of events tells what happens first, next, and last in the story.

In "Red Writing Hood," Red changes the outcomes of familiar fairy tales and nursery rhymes by changing events in the stories. In the chart, look at the familiar version of "Little Miss Muffet" and Red's version of the same nursery rhyme.

Familiar Version	Red's Version
Miss Muffet sits on a tuffet, eating curds and whey.	Miss Muffet sits on a tuffet, eating curds and whey.
↓	↓
A spider sits down beside her.	Prince Charming invites her to his palace.
↓	↓
Miss Muffet runs away.	Cinderella looks for Prince Charming, who is supposed to go to the ball with her.
	↓
	Red brings in a second Prince Charming, and everyone is confused.

Red changed one event in the story by having Prince Charming arrive instead of the spider. Changing that one event changed the sequence of events that followed it. How would changing the sequence of events in other stories you know change the outcomes?

Visit *The Learning Site!*
www.harcourtschool.com

See *Skills* and *Activities*

Test Prep

Sequence

NC STANDARDS: ELA 5.08b demonstrate language cohesion/use time order sequence of events

▶ **Read the story. Then answer the questions.**

Rumpelstiltskin

A miller claimed that his daughter could spin straw into gold. The king put her in a room filled with straw and ordered her to spin it into gold. She wept, and a little man appeared. He said he would spin the straw into gold for her, but she must promise him her firstborn child.

When the king found the room filled with gold, he asked the miller's daughter to be his queen. The next year, they had a baby daughter. The strange little man appeared again. He said the queen could keep the child if she could guess his name.

When the queen guessed his name, the little man was very angry. He stamped a deep hole, fell into it, and was never heard from again.

COGNITION / ORGANIZING

1. Which event happens first?

A The little man appears.

B The girl begins to weep.

C The king puts the girl in the room.

D A miller claims that his daughter can spin straw into gold.

Tip

Think about the order in which events happen in the story.

COGNITION / ORGANIZING

2. How would the outcome of the story change if the miller's daughter escaped from the room before morning? Write your response on a separate sheet of paper.

Tip

What might happen next after the daughter escapes? How might the story end?

▲ One Grain of Rice

Vocabulary Power

"One Grain of Rice" is a folktale about a raja who will not help his people when they don't have enough to eat. Read the story below to see how another ruler handles the same problem.

plentifully

trickle

famine

decreed

implored

Water once flowed **plentifully** in a rushing river here. Now, with the lack of rain, there is just a **trickle** in a thin stream. Without water, crops can't grow. If it doesn't rain soon, there won't be enough food for my people. In time this dry spell could lead to a **famine**. Such a widespread lack of food would cause the people of my kingdom to become very hungry. I wonder what I can do.

I remember that another king had the same problem. He **decreed**, or formally ordered, that the water problem was to be solved by his ministers. I think this is being too bossy, so I won't do that.

Another king, from a different kingdom, **implored**, or begged, his ministers to find ways to help his people. This made the problem seem worse and scared his people.

What I'll do is have a meeting with my ministers. We will sit down together and listen to each other's ideas. I will choose the best idea after speaking with my ministers.

Vocabulary-Writing CONNECTION

The kings in this story looked for ways to make water flow **plentifully** in the rivers. Think of a place where water is plentiful and write a few sentences describing it.

Genre

Folktale

Folktales are stories that were first told orally. They reflect the customs and beliefs of a culture.

In this selection, look for

- **A plot that teaches a lesson**
- **A main character who reflects the values of a culture**

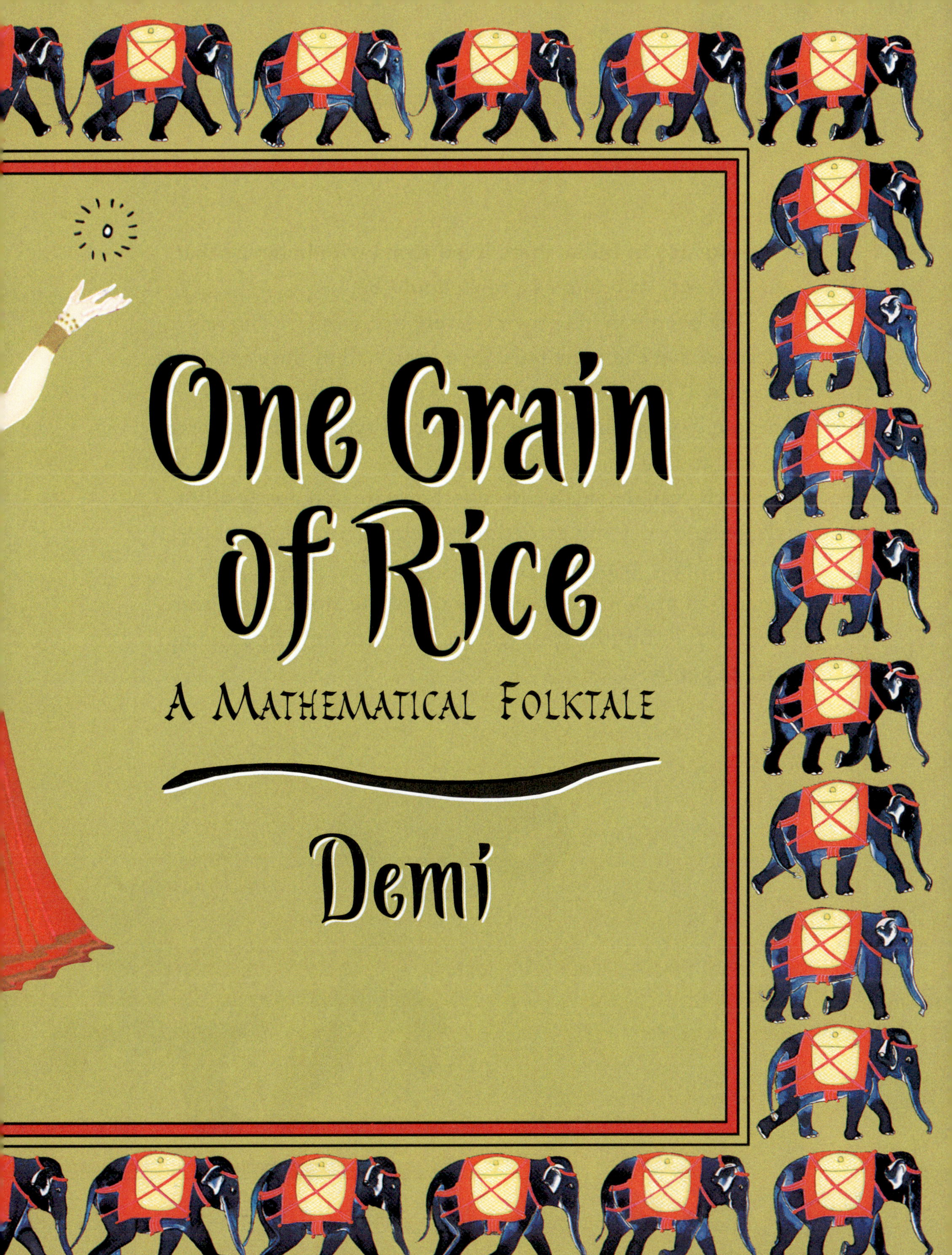
One Grain of Rice
A Mathematical Folktale
Demi

Long ago in India, there lived a raja who believed that he was wise and fair, as a raja should be.

The people in his province were rice farmers. The raja decreed that everyone must give nearly all of the rice to him.

"I will store the rice safely," the raja promised the people, "so that in time of famine, everyone will have rice to eat, and no one will go hungry."

Each year, the raja's rice collectors gathered nearly all of the people's rice and carried it away to the royal storehouses.

For many years, the rice grew well. The people gave nearly all of their rice to the raja, and the storehouses were always full. But the people were left with only just enough rice to get by.

Then one year the rice grew badly, and there was famine and hunger. The people had no rice to give to the raja, and they had no rice to eat.

The raja's ministers **implored** him, "Your Highness, let us open the royal storehouses and give the rice to the people, as you promised."

"No!" cried the raja. "How do I know how long the famine may last? I must have the rice for myself. Promise or no promise, a raja must not go hungry!"

Time went on, and the people grew more and more hungry. But the raja would not give out the rice.

One day, the raja ordered a feast for himself and his court—as, it seemed to him, a raja should now and then, even when there is famine.

A servant led an elephant from a royal storehouse to the palace, carrying two full baskets of rice.

A village girl named Rani saw that a **trickle** of rice was falling from one of the baskets. Quickly she jumped up and walked along beside the elephant, catching the falling rice in her skirt. She was clever, and she began to make a plan.

At the palace, a guard cried, "Halt, thief! Where are you going with that rice?"

"I am not a thief," Rani replied. "This rice fell from one of the baskets, and I am returning it now to the raja."

When the raja heard about Rani's good deed, he asked his ministers to bring her before him.

"I wish to reward you for returning what belongs to me," the raja said to Rani. "Ask me for anything, and you shall have it."

"Your Highness," said Rani, "I do not deserve any reward at all. But if you wish, you may give me one grain of rice."

"Only one grain of rice?" exclaimed the raja. "Surely you will allow me to reward you more **plentifully**, as a raja should."

"Very well," said Rani. "If it pleases Your Highness, you may reward me in this way. Today, you will give me a single grain of rice. Then, each day for thirty days you will give me double the rice you gave me the day before. Thus, tomorrow you will give me two grains of rice, the next day four grains of rice, and so on for thirty days."

"This seems still to be a modest reward," said the raja. "But you shall have it."

And Rani was presented with a single grain of rice.

The next day, Rani was presented with two grains of rice.

And the following day, Rani was presented with four grains of rice.

On the ninth day, Rani was presented with two hundred and fifty-six grains of rice. She had received in all five hundred and eleven grains of rice, only enough for a small handful.

"This girl is honest, but not very clever," thought the raja. "She would have gained more rice by keeping what fell into her skirt!"

On the twelfth day, Rani received two thousand and forty-eight grains of rice, about four handfuls. On the thirteenth day, she received four thousand and ninety-six grains of rice, enough to fill a bowl.

On the sixteenth day, Rani was presented with a bag containing thirty-two thousand, seven hundred and sixty-eight grains of rice. All together she had enough rice for two full bags.

"This doubling adds up to more rice than I expected!" thought the raja. "But surely her reward won't amount to much more."

On the twentieth day, Rani was presented with sixteen more bags filled with rice.

On the twenty-first day, she received one million, forty-eight thousand, five hundred and seventy-six grains of rice, enough to fill a basket.

On the twenty-fourth day, Rani was presented with eight million, three hundred and eighty-eight thousand, six hundred and eight grains of rice—enough to fill eight baskets, which were carried to her by eight royal deer.

On the twenty-seventh day, thirty-two Brahma bulls were needed to deliver sixty-four baskets of rice.

The raja was deeply troubled. "One grain of rice has grown very great indeed," he thought. "But I shall fulfill the reward to the end, as a raja should."

On the twenty-ninth day, Rani was presented with the contents of two royal storehouses.

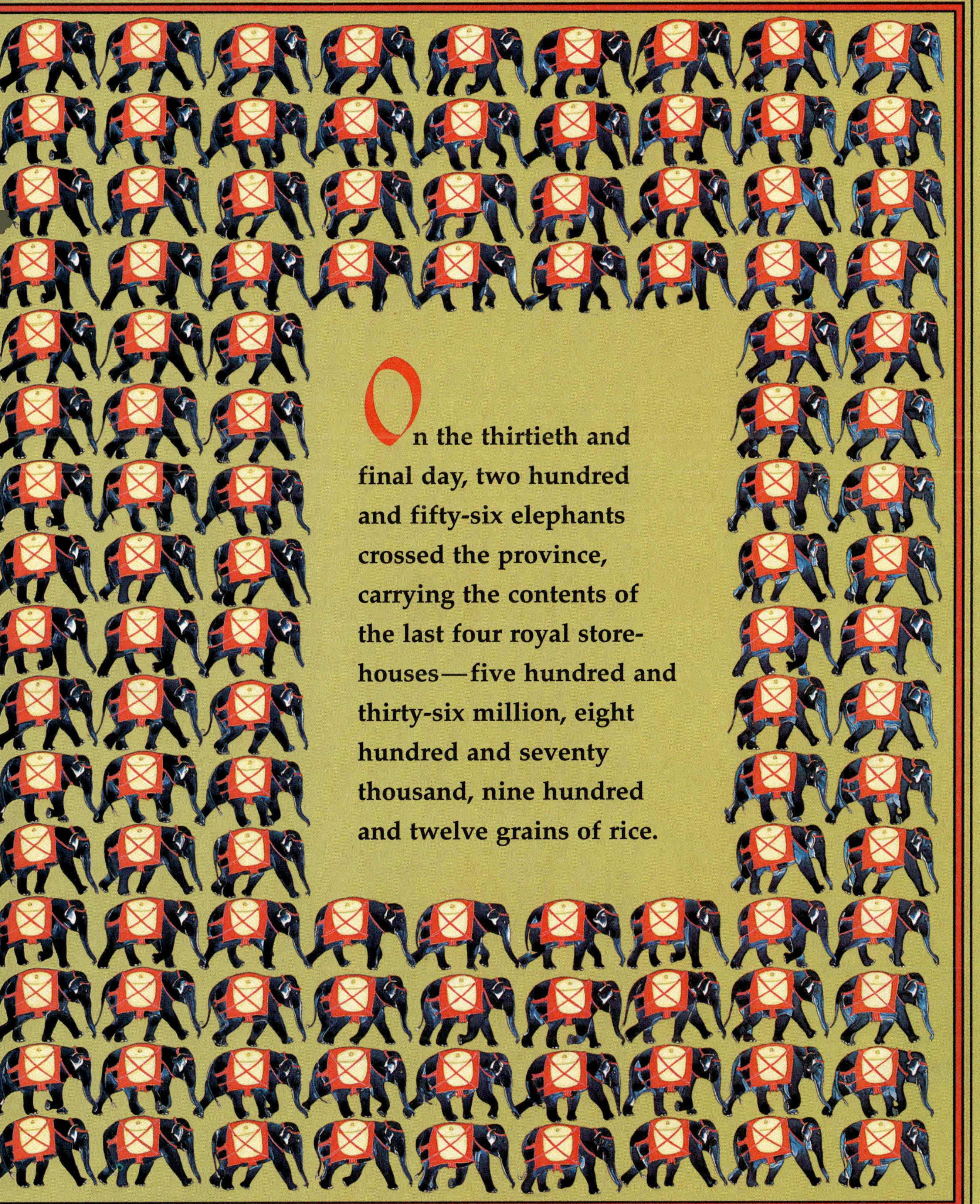

On the thirtieth and final day, two hundred and fifty-six elephants crossed the province, carrying the contents of the last four royal storehouses—five hundred and thirty-six million, eight hundred and seventy thousand, nine hundred and twelve grains of rice.

All together, Rani had received more than one billion grains of rice. The raja had no more rice to give. "And what will you do with this rice," said the raja with a sigh, "now that I have none?"

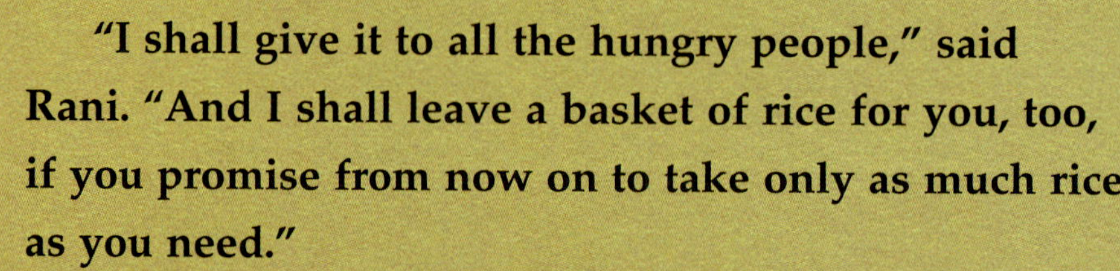

"I shall give it to all the hungry people," said Rani. "And I shall leave a basket of rice for you, too, if you promise from now on to take only as much rice as you need."

"I promise," said the raja.

And for the rest of his days, the raja was truly wise and fair, as a raja should be.

From One Grain of Rice to One Billion

Each day, Rani received double the amount of rice as the day before. See how quickly one grain of rice doubles into so much more.

To count how many grains of rice Rani received in all, add all of these numbers together. The answer: 1,073,741,823—more than one billion grains of rice!

DAY 1 1	DAY 2 2	DAY 3 4	DAY 4 8	DAY 5 16
DAY 6 32	DAY 7 64	DAY 8 128	DAY 9 256	DAY 10 512
DAY 11 1,024	DAY 12 2,048	DAY 13 4,096	DAY 14 8,192	DAY 15 16,384
DAY 16 32,768	DAY 17 65,536	DAY 18 131,072	DAY 19 262,144	DAY 20 524,288
DAY 21 1,048,576	DAY 22 2,097,152	DAY 23 4,194,304	DAY 24 8,388,608	DAY 25 16,777,216
DAY 26 33,554,432	DAY 27 67,108,864	DAY 28 134,217,728	DAY 29 268,435,456	DAY 30 536,870,912

Think and Respond

1. How does Rani save the people from **famine**?
2. How does the raja change from the beginning of the story to the end? Why do you think he decides to change?
3. Why does the raja keep giving Rani more and more rice, even after he sees what is happening?
4. Were you surprised by the amount of rice Rani got in thirty days? Why or why not?
5. What reading strategies did you use as you read "One Grain of Rice"? Give an example of how you used a strategy.

Meet the Author and Illustrator

DEMI

As a child, Charlotte Dumaresq Hunt was nicknamed Demi. She now writes and illustrates books under that name. She comes from a family of artists.

Demi has studied art in several countries. She lived in India for two years and became interested in Indian art and culture. She also loves Chinese painting and uses many of its ideas in her work. Demi's husband is from China. He tells her the folktales and fables he heard as a child, and Demi retells the tales in her books.

Demi's work has been shown in museums across the country. She has created murals, mosaics, puppet toys, scroll paintings, and Chinese paper objects.

Demi

Visit *The Learning Site!*
www.harcourtschool.com

Genre
Magazine Article

It's Just Math

by Linda O. George
illustrated by Barbara Emmons

TRICKS WITH NUMBERS can be fun. Here's one you can try with your friends:

1. Think of a number.
2. Add 3 to this number.
3. Multiply your answer by 2.
4. Subtract 4.
5. Divide by 2.
6. Subtract the number you started with.

If you did everything right, your answer will be 1. Try the trick again using a different number. Your answer will still be 1.

Here's another example. Since we can start with any number, let's pick 5.

1. Think of a number.	5
2. Add 3.	5 + 3 = 8
3. Multiply by 2.	8 x 2 = 16
4. Subtract 4.	16 − 4 = 12
5. Divide by 2.	12 ÷ 2 = 6
6. Subtract the original number.	6 − 5 = 1

Is this magic? No! Math is magic only for people who don't understand it. There is a reasonable explanation for every number trick.

Let's use pictures. If we pretend that our numbers represent buttons, we can see what happens in this trick.

1. Think of a number.
   Since we can start with any number of buttons, let's hide them in a bag.

2. Add 3.
   Our bag of buttons and 3 more buttons.

3. Multiply by 2.
   Now we have 2 bags and 6 buttons altogether.

4. Subtract 4.
   Take away 4 buttons.

5. Divide by 2.
   That leaves us with 1 bag and 1 button.

6. Subtract the original number.
   Take away the bag of buttons we started with, and we are left with 1 button!

This will happen every time. Remember that the bag of buttons could hold any number of buttons, and we did not do anything to change the buttons inside the bag. So we will always end up with 1 lone button at the end of this trick. This lone button stands for 1.

The next time you see a number trick, try to figure out why it works. You can be sure that if it's math, it isn't magic.

Think and Respond

Do you think the buttons and bags example is a good explanation of the trick? Explain your answer.

▲ One Grain of Rice

Making Connections

Text to Self • Text to Text • Text To World

Compare Texts

NC STANDARDS: ELA 2.02a interact with text/set purpose for reading, 2.05 support inferences/conclusions, 3.02 analyze/compare texts, 3.03 examine effect of language/visuals

1. Why is Rani's creative solution in "One Grain of Rice" such a good one? INTERPRETATION / ANALYZING
2. How do the illustrations on pages 482–487 aid readers in understanding the story? COGNITION / ORGANIZING
3. What viewpoint does the author express in "It's Just Math"? How is this like or unlike the viewpoint of the author of "One Grain of Rice"? CRITICAL STANCE / ANALYZING
4. What is another folktale that you have read in which one character tricks another? Compare and contrast the characters' traits and the reasons for their tricks. CRITICAL STANCE / ANALYZING
5. Which topic most interests you as a result of reading "One Grain of Rice"— India, rice, or mathematics? INTERPRETATION / EVALUATING

Write a Journal Entry

On the last day of Rani's reward, the raja realizes he has no rice left. Think about what the raja might have written in his journal that day. Write to express the raja's thoughts and feelings. Use a graphic like the one shown here to organize your thoughts.

What I (the raja) thought of Rani's plan at first:
Events that happened:
What I think of Rani's plan now:
Thoughts and feelings about Rani and the events:

Writing CONNECTION

Measuring Volume

Math CONNECTION

The space inside a container such as a storehouse or a box is called its volume. Find a box, such as a shoe box, and measure the volume. Use this formula: **Volume=length x width x height**. Fill the shoe box with rice. Then find another box and measure its volume to determine if it will hold the same amount of rice. Test the accuracy of your measurement by carefully transferring the rice from the first container to the second container.

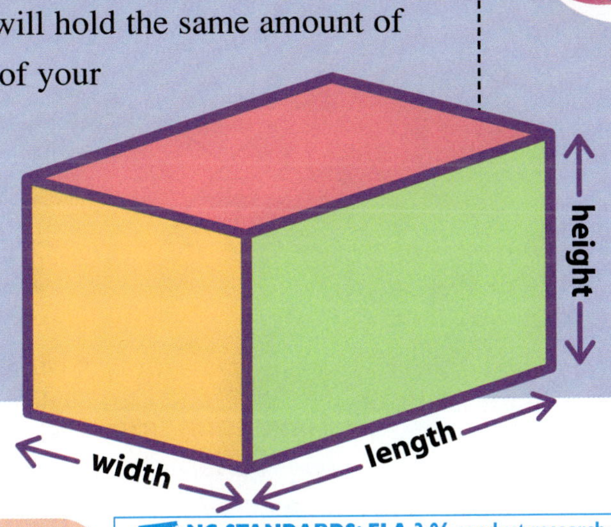

NC STANDARDS: ELA 3.06 conduct research using a variety of tools; Social Studies 4.04 understand how local/state governments work in NC

Create a Fact Sheet

Social Studies CONNECTION

In "One Grain of Rice," the raja ruled the land. In the United States today, we have a very different system of government. Research the government of the state where you live. What kind of government did it have before becoming a state? When and how did it gain statehood, and what kind of government was established at that time? Create a fact sheet to share the information you find.

California Fact Sheet

California became a state in 1850.

It was the 31st state of the United States.

▲ One Grain of Rice

Compare and Contrast

Folktales often share similar themes, situations, and types of characters. You can compare and contrast "One Grain of Rice" and "In the Days of King Adobe" in a Venn diagram to show how they are alike and different.

One Grain of Rice

- Main character: young girl, Rani
- Problem: The raja will not give rice to his hungry people.
- Solution: Rani outsmarts the raja.
- The raja learns to rule with kindness.

Both

- Folktales
- Time: long ago
- Main character uses cleverness to solve a problem.
- A lesson is learned.

In the Days of King Adobe

- Main character: old woman
- Problem: Two rascals try to steal the old woman's ham.
- Solution: The old woman outsmarts the rascals .
- The rascals learn not to take advantage of hospitality.

Think about other folktales you know. Compare and contrast the characters, settings, and plots.

Visit *The Learning Site!*
www.harcourtschool.com
See *Skills* and *Activities*

Test Prep
Compare and Contrast

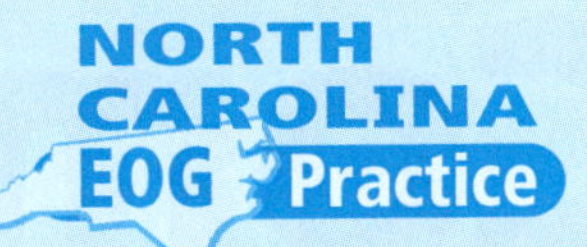

▶ **Read the story and look at the Venn diagram. Then answer the questions.**

Busy Mouse and Lazy Mouse

Once there were two mice. One worked all summer gathering food for the long winter. The other spent all her time dancing. When winter came, the lazy mouse hurried to gather food, but it was too late. She went hungry.

Busy Mouse and Lazy Mouse | **Both** | **One Grain of Rice**

CRITICAL STANCE / ANALYZING

1. Which phrase does *not* belong with "One Grain of Rice"?

- **A** main character: a girl
- **B** uses knowledge of math
- **C** main character's goal: to help others
- **D** character's problem not solved

Tip

Pay attention to the word *not* in the question. Identify the one phrase that does not tell about "One Grain of Rice."

CRITICAL STANCE / ANALYZING

2. Which phrase does *not* belong with "Busy Mouse and Lazy Mouse"?

- **F** contrasts the actions of two characters
- **G** shows why the powerful also need to be wise
- **H** shows time running out
- **J** teaches the value of hard work

Tip

Find the answer choice that does not tell about "Busy Mouse and Lazy Mouse."

THEME 5

Community Ties

CONTENTS

▲ Fire!

Vocabulary Power

The firefighters described in "Fire!" risk their lives to keep others safe. So do police officers, and communities depend on their help, too. Look at this community police officer's scrapbook.

- dedication
- curfew
- ventilate
- billowing
- flammable
- brigade

Presented to Officer Keziah Morgan for her **dedication**. She is always willing to work hard and never willing to give up. She is an example to others.

YOUNGSTERS IN BY NINE

Since last week, young people in our city have had a **curfew**. This law states that youths under the age of sixteen must be off the streets by 9 P.M. unless they are with a parent or other responsible adult. So far, the law seems to be working well. Officer Keziah Morgan reports that she hasn't seen any children on the streets after 9 P.M. without a responsible adult.

Dear Officer Morgan,

Thank you for reporting the apartment house fire. The fire started because a window had been opened to **ventilate** the house, allowing air to flow in and out. The breeze caused the curtains to move back and forth. The **billowing** curtains came too close to a lighted candle on a table. Because the curtains were **flammable**, they readily burst into flames.

After your fast action, the fire **brigade** arrived quickly and put the fire out. Thank you again for your help.

Yours truly,

Fire Chief Downing

Vocabulary-Writing CONNECTION

Because many of the things that we use in our everyday lives are **flammable**, fire safety is important. Make a list of things you could do to prevent a fire in your home.

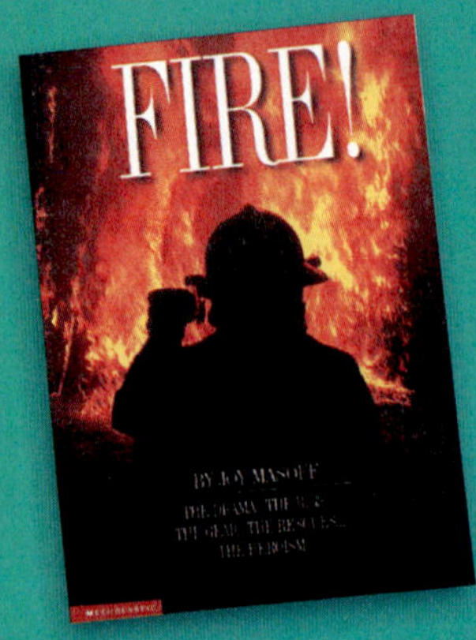

Genre

Expository Nonfiction

Expository nonfiction presents and explains information and ideas.

In this selection, look for

- **Facts and details about a subject or topic**
- **Text features such as photographs, captions, headings, and subheadings**

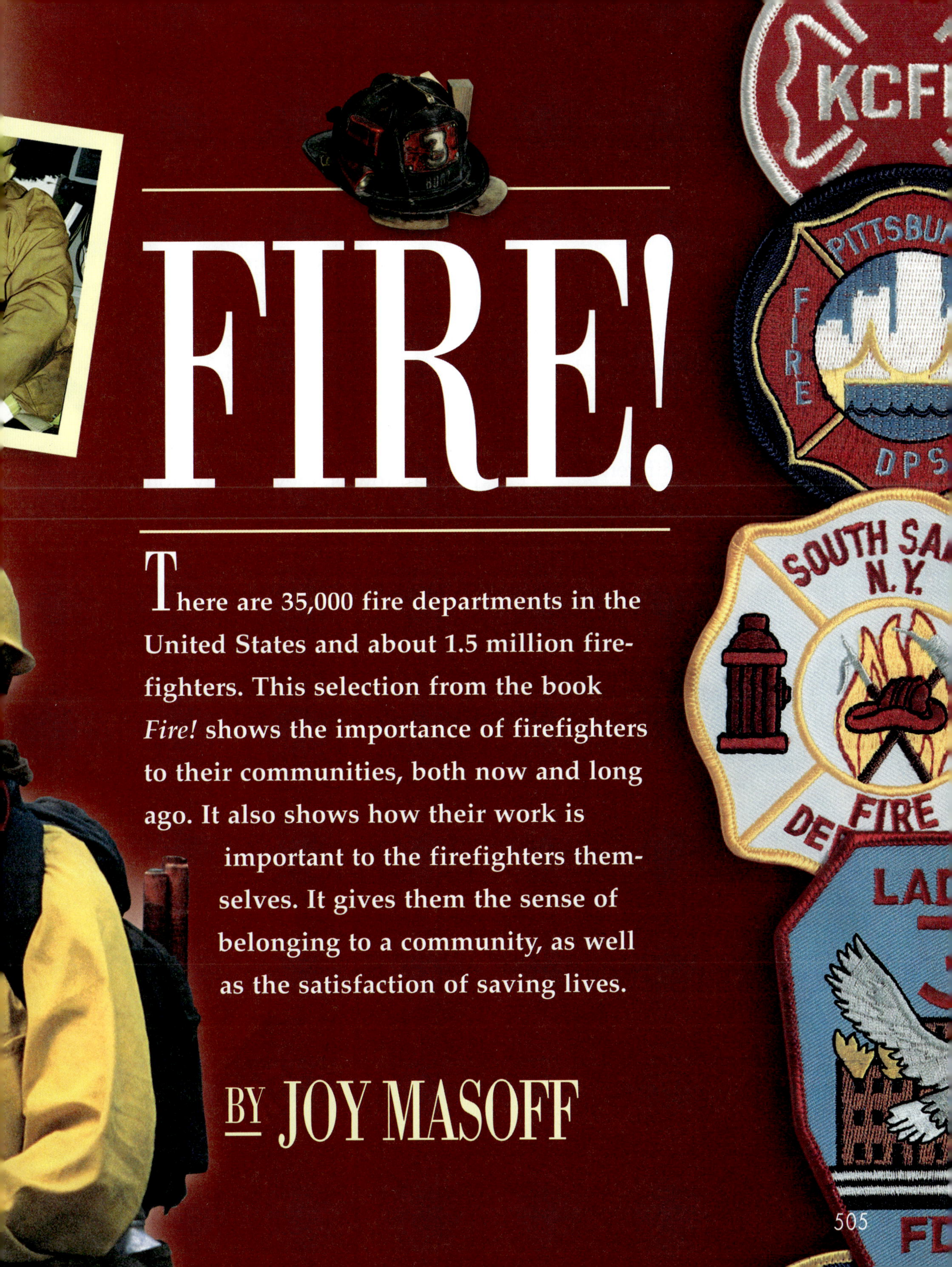

FIRE!

There are 35,000 fire departments in the United States and about 1.5 million firefighters. This selection from the book *Fire!* shows the importance of firefighters to their communities, both now and long ago. It also shows how their work is important to the firefighters themselves. It gives them the sense of belonging to a community, as well as the satisfaction of saving lives.

BY JOY MASOFF

Different...Yet the Same

When a call comes in—whether it's a report of flames at a country farm or smoke on the forty-eighth floor of a skyscraper—firefighters feel the same emotions. What will it be like? Will I be able to help? But every town is different; every department does things a different way.

They all have different names for their equipment and different systems for getting things done. In big cities, people get paid to be firefighters. In small towns, they usually don't. But one thing is the same. It's *always* challenging, always demanding... always thrilling.

In big cities, firefighters can answer a dozen calls a day. City firefighters stay at the station house.

In small towns, many firefighters are volunteers. There are almost one million volunteer firefighters in the United States.

Answering the Call

You are a firefighter. People count on you to come the moment they call. But you never know when that call will happen, so you are always ready. You check your equipment. You check your equipment again. You might sleep at the fire station a few nights each month or you might sleep in your house with a beeper at your bedside. But you always wait for that moment when you hear the call for help.

The station house is a second home to you. The people you work with are more than just your co-workers. They are the people you trust with your life. They have become like family—brothers and sisters you love fiercely, even if sometimes you get on one another's nerves.

You wait and check and practice. And then it happens. . . .

When the bells and buzzers sound in the station house, there is a great burst of activity. Poles are slid down, gear is pulled on. Firefighters call these runs JOBS or WORKERS. Let's pretend that for just one day, *you* are a big-city firefighter. You've got a worker!

YOUR ASSIGNMENT: ENGINE 21

Unlike small-town fire departments, which keep all their equipment in one place, big-city fire departments keep their trucks in buildings all over town, just a few trucks to each building.

Each truck has a team. There's a DRIVER (who takes care of the rig), an OFFICER (who's in charge of the crew), and FIREFIGHTERS (who tackle the flames or mount the rescues). In the old days, those firefighters were called "back-steppers" because they used to ride on the back of the truck, hanging on for dear life. This was very dangerous, so new trucks carry them inside.

You will work on a shift—usually a 24-hour period when you live at the station, eating and sometimes sleeping there. Remember, fire doesn't take vacations. Accidents never take the night off.

LIFE IN THE HOUSE

When you arrive for your shift, you pull out your gear and get it set up near your rig. If you're going to be working at night, you make your bed and help clean up the station house. There are usually training sessions to attend. You might even shop for groceries and cook dinner. There's always a lot to do.

The calls will come in to DISPATCH via the 911 network, and you never know what they will be. A child locked in a bathroom, a car that hit a stop sign, a burst pipe, a funny smell, a cat stuck inside a wall . . . people call the fire department for help with *everything*.

▶ ***These bunker pants are already tucked into boots, ready to be pulled on at a second's notice.***

STRUCTURE FIRE, CORNER OF PARK AND MAIN

But a fire call is something special. And now, just before lunch, a call has come in. Smoke is billowing from a store downtown. You hear your truck number called. In many fire stations you slide down the pole and slide into your turnout gear. Then, with your heart racing, you hop on your rig.

ALL ABOARD

The sirens are on, the lights flashing. You're on your way. You try to imagine what's waiting for you, and all the time your mind is racing along with your heart. You feel excited. This is what you've trained for.

▶ ***Pull on your hood, pull on your mask, check the airflow, and head on in!***

OUT OF CONTROL

When you get to the scene, the crew breaks up into teams. Some of you pull in the attack hoses to cool the flames. Some set the bigger discharge lines. Others are part of SEARCH AND RESCUE, looking for people or pets. Still others ventilate the building by breaking windows or cutting holes in the roof.

When it is all over and the fire is almost KNOCKED DOWN, you shovel up the cinders and toss outside anything that might still burn, then soak it until you can touch it with your bare hands. This is called the OVERHAUL.

The one word firefighters never want to hear is REKINDLE . . . a fire they thought was out but wasn't.

Three hours after the first alarm, it's back to the station, into a quick shower, and finally it's time for a very late lunch.

Eat Like a Firefighter

Firefighter McNulty's Four-Alarm Chicken

Ask a grown-up to help you whip up this reheat-and-eat dinner. Serves an entire firehouse (6–8 people).

4 cups cut-up boneless chicken breasts
2 cups celery, thinly sliced
$\frac{1}{4}$ cup chopped green pepper
$\frac{1}{4}$ cup chopped red pepper
2 tsps. lemon juice
$1\frac{1}{2}$ cups spaghetti sauce
1 cup bread crumbs
1 tablespoon melted butter
1 cup grated cheddar cheese

For a spicier dish add $1\frac{1}{2}$ tbsps. Worcestershire sauce and 1 tsp. Tabasco sauce.

Combine all the ingredients except the bread crumbs, butter, and cheese. Pour into a baking dish. Top with grated cheese. Toss the bread crumbs with melted butter and sprinkle over the top. Bake at 350° for 40 minutes. Can be reheated whenever a rescue interrupts.

Firefighting Long Ago

In 1607, Jamestown, Virginia, became the first English settlement in America, and in 1608 it burned to the ground. Life in this "new world" seemed to be one big fire after another. Year after year people built homes only to see them go up in flames. Here's why. . . .

THE FIRST LITTLE PIG BUILT HIS HOUSE OF STRAW

The first homes in our country were built quickly, using easily found materials such as brush, tree limbs, clay, and grasses. The roofs were made of thatch (which is made from bundles of straw lashed together) and mud. If you've ever been to a campfire, you know that a lot of those things make for a mighty flame. There was no heat or hot water and no electric stoves, so people kept fires going all day long in poorly constructed hearths.

▲ ***It's easy to see why Jamestown, Virginia, kept burning down. The houses were made of campfire ingredients.***

EVEN CHILDREN WERE FIREFIGHTERS

If you lived in the 1600s you would have been a part of the firefighting force. It took the whole town to stop a blaze. Every single home had a leather bucket hanging near the door just for putting out fires. Unlike today, when you just turn on a faucet to get water, townspeople had to get water from ponds, rivers, or wells. When a fire broke out, people formed a BUCKET BRIGADE.

CUSTOM HOUSE
2

Two lines stretched from the town's water source, everyone armed with a bucket. The men would fill the buckets and pass them toward the fire; the women and children would send the empty ones back to be filled. Most times it was too little water, too late. Town after town burned to the ground.

IT'S 9 P.M. IS YOUR FIRE OUT?

Wisely, the elders knew things had to change. Laws were passed forbidding the use of flammable building materials such as thatch. And because most fires occurred at night, while people slept, their fireplaces still lit for warmth, a curfew (which comes from the French for "cover the fire") was ordered. You could not have a fire going between 9 P.M. and 4:30 A.M. If you broke the law, you paid a heavy fine, and the money went toward big buckets, ladders, hooks, and rope.

▼ Women are firefighters, too. The first American woman firefighter on record was Molly Williams, who lived in the late 1700s. By the early 1900s there were all-woman companies like this one in Silver Spring, Maryland.

THE RATTLE WATCH

In the quickly growing cities, more and more houses were being built, all packed in close together. When one caught on fire, dozens ended up burning. In some cities, men were appointed to wander the streets at night to watch for fires. They carried big wooden rattles that made an alarming sound when twirled.

▲ *When Ben Franklin wasn't flying kites in lightning storms, he was busy improving day-to-day life.*

WHO INVENTED THE FIRE DEPARTMENT?

Benjamin Franklin, one of the greatest Americans ever, convinced a group of Philadelphia's leading citizens to band together to form the Union Fire Company. Willing to drop what they were doing to rush to the scene, they brought with them a great sense of dedication and loyalty—the true spirit of firefighting to this day. Franklin also published an important newspaper, and he frequently printed articles urging people to be more careful. He came up with the phrase "an ounce of prevention is worth a pound of cure" to keep people from carrying hot coals on shovels from room to room. George Washington, Paul Revere, and Thomas Jefferson were all volunteer firefighters, along with many other patriots. It was the right thing to do for a growing country.

Tools of the Trade

You wouldn't go out to play in the snow and ice in a bathing suit, would you? Just as you depend on gloves, a hat, a warm coat, and boots to protect you, firefighters depend on their turnout gear. That gear can mean the difference between a successful rescue and disaster.

Total weight of the average turnout gear: 68 pounds!

Think and Respond

1. What are some things that a firefighter might do during a 24-hour shift?
2. If you wanted to reread a specific piece of information in this article, how would you find that information?
3. Why do you think the author included the section about firefighting long ago?
4. Do you agree with the author that a sense of **dedication** and loyalty is the true spirit of firefighting? Why or why not?
5. Where in the selection did you use a reading strategy? How did using the strategy help you?

Meet the Author

Joy Masoff is a writer and art director in advertising. As a scout leader, she took her troop to visit the fire station that sponsored it. There she developed an admiration for the job firefighters do for the community. *Fire!* is her first book. Ms. Masoff visited many fire stations and museums and talked with firefighters to get the information for this book. She tries to capture the danger and the excitement of firefighting and possibly inspire young people to choose this important job as a career. Continuing her interest in careers that help the community, she has written a second book titled *Emergency!*

Joy Masoff

Visit *The Learning Site!*
www.harcourtschool.com

▲ Fire!

Making Connections

Text to Self • Text to Text • Text To World

Compare Texts

NC STANDARDS: ELA 2.07 evaluate usefulness of content, 3.02 analyze/compare texts

1. Do you think that the selection "Fire!" is a good choice for the theme Community Ties? Explain your answer. CRITICAL STANCE / EVALUATING
2. How is the section "Answering the Call" different from the section "Firefighting Long Ago"? INTERPRETATION / KNOWLEDGE
3. How is this selection similar to other selections that you have read about this topic? CRITICAL STANCE / ANALYZING
4. Think of a nonfiction selection you have read that did not include photographs, diagrams, or headings. Did you find that selection easier or harder to understand than "Fire!"? Explain. CRITICAL STANCE / ANALYZING
5. How would you find out more information about fire prevention? INTERPRETATION / EVALUATING

Write a News Story

Major fires and daring rescues are important news. Imagine a fire and rescue, and think about what you would tell in a newspaper article about these events. Write to inform readers about what happened. Use a graphic organizer like the one shown here to plan your news story.

Who?
What?
When?
Where?
Why?
How?

NC STANDARDS: ELA 4.05 use planning strategies to organize ideas, 4.07 compose fiction/nonfiction/poetry/drama

Make a Poster

Science CONNECTION

Think of a question you would like to answer about fire. Here are some ideas.

- **What is fire?**
- **What causes something to burn?**
- **Why does water usually put out fire?**
- **Is there any material that will not burn?**

Research your question. Then make a poster that shows your question and the answer. Include a diagram, a chart, or a drawing.

NC STANDARD: ELA 4.03a use visual aids

Plan a History Video

In "Fire!" the author tells about events in Jamestown in the 1600s and in Philadelphia in the 1700s. What historical events took place in your state in the 17th and 18th centuries? Research one event and plan an educational video about it. Your plan should tell what happened, when it happened, the causes of the event, the effects of the event, and why it was important to the history of your state.

Video Plan

Introduction: Built between 1672 and 1695, the fort of Castillo San Marcos protected the city of St. Augustine until the middle of the 1700s.

▲ Fire!

NC STANDARDS: ELA 2.04c identify main idea/details

Elements of Nonfiction

Nonfiction writing that gives information about a topic is called expository writing. The information may be organized according to main idea and details, cause and effect, sequence of events, or comparison and contrast.

The selection "Fire!" is organized according to main idea and details. It is divided into four main sections with headings that express the main ideas. Within each main section, there are smaller sections called subsections. Most of the subsections are also organized by main idea and details.

Main Idea and Details

The station house is a second home to you. The people you work with are more than just your co-workers. They are the people you trust with your life. They have become like family—brothers and sisters you love fiercely, even if sometimes you get on one another's nerves.

Main Idea: The station house is a second home to you.

Visit *The Learning Site!*
www.harcourtschool.com

See *Skills* and *Activities*

Test Prep

Elements of Nonfiction

NC STANDARD: ELA 2.04c identify main idea/details

▶ **Read the passage. Then answer the questions.**

Fire Facts

Fire gives off heat and light. The heat of a fire can be very intense. The light, or flame, is made up of glowing bits of whatever is burning, plus gases that glow at that temperature.

Fire can be started by rubbing together two pieces of wood. This can create enough heat to cause the wood to catch fire. Fire can also be produced by using a lens, such as a magnifying glass. Rays of sun shining through the lens can produce enough heat to cause certain materials to burn.

CRITICAL STANCE / INTEGRATING

1. **The first paragraph of "Fire Facts" is organized according to—**

   A cause and effect

   B main idea and details

   C sequence

   D none of these patterns

Determine whether the paragraph is organized by main idea and details, cause and effect, or sequence of events.

CRITICAL STANCE / INTEGRATING

2. **The second paragraph of "Fire Facts" is organized according to—**

   F cause and effect

   G main idea and details

   H sequence

   J none of these patterns

Look for signal words or phrases that may help you decide how the paragraph is organized.

▲ A Very Important Day

Vocabulary Power

"A Very Important Day" tells about a goal many people share—to become a citizen of the United States. They want to have the right to express their ideas about what goes on in their country. The newspaper article below reports on how citizens in one town expressed their ideas about a problem.

- petitioners
- certificate
- examiner
- enrich
- apologized
- obliged
- resounded

Mayor Agrees to Save Tree

A group of citizens came to see the mayor with an official request. These **petitioners** did not want the old tree in the main square to be cut down. Thelma Jones showed the mayor a **certificate**. The document stated that Jones is a tree expert. She passed exams at a special school by correctly answering questions that an **examiner** asked her. Thelma Jones told the mayor that there is no good reason to cut down the healthy old tree.

Others in the group pointed out that trees **enrich** our lives by adding natural beauty. Trees also help fight air pollution.

This tree will go on standing in the main square, as it has for over fifty years.

The mayor **apologized**, saying he was sorry he had ordered the tree cut down. He said he would cooperate with the group members, and he **obliged** them by signing a new order. It names Ms. Thelma Jones as caretaker for the tree. A cheer **resounded** through the mayor's office, filling the room with the sound. Everyone was pleased with the decision.

Vocabulary–Writing CONNECTION

In this story you read about two ways trees **enrich** our lives. Write a paragraph describing other ways in which trees make our lives better.

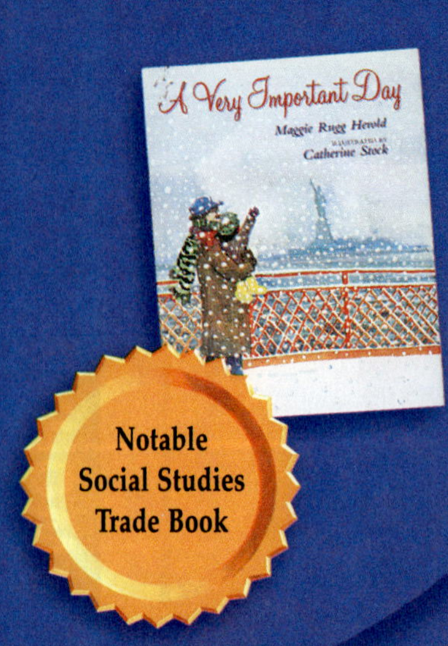

Genre

Informational Narrative

An informational narrative is a story that presents information and facts.

In this selection, look for

- **Information about a topic**
- **Characters and events that are realistic**

A Very Important Day

by Maggie Rugg Herold
illustrated by Catherine Stock

Nelia Batungbakal (NEL-i-ah bah-TUHNG-bah-KAHL) was too excited to sleep. She was looking out her window, listening to music on her Walkman, when she thought she saw snow!

Sure enough, before long the station DJ came on. "It's three A.M. here in New York City, and it's snowing. Four to six inches are expected by noon."

Nelia's mind raced. Imagine, snow on such a very important day. This would never happen in the Philippines. Her son and daughter-in-law and the grandchildren were fast asleep. She would need to awaken them early, to allow extra time for the trip downtown.

"Wake up, Miguel (mee-GEL). It's snowing," Rosa Huerta (ROE-sah WHERE-tah) called to her brother. "There are at least two inches on the fire escape."

"All *right*!" said Miguel, bounding from his room. He opened the window and scooped up some snow.

"Close that window," their father ordered. "It's cold in here, and—Miguel, is that snow in your hand?"

"Yes, Papa, the first this year."

"Back outside with it before it melts. And on such a very important day. This would not happen in Mexico, at least not in the south."

"Let's move quickly," urged their mother. "It's six-thirty. We can get an early start downtown."

Veena Patel (VEE-nah pah-TEL) had just set the table when the doorbell rang. "That will be the children," her husband, Mohandas (moe-HAHN-dahs), said.

But it was their neighbors, the Pitambers (pi-TAHM-buhrs). They apologized for stopping by so early. "We were afraid of missing you, and we wanted to wish you well on this very important day."

"Join us for breakfast," said Veena. "Our daughter and her family will be here any minute. They think we must allow extra time, that the snow will slow us down. That's one worry we never had in India."

The doorbell rang again, and this time it was the children. Everyone gathered quickly at the table, talking eagerly about the special morning ahead.

Out the door and down the steps came the Leonovs (lay-OH-nufs)—first Eugenia (yev-GAY-nee-ah), then her brother, Lev (LEF), followed by their grandfather, grandmother, mother, and father.

"Snow reminds me of Russia," said their mother.

"I love snow!" exclaimed Eugenia.

Her grandfather stooped, grabbed two handfuls, and threw them at his grandchildren.

The fight was on.

Just then Mr. Dionetti (dee-on-ET-ee) lobbed a snowball from the door of his corner grocery. "Is this the big day?" he called out. "Are you headed downtown?"

"Yes," answered their father. "This snowball fight is headed for the subway."

"Congratulations!" cried Mr. Dionetti. And tossing a big handful of snow straight up in the air, he crossed the street to shake their hands.

Kostas and Nikos Soutsos (KOS-tahs and NEE-kose SOO-tsose) were clearing the sidewalk in front of the family restaurant when their mother came out the side door from their apartment above. She was carrying their baby sister, Kiki (ki-KEE).

"Kiki, this is snow," said Kostas.

"How do you like it?" Nikos asked.

Kiki seemed puzzled by the flakes that hit her nose.

Their mother laughed. "She'll get used to it, living here. Not like Greece, where it snows maybe once in ten years. But where's your father? We should be on our way."

"He went to make a sign for the door. See, there he is."

"Set those shovels inside, and let's be off," their father called. "And read this sign, everyone. What does it say?"

They chorused together, "Closed for a very important day."

"Finally! There's the bus," said Duong Hao (ZUNG HAH-oh). He and his older sister, Trinh (CHRIN), brushed snow off each other and followed their mother on board. It was crowded at first, but a few stops later they all got seats.

"Here we are," said their mother, "in the middle of a snowstorm on the most important day since we arrived from Vietnam—"

Suddenly the driver braked hard.

They were all thrown forward.

"Car skidded at the light and couldn't stop," the driver yelled. "Everybody okay?"

Fortunately only bundles had landed on the floor.

"That was close," said their mother.

"Yes," said Trinh, "but our driver's good."

Duong nodded. "Maybe he knows that today of all days we just have to get downtown."

"I love the ferry," said Jorge Báez (HOR-hay BYE-es).

"So do I," agreed his cousin Pedro Jiménez (PAY-droe hee-MAY-nes), "especially in snow. Let's go up on deck."

"Not by yourselves, but I'll go with you," said Pedro's father.

"And I'll keep you company," Jorge's father added.

"Me too," begged Jorge's sister. "I want to go outside."

"All right," said her father. "You are old enough."

They went up on deck, leaving the little ones inside with Jorge's mother and aunt.

"I'm so glad this day takes us across the harbor," said Pedro's father. "I never tire of the ride."

"Neither do I," said Jorge's father. "Even in snow, this view is the best in the city. And now we will all remember it as part of the most important day since we came from the Dominican Republic."

Through the narrow streets on the unshoveled sidewalks the Zeng (DZENG) family made their way on foot. Suddenly, from above them, a voice called out.

Yujin's (EEOO-JING) friend Bailong (BYE-LONG) was leaning out the window. "I've been watching for you," he said. "Don't open this until later. Catch!"

Down through the snowflakes came a small brightly wrapped package, straight into Yujin's outstretched hands.

"Thanks, Bailong."

"Thanks for remembering."

"This is such an important day."

"The most important since we arrived from China."

Yujin tucked the package safely inside his coat, and with waves and good-byes the Zengs set off again, heading south.

Jihan Idris (ji-HAN i-DREES) and her parents had also left home early to make the trip downtown. Now their subway ride was over, and there was time for breakfast.

"I see a coffee shop ahead," Jihan's mother called out.

"I want to sit at the counter!" Jihan exclaimed.

They entered and sat on three stools, Jihan in the middle.

"I'd like waffles," Jihan told their waitress.

"And I'll have pancakes," said her father. "With coffee and grapefruit juice."

"Scrambled eggs and a toasted bagel, please," said her mother. "With orange juice and tea."

Quickly the waitress was back with their breakfasts. "What brings you out so early on a snowy day like today?" she asked.

"Can you guess?" said Jihan's mother.

"It's the most important day for us since we came from Egypt," said Jihan's father.

"And I'm celebrating with waffles," said Jihan. "I never get them at home."

"There's the courthouse," said Kwame Akuffo (KWA-mee ah-KOO-foo) to his wife, Efua (eh-foo-WAH), as they rounded a corner, walking fast.

She stopped. "Only two blocks to go. I'll race you to the steps."

He stopped, too. "Are you crazy?"

"It's not slippery."

"You're on! Ready?"

She nodded.

"On your mark, get set, go!"

And off they dashed, down the sidewalk.

"Tie," Efua declared at the bottom of the steps.

"I used to run in Ghana," Kwame said, "but never in snow."

"Wait," said Efua, taking a camera from her purse.

"Before we go in on this very important day, let's get someone to take our picture."

So they asked a stranger, who gladly obliged, and then hand in hand they climbed the courthouse steps.

As Robert MacTaggart came through the courthouse door, he heard familiar voices calling, "Robert. Over here."

Near the entrance stood his friends Elizabeth and Alan. Each of them gave him a big hug.

"You made it," Robert said. "Thank you so much for coming. I was afraid the snow would stop you."

"Oh, no, not on such an important day," said Elizabeth.

"We were getting worried about *you*, though," said Alan.

Robert chuckled. "A few snowflakes defeat a man from the highlands of Scotland? Come on. Let's find the chamber. It's on this floor."

Leaving relatives and friends to wait in the hall outside, Alvaro Castro (AL-vah-roe CA-stroe), his wife, Romelia (roe-MAY-lee-ah), and their children entered the crowded chamber. They were among the last to find seats.

Soon the examiner appeared, and the room became quiet. "When I call your name," he said, "please come forward to receive your certificate."

Many names were called; many people went forward. Then, "Alvaro and Romelia Castro and children Marta, José, and Oscar."

The Castros approached the examiner.

"Please sign here," he said to Alvaro. "And here," he said to Romelia. "These are your papers."

"Thank you," said Alvaro. "This is a proud moment."

The Castros returned to their seats. "The long journey from El Salvador has ended," Romelia whispered to her husband, and he squeezed her hand.

When the examiner had finished, he said, "Please open the door to relatives and friends."

People poured in. There were so many they filled the aisles and lined the walls at the back and sides of the chamber.

"Everyone please rise," said the examiner, and as everyone did, a judge entered the chamber.

"Your Honor," said the examiner, "these petitioners have qualified for citizenship in the United States of America."

"Then," said the judge, "will you repeat after me the oath of citizenship. Let us begin. 'I hereby declare, on oath . . .' "

"I hereby declare, on oath . . ."

Echoing the judge phrase by phrase, sentence by sentence, the many voices resounded as one, swearing loyalty to the United States of America.

"Congratulations," said the judge. "Those of you who can be, please be seated."

As the room became quiet again, the judge cleared his throat. "Two hundred nineteen of you from thirty-two countries

have become United States citizens here today. You are carrying on a tradition that dates back to the earliest days of our country, for almost all Americans have come here from somewhere else. May citizenship enrich your lives as your lives enrich this country. Welcome. We are glad to have you. This is a very important day."

Everyone then rose and joined the judge in the Pledge of Allegiance.

Family and friends and strangers turned to one another. "Best wishes!" "I'm so happy for you." "You must be so proud." "Isn't it wonderful?" "What a day!" "Let me shake your hand." "Let me give you a kiss." "Let me give you a hug."

Zeng Yujin tore open the package from his friend Bailong. Inside he found small American flags, a dozen or so, enough to share with everyone in his family and with other new citizens surrounding him.

In a wave of excitement, they all made their way out of the chamber, through the hallway, and back to the courthouse door.

"Look!" they exclaimed, everybody talking at once. "The snow has stopped." "The sun is shining." "It will be easy to get home and go on celebrating." "This has become our country on this very important day!"

Think and Respond

1. How are the people in this story different from one another? How are they alike?
2. Why doesn't the author reveal what the important day is until the end of the story?
3. How might someone seeing the story characters on the street have known that it was a special day for them?
4. In the story, the judge says to the new citizens, "May citizenship **enrich** your lives as your lives enrich this country." What does he mean by these words?
5. What reading strategies did you use as you read this selection? How were they helpful?

MEET THE AUTHOR
Maggie Rugg Herold

MEET THE ILLUSTRATOR
Catherine Stock

A book review tells about a book and gives an opinion. It might look like this.

Books on America: Top Picks

If you're looking for good books on citizenship, one to check out is *A Very Important Day*. This colorful picture book is written by Maggie Rugg Herold and illustrated by Catherine Stock.

On a snowy day in New York, people from all over the world make their way downtown. At the turn of each page, readers meet a new family with the same plans. Herold keeps readers guessing about what is so important, and Stock's bright watercolors set a happy mood.

The author and illustrator are a good team for a book like this one. Herold has made her career in children's book publishing. Stock is both an author and an illustrator, and many of her books celebrate special days such as holidays. Stock lives in New York City, and Herold lives in nearby Montclair, New Jersey.

This is a book about the true meaning of citizenship that any reader will enjoy.

Visit *The Learning Site!*
www.harcourtschool.com

▲ A Very Important Day

Making Connections

Text to Self • Text to Text • Text To World

Compare Texts

NC STANDARDS: ELA 1.02 use roots/prefixes/suffixes to decode/infer meanings, 1.03 use planning strategies for key word meanings/relationships, 1.04h increase vocabulary/examine author's craft, 2.04b identify theme

1. How does "A Very Important Day" give readers a better understanding of community? INTERPRETATION / EVALUATING
2. Why do you think the author has characters compare the snow in New York with the amount of snow in the lands they came from? INTERPRETATION / KNOWLEDGE
3. Besides entertaining readers, what other purpose did the author have for writing "A Very Important Day"? CRITICAL STANCE / EVALUATING
4. How is this informational narrative different from realistic fiction stories you have read? COGNITION / INTEGRATING
5. What are some topics you might want to learn more about after reading "A Very Important Day"? INTERPRETATION / EVALUATING

Write a Speech

Writing CONNECTION

The judge in "A Very Important Day" welcomes the new citizens with a speech. Think about what you would say in a speech to welcome people who are new to your community. Write a short speech, practice it, and present it to your classmates. Jot down ideas for your speech in a web like this one.

Welcoming Speech

Make a Line Graph

NC STANDARD: ELA 3.05 use graphs/charts/maps to expand understanding

Social Studies CONNECTION

The characters in "A Very Important Day" were recent immigrants to the United States. Find out how many people immigrated to the United States between 1840 and 2000. Use an almanac or an encyclopedia article about immigration. On a sheet of graph paper, set up a graph like the one below. Then make a line to show the number of people who immigrated to the United States each year.

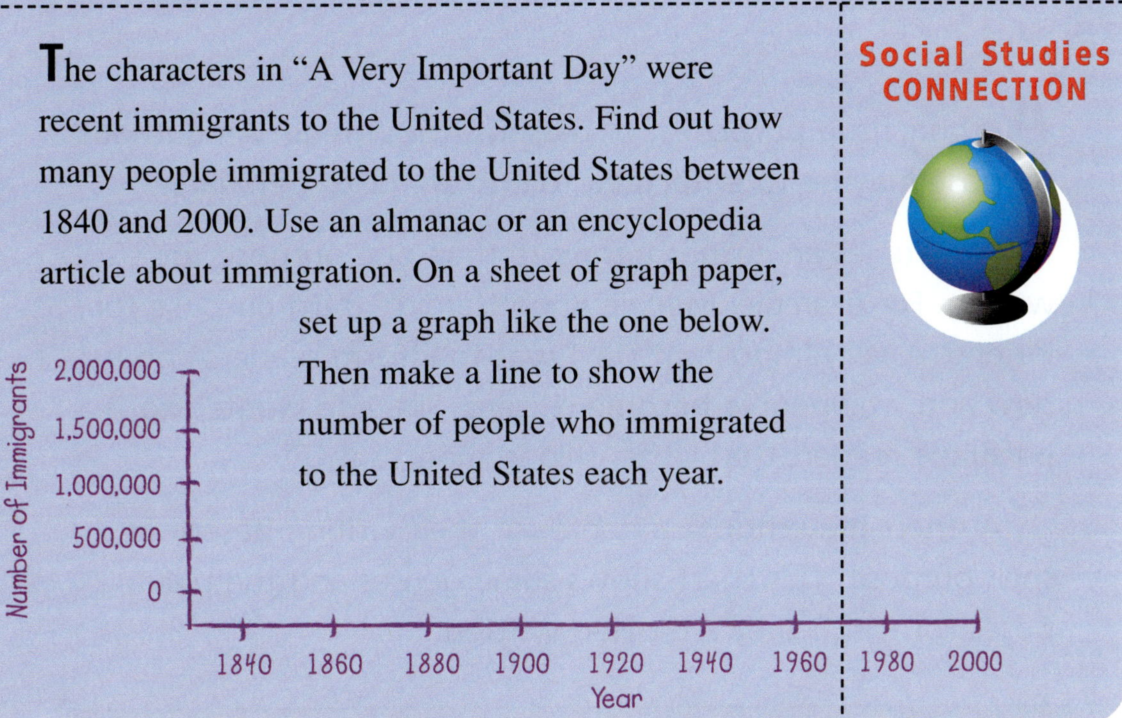

Research a Scientist

NC STANDARD: ELA 3.06 conduct research using a variety of tools

Science CONNECTION

In "A Very Important Day," the judge tells the new citizens that their lives will enrich the United States. Many important scientists and inventors, such as Albert Sabin and Alexander Graham Bell, were immigrants to the United States. Research a scientist or an inventor who was an immigrant. Prepare a brief oral report about the person you chose. Tell about the most important things he or she did. You may want to include a photograph or drawing of the person as part of your presentation.

▲ A Very Important Day

NC STANDARD: ELA 1.04h increase vocabulary/examine author's craft

Author's Purpose

Authors have **purposes**, or reasons, for writing. An author's purpose may be to **entertain**, to **inform**, or to **persuade**.

Sometimes an author has more than one purpose for writing. For example, Maggie Rugg Herold's main purpose for writing "A Very Important Day" was to inform readers about how and why people become citizens. She also wanted to persuade readers that citizenship is important.

Authors may choose a genre for their writing based on their purpose. This chart shows some genres and the purposes for which they are often written.

Author's Purpose	Genres
to entertain to give readers enjoyment or amusement	realistic fiction stories fantasy stories
to inform to explain or give information	biographies autobiographies nonfiction books and articles informational narratives how-to books and articles road signs
to persuade to convince readers to do or believe something	advertisements letters to a newspaper editor

Visit *The Learning Site!*
www.harcourtschool.com

See *Skills* and *Activities*

Test Prep
Author's Purpose

ELA 1.04h increase vocabulary/ examine author's craft

▶ **Read each paragraph and answer each question.**

> **Paragraph 1**
>
> **There are many reasons why people leave their homelands and move to other countries. One of the main reasons has always been to seek better jobs, better pay, and a more comfortable way of life.**

COGNITION / EVALUATING

1. What is the author's purpose for writing Paragraph 1?

A to entertain

B to inform

C to persuade

D to amuse

Ask yourself whether the author is telling a story, giving information, trying to get you to do something, or explaining how to do something.

> **Paragraph 2**
>
> **Becoming a citizen of the United States is a wonderful thing! Everyone who has the chance should definitely do so. If you are not a citizen now, I urge you to begin the process today!**

COGNITION / EVALUATING

2. What is the author's purpose for writing Paragraph 2?

F to entertain

G to inform

H to persuade

J to explain

Look for signal words. Ask yourself for what purpose an author might use words like *should* and *urge*.

▲ Saguaro Cactus

Vocabulary Power

- habitat
- teeming
- perch
- nectar
- brush
- spiny
- topple
- decomposes

Welcome to the desert! This is a very "cool" place to live, although the temperature here can rise as high as 130 degrees Fahrenheit. As you read these pages, you will learn more about this unusual place.

Because of the heat and dryness, the desert seems to be an unfriendly **habitat**, or place to live, for plants and animals. If you look closely, however, it is **teeming** with all kinds of life.

Mighty mountain lions **perch** at the top of the cliff, looking down. Small birds dip their beaks into cactus flowers to sip the sweet **nectar**.

Out of the desert **brush**, the small trees and shrubs that dot the landscape, rises a strange and wonderful life form. It can take many different shapes, but you will recognize it by its **spiny**, green thorns. It is a cactus!

A strong cactus can stand tall for two centuries before winds and other forces cause it to **topple** over. Then it finally lies flat and **decomposes** on the desert floor.

Vocabulary-Writing CONNECTION

Write for five minutes about a **habitat** you know well. Tell about what you can see, hear, and smell there.

Genre

Expository Nonfiction

Expository nonfiction presents and explains information or ideas.

In this selection, look for

- **Events in time-order**
- **Facts about desert life**

The Sonoran Desert is a small bit of land in the southwestern United States. The weather is hot and dry there for most of the year. It is a very difficult place for plants to grow.

Yet, rising out of the desert sand and scrub **brush** is an amazing sight—the giant saguaro (pronounced suh WAH row) cactus.

SAGUARO CACTUS

by Paul and Shirley Berquist

▲ The elf owl is only 5 inches long (13 centimeters). It is the smallest owl in the world. The elf owl is only one of the many birds that find a safe, dry home inside the cool saguaro.

A saguaro can live as long as 200 years. It can grow to 50 feet tall (15 meters) and weigh as much as 10 tons (9 metric tons). That's the weight of three or four automobiles.

From all over the desert, animals and birds walk, crawl, and fly to the saguaro. That's because a saguaro is much more than just a giant plant. It is the center of life for hundreds of creatures, including the tiny elf owl.

Life for a new saguaro begins in the summer, when warm rains come to the desert. This is also when the bright red fruit of a full-grown cactus falls to the ground. For desert creatures, it is time to feast!

Insects and birds feed on the sweet, juicy pulp of the saguaro's fruit. Mice and rabbits gobble up the soft, black seeds. By chance, a seed may stick to a mouse's paw or to a rabbit's ear. Perhaps the seed will travel with the animal to another place in the desert. And maybe it will fall to the ground and take root.

The desert is a harsh place for young saguaros. Most cactus seedlings die in the blazing heat. But a few lucky plants take root in shady spots, safe from the burning sun. In the shadow of a mesquite (mess KEET) tree, this ten-year-old saguaro is off to a good start.

The saguaro grows very slowly. After 50 years it stands only 10 feet tall (3 meters). Every spring lovely flowers appear. Each flower blooms for only one full day.

On this day, birds, bats, and insects may come to drink the nectar. This is the sweet liquid inside a flower. As the creatures drink, bits of flower dust, called pollen, stick to their bodies. At the next flower, a bit of pollen might fall off and start a new cactus.

The saguaro has long folds on its skin called pleats. These pleats allow the cactus to stretch. As it takes in water, the saguaro grows fatter and fatter. A fully grown saguaro can stretch until it holds several thousand pounds of water!

The saguaro's roots do not grow deep. They stay shallow to catch any bit of rainwater that drips through the ground. The roots spread out as much as 90 feet (27.5 meters), forming the shape of a giant bowl.

When there is no more nectar to drink, most of the creatures leave. But not the gila woodpecker. With its long, sharp beak the bird tap . . . tap . . . taps through the saguaro's tough skin to build a nest.

Soon, the woodpecker has drilled a hole that reaches deep inside the cactus. The dark hole makes a cool nesting place for the woodpecker's family. Safely inside, the birds hunt and feast on insects that would otherwise harm the saguaro.

A woodpecker family does not stay in the same nest for long. When the babies are ready to fly, the family moves on. Soon the family is tapping a new hole either in that cactus or in another.

As the woodpecker drills, a hard wall grows around the hole in the cactus's skin. This wall, called a boot, keeps the hole dry. It also keeps air from drying out the rest of the saguaro.

Even after the cactus dies, the boot stays hard and strong. No wonder the people of the desert look for cactus boots to use as dishes and bowls!

Old woodpecker nests do not stay empty. As soon as one kind of bird moves out, another moves in. Elf owls are among the first to take over. Unlike woodpeckers, however, these little owls may stay in the same hole for years.

Other birds, such as this starling, follow close behind. High up in the spiny saguaro, the birds find a safe, cool place to raise their families.

At 60 years of age, the cactus is almost 18 feet tall (5.5 meters). Now branches reach out from its sides like arms. There, white-winged doves build cozy nests. Red-tailed hawks and horned owls also find homes on the growing saguaro. Somehow, the sharp spines of the cactus do not get in their way.

By the time it is 75 years old, the saguaro is nearly 50 feet tall (15 meters) . . . and teeming with life! It is more like a crowded village than a plant.

Birds aren't the only creatures in search of a cool cactus home. Lizards, insects, and spiders also fill empty nest holes. The insects feed on the cactus. The lizards and spiders feed on the insects.

Mule deer and other animals come to eat the tender plants that grow in the shade of the saguaro. Still other creatures, such as the ringtail cat, perch at the top. Up here, they stay safe from coyotes and are free to spy on small prey.

Keen-eyed coyotes and bobcats hunt in the brush around the saguaro. Perhaps one of them will dine on a jackrabbit tonight.

▲ Coyotes are members of the dog family. Although they are excellent hunters, coyotes eat just about anything. Rabbits, gophers, rats, squirrels, reptiles, and insects are all food for coyotes. So are antelope, goats, and sheep. But when necessary, coyotes will even eat berries, melons, and beans!

For 150 years or more, the saguaro provides an important habitat for many desert creatures. But, in the end, old age and disease weaken the trunk of the great plant.

When this happens, desert winds topple the dead plant to the ground. Creatures living in the saguaro must move to a new cactus home.

After the saguaro dies, it is still necessary to desert life. Now the plant becomes a cool, shady home for creatures that live close to the desert floor.

Among others, scorpions, rattlesnakes, and horned lizards come to the dead saguaro looking for food and shelter.

Very, very slowly, the dead cactus decomposes, or rots away. Over time, it will return to the earth. For now, though, animals such as this javelina drop by. Using all its strength, the javelina tears at the fallen cactus. Could a meal of tender young plants lie beneath it?

But look! Just behind the javelina, a young, healthy saguaro is growing. Perhaps the javelina won't harm it.

With a good deal of luck, the young saguaro will continue to grow upward and outward into a grand cactus. And if it succeeds, it too will one day become home to the many creatures of the Sonoran Desert.

▲ Beneath the cactus's tough, spiny skin are long wooden ribs. These ribs hold up the giant plant. For hundreds of years they have been used by desert people for fences, roofs, and firewood.

▲ Javelinas are distant cousins of wild hogs. They have rough, gray-ish- black coats with silvery collars. Although javelinas feed mostly on roots, they sometimes prey on small animals.

Think and Respond

1. Why is the saguaro cactus an important **habitat** for creatures of the Sonoran Desert?
2. What pattern or structure do the authors use to organize the information in this selection?
3. Why do you think the authors decribe the saguaro cactus as **teeming** with life and more like a crowded village than a plant?
4. How does the desert compare with the area where you live?
5. What reading strategy did you use as you read "Saguaro Cactus"?

More About This Habitat

Desert Tortoise

With its strong legs and sharp claws, the desert tortoise is a great digger. At the end of fall, it digs a deep burrow in the sand where it will spend the winter.

Gila Woodpecker

Both gila woodpecker parents share the task of feeding and caring for their young. But at night, the father may sleep in a separate hole near the nest.

Wolf Spider

Wolf spiders are active hunters. Many stalk insects. They pounce on their prey the same way tigers do.

Mesquite Tree

The hardy mesquite tree grows where very few other plants can survive. It has many uses. Gum from its sap is even used to make candy!

Starling

The starling originally came from Europe. In 1890, about 60 starlings were set free in Central Park in New York City. Millions of starlings now live in the United States.

Bobcat

Bobcats sneak around dead saguaros, hunting for mice, pack rats, rabbits, and other small animals. Their fine senses of sight and hearing help them to catch their prey.

Meet the Authors

Paul and Shirley Berquist

When Paul and Shirley Berquist went to Arizona in 1968 on a job for the military, they decided to stay. In their years living in the desert southwest, they have made a second career out of photography. Their work has appeared on postcards and in books, magazines, and calendars. They have done educational programs for the Arizona–Sonora Desert Museum. Their photos have been used in several projects for Saguaro National Park. Although the Berquists have been as far away as Africa and South America with a camera, they especially like taking photographs of the wildlife near their home area.

Paul Berquist

Shirley Berquist

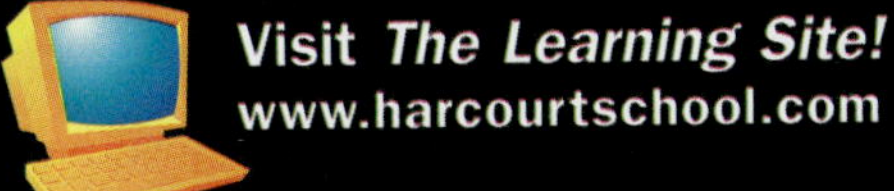
Visit *The Learning Site!*
www.harcourtschool.com

Genre
Poem
Award-Winning
Author
CACTUS POEMS
FRANK ASCH
&
TED LEVIN
Saguaro

Stand
still.
Grow
slow.
Lift
high
your arms to the sun.

Stand
still.
Grow
slow.
Lift
high
your
flowers to the sky.
Stand
still.
Grow
slow.
Hold
tight
your
water
inside.
Stand
still.
Grow
slow
and let your roots spread wide and let your roots spread wide.

by Frank Asch
photographs by Ted Levin

▲ Saguaro Cactus

Making Connections

Text to Self • Text to Text • Text To World

Compare Texts

NC STANDARDS: ELA 1.01 use word identification strategies, 1.02 use roots/prefixes/suffixes to decode/infer meanings, 3.01e interpret/evaluate text/draw inferences/conclusions, 3.02 analyze/compare texts

1. How is a saguaro cactus like a human community? CRITICAL STANCE / ANALYZING
2. Reread the photo captions in "Saguaro Cactus." How does the information in these captions differ from the information in the rest of the selection? COGNITION / EVALUATING
3. How do the authors of "Saguaro Cactus" and the poem "Saguaro" differ in their purposes and in the way they treat the same subject? CRITICAL STANCE / ANALYZING
4. How is the poem "Saguaro" different from most of the other poems you have read? CRITICAL STANCE / ANALYZING
5. Where would you look to find what national parks or wildlife refuges exist in the Sonoran Desert? INTERPRETATION / EVALUATING

Write a Persuasive Essay

Some people go into wilderness areas and dig up saguaros to sell. Think of reasons why saguaros should be protected. Write to persuade your audience to protect saguaros. Use a graphic organizer like this to arrange your ideas.

Audience: Opinion:
Reason 1: Examples/details:
Reason 2: Examples/details:
Opinion restated/action requested:

NC STANDARDS: ELA 3.01e interpret/evaluate text/draw inferences/conclusions, 3.05 use graphs/charts/maps to expand understanding; Science 1.01 observe/describe how an animal is affected by living/nonliving things

Develop a Chart

An ecosystem is made up of both living and nonliving things. Look back through the selection "Saguaro Cactus." Develop a two-column chart showing living and nonliving members of this desert ecosystem.

living	nonliving
cactus snakes	sand rocks

NC STANDARDS: ELA 3.05 use graphs/charts/maps to expand understanding; Math 4.03 compare two sets of data

Make a Bar Graph

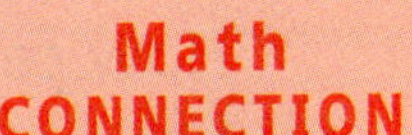

A saguaro may grow as tall as 50 feet. That is taller than some trees. Do research to find out how tall three different types of trees can grow. Look for information in an encyclopedia (in print or online) or in a book about trees. Create a bar graph to compare the heights of these three plants.

▲ Saguaro Cactus

NC STANDARDS: ELA 2.04c identify main idea/details

Elements of Nonfiction

Authors organize expository texts in different ways, including main idea and details, cause and effect, or sequence of events. Knowing how a text is organized can help you understand the selection. It can also help you find information in it.

"Saguaro Cactus" is organized according to the sequence of events in the life of a saguaro cactus. This time line shows some of those events.

Life of a Saguaro Cactus

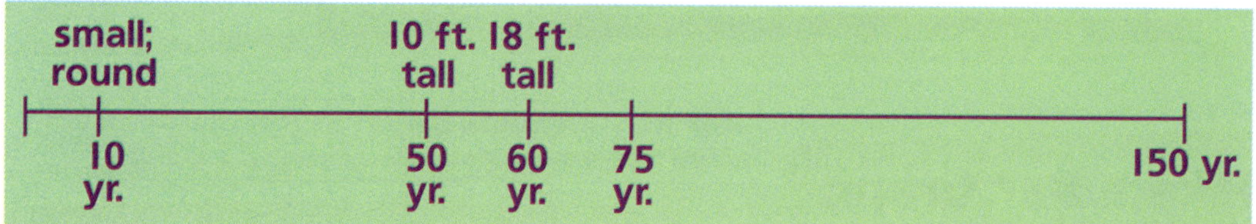

How can you find the information to complete the time line? Because the selection is organized by sequence, you know that you need to look toward the middle of the selection to find out what the saguaro is like when it is 75 years old. Where would you locate facts about the saguaro when it is 150 years old?

You can use the headings, illustrations, and other graphics in this selection to help you find information, too. For example, if you wanted to locate information about coyotes, the photograph of a coyote on page 557 would help you know where to look in the text.

Visit *The Learning Site!*
www.harcourtschool.com

See *Skills and Activities*

Test Prep
Elements of Nonfiction

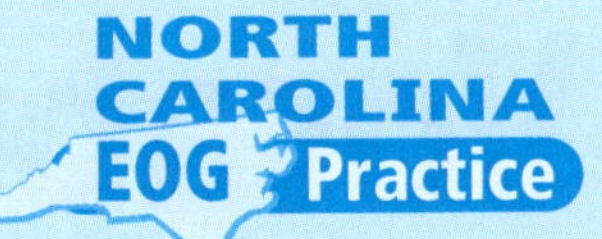

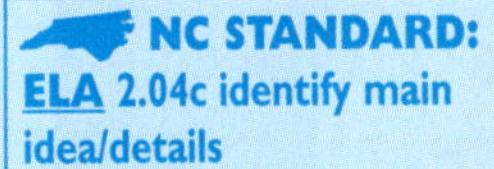

ELA 2.04c identify main idea/details

▶ **Read the passage. Then answer the questions.**

The Mesquite Tree

DESCRIPTION OF A MESQUITE TREE

Mesquite trees grow in the southwestern United States. Its flowers grow on a long stalk. Its fruit is in the form of a pod.

PRODUCTS FROM MESQUITE TREES

The wood of the mesquite tree is used to make railroad ties and fence posts. Mesquite pods are used as feed for livestock.

CRITICAL STANCE / INTEGRATING

1. What is the function of the phrase *Description of a Mesquite Tree*?

A It is the title of this article.

B It introduces a sequence of events.

C It is a caption for an illustration.

D It is a heading that tells the main idea of the section.

Tip

Find the phrase in the passage and reread it. Ask yourself how it is related to the passage.

CRITICAL STANCE / INTEGRATING

2. What information would you *not* expect to find in a section called *The Habitat of the Mesquite Tree*?

F other plants and animals that live in the same place

G the kind of climate where mesquite trees grow

H how the mesquite tree survives in its environment

J how the mesquite tree got its name

Pay attention to the word *not* in the question. Which detail is *not* about where mesquite trees grow?

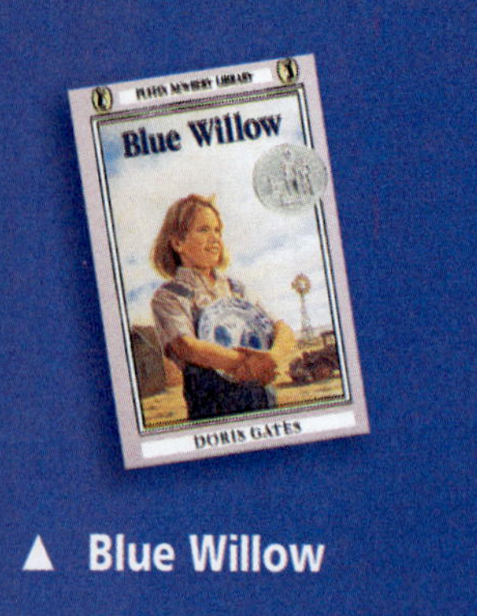

▲ Blue Willow

Vocabulary Power

- sulkily
- certainty
- indifferent
- undoubtedly
- heartily
- protruded
- loathe

In "Blue Willow," a girl named Janey expects her new school to be as bad as all the others she has attended. The girl in the sketches below expects her brother to draw her looking silly, as he usually does. Expecting new experiences to match earlier ones can be useful, but it can also result in surprises.

Here's Tammy looking at me **sulkily**. She's unhappy because she thinks it's a **certainty** that I'll draw her with a clown's nose or elephant ears. She is sure that I'll make her look silly.

This is Tammy pretending to be **indifferent**. She's acting as if she doesn't care what happens.

Now Tammy's watching TV. She's **undoubtedly** watching a funny show. I know it without a doubt because she's laughing **heartily**, with great enthusiasm.

Here's how Tammy would look if a carrot **protruded** from the top of her head. This giant one really sticks out! Tammy hates pictures like this. I know she would **loathe** this one.

This is Tammy looking surprised. She says my sketches really look like her. (I didn't show her the one with the carrot!)

Most people have a chore that they loathe. Pick a chore you especially dislike, and make a list of ways to make it more enjoyable.

BLUE

Genre

Realistic Fiction

Realistic fiction tells about characters and events that are like people and events in real life.

In this selection, look for

- **A setting that could be a real place**
- **Realistic characters and events**

WILLOW

by Doris Gates
illustrated by Robert Crawford

Janey's father works in the fields, picking crops. Her family, like those of many other migrant workers in the 1940s, must always move on to wherever workers are needed. The family takes only basic necessities with them, except for a blue willow plate that belonged to Janey's great-great-grandmother. To Janey, the plate is a reminder of the time when they had a home. When she discovers a place that reminds her of the picture on the plate and finds a friend, Lupe, she begins to hope that this time they will stay.

Janey and Dad were on their way to the cotton fields. Dad was going to work; Janey was going to school. It was October now. The sun, though bright and warm, was not hot as it had been a month ago, and the mountains, as if rewarding the valley for milder weather, were allowing their blue outlines to be seen. Wild sunflowers turned bright faces to the east, and occasional dust devils went spiraling off across the plain in merry abandon. But Janey, huddled in a corner of the ragged front seat, was sulkily indifferent to the world around her. The corners of her mouth sagged, her lower lip protruded in something close to a pout, and her eyes glowered darkly. She wasn't glad to be going to school, not this school at any rate. If only she were being taken to the town school, the one where Lupe and all the other children of the district went! That is, they did if they belonged to the district. Janey was well aware that actually she herself could have attended that school, too. There was no law forbidding it. But it was a fact, too, that in some communities she

would have been extremely unwelcome, and Dad, knowing this, had made his own law in respect to Janey.

"We'll keep with our own kind," he had once said when she had remonstrated with him. "The camp schools are put there for us to use and so we'll use them and be thankful. Besides, a body can learn anywhere if he's a mind to."

Janey hadn't argued further with him on that occasion and she had no desire to do so today. She knew that going to the "regular" school would no longer satisfy her anyway, for just going there couldn't make her really belong. Since she had begun to want to stay in this place, merely going to the district school was no longer enough. What Janey wanted was to belong to this place and to go to the district school because as a member of the community it was her right to go there. The camp school would now be a daily and forceful reminder of the fact that she didn't belong, and so she dreaded it.

She knew what the camp school would be like. No two of the children would have learned the same things, and it would all be a jumble. In some lessons, Janey would find herself way

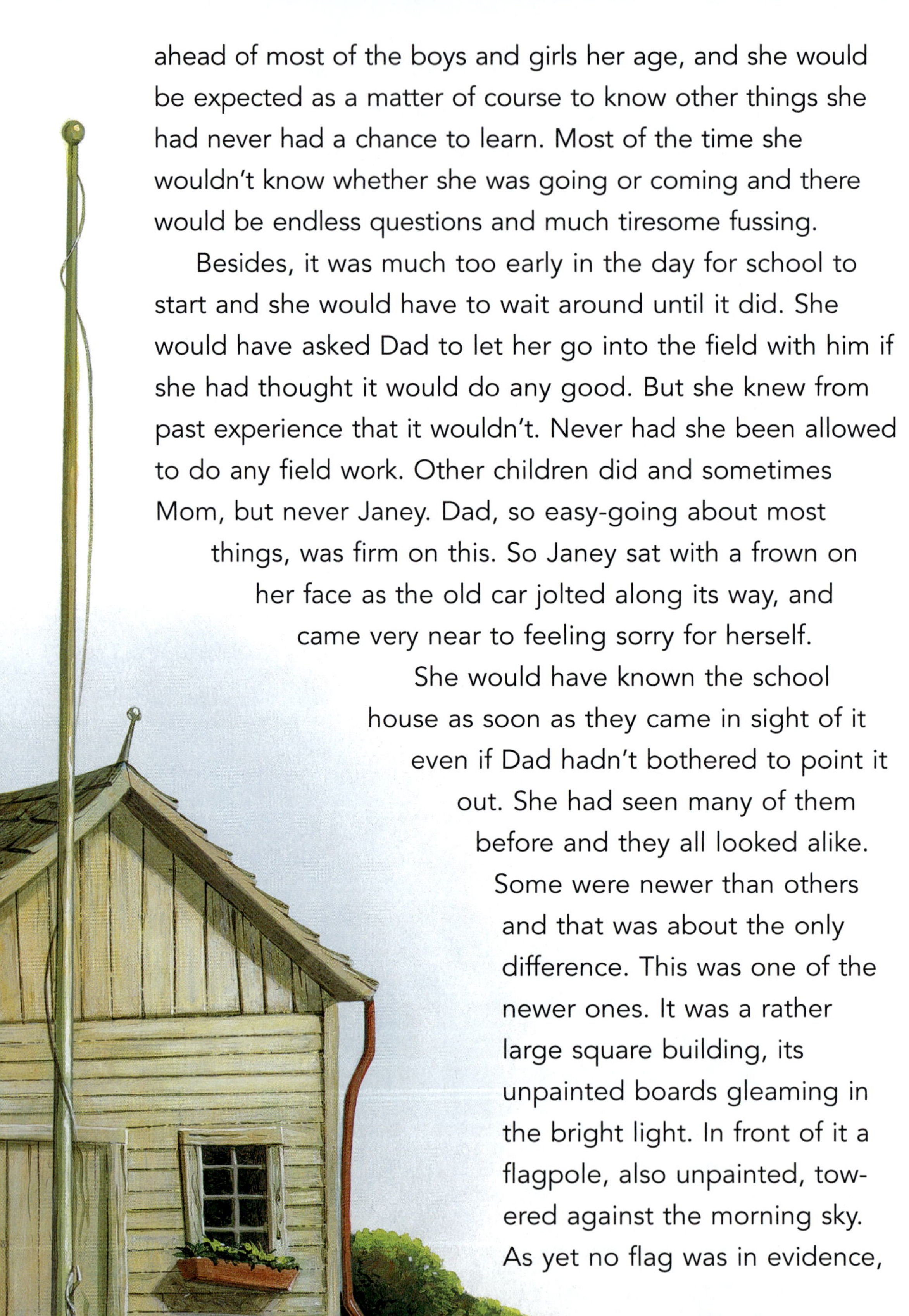

ahead of most of the boys and girls her age, and she would be expected as a matter of course to know other things she had never had a chance to learn. Most of the time she wouldn't know whether she was going or coming and there would be endless questions and much tiresome fussing.

Besides, it was much too early in the day for school to start and she would have to wait around until it did. She would have asked Dad to let her go into the field with him if she had thought it would do any good. But she knew from past experience that it wouldn't. Never had she been allowed to do any field work. Other children did and sometimes Mom, but never Janey. Dad, so easy-going about most things, was firm on this. So Janey sat with a frown on her face as the old car jolted along its way, and came very near to feeling sorry for herself.

She would have known the school house as soon as they came in sight of it even if Dad hadn't bothered to point it out. She had seen many of them before and they all looked alike. Some were newer than others and that was about the only difference. This was one of the newer ones. It was a rather large square building, its unpainted boards gleaming in the bright light. In front of it a flagpole, also unpainted, towered against the morning sky. As yet no flag was in evidence, so Janey knew for sure that school had not yet started. Her father let her off at the front steps, then drove over to park beside a row of cars that looked as if they might all have come from the same junk pile. Janey sat down to wait, her package of lunch beside her.

Across from her were the cottages, row upon row, that comprised the camp. Looking at these little one-room sheds so close together that their eaves almost touched, she was thankful for their own shack and the spreading country around it. Of course there was plenty of country spread around here. But the camp itself was squeezed into as small a space as possible so as not to use up any more of the cotton ground than was absolutely necessary. The deep green of the cotton plants reached in every direction almost as far as the eye could see. And here and there against the green of every bush a gleam of white showed clearly. That was where a cotton boll had burst open to free the fluffy fibers which would be picked by hand from each boll. There would be thousands, perhaps millions, of these little white bunches and it would take many fingers working many hours a day to pick all the ripening cotton. That is why there was a village of little houses at this place with a school house at hand. During the picking season hundreds of people lived here and worked here until the day should come when all the cotton was harvested. Then they would load their cars with what household goods they owned, and with their boys and girls the cotton pickers would move on to some other part of the country which needed their hands and their heads.

Of course, Janey wasn't thinking of all this while she sat on the steps of the school house. It was so much a part of her life that she didn't bother to think about it any more than she bothered to think about the processes of breathing when she drew fresh air into her lungs.

For perhaps ten minutes, Janey sat there, a blue-overalled figure of gloom, when all at once she caught a movement in the dust in front of her. It was so slight a movement that at first she thought her eyes were playing her tricks. But in the next second, the dust was again stirred, and then she was off the school house steps in one lunge. Flat on the ground she hurled herself, one arm reaching out ahead of her. Slowly she drew in her arm, her hand tightly closed, and gathered herself up. From head to foot she was coated with fine dirt, but she didn't care. She didn't even stop to brush herself off before she slowly began to open her fingers, squinting closely at what she held there. A smile widened across her face, for in the shadowy hollow of her palm was a small horned toad. Its eyes, mere pinheads of glistening black, stared fiercely at her, and its chinless mouth was set grimly. But Janey was not alarmed. She had captured many horned toads before this and knew that for all their fierce expression and spiky covering, they were quite harmless creatures. Slowly she lowered herself onto the school house steps once more to inspect her captive. To most people he would have appeared far from beautiful, but to Janey he seemed an object of delight. His four tiny feet with their minute claws were perfect, and from the fringe of miniature scales outlining what should have been his chin, to the last infinitesimal spike on the end of his brief tail, he was finished and complete. Janey loved him at once and began cautiously to draw her finger across his hard little head.

Suddenly an idea occurred to her. She would use this horned toad to test the new teacher. In every school she had ever been, someone had always solemnly assured her whenever she happened to mention a "horned toad" that she should call them "horned lizards," for they were not really toads at all. Janey had always been entirely willing to accept the fact that they were not, strictly speaking, "horned toads," but to call them anything else just wasn't possible. The minute you said "horned lizard" you turned a perfectly good horned toad into a new and unattractive animal. She would loathe having anyone refer to her new pet as a horned lizard, and if the new teacher did so, Janey's respect for her as a human being would be completely shattered. It would be, she thought, like saying "It is I" instead of "It's me." If you used the former, you would be correct, but you wouldn't be a friend. She was determined to discover whether the new teacher was a friend or merely correct.

She and the horned toad had not long to wait. Janey had hardly got some of the dirt brushed off when a dusty sedan rolled to a halt in the shade of the school house and a fat and smiling woman got out of it. Janey felt hopeful.

"Hello," called the woman. "No ten-o'clock-scholar about you, is there?"

Janey felt increasingly hopeful as she rose to meet this stranger who was undoubtedly the teacher. Surely no one who quoted Mother Goose to you before she had asked your name would call a horned toad a horned lizard. More than that, she would know what to do with you if you were good in reading and poor in arithmetic. Suddenly the whole tone of the day was changed. But the final test was yet to come.

"Look," said Janey, holding out her captive.

"Well, bless my soul," said the woman heartily, bending over Janey's hand, "a horned toad! Did you catch it?"

Janey nodded, too delighted for the moment to speak, then: "But I haven't named him yet."

"Can't let him go without a name. Let's see." The woman thought a moment. Then, "I have it. Let's call him Fafnir. He was a first-class dragon when giants ruled the

earth. And this fellow looks a lot like a dragon. A fairy dragon. Does Fafnir appeal to you?"

Janey nodded.

The teacher chuckled. "I suppose the proper thing would be to let the horned toad decide such an important matter for himself. But from the look of him I should say that he wasn't quite on speaking terms with us yet."

She looked at Janey with eyes that were merry and direct. Trustworthy eyes with friendly secrets in their depths.

"I am Miss Peterson," she said.

"I'm Janey Larkin."

A stout arm encircled Janey's narrow shoulders and for a brief moment she felt herself squeezed against Miss Peterson's warm and well-cushioned side.

"Welcome to Camp Miller school, Janey. Come on inside. We'll start the day together."

No questions, no fussing. Just "Come on in," as if she had known you always. Janey slid an arm around Miss Peterson's ample waist and together they entered the building, the small girl walking on tiptoe, to her teacher's secret amusement. Miss Peterson would have been surprised

to know she was the innocent cause of that strange behavior. For Janey was thrilling to the certainty that this very morning, unexpectedly and alone, she had discovered the most wonderful teacher in the world. That was enough to make anyone prance on tiptoe! A few minutes ago she had been feeling sorry for herself and all the time there had been Fafnir and Miss Peterson. Not even Lupe going to the "regular" school could possibly have enjoyed such luck as that!

During the next half hour Janey helped Miss Peterson prepare for the day's work. She cleaned the blackboards and put the tables and benches in order. Some pink petunias were blooming in a window box and Janey watered them from the standing pipe outside the door. Then she picked off the withered blossoms, which left her fingers so sticky she had to return to the water pipe to wash her hands. Soon the boys and girls began to arrive. The school day started at nine o'clock when one of the boys carried the flag out to the unpainted pole

and fastened it to the rope neatly secured there. While the whole school stood grouped at attention, the flag was drawn slowly up into the morning sky until at last it came to rest at the pole's very top and the Stars and Stripes was unfolded above the school and the camp. The little ceremony ended, they all trooped to their lessons.

As the morning advanced, Janey's regard for Miss Peterson increased, if that were possible. Because they were crowded on the benches, and because their legs were not all long enough to reach the floor, she saw to it that the children were given time to move around and rest. And it seemed to be the custom for two or three of the children to tell the others each day which part of the country they had thought the most interesting in their traveling around. Janey, listening to the others this morning, decided, when her turn came, to tell about the place by the river which she had discovered the other day. The place like the willow plate.

Think and Respond

1. Why is Janey **sulkily indifferent** at the beginning of the story? How and why do her feelings change?
2. Why is the horned toad important to the plot of the story?
3. What reason might Janey's parents have for not allowing her to do field work?
4. Do you think Janey will have a better experience at her new school than she has had in other camp schools? Explain your answer.
5. As you read "Blue Willow," what reading strategies did you use? How were they helpful?

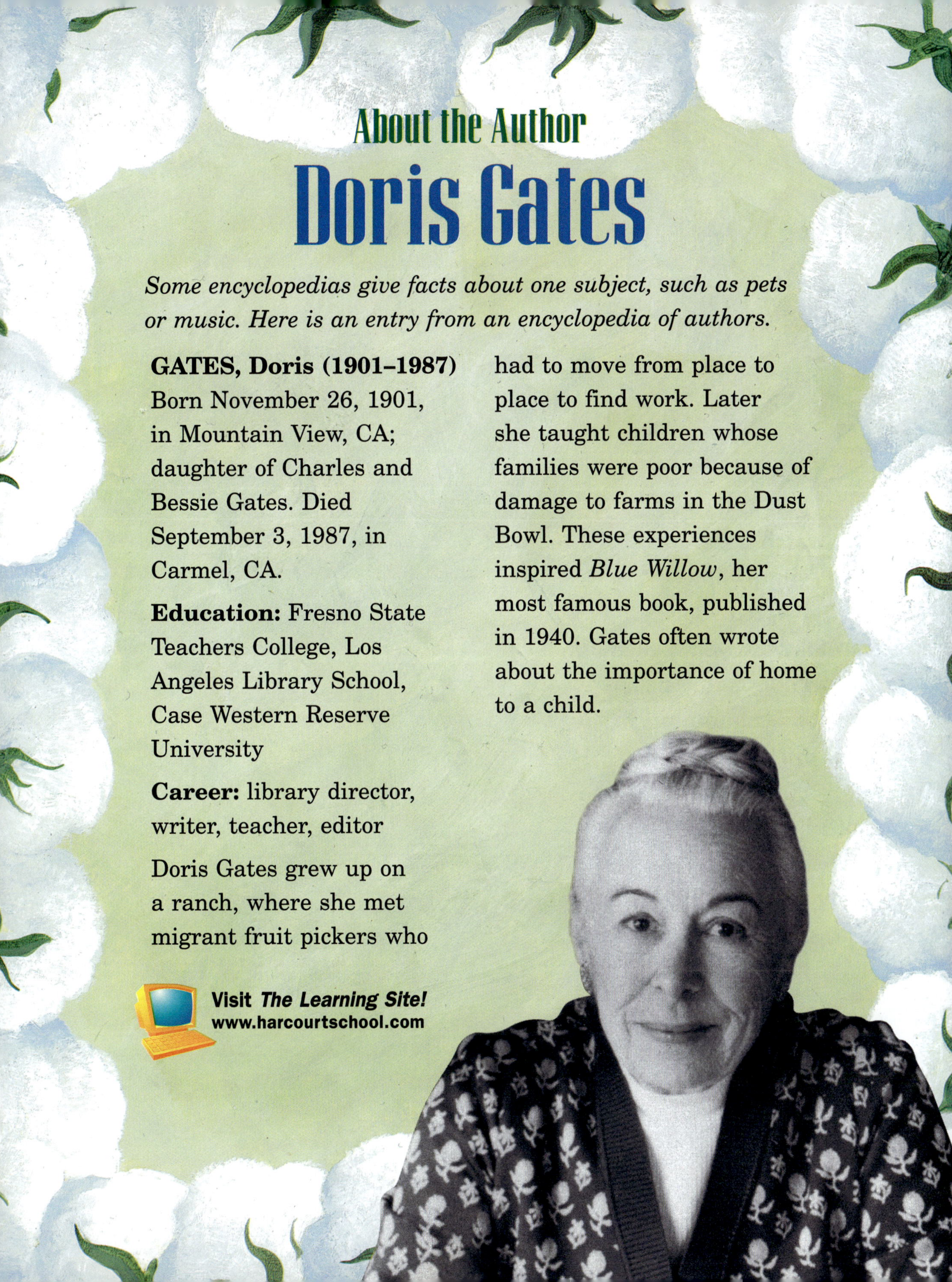

About the Author

Doris Gates

Some encyclopedias give facts about one subject, such as pets or music. Here is an entry from an encyclopedia of authors.

GATES, Doris (1901–1987) Born November 26, 1901, in Mountain View, CA; daughter of Charles and Bessie Gates. Died September 3, 1987, in Carmel, CA.

Education: Fresno State Teachers College, Los Angeles Library School, Case Western Reserve University

Career: library director, writer, teacher, editor

Doris Gates grew up on a ranch, where she met migrant fruit pickers who had to move from place to place to find work. Later she taught children whose families were poor because of damage to farms in the Dust Bowl. These experiences inspired *Blue Willow*, her most famous book, published in 1940. Gates often wrote about the importance of home to a child.

Genre
Poem

Horned Lizard

Still as a rock,
you watch bees, ants,
your wriggly lunch.
I watch you,
carefully put you, bellybulge
pincushion, in my palm,
just for a minute touch
your prickly top.
Puff. A warm balloon
puffs in my hand.
Plop
away you hop across hot sand,
soft, spiny desert creature,
like me.

by **Pat Mora**
pictures by **Steve Jenkins**

Award-Winning
Author

▲ Blue Willow

Making Connections

Text to Self • Text to Text • Text To World

Compare Texts

NC STANDARDS: ELA 3.01e interpret/evaluate text/draw inferences/conclusions, 3.02 analyze/compare texts

1. Why do you think "Blue Willow" is included in the theme Community Ties? INTERPRETATION / ANALYZING
2. How is the Camp Miller school different from what Janey expects? CRITICAL STANCE / ANALYZING
3. Compare the viewpoints of the authors of "Blue Willow" and "Horned Lizard" on the subject of horned lizards. CRITICAL STANCE / ANALYZING
4. Think of another realistic fiction story you have read that tells about a character's experiences in school. Which character's experiences seemed more realistic to you, and why? CRITICAL STANCE / EVALUATING
5. After reading the excerpt from *Blue Willow*, would you want to read the rest of the novel? Why or why not? INTERPRETATION / EVALUATING

Write a Description

Writing CONNECTION

Both "Blue Willow" and "Horned Lizard" give vivid descriptions of horned lizards. Choose an animal to describe. Then write a clear, colorful description of the animal. Use a graphic organizer like this one to decide on sensory details you want to include in your description.

Details:

Sight	Hearing	Touch	Smell

NC STANDARDS: ELA 1.05 use reference materials to find word meanings, 3.05 use graphs/charts/maps to expand understanding

Make a Cause-and-Effect Chart

Social Studies CONNECTION

Many Americans became migrant workers after the Dust Bowl in the 1930s destroyed their farms. Do research to learn more about the Dust Bowl. Find out what caused it and what effect it had on people's lives. Organize your information in a cause-and-effect chart like this.

The Dust Bowl

Cause	→	Effect
Cause	→	Effect

NC STANDARDS: Science 1.03 observe/discuss how an animal's behavior/body aids survival

Research an Animal

Science CONNECTION

Although the horned lizard appears fierce, it is actually very gentle. Like many gentle animals, the horned lizard has several unique ways of protecting itself from predators. Research the horned lizard or a similar animal that lives in your region. Find out how it defends itself. Draw a picture that illustrates the animal's method of self-defense. Then write a caption beneath your picture to explain it.

▲ Blue Willow

NC STANDARDS: ELA 1.04h increase vocabulary/examine author's craft, 2.01a use strategies to clarify text/vocabulary/reread

Author's Purpose

Doris Gates wrote "Blue Willow" to entertain readers. You know that an **author's purpose**, or reason, for writing may be to entertain, to inform, or to persuade. An **author's perspective**, or viewpoint, is the way he or she feels about a topic.

You can figure out an author's perspective by thinking about the details the author includes. Knowing something about the author can also help you understand his or her perspective.

Details from Story

Migrant workers move from place to place.

Not all children in camp have learned the same things.

Janey is happy because Miss Peterson cares about the children and seems to understand their needs.

About Doris Gates

She grew up on a ranch.

She met migrant fruit pickers.

She was a teacher of farm children whose families were poor as a result of the Dust Bowl.

Author's Perspective

All children deserve good schools and good teachers.

To figure out the author's perspective, ask yourself:

- How does the author seem to feel about the topic?
- How can I tell?

Visit *The Learning Site!*
www.harcourtschool.com

See *Skills* and *Activities*

Test Prep
Author's Purpose

ELA 1.04h increase vocabulary/examine author's craft

▶ **Read the passage. Then answer the questions.**

> **The horned lizard, also known as a horned toad, is a lizard but has the rounded shape of a toad. Its horns are actually spikes on the back of its head and along the sides of its body.**
>
> **Horned lizards puff up their bodies and spray blood from the corners of their eyes when they feel they are in danger. It is best to observe them in their own habitats rather than to keep them as pets. The Texas horned lizard can no longer be found in many areas where it once lived. It is now protected by the state of Texas.**

COGNITION / EVALUATING

1. What is the author's main purpose for writing this article?

A to entertain

B to inform readers about a topic

C to persuade

D to sell a product

Ask yourself whether a passage is fiction or nonfiction to help you narrow your choices.

COGNITION / EVALUATING

2. What is the author's perspective in this article?

F There is no need to protect horned lizards.

G Lizards are dangerous and should be avoided.

H Horned lizards make interesting pets.

J Horned lizards should be left in their own habitats.

Remember to ask yourself how the author feels about the topic and how you can tell.

▲ In My Family

Vocabulary Power

"In My Family" tells about some of the traditions one family follows. In the story below, another family has its own special customs and favorite foods for celebrating the Fourth of July.

- barbecue
- chile
- mesquite
- accordion
- confetti
- culture

Every year on the Fourth of July, my family gets together for a picnic. We always use a **barbecue** grill to cook the hot dogs and hamburgers. This special kind of grill gives the meat a delicious flavor!

I like spicy food, so I usually put a sliced **chile** pepper on my hamburger. My mother and I are the only people in our family who can handle eating this type of pepper. The others think chiles are too hot to eat.

After I finish eating, I relax in the shade of a **mesquite** tree. This kind of tree grows in the southwestern United States and Mexico.

I always bring along my **accordion** to play at the picnic. This musical instrument has lots of buttons, and it was hard to learn to play it. After I perform, all my family members applaud and shower me with **confetti**. It takes a long time afterward to pick up these tiny pieces of colored paper!

I'm glad that Fourth of July picnics are a part of our United States **culture**. This custom is so much fun! My family believes it is important for us all to celebrate this special holiday together.

Vocabulary–Writing
CONNECTION

A **chile** is very spicy. Write a few sentences describing what it feels like to eat a spicy food.

Award-Winning Author/ Illustrator

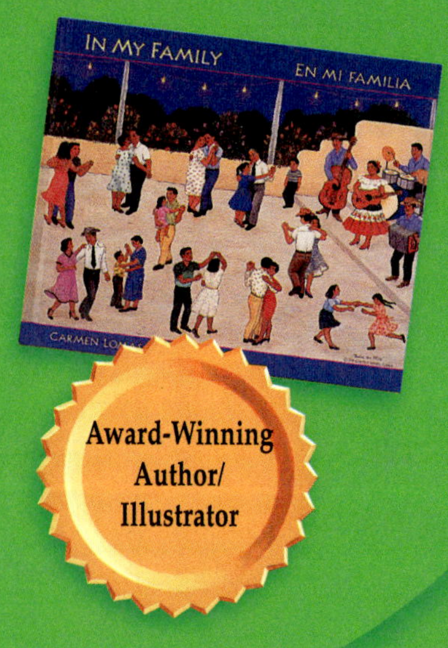

In My

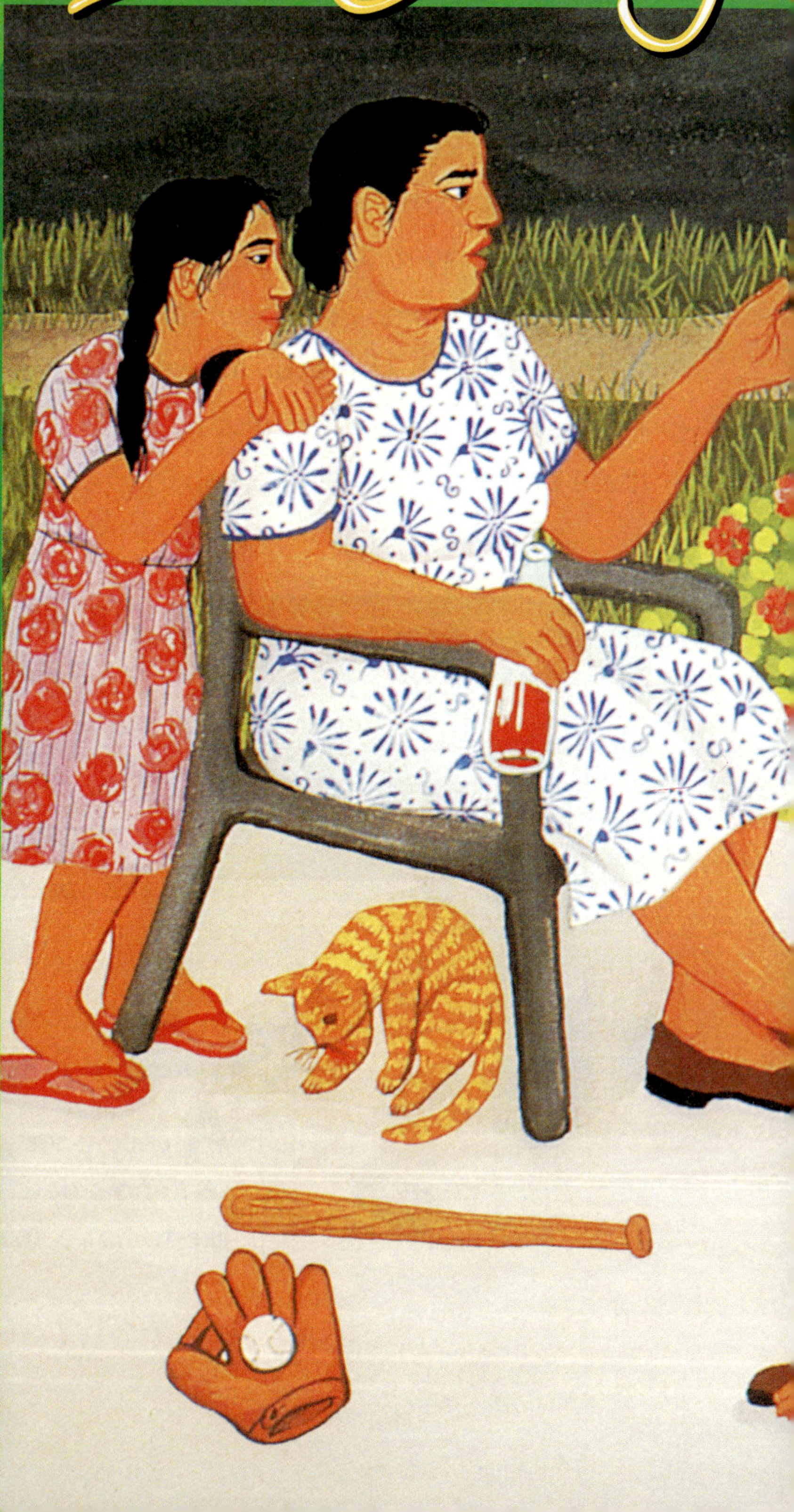

Genre

Autobiography

An autobiography is a person's account of his or her own life.

In this selection, look for

- **The first-person point of view**
- **Details about important events in the author's life**

Family

by Carmen Lomas Garza

*Every time I paint, it serves a purpose—to bring about pride in our Mexican American **culture**. The paintings and stories in this book are my memories of growing up in Kingsville, Texas, near the border with Mexico.*

— Carmen Lomas Garza

The Horned Toads

When we were kids, my mother and grandmother would get mad at us for playing in the hot sun in the middle of the day. They'd say we were just like the horned toads at high noon, playing outside without a care.

I was fascinated by the horned toads. They're shaped like frogs, but they're not frogs. They're lizards. They have horns all over their bodies to protect them from bigger animals that want to eat them.

Here's my brother Arturo, trying to feed an ant to a horned toad. I'm behind him, on my toes, because I don't want the ants to crawl up on me. Those are fire ants. They can really sting.

Cleaning Nopalitos

This is my grandfather, Antonio Lomas. He's shaving off the thorns from freshly-cut cactus pads, called *nopalitos*. My sister Margie is watching him work.

Nopalitos are called "the food of last resort," because back when there were no refrigerators and your winter food supply would run out, you knew you could eat the cactus pads through the last days of winter and the early days of spring.

My grandmother would boil the *nopalitos* in salt water, cut them up, and stir-fry them with chile and eggs for breakfast.

Empanadas

Once every year my Aunt Paz and Uncle Beto would make dozens and dozens of *empanadas*, sweet turnovers filled with sweet potato or squash from their garden. They would invite all the relatives and friends to come over, and you could eat as many as you wanted. They lived in a little one-bedroom house, and every surface in the house was covered with a plate of *empanadas*. There was no place to sit down.

There's Uncle Beto, rolling out the dough. Aunt Paz, in the yellow dress with the red flowers, is spreading in the filling. My mother and father are drinking coffee. That's me in the blue dress.

Birthday Barbecue

This is my sister Mary Jane's birthday party. She's hitting a piñata that my mother made. My mother also baked and decorated the cake. There she is, bringing the meat that's ready to cook. My father is cooking at the barbecue, which he designed and built himself. My grandfather is shoveling in the coals of mesquite wood.

Underneath the tree are some young teenagers, very much in love. My great uncle is comforting my young cousin, who was crying, and encouraging him to hit the piñata. My grandmother is holding a baby. She was always holding the babies, and feeding them, and putting them to sleep.

Easter Eggs

This is my parents' dining room. My mother and brothers and sisters and I are gathered around the table decorating eggshells, *cascarones*, for Easter Sunday. We would fill them with confetti, which we made by cutting up newspapers and magazines.

On Easter Sunday, after church, we would go swimming. After swimming, we'd eat, and after eating, we'd bring out the *cascarones*. We would sneak up on our brothers or sisters or friends, break the *cascarones* on their heads, and rub the confetti into their hair. Sometimes my brothers would put flour into the eggshells, so that when they broke them on your wet head, the flour would turn to paste. That's how sneaky my brothers were sometimes.

Dance at El Jardín

This is a Saturday night at *El Jardín*, a neighborhood restaurant in my home town. It's the summer, so warm that you can dance outside. A *conjunto* band is playing—drums, accordion, guitar, and bass. This is the music I grew up with. Everybody's dancing in a big circle: the young couples, the older couples, and the old folks dancing with the teenagers or children. Even babies get to dance.

I learned to dance from my father and grandfather. This is where my love of dance started. To me, dance means *fiesta*, celebration. You have the music, the beautiful clothes, and all the family members dancing together. It's like heaven. It is heaven.

Think and Respond

1. How does the author feel about her childhood? Use the paintings to help you answer the question.
2. How does the author give information about Mexican American **culture** through her paintings?
3. How can you tell that the author grew up in a desert region?
4. Which of the paintings do you like best? Why do you like it?
5. What reading strategy did you use as you read this selection? Give an example of how using this strategy helped you.

Meet the Author and Illustrator

Carmen Lomas Garza

How old were you when you started making art?

I was thirteen years old when I decided to become an artist. I taught myself how to draw by practicing every day. I drew whatever was in front of me—books, cats, my left hand, my sisters and brothers, chairs, chilies, paper bags, flowers—anything or anybody that would stay still for a few minutes.

How long does it take you to make a painting?

It takes from two to nine months to complete a painting. I can paint for about six hours a day and then my fingers and eyes get tired. I do not paint every single day because I also have to work in my office to write letters, make telephone calls, and keep records for my art business.

Answers Questions from Children

Do you sell your artwork?

I have sold most of my paintings and lithograph prints. Sometimes it is very difficult to let go of paintings because I get very attached to them—just like parents get very attached to their children and do not want them to move out of their home.

Which painting is your favorite?

I can't really say which painting is my favorite, but I do like to paint interiors like bedrooms and kitchens. My favorite thing to paint is clothing. I can still remember some of the colors and designs of the clothing that my mother sewed for me.

CARMEN LOMAS GARZA

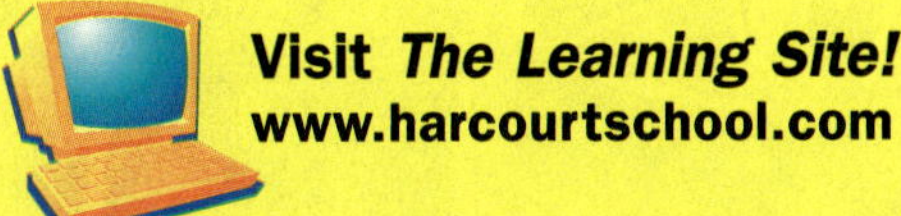

Visit *The Learning Site!*
www.harcourtschool.com

Did you go to college?

I have three college degrees. When I was in high school I could hardly wait to graduate so I could go to college and study art. My parents insisted that all of us go to college to study whatever we wanted.

My Village

by Isaac Olaleye
illustrated by Stéphan Daigle

Ẹ̀rín is the name
Of my African village.
Laughter is what Ẹ̀rín means
In the Yoruba language.

In streams,
Women and children
Still collect water in gourds and clay pots,
Which they balance on their heads.

Electric light has not shone in my village.
With ruby-red palm oil
Poured into a clay vessel
We see at night.

My village of Ẹ̀rín is peaceful,
Like a hidden world.
It's ringed by radiant green
And surrounded by five streams.

Like a stream,
The love
For my village
Flows.

▲ In My Family

Making Connections

Text to Self • Text to Text • Text To World

Compare Texts

NC STANDARDS: ELA 2.04b identify theme, 2.04c identify main idea/details, 3.01d interpret/evaluate text/analyze differences among genres, 3.02 analyze/compare texts

1. Why is the selection "In My Family" included in a theme called Community Ties? INTERPRETATION / EVALUATING
2. How are the first two paintings different from the rest? INTERPRETATION / APPLYING
3. How are Carmen Lomas Garza's autobiography and Isaac Olaleye's poem "My Village" alike? How are they different? CRITICAL STANCE / ANALYZING
4. What other autobiography have you read? How is it similar to and different from "In My Family"? CRITICAL STANCE / ANALYZING
5. What topics in "In My Family" did you find especially interesting? How could you find out more about them? INTERPRETATION / EVALUATING

Write a Personal Narrative

Writing CONNECTION

In this selection, the author tells about important events and celebrations from her childhood. Think about an important event or celebration in your childhood. Write a personal narrative to tell about this experience. You may want to use a graphic organizer like the one shown here to help you plan.

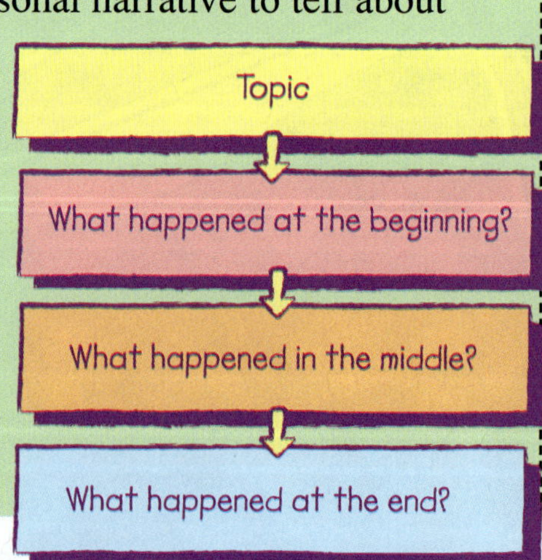

NC STANDARDS: ELA 1.05 use reference materials to find word meanings, 3.05 use graphs/charts/maps to expand understanding, 3.06 conduct research using a variety of tools

Compare and Contrast

Science CONNECTION

The author points out that a horned toad is not really a toad. It is a lizard. Lizards are reptiles. Toads are amphibians. Research the characteristics of reptiles and amphibians. Then make a Venn diagram to show the similarities and differences between reptiles and amphibians.

Reptiles
dry skin

Both
cold-blooded

Amphibians
moist skin

NC STANDARD: ELA 4.03a use visual aids

Paint a Scene

Art CONNECTION

The paintings in "In My Family" are like photographs from the artist's childhood. Ask a family member or friend to lend you a photograph from their past. Talk with the person to find out more information about what is happening in the photograph. Paint a picture based on the photograph and on details from your conversation. Write a paragraph about the scene, and display it with your painting.

▲ In My Family

Sequence

NC STANDARD: ELA 5.08b demonstrate language cohesion/use time order sequence of events

In the selection "In My Family," Carmen Lomas Garza uses paintings and text to tell about events from her childhood.

In a story, the plot is organized according to sequence. In expository writing, passages or whole articles may be organized according to sequence.

In this selection, Carmen Lomas Garza often organizes information according to sequence. The chart below shows the sequence of events in the selection called Easter Eggs.

Before Easter, the family gathers around the table to make *cascarones*.

↓

The eggs are filled with confetti.

↓

On Easter Sunday, the family members go to church.

↓

They go swimming.

↓

They eat.

↓

They bring out the *cascarones* and break them on the heads of family and friends.

What other sections in "In My Family" are organized by sequence?

Visit *The Learning Site!*
www.harcourtschool.com

See Skills and Activities

Test Prep

Sequence

NC STANDARD: ELA 5.08b demonstrate language cohesion/use time order sequence of events

▶ **Read the article. Then answer the questions.**

The exhibition of paintings by Carlos Puente opened today at the Fine Arts Gallery. Puente's work features scenes from his childhood in Puerto Rico.

In an interview, Mr. Puente explained how he creates each painting. He says, "First, I choose photographs from my childhood. Next, I choose strong, lively colors. Then, I let my imagination take over."

Carlos Puente closed the interview by encouraging people to come see his exhibit at the Fine Arts Gallery.

COGNITION / ORGANIZING

1. What does Carlos Puente do before he chooses colors?

A He chooses photographs.

B He lets his imagination take over.

C He explains why he paints.

D He exhibits his other paintings.

Tip

Look for words such as *first*, *next*, and *then* to help you understand the sequence of events.

COGNITION / ORGANIZING

2. How is the information in the interview organized?

F by main idea and details

G by cause and effect

H by sequence of events

J in order of importance

Tip

Think about how to organize the steps in a process.

THEME
6
NEW
LANDS
N
E
S
W

CONTENTS

▲ The Gold Rush

Vocabulary Power

abandoned

rugged

profitable

beckons

multicultural

fares

Sometimes events occur that cause people to move from one place to another. You will learn about one such event in "The Gold Rush." There are also many other reasons why people move to a new place.

This barn was **abandoned**, or deserted, years ago. The people who lived on the farm left. Why? Maybe they left because the land was too **rugged**, or rough, for them to make a living. Maybe they left because the farm was not **profitable** and they needed to earn more money.

Sometimes the promise of an easier life in the city **beckons** to farmers. City life attracts them by offering them a chance to leave their long days of hard work behind. Whatever the reason, something convinced the owners of that old barn that they could have a better life somewhere else.

Today it is fairly simple to move to a new place. Places all over the world are becoming more **multicultural** as people from different cultures and backgrounds move there to make their homes. People who can afford the **fares**, or costs of travel tickets, often go to visit lands with different cultures, too.

Will you make your home in a new place someday? Maybe you already have. If not, you may know someone who has.

Vocabulary-Writing CONNECTION

What do you like about living in a **multicultural** society? Write a paragraph stating three reasons why it is good to live in a society like ours.

Genre

Expository Nonfiction

Expository nonfiction presents and explains information or ideas.

In this selection, look for

- Illustrations with captions
- Interesting historical information

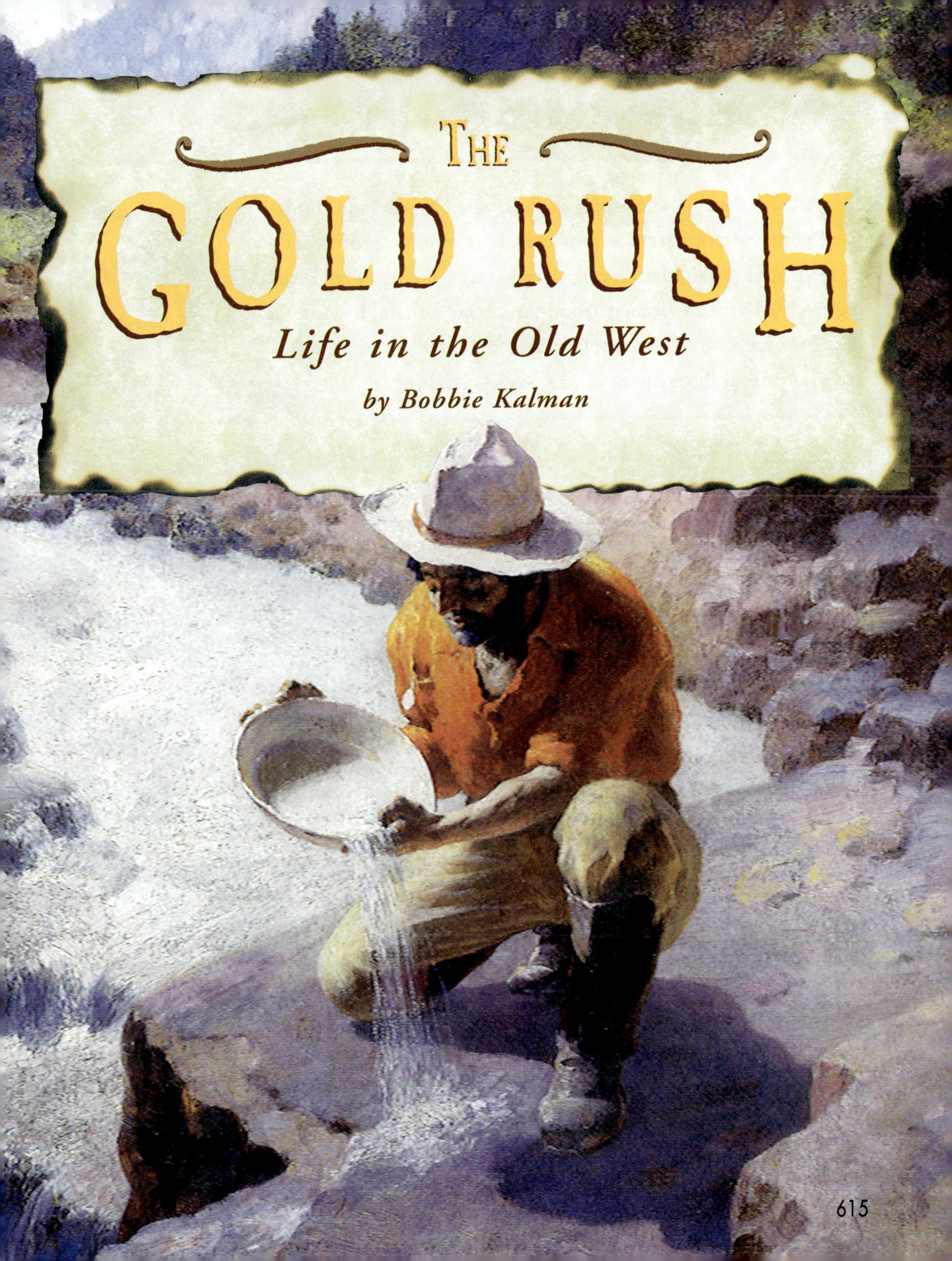
THE
GOLD RUSH
Life in the Old West
by Bobbie Kalman

GOLD STRIKE

In the 1800s, most of the people in the United States and Canada lived in the eastern states and provinces. Communities, roads, and pastures marked the landscape. Eastern towns and cities were becoming crowded with newcomers from Europe and Britain. Land in the East was expensive. Many people wanted to have their own land and escape from the cramped conditions of city life.

The West

In the early 1800s, the western areas of the United States and Canada were mainly unsettled. Miles of grassy plains and steep mountains lay to the west of the busy, populated eastern cities. At first, only a small number of people made the long and difficult journey west. Most of them were men who went to start ranches or work as cowboys.

Gold Beckons

In the mid-1800s, gold was discovered in the rivers of western North America. It took time for people to learn of this discovery. When the news of gold findings traveled east, many people did not believe these reports to be true. When some of the gold was brought to the East, however, people quickly became interested! Rumors and newspaper headlines convinced people that there really was gold in the West. People across the continent were eager to make a claim and become rich. Thousands of people made the trip west in search of their fortune. A great migration of people to the West in search of gold was known as a gold rush.

The Prospectors

The people who headed west to search for gold were called prospectors. When they arrived, there were plenty of opportunities for them to become miners. Anyone who came to the gold fields had a chance of striking gold.

THE GREAT GOLD RUSHES

There were many gold rushes, and each brought people to different areas of the rugged, unsettled West. Some gold rushes brought thousands of people and lasted several years. In addition to miners, business people also came. They opened shops and offices in the busy towns that developed around the mines. The increase in businesses helped small towns grow into large cities. Other gold rushes lasted less than a year. The towns in those areas were abandoned after all the gold was taken.

The California Gold Rush

The first gold rush in the North American West was the California gold rush. In January of 1848, James Marshall was hired by a logging company to build a sawmill on the American River in California. He found flakes of gold in the riverbed. News of his find traveled quickly and, by 1849, the California gold rush was under way. People from all over the world left their families and businesses to travel to California in search of gold. These prospectors were known as the "forty-niners." Due to this gold rush, California's population jumped from under 30,000 to more than 300,000 in just ten years!

James Marshall was the first newcomer to discover gold in the West. Unfortunately he never became rich. In this picture he is standing in front of the mill he built, which was known as Sutter's mill.

Some miners in the Klondike were known as sourdoughs. Sourdough is a type of bread that the miners ate. It was often the only food they had available in a mining camp or on the journey north to find gold. In the picture above, this sourdough in Dawson City is using a team of dogs to pull his equipment.

Gold Fever

Gradually, prospectors moved farther away from the California gold fields in search of more gold. Great amounts of gold and silver were soon discovered in Nevada. These precious metals are still mined in Nevada today. As some prospectors moved east to Nevada, others struck gold in the North between Oregon and British Columbia. In the 1890s, some Californian miners decided to return to the East after they could no longer find gold. Along the way they stopped in Colorado and struck gold there. Prospectors flocked to any place gold was found.

The Klondike Gold Rush

Another famous gold rush was the Klondike gold rush. The Klondike is a region of the Yukon territory in Canada and is near the Arctic. The Klondike gold rush began in 1896—almost fifty years after the California gold rush. Gold was found in mountainous and forested regions that had long, freezing winters. The precious nuggets were first discovered in a creek stemming from the Klondike River. The creek where this gold was found was known as Bonanza Creek. A bonanza is a rich source of precious metal. Ten million dollars worth of gold was mined in the Klondike during that gold rush!

GETTING TO THE

GOLD FIELDS

Business people, farmers, and factory workers left their homes and families in the East to travel to the gold fields. Others came from distant countries. They packed their tools, clothing, and food and said goodbye to their friends. The travelers knew the journey would be dangerous, and they were not sure if they would ever return home.

On Their Own

Many prospectors left their loved ones behind. The journey through unknown territories would put women and children at risk. Some could not afford to pay the additional travel costs to take their family along. Other miners left family members at home to run their business in case they did not strike it rich.

The Sea Voyage

People who came from great distances to the gold fields traveled over land or by sea. Reaching the gold fields by sea was difficult. Large ships had expensive fares, and small boats were often cramped, dirty, and dangerous. An overseas trip could take from five weeks to seven months. When the boat finally arrived at the port, the travelers still had to make a long overland journey.

This map shows the land and sea routes used to reach the California and Klondike gold rushes. Which route looks the most difficult?

Thousands of settlers used covered wagons like this one to travel to the West. People often walked alongside the wagon and helped push its heavy load.

Traveling by Wagon Train

The journey by land to California was often more difficult than the journey by sea. Some people traveled across the entire continent to reach the gold fields! These miners used covered wagons pulled by horses or mules to transport their belongings. They often traveled together in groups called wagon trains. Traveling in a group was safer than traveling alone. The miners were able to help one another find food or repair broken wagons. Each day, from sunrise to sunset, the wagon train would continue its journey with brief stops to eat and feed the animals.

Hazards of the Overland Trip

Some people traveled to the gold fields on foot and carried their possessions on their backs. Whether by wagon or on foot, the overland journey was extremely dangerous. Travelers had to cross swift rivers and steep mountains in sweltering heat and freezing temperatures. There was little food to eat, and people often became ill. Many travelers died trying to get to the gold fields. A large number of gold seekers gave up and turned back before reaching the gold fields.

Difficult Terrain

Determined travelers overcame obstacles such as rivers and steep inclines. They built scows, or rough boats, to cross lakes and rivers. In the Klondike, they had to carry supplies over steep, icy slopes and rugged landscapes. In later years, tramways powered by horses or steam engines also hauled heavy loads of goods and supplies up steep mountainsides. Tramway operators charged customers by the weight of their load.

Staking a Claim

When prospectors first arrived at a gold field, they began searching for gold wherever they could. When they found an area of unsettled land, they "claimed" it as their own by leaving their tools on the ground. The tools showed other prospectors that the spot was taken. As greater numbers of people began arriving at the gold fields, many prospectors began mining for gold on land that was being mined by someone else. To settle land disputes, miners set up rules so that each miner would have his or her own property on which to search for gold. Marking property was called staking a claim.

Claim Regulations

When miners found an area suitable for mining, they marked their claim. Some hammered shovels or stakes into the ground. Others made piles of rocks or put up a sign with their name on it. Claims in popular areas, such as along rivers, could be as small as ten square feet (3 square meters). Claims that were farther away from the river could be more than fifty square feet (15 square meters). Abandoned claims could be taken by anyone. In some places, a claim had to be left for a week before it was considered abandoned. In others, a two-day waiting period was enough.

This woman in the Klondike is staking a claim by sticking a marker in a tree.

Registering Claims

As more people arrived, the competition for land and gold became fierce. People tried to claim jump, or take over the claims of others. Eventually, prospectors had to register their claims at a commissioner's office. Having a registered claim provided proof of ownership and allowed miners to buy and sell their claims.

HOW WAS

GOLD FOUND?

Gold was found in the form of small flakes, nuggets, or dust. Some was scattered in the dirt and gravel at the bottom of riverbeds, and some was buried underground. The gold came from larger deposits that were buried deep in underground rock. These deposits are called lodes or vein deposits because they are spread throughout the narrow seams of the rock like veins in a leaf.

Golden Streams

Over thousands of years, water from rivers and streams eroded, or washed away, hard rock. Gradually, particles of gold in the rock were loosened and carried away with the moving water. This gold, found in rivers, streams, and other areas just below the ground's surface, was called placer gold. Much of the placer gold was found in the bends of rivers and streams, where the current of the water slowed, and the gold settled at the bottom.

How Did Miners Get the Gold?

Gold is eight times heavier than sand and stones. Prospectors washed the gold in a lake or river to separate it from the dirt. When the dirt containing gold was washed, the gold settled on the bottom of the pan. By swirling the pan around, the dirt mixed with the water. When the water was tipped out of the pan, the dirt poured out as well. The gold-laden dirt at the bottom of the pan was washed over and over again until nothing remained but the gold.

Teamwork

Prospectors often worked together on one claim to mine for gold. The job was much easier with five or six pairs of hands! Some prospectors learned how to mine for gold by trial and error, but it was much easier to learn from someone with more experience. Experienced miners sometimes helped the new miners, who were called greenhorns. They showed greenhorns the best methods for finding gold.

Buried Gold

In order to find buried gold, miners dug holes as deep as 100 feet (30 meters). A miner at the bottom of a deep hole put dirt and gravel into a bucket that was attached to a rope. The miners above ground pulled up the bucket. Then they washed the dirt hoping to see the gleam of gold.

TOOLS OF THE TRADE

When prospectors arrived at the gold fields, some had tools they brought from home. Many had no tools at all. Tools could be bought from small tent stores at the gold fields. Most prospectors, however, bought only a few necessary tools because they had little money and store-bought items were expensive.

The basic mining tools were a shovel, a pick, and a pan. A miner used the pick to break away or loosen pieces of rock. The shovel was needed for moving dirt and gravel to the location of the other mining equipment.

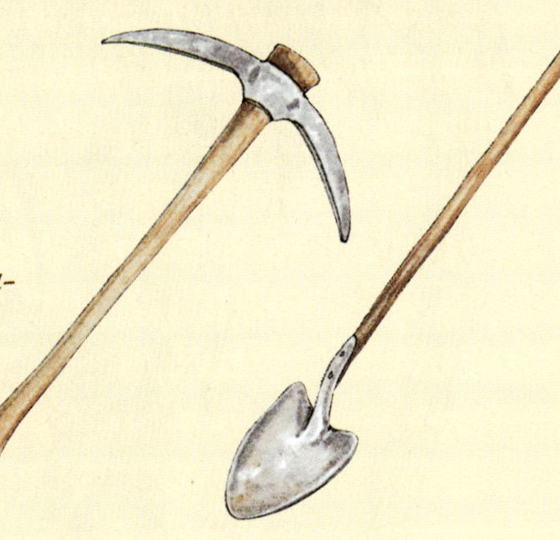

Miners used a cradle to wash large amounts of gold. A miner shoveled dirt onto the metal sieve at the top and poured water into the box. He or she used the handle to rock the cradle back and forth in order to separate the gold from the dirt. The dirt and water came out the other end, and the gold flakes settled at the bottom of the cradle.

Prospectors separated the gold from dirt using a pan. Some miners panned all day long for gold. Others used the pan to test if there was gold in a certain area. When gold was found, the miners used larger equipment to separate the gold from the dirt and rock.

Sluices were also used to wash gold. A sluice was a long wooden trough through which water could flow. Dirt was shoveled into the sluice, where running water washed over it. The gold sank to the sluice bottom, where it was caught by wooden riffles, or ridges. Large sluices called long toms could wash dirt at the same rate as two or three people using pans.

Hydraulic Mining

Hydraulic mining was a method used in the later years of gold mining, after most of the placer deposits had been taken. It enabled miners to get gold located deep in hard rock deposits. Large flumes, or channels, directed water from a dammed stream to the mining site. A metal pipe attached to the end of the flume sent out a high-pressure spray of water. The spray from the pipe was strong enough to blast away rock and soil. The runoff water carrying dirt and gravel was directed into sluices, where the gold was separated.

LIFE AT THE MINES

The California gold rush attracted people from all over the world. Hopeful prospectors from Britain, Europe, Australia, China, Portugal, and Mexico flooded into San Francisco in 1849, when gold was discovered there.

Many African American people who were brought to the gold fields as slaves were able to find enough gold to buy their freedom.

These American and Chinese miners are working together.

This little "miner" is ready for the gold fields. Do you think she became a miner when she grew up?

These two women made a lot of money but not on the gold fields. They sold food to hungry miners in the Klondike.

The life of a miner was often lonely. Many prospectors spent their spare time doing chores such as scrubbing dirty laundry.

This large group of miners took a break from a long day of mining to pose for a photograph.

Boomtowns

As thousands of people moved to the West, settlements began forming quickly. Within days, unsettled areas became busy towns. A town was likely to appear anywhere prospectors were mining. These new towns were called boomtowns. A boomtown is a town where the population grows quickly, or booms.

Boomtown Homes

The first buildings in a boomtown were rough shacks that were built to provide the miners with shelter. When people began making enough money, they built more comfortable places to live and work. A gold-rush town often had well-built, two-story structures as well as rough and dirty camps.

Busy Roads

Boomtowns were busy places. People hurried through the streets on foot, on horseback, and in wagons or carriages. The roads were made of packed dirt that turned into deep, sticky mud when it rained. Instead of concrete sidewalks, gold-rush towns had wooden boardwalks.

Boomtown Business

In addition to prospectors, merchants and other business people moved to a boomtown in order to set up stores, hotels, and restaurants. Businesses made money selling goods and services to the miners. The success of these businesses attracted more people to the town.

Going to Town

Many prospectors lived outside the towns but went into town for supplies, entertainment, and news. In a boomtown there were plenty of jobs for unsuccessful

To get mail from home, the prospectors in San Francisco waited for hours in line at the post office.

miners. They worked in stores, hotels, and restaurants. Some even abandoned the gold mines and stayed in town to make money running a business.

The people of Dawson City are gathered around a rare sight—a hot air balloon.

Long Visits

During warm weather, the miners worked hard on their claims, but in the winter many moved into town. In the Klondike, most of the miners remained in town for the entire winter. Winter on the claims was long, cold, and extremely lonely. Creeks and rivers became frozen or too cold to pan. Miners could not dig into the frozen ground. It was much easier to spend the season in a place where there were jobs and people.

Have you ever heard someone talk about "hitting pay dirt"? This expression comes from the gold rush. To prospectors, pay dirt was dirt that had the glitter of gold in it. Nowadays, pay dirt means discovering something useful or profitable.

When miners struck gold, they often built their family a large Victorian-style house on the outskirts of a boomtown. Living in a fancy home made them feel wealthy and civilized, like their friends back east. People liked to show off their newfound wealth. Building a large house was a good way to show off!

Millionaires of the Gold Rush

Not everyone found their fortune, but a few miners made over a million dollars by digging on one small claim! Prospectors were not the only ones who could make a fortune, however. Landowners made huge profits selling land to eager settlers. Many business people earned a lot of money by operating businesses such as stores, hotels, and law firms.

Not everything that glittered was gold. Prospectors had to keep from being fooled by fool's gold. Fool's gold was a hard substance called iron pyrite that looked like gold but was not valuable. Fool's gold shattered when it was hammered, and it felt gritty. True gold, however, could be hammered thin and was smooth to the touch.

Grubstaking

Many prospectors spent all their money in traveling to the gold fields. They did not have enough left over to buy mining equipment. Often, wealthy miners or townspeople loaned them a grubstake. A grubstake was a supply of equipment, food, or money that allowed the prospector to get started. In return, the miner had to promise to give the lender of the supplies a share of the profits. Giving money to a person or business in return for a share of the profits is also known as investing.

Wasted Money

Few miners struck it rich, and even fewer managed to stay rich. Some successful miners spent all their money on clothing and travel. Others invested their money in promising businesses. Unfortunately, the companies they supported often went out of business, and the investors lost their money as a result.

THE END OF THE GOLD RUSHES

Eventually, the supply of gold began to run out. To get at the gold that remained, big equipment such as dredges was needed. Dredges were huge machines powered by an engine that scooped gravel from deep rivers and lakes.

Only large companies could afford such expensive equipment. Individual miners found that they could no longer mine on their own and went to work for large companies. Company miners worked for wages. Any gold that they mined went to the company and not to them. There were no more overnight millionaires! The rush of people slowed and then stopped altogether. Eventually, people began to pack up and leave.

Effects of the Gold Rushes

The gold rushes played an important role in North American history. The discovery of gold caused people to make journeys to faraway places such as California and the Klondike. In the process of searching for gold, roads were built and buildings were constructed. Newcomers from other countries became part of North America's multicultural heritage. Thousands of people stayed in the West and started new lives. In California, ex-miners turned to farming the fertile Sacramento Valley. Cities such as Sacramento and San Francisco continue to grow and thrive.

The California gold rush brought thousands of settlers west, causing towns like San Francisco to grow into huge cities.

MEET the AUTHOR

Bobbie Kalman is the author and publisher of more than 150 children's books. She has done some exciting things while doing research for her books. For example, she went helmet-diving to gather information for her book *What Do You See Under the Sea?*

Bobbie Kalman began her working life in Nassau, Bahamas, as a special-education teacher. She likes teaching and has taught children of different ages.

Kalman makes her books interesting to read and fun to look at. She likes her books to be as enjoyable to read as they were to write!

Bobbie Kalman

Think and Respond

1. How did gold rushes change areas where they took place?
2. How does the author organize the information and make it easier for you to understand?
3. How were the gold rushes **profitable** for people who were not prospectors?
4. Do you think you would enjoy prospecting for gold? Why or why not?
5. How did using a reading strategy help you as you read this selection?

Visit *The Learning Site!*
www.harcourtschool.com

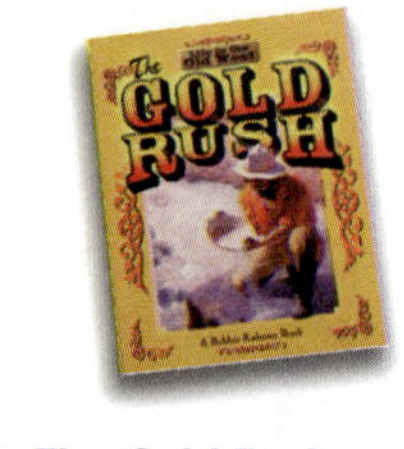

▲ The Gold Rush

Making Connections

Text to Self • Text to Text • Text To World

Compare Texts

NC STANDARDS: ELA 2.02e interact with text/connect text to own experiences, 2.04b identify main idea/details, 3.02 analyze/compare texts

1. How is the selection "The Gold Rush" related to the theme New Lands? INTERPRETATION / EVALUATING
2. How is the section called "Life at the Mines" different from the other sections of "The Gold Rush"? INTERPRETATION / KNOWLEDGE
3. The author explains that there were many gold rushes. How were the gold rushes different from each other? CRITICAL STANCE / ANALYZING
4. Name another nonfiction selection you have read that is similar to "The Gold Rush" in its tone, style, structure, or format. Explain how the two selections are alike. COGNITION / EVALUATING
5. After reading "The Gold Rush," what other questions do you have about this topic or related topics? INTERPRETATION / EVALUATING

Write a Letter

Writing CONNECTION

Many prospectors left their families behind while they searched for gold. Think about what a prospector might write home to his family after first arriving at a gold field. Write to express the miner's ideas and feelings. Jot down ideas for your letter in a graphic organizer like the one shown here.

What I (the prospector) saw and heard at the gold field:
My thoughts and feelings about my experience so far:
My future plans:

NC STANDARDS: ELA 3.06 conduct research using a variety of tools, 4.02b use oral language to communicate with others

Role-Play a Person in History

"The Gold Rush" tells some of the effects of the California gold rush. Choose one of the following people: John Sutter, Mariano Guadalupe Vallejo, or Louise Clapp. Do research to find out what role he or she played in the gold rush. Role-play the person you chose. Tell important facts about his or her life, and about the gold rush and its impact on life in California.

John Sutter

Demonstrate a Process

Science
CONNECTION

You learned in "The Gold Rush" that gold is found in riverbeds and in underground deposits. Research different types of geological deposits and how they are formed. Choose one type and show what it is and how it forms. You may use pans of water, gravel, sand, clay, or other materials to give a demonstration, or create diagrams that show the process. Present your demonstration or diagrams to classmates.

Some Kinds of Deposits

- alluvial deposit
- vein deposit
- stalactite or stalagmite
- terminal moraine
- esker
- sand dune
- loess

NC STANDARDS: ELA 3.06 conduct research using a variety of tools, 4.02b use oral language to communicate with others; Science 2.04 show different rocks/different properties

▲ The Gold Rush

Fact and Opinion

 **NC STANDARD:** ELA 3.01a interpret/evaluate text/assess impact of work choice

In "The Gold Rush," the author gives many facts about gold rushes that began in the mid-1800s. A **fact** is a statement that can be proved. The author also makes some statements of **opinion**, statements she believes to be true but cannot be proved. The chart below shows examples of a fact and an opinion from the selection.

	Characteristics	Examples
Fact	• can be proved • describes something that can be seen or that really occurred	Gold is eight times heavier than sand and stones.
Opinion	• tells how the writer or speaker feels about something • cannot be proved • may include signal words or phrases, such as *should, must, ought, I think, I believe,* or *in my opinion*	When they [gold seekers] arrived, there must have been plenty of opportunities for them to become miners.

Discuss the examples in the chart. How is the fact different from the opinion? What signal words in the opinion make it an opinion?

Visit *The Learning Site!*
www.harcourtschool.com
See *Skills* and *Activities*

Test Prep
Fact and Opinion

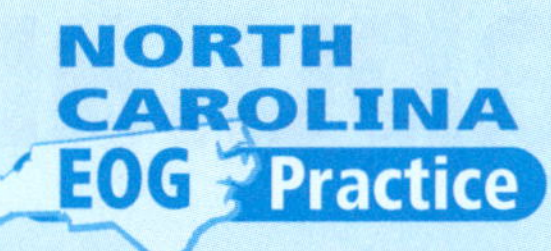

NC STANDARD: ELA 3.01a interpret/ evaluate text/assess impact of word choice

Focus Skill

▶ **Read the passage. Then answer the questions.**

The Sierra Nevada is a mountain range located mostly in eastern California. It is about 400 miles long. Years ago, it must have been difficult for travelers to cross this mountain range. Then James Beckwourth came to the Sierra Nevada with a party of gold seekers. Beckwourth was seeking a pass, an opening through the mountains. He did find a pass. It opened onto a lovely green valley. The pass was used by thousands of gold seekers on their way to California. James Beckwourth discovered something special.

CRITICAL STANCE / EVALUATING

1. **Which statement from the selection is a fact?**

   A It must have been difficult for travelers to cross this mountain range.

   B The Sierra Nevada is about 400 miles long.

   C Beckwourth discovered something special.

   D Gold was discovered in the rivers of western North America.

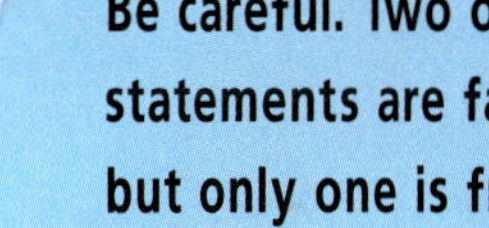

Tip Be careful. Two of these statements are facts, but only one is from the passage.

CRITICAL STANCE / EVALUATING

2. **How do you know that the last sentence expresses an opinion? Write your answer on a separate sheet of paper.**

Tip Look for a clue in the sentence that signals an opinion. Explain how you used this clue.

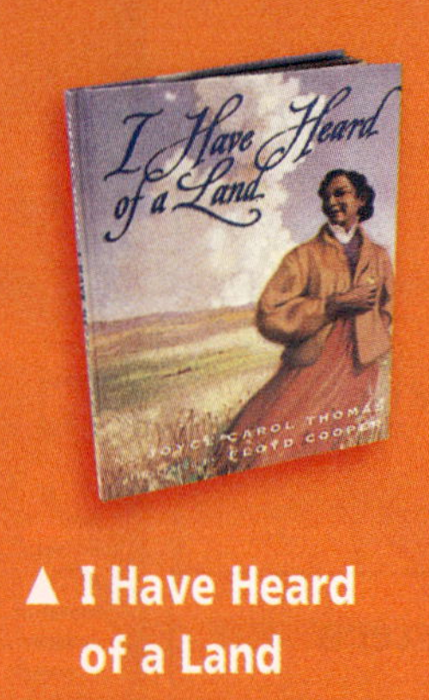

▲ I Have Heard of a Land

Vocabulary Power

The selection "I Have Heard of a Land" tells about a pioneer woman making a home in a new place. The things below were kept in a scrapbook by another woman to help her remember her first days in her new home.

- arbor
- fertile
- harmony
- pioneer
- possibilities

There is an **arbor**, a shelter of vines and branches, in back of our new house. These petals are from the sweet-smelling roses that grow there. The soil *must* be very **fertile** because there are flowers, vines, and shrubs growing everywhere I look.

I like going into the town. It's much smaller than I'm used to, but there's always something interesting going on. I drew these musicians in the square. They were singing in **harmony**. Their voices blended to make such a pleasing sound. You can see the statue of Horace Goodwin, too. He was one of the first people to settle in this region—a true **pioneer**.

The family across the street left this card at our front door. It invites us to dinner at their house tomorrow night. There seem to be many **possibilities** for fun and friendship here. Good things seem likely to happen in our new home!

Vocabulary-Writing CONNECTION

Every new school year is filled with **possibilities**. Write a paragraph telling about some of the possibilities for your next school year.

Genre

Historical Fiction

Historical fiction is a story that is set in the past and portrays people, places, and events that did happen or could have happened.

In this selection, look for

- A real time and place in the past
- Vivid words that describe the setting

I Have Heard of a Land

BY JOYCE CAROL THOMAS

ILLUSTRATED BY FLOYD COOPER

I have heard of a land
Where the earth is red with promises
Where the redbud trees catch the light
And throw it in a game of sunbeams and shadow
Back and forth to the cottonwood trees

I have heard of a land
Where a pioneer only has to lift up her feet
To cast her eyes on the rocks
The fertile earth, the laughing creek
Lift up her feet running for the land
As though running for her life
And in the running claim it
The stake is life and the work that goes into it

I have heard of a land
Where the cottonwood trees are innocent
Where the coyote's call is a lullaby at night
And the land runs on forever
And a woman can plant her crop and
    walk all day and never come to the end of it

I have heard of a land
Where the imagination has no fences
Where what is dreamed one night
Is accomplished the next day

I have heard of a land where the flapjacks
Spread out big as wagon wheels
Where the butter is the color of melted sun
And the syrup is honey
Stirred thick by a thousand honeybees

I have heard of a land
Where winter brings storm warnings
And pioneers wonder whether
The scissortail in spring will ever sing

I have heard of a land where the children
Swing in homemade swings strung from
The strong limbs of trees

I have heard of a land
Where the crickets skirl in harmony
And babies wrapped to their mothers' backs in the field
laugh more than they cry

I have heard of a land where worship
Takes place in an outdoor church
Under an **arbor** of bushes
And the hymns sound just as sweet

I have heard of a land
Where a woman sleeps in a sod hut
  dug deep in the heart of the earth
Her roof is decorated with brush
A hole in the ground is her stove
And a horse saddle is her pillow
She wakes thinking of a three-room log cabin

And soon that morning her neighbors
    and their sons and daughters
Help lift the logs and chock them into place
Together they hoist the beams high
After dinner, they finish the porch
    where they sit and tell stories
Finally when everyone else has gone home
She saws the planks for the steps
    by herself

That night by the glow of an oil lamp
She writes in her journal:

I raise nearly everything I eat
The land is good here
I grind corn for meal
Raise me some cane and make sorghum syrup
And if I feel real smart
I make hominy grits from scratch

I have heard of a land
Where the pioneer woman still lives
Her possibilities reach as far
As her eyes can see
And as far as our imaginations
can carry us

Think and Respond

1. What good things does the poem tell about that would make a *pioneer* want to come to this land?
2. Why do you think the author repeats the phrase *I have heard of a land* many times in the poem?
3. Why do you think the author wrote this poem about the pioneers? Explain your answer.
4. Which pictures and descriptions of the land do you like best? Why do you like them?
5. What reading strategies did you use as you read this selection?

Meet the Author
Joyce Carol Thomas

Question: Why did you write *I Have Heard of a Land?*

Joyce Carol Thomas: I wanted to tell my family stories. Slaves who were set free were given land if they settled in the Oklahoma Territory. In the book I imagine the feelings of my great-grandmother, who traveled to Oklahoma from Tennessee to establish a homestead.

Several of my other books are also set in Oklahoma, where I was born.

Question: How did you prepare to become a writer?

Thomas: I read many books as a child and made up songs, poetry, and plays. I studied at California State University and at Stanford University. I taught in middle schools, community colleges, and universities before I became a full-time writer.

Question: You write poetry. Do you think that influences the way you write stories?

Thomas: Yes. The words, even when I write stories, must have a singing rhythm.

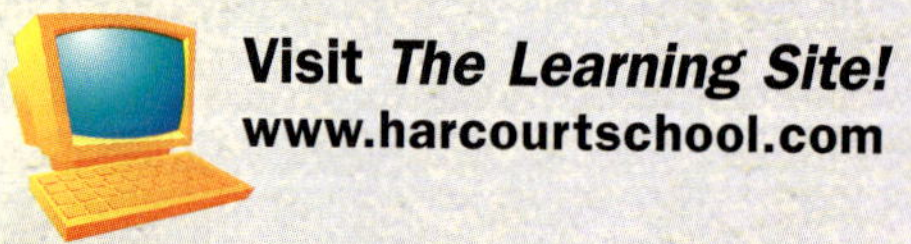

MEET THE ILLUSTRATOR

Floyd Cooper

Question: Do you have any personal connections to *I Have Heard of a Land*?

Floyd Cooper: Yes. My great-grandparents ran for the land in Oklahoma. I was born and raised in Tulsa, and I studied at the University of Oklahoma.

Question: What made you want to be an artist?

Cooper: When I was in the second grade, my teacher hung my sunflower art on the wall. Everyone else's picture was on the wall, too, but I felt so proud to see mine displayed. I thought, this is what it is like to be an artist.

After college I worked for a greeting card company. I didn't feel I could be creative doing greeting cards. I tried advertising for a while. Then I discovered the world of children's book illustrating.

Question: How did you paint the pictures in *I Have Heard of a Land*?

Cooper: I worked with a kneaded rubber eraser. First I painted a background on paper glued to cardboard. Then I rubbed shapes onto the background with the kneaded eraser. Then I applied color—very thin washes of oil paint. This is the technique I use for all my paintings now.

▲ I Have Heard of a Land

Making Connections

Text to Self • Text to Text • Text To World

Compare Texts

NC STANDARDS: ELA 2.02e interact with text/connect text to own experiences, 3.01b interpret/evaluate text/examine characters' actions/motives, 3.02 analyze/compare texts

1. How does the pioneer woman in "I Have Heard of a Land" feel about the new land where she has made her home? Why does she feel this way? INTERPRETATION / EVALUATING
2. How is the pioneer woman's journal entry on page 659 different from the rest of the selection? INTERPRETATION / KNOWLEDGE
3. What contrast is shown by the illustrations on pages 650–651 and pages 652–653? CRITICAL STANCE / ANALYZING
4. Think of another historical fiction selection that you have read. How is that selection like and unlike "I Have Heard of a Land"? CONNECTIONS / ANALYZING
5. What questions would you like to ask the author of this selection? INTERPRETATION / EVALUATING

Write a Journal Entry

Writing CONNECTION

The pioneer woman in "I Have Heard of a Land" writes an entry in her journal. Think about what you would write in your journal if you were one of the neighbors who helped the woman build her new home. Write to express your ideas and feelings about the events of that day. Use a graphic organizer like this one to plan.

Events to Include in Journal Entry	Thoughts and Feelings

NC STANDARDS: ELA 4.02a use writing to communicate with others; Social Studies 3.02 identify people/symbols/events/documents key to North Carolina's history

Create a Quilt Square

Social Studies CONNECTION

The author of "I Have Heard of a Land" mentions two symbols of Oklahoma. The scissortail is Oklahoma's state bird, and the redbud is the state tree. Choose a symbol that represents an important person, place, or event in your state's history. Then create a quilt square with that symbol. Explain your symbol to classmates. Work with them to sew all your squares into a class quilt.

Learn a Song

Many pioneers wrote songs about their new homes. Look in a children's book of folk songs for songs about the West. Learn one of the songs, and teach it to your classmates.

NC STANDARDS: ELA 3.06 conduct research using a variety of tools

▲ I Have Heard of a Land

Word Relationships

NC STANDARDS: ELA 1.04c increase vocabulary/use synonyms/antonyms, 1.04d increase vocabulary/use homophones/homonyms, 1.04e increase vocabulary/use multiple meaning words

Readers often use context to figure out the meanings of unfamiliar words. Understanding **word relationships**, or how words are related, can help you use context to understand what you read.

How Words are Related	Examples
synonyms: words that have similar meanings	Neighbors help lift the logs. Together they hoist the beams high.
antonyms: words that have opposite meanings	A woman sleeps in a sod hut. She wakes thinking of a three-room log cabin.
homophones: words that sound the same but have different meanings and spellings	A hole in the ground is her stove. They work the whole day building the cabin.
homographs: words that are spelled the same but have different meanings and pronunciations	The pioneer woman still lives in this land. The pioneers' lives are filled with work and joy.
multiple-meaning words: words that have more than one meaning	The redbud trees catch the light. Now she will light her oil lamp.

When you read, think about how words are related. Use context to figure out how a homograph or a multiple-meaning word is being used in a sentence. If a word is unfamiliar, you might look for a synonym or antonym to help make the meaning of the word clear.

Visit *The Learning Site!*
www.harcourtschool.com

See *Skills* and *Activities*

Test Prep
Word Relationships

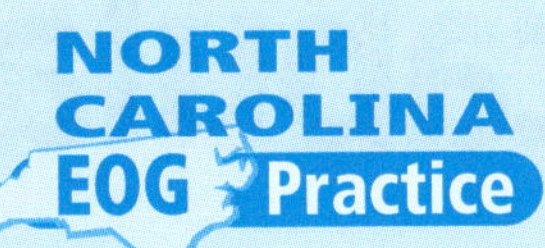

NC STANDARDS: ELA 1.04c increase vocabulary/use synonyms/antonyms, 1.04e increase vocabulary/use multiple meanings words

▶ **Read the passage. Then complete the items.**

The children were glad to climb down from the wagon. They drank cool water from the stream. Then they washed and splashed while their parents filled the water jugs. After they emptied the <u>creek</u> water from their shoes and pockets, they climbed back into the covered wagon. Soon the sun would set, and the gentle creak and sway of the wooden wagon would <u>rock</u> the children to sleep.

COGNITION / ORGANIZING

1. Which word in the paragraph is a synonym for <u>creek</u>?

A wagon

B water

C stream

D sway

Think about what the word means. Look for a word with a similar meaning.

COGNITION / ORGANIZING

2. The word <u>rock</u> in this paragraph means—

F a small piece of stone

G a kind of music

H to move from side to side

J to disturb

In two of the answer choices, *rock* is a verb. Look closely at the meanings of the verbs.

▲ Paul Bunyan and Babe the Blue Ox

Vocabulary Power

In "Paul Bunyan and Babe the Blue Ox," you will read about a larger-than-life logger and his unusual pet. Tall tales, such as the story about Paul Bunyan and the story below, include wild exaggerations and fantastic details.

gadgets

bellowing

tragedy

fateful

softhearted

ration

Today was quite a day! Dave was outside, working on one of his **gadgets**. He likes to invent small machines and mechanical tools.

I had baked a cherry pie and set it on the counter. Suddenly I heard the most terrible **bellowing** I'd ever heard in my life. The loud, deep roaring was coming from the kitchen. Dave heard it, too, and we both ran to see what it was.

"Look! It's an elephant!" Dave shouted.

Sure enough, there was an elephant with its trunk stuck in the kitchen window. It was trying to reach my cherry pie. The elephant was pushing so hard that the house was about to fall down. What a **tragedy** that would have been!

Luckily, Dave is a quick thinker. Without him, it would have been a **fateful** day, bringing disaster for us and the elephant. He grabbed a

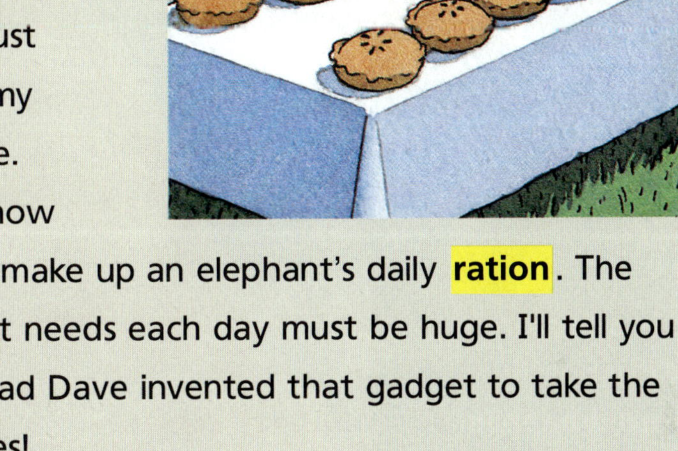

pepper shaker and emptied it into the end of the elephant's trunk. One big sneeze was all it took. The elephant pulled his trunk out of the window, and our house was saved.

Now, Dave is a kind, **softhearted** fellow. He felt sorry for the elephant. The poor animal just wanted some of my delicious cherry pie.

I don't know how many cherry pies make up an elephant's daily **ration**. The amount of food it needs each day must be huge. I'll tell you one thing—I'm glad Dave invented that gadget to take the pits out of cherries!

Vocabulary-Writing CONNECTION

Think about a **gadget**, such as a pencil sharpener, that you use in your everyday life. Write a paragraph for someone who has never seen it, explaining how to use this gadget.

Paul Bunyan

Genre

Tall Tale

A tall tale is a humorous story about impossible or exaggerated happenings.

In this selection, look for

- **Events that could not happen in real life**
- **Exaggerations about the strength and abilities of a hero**

and Babe the Blue Ox

from *Larger Than Life: The Adventures of American Legendary Heroes*

retold by Robert D. San Souci • illustrated by Andrew Glass

Paul Bunyan, the greatest logger of all time, the giant who pretty much invented the lumber industry, was born and raised in Maine. He had logged off the better part of that state before he turned twenty. After that he did some work in Canada, before he turned up in Michigan. He became boss of a camp on the Big Onion River, where he would cut down so much timber in a day that three hundred mule drivers would have to work day and night to haul his logs to the river. He headed a campful of mighty men, including French Canadians, Swedes, Irishmen, Scots, and any other logger who could give a good account of himself.

But his truest companion was Babe the Blue Ox.

There are different stories of how the two met. One story is that Paul found Babe during the Winter of the Blue Snow.

On that special morning, Paul woke just before dawn, broke up the ice on a little lake nearby and washed his face, parted his hair with a hand ax, and combed his beard with a crosscut saw. Then he went out looking for a stand of trees to cut down, walking through the blue snow that filled the woods. Suddenly he heard bellowing from the direction of the frozen river. There he discovered a young ox, already bigger than a full-grown steer, splashing in the water where the ice had given way under it.

"Hold on!" cried the softhearted logger. Kneeling down on the snowy bank, he fished out the soggy calf. The poor thing had been white when he had fallen in, but had turned bright blue from the cold before Paul pulled him out of the icy river.

Paul carried the creature back to camp through a blue blizzard, saying, "There, there, poor little baby." When they reached Big Onion Camp, Paul built a barn for the ox he had already begun to call "Babe." Then he searched the mountains around for moose moss to make soup for the calf.

As it turned out, when Babe was spoon-fed love and soup, he grew so fast, that the next morning, Paul found

the barn he had built sitting on the ox's back. Then Paul put his hands on his hips and said with a smile, "You're sure gonna be something t' reckon with." Then he scratched at his beard thoughtfully, and added, "You have so much power, it shouldn't be wasted. When you're grown up, I'll find you some useful work."

Babe made a soft, chuckling sound, as if to say, "That's fine with me."

Paul kept on feeding Babe, and pretty soon the animal was up to full size, measuring forty-two ax handles between the eyes. An ordinary person standing at Babe's head or tail would have to use a telescope to see what was happening at the other end.

Some people say that Paul dug the Great Lakes so that Babe would always have fresh water. A lot of the smaller lakes in Wisconsin and Minnesota, they add, are simply Babe's hoofprints filled with water.

Babe's shoes were made by the blacksmith Ole Olsen, who sank to his knees in solid rock the first time he tried to carry one.

At first there was a lot of grumbling, because Paul put part of his crew to work bringing in enough hay to feed Babe. "That critter's a waste of hay and time," some men said.

The matter was settled by Johnny Inkslinger, Paul's bookkeeper. He used a special fountain pen that was eighteen feet long and connected by a three-foot hose to thirty-eight barrels of ink on the shelf over his desk. Always looking for a way to save a penny, Johnny once saved nine barrels of ink over a winter by not crossing his t's or dotting his i's. He pointed out, "Babe really *saves* us money. He can haul the lumber in one trip that we needed three hundred mule drivers for. Thanks to him, we make more money. That means your paychecks are bigger."

This fact—if not the milk of human kindness—quickly made the blue ox popular with the loggers.

Babe, who could haul anything, was a great worker who could drag 640 acres of timberland to the river at one time—all in one piece. There, Paul's crew chopped down the trees. Then the blue ox hauled the cleared land back into place.

Paul would also use the blue ox in plenty of other ways. Once, when one of Paul's men sent the wrong lumber down the Mississippi to New Orleans, Paul was faced with the problem of getting the lumber back upstream. What would have seemed impossible to anyone else just needed a little thinking on Paul's part. He simply fed Babe an extra-big salt ration, then led him to the Mississippi to drink. Babe was so thirsty, he drained the river dry, sucking the water upstream, so that the logs came back faster than they had gone down.

Babe was a fine pet. When he was happy, he would chortle and roll his big blue eyes and stick out his tongue to lick Paul behind the ear or on the back of the neck. This would always send the giant logger into roars of laughter that made folks miles away think thunder was rolling down the mountains.

But Babe loved to play jokes on Paul's crew, and this could make the men angry. He would sometimes go to the lake from which the men got water, and drink it dry in a single swallow. Then the men would have to go thirsty and dirty until the lake filled up again. Once he lay down in the river and dammed it up, not moving until Paul drew him away with a sandwich made of two giant flapjacks with a filling of clover hay.

But even with all of his joking, Babe helped Paul to keep the money rolling in. Paul added more and more men to his crew, building bunkhouses so long that it took three days to walk from one end to the other. To keep his men well fed

and happy, Paul hired the best camp cooks around, including Hot Biscuit Slim, Joe Muffinton, Sourdough Sam, Pea Soup Shorty, and Cream Puff Fatty, who made desserts.

At Round River Camp, Paul built a cooking stove so big that it took three hundred cooks standing shoulder to shoulder to keep it going, and a special crew just to supply firewood. When it was time to make flapjacks, a griddle would be lowered onto the stove, and this was greased by the kitchen workers skating along with bacon slabs tied to their feet.

Meals were served by men on roller skates, who raced up and down the long tables Paul had built.

When they were ready to move on to the next camp in North Dakota, Paul got the bright idea of tying all the camp buildings together, with the cookhouse in the lead, and having Babe haul the camp to Red River.

When he yelled, "Gee! Haw! Yay!" Babe pulled the camp over mountains and plains, while the loggers leaned out the cabin windows, waving to anyone they happened to see—though, for the most part, only the wild creatures of the woods saw them pass.

One winter Paul logged off North Dakota with the Seven Axemen, his finest lumberjacks. Stories about the height and weight of the Seven Axemen are different, but people say that they used four-foot logs as toothpicks. When they got working along with Paul, their axes often flew so fast, they sometimes came close to setting fire to the forests.

In the Dakotas, they all got carried away and logged off the whole of the state, until there wasn't much left but bushes. Looking around and feeling a little bad, Paul said, "I think maybe we shoulda stopped a while back."

Sitting on a big stump, Babe beside him, Paul looked out over the sorry wasteland he had helped make. To Babe he said, "I won't let this happen again. It isn't good for the land. And there's nothing left for an honest logger to make a living from."

True to his spirit of making the best of the worst, Paul got up, took a big hammer, and pounded down the stumps into the ground. He turned the Dakotas into smooth, rolling plains that became fine farmland.

But Paul was never able to cross the Dakotas without thinking of the great forests that had disappeared under his ax.

When Paul and his men returned to the North Woods, they found that pine trees, loggers, and a certain blue ox were not the only things that came big-sized there. They were attacked by giant mosquitoes that had to be fought off with pikes and axes. When they tried to escape into a cabin, these monsters would tear off the roof or chew through the log walls.

Paul decided to fight fire with fire, so he sent Sourdough Sam back to Maine for some of the giant bees Paul remembered from his boyhood. Sourdough had to bring the insects back on foot, with their wings tied, because they could not be controlled if they were allowed to fly. He collected their stingers, gave them boots, and marched them two by two to Paul's camp.

But when Paul let the bees go, thinking they would chase away the mosquitoes, he found he had planned wrong. The bees and mosquitoes intermarried, producing offspring with stingers in front and behind, and they got Paul's men coming and going.

Paul got rid of them by sending ships full of sugar and molasses out to the middle of Lake Superior.

The insects, who had a bee-like hunger for sweets, swarmed over the ships, eating so much sugar they could not fly, and they drowned trying to get back to shore.

The following year, Paul decided to try his luck among the tall trees of Oregon and Washington, on the Pacific Coast. Since both he and the blue ox were getting a little on in years, Paul bought several thousand oxen to help Babe with the hauling. This worked out fine for several weeks, until tragedy struck.

On the fateful day, one of Paul's crew tied all the oxen together, with Babe in the lead, to haul lumber to the ocean. All went fine until they reached a deep valley. Babe, marching along in front, started up the far side of the valley before the rest of the team had finished coming down. As a result, all the normal-sized oxen were quickly and fatally strung across the valley like laundry drying on a clothesline.

By the time Paul discovered what had happened, there was not much to do but tell the men back at camp that there would be plenty of beef for breakfast, lunch, and dinner.

After that, Babe continued to do the hauling alone. But Paul could see the blue ox was slowing down a bit. And, to tell the truth, he felt himself slowing down some.

To Babe, he said, "All these logging trucks and chain saws and sawmills full of fancy gadgets are making me feel a little useless—even if I invented half the stuff myself."

Babe made a soft sound as if to say, "I agree."

Not long after, they took themselves up to Alaska, where they enjoyed some old-fashioned logging. When they had had their fill of the Arctic, they came back. In a deep woods—in Oregon or Minnesota or Maine, depending on who tells the story—Paul built a cabin for himself and a barn for Babe.

There he keeps two big iron kettles bubbling all the time: one full of pea soup for himself, and one full of moose moss soup for Babe.

In the evenings, Paul sits on his porch and Babe rests nearby, and they listen to the trees growing, which is a joy they had never shared before. And that green, growing power fills them so that they know they will be around as long as a single tree endures.

Think and Respond

1. What humorous explanations does the story give for natural features in certain parts of our country?
2. What parts of the story show that it is a tall tale? Give some examples.
3. Why do **gadgets** such as trucks and chainsaws make Paul feel useless?
4. Which part of the story do you think is the funniest? Why is it funny?
5. What reading strategy did you use as you read this tall tale? Tell how it helped you understand or enjoy the story.

Meet the Author

Robert D. San Souci

Robert D. San Souci likes to travel, and his writing includes many folktales from around the world. Some of his ideas have come to him in interesting ways. Once, on a cross-country trip, his car broke down in Pecos, Texas, and he decided to visit the towns nearby. There he learned Native American legends that he later used in a book!

In addition to retelling folktales and writing novels, Mr. San Souci has worked as a story consultant for Walt Disney Feature Animation. When asked how long he plans to keep writing, he says, "as long as I have stories to tell—and an audience that is willing to listen."

Robert D. San Souci

Visit *The Learning Site!*
www.harcourtschool.com

Genre
Poem

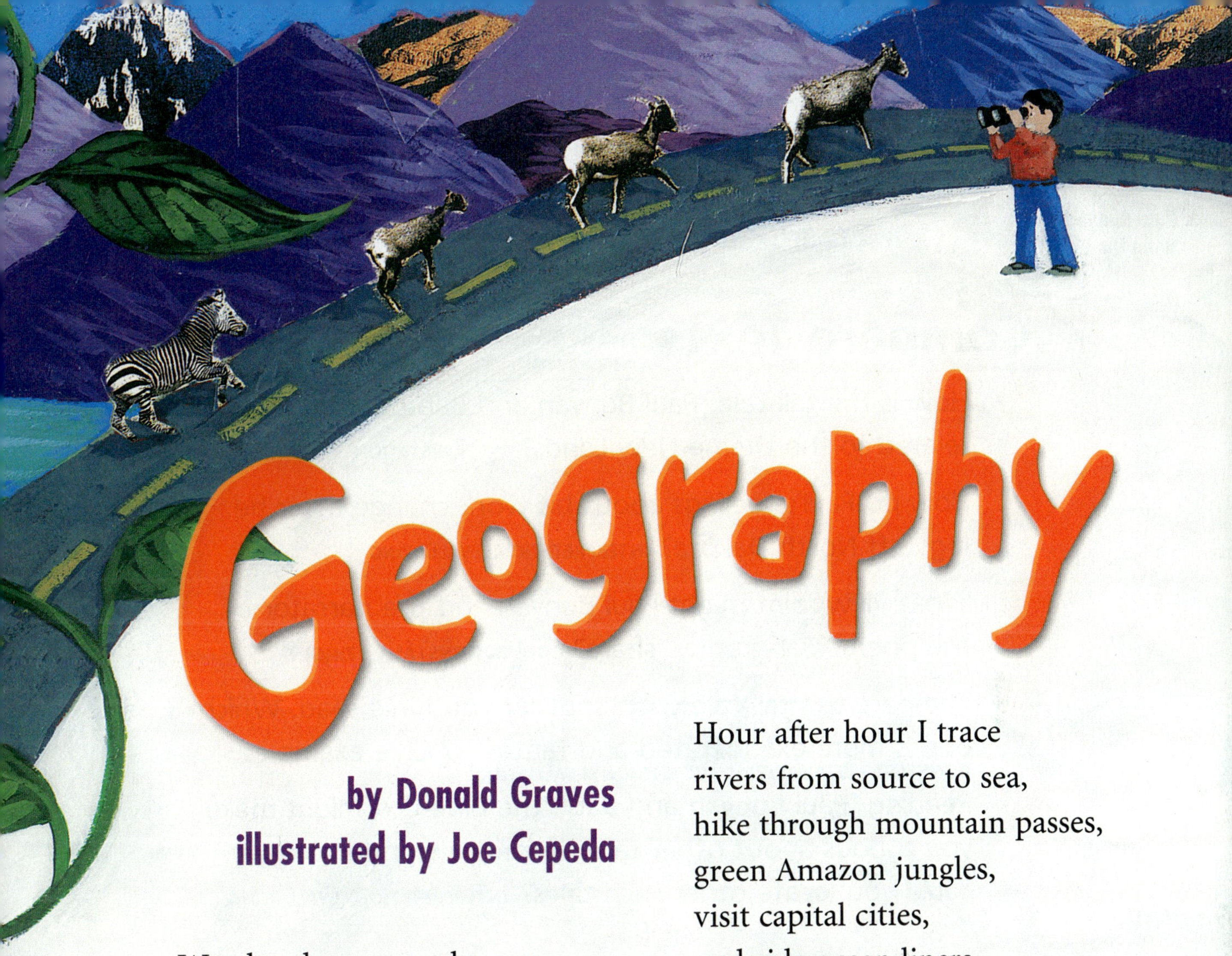

Geography

by Donald Graves
illustrated by Joe Cepeda

We play the geography game.
Miss Adams pulls down a map,
any map in the world.
She says, "Find Ethiopia."
My hand is up first;
I whiz to the front
of the room and put
my finger on Ethiopia.

At home I shut my bedroom door,
pull out the bottom drawer
to my desk, and slowly turn
the Atlas pages.

Hour after hour I trace
rivers from source to sea,
hike through mountain passes,
green Amazon jungles,
visit capital cities,
and ride ocean liners
across the Atlantic
to England or France.

I beg for free road maps
at the corner Texaco station
and plot auto trips
to the White Mountains,
find the best way to a ballgame
at Fenway Park,
or imagine traveling
to Grandmother's house
for Christmas.

▲ Paul Bunyan and Babe the Blue Ox

Making Connections

Text to Self • Text to Text • Text To World

Compare Texts

NC STANDARDS: ELA 2.04b identify theme, 3.01b interpret/evaluate text/examine characters' actions/motives, 3.02 analyze/compare texts

1. How is the tall tale "Paul Bunyan and Babe the Blue Ox" related to the theme New Lands? INTERPRETATION / EVALUATING
2. How do Paul's feelings about his work change after he logs off North Dakota? INTERPRETATION / EVALUATING
3. What viewpoint might Paul Bunyan and the narrator of the poem "Geography" share? CONNECTIONS / ANALYZING
4. Compare this tall tale with another you have read. Which one is more exaggerated and fantastic? Give examples. CONNECTIONS / ANALYZING / COGNITION / EVALUATING
5. Reading "Paul Bunyan and Babe the Blue Ox" might make you curious about other tales from the frontier. How could you locate other such tales? INTERPRETATION / EVALUATING

Write a Tall Tale

The story says that Paul Bunyan made the Great Lakes and the Dakota plains. Think of a natural or human-made landmark in the area where you live. Write a tall tale about how it came to be. You can use Paul Bunyan and Babe as the characters or make up new characters.

Writing CONNECTION

Characters	Setting
Main Events	

NC STANDARDS: ELA 2.02d interact with text/locate information; Social Studies 1.05 assess how physical environment affects human movement

Map a Route

Social Studies CONNECTION

The speaker in "Geography" looks at maps and imagines going places. With a partner, find a map of the United States in an atlas and trace the outline on a sheet of paper. Next, list all of the places the characters in "Paul Bunyan" went. Mark and label each place on your map. Draw a line connecting the places to show a possible route for Paul Bunyan's travels.

Research Reforestation

Science CONNECTION

Wood is one of our most valuable natural resources. It is used to make many things, including the paper on which you write. Find out how forests are renewed after trees have been cut down to make products from wood. Research the process of reforestation. Prepare an oral presentation to share your information with your classmates.

NC STANDARD: ELA 4.02b use oral language to communicate with others

▲ Paul Bunyan and Babe the Blue Ox

Fact and Opinion Focus Skill

NC STANDARD: ELA 3.01a interpret/evaluate text/assess impact of word choice

A **fact** is a statement that can be proved. An **opinion** expresses someone's thoughts or feelings. In imaginative literature, such as stories, myths, folk tales, and tall tales, facts are statements that tell what has happened in the story and can be proved. They do not have to be true in real life. An opinion is what a character thinks or believes. Look at these examples of fact and opinion from "Paul Bunyan and Babe the Blue Ox."

Fact

Paul kept on feeding Babe, and pretty soon the animal was up to full size, measuring forty-two ax handles between the eyes.

This statement is a fact because in the story, it could be proved by measuring Babe.

Opinion

When Paul sits down and looks at the Dakotas, he says, "I think maybe we shoulda stopped a while back."

This is Paul's opinion because it's what he believes. He uses the words *I think*. His opinion may be right, but that doesn't make it a fact. Even if many people agree with him, his statement is still an opinion.

Visit *The Learning Site!*
www.harcourtschool.com
See *Skills* and *Activities*

Test Prep
Fact and Opinion

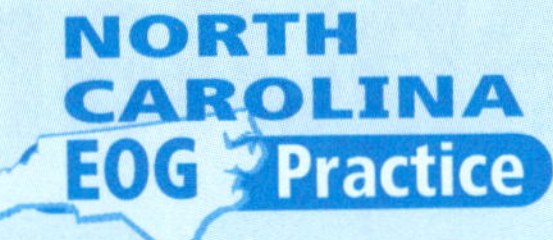

NC STANDARD: ELA 3.01a interpret/evaluate text/assess impact of word choice

▶ **Read the passage. Then answer the questions.**

One day Millie heard a giant slurping noise. She ran to the Rattlesnake River. In sixteen and a half seconds, the riverbed was dry.

Millie set off to find out where all the water had gone. She came upon Paul Bunyan and Babe, his giant blue ox. She spotted a dribble of water running down Babe's chin. "That ox ought to be kept in a pen!" she bellowed. "He's gone and drunk up the Rattlesnake River!"

CRITICAL STANCE / EVALUATING

1. **Is the statement *She ran to the Rattlesnake River* a fact or an opinion?**

   A an opinion, because it tells what Millie thinks

   B a fact, because it tells about an event that happens in the story

   C an opinion, because the story is not true

   D a fact, because it tells about an event in real life

Each choice includes both an answer and a reason. Be sure that both parts are correct.

CRITICAL STANCE / EVALUATING

2. **Which of these statements from the story expresses an opinion?**

   F "That ox ought to be kept in a pen."

   G In sixteen and a half seconds, the riverbed was dry.

   H She came upon Paul Bunyan and Babe.

   J Millie heard a giant slurping noise.

To find the opinion, look for signal words and phrases such as *I think*, *I believe*, *ought*, and *should*.

▲ Fly Traps! Plants That Bite Back

Vocabulary Power

You can probably name quite a few animals that eat meat, but how many plants can you think of that do that? Learn more about how plants and animals depend on each other for food.

- carnivorous
- victim
- boggiest
- accidentally
- chemicals
- fertilizer
- dissolve

Many animals are **carnivorous**, or meat-eating. When a lion is hungry, it must attack another animal, which becomes its **victim**. Other animals, such as deer and cattle, eat only plants. A number of animals eat both plants and meat.

The diagram below shows that all animals depend on plants. Plants grow in the dry deserts and in the **boggiest** places, where the ground is watery and spongy.

Early humans gathered food they found **accidentally**, without planning to look for it. Later, people learned to grow their food on farms. Crops take in **chemicals**, or substances with certain properties, from the soil. Then farmers need to add those chemicals back to the soil as **fertilizer** to help later crops grow properly. They may add dry fertilizer directly or **dissolve** it in water to change it from solid to liquid. Fertilizers often include animal wastes and bones, so in a way, plants need animals, just as animals need plants.

Vocabulary–Writing CONNECTION

Sometimes accidents turn out surprisingly well. Write a paragraph telling about a time when you **accidentally** did something that worked out for the best.

Fly

Genre

Informational Narrative

An informational narrative is a story that presents information and facts.

In this selection, look for

- Information about a topic
- Characters and events that are realistic

by Martin Jenkins
illustrated by David Parkins

Traps!

Plants That Bite Back

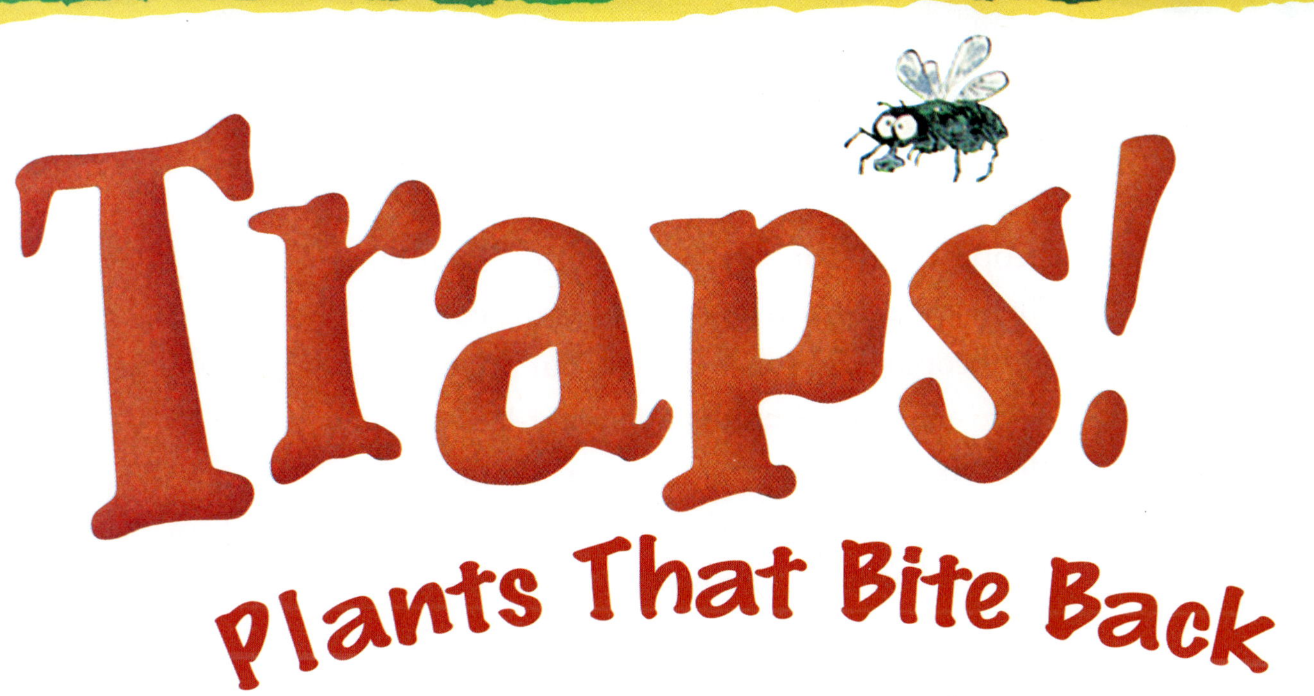

Plants that eat animals are called carnivorous plants. There are hundreds of different kinds and they grow all around the world.

People do all sorts of things in their spare time. There are people who collect yogurt containers and people who make models out of bottle tops. There are beetle hunters and giant-leek growers. Me, I like watching plants that eat animals.

It all started with a plant I found in a pond. It had little yellow flowers sticking out of the water. Under the water there were tangled stems with hundreds of tiny bubbles on them. A friend told me it was called a bladderwort.

There are over 200 different kinds of bladderworts. Most of them grow in ponds and rivers. They are usually very small, with narrow leaves and stems.

She said the bubbles on the stems were the bladders. Each one had a trap door shut tight, with little trigger hairs around it.

Whenever a water flea or other bug touched a hair, the trap door swung back and in the bug went.

Then the trap door slammed shut and there was no way out. And it all happened in the blink of an eye.

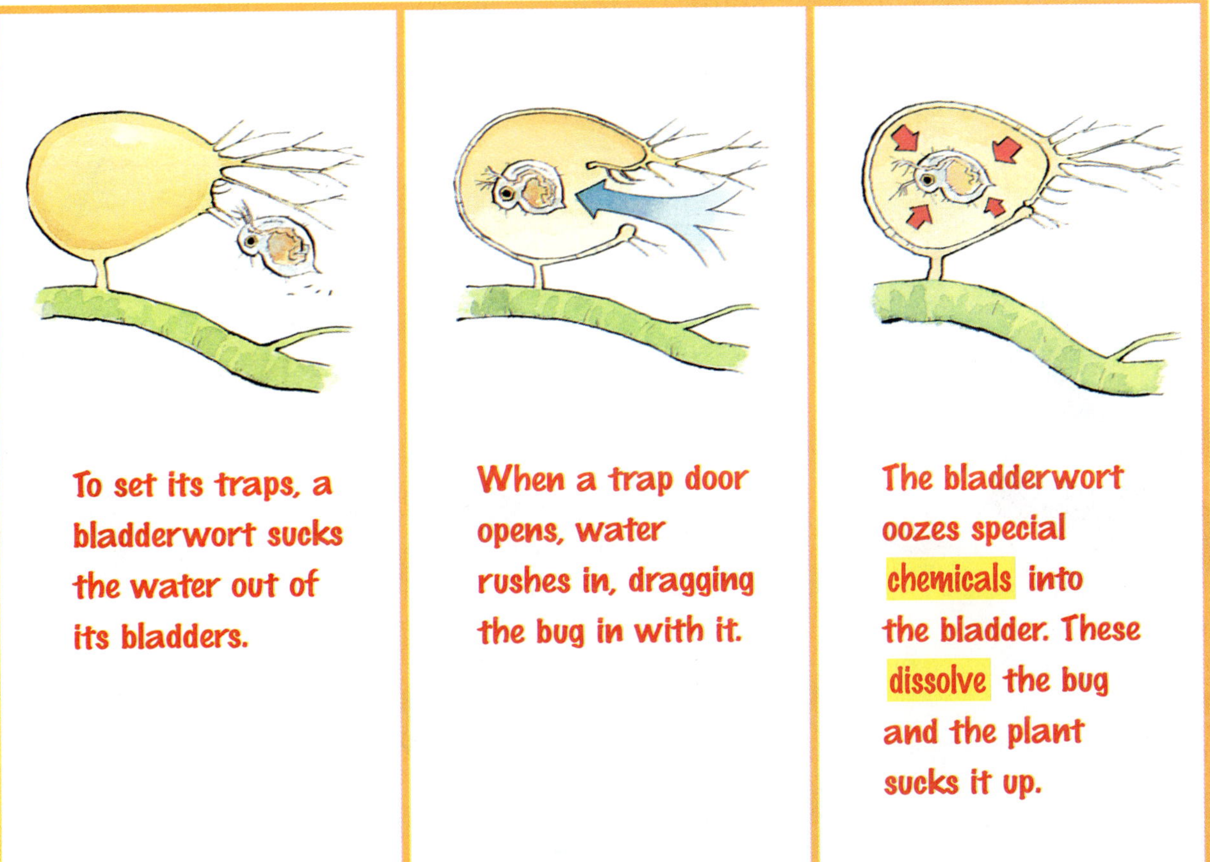

Wow, that's neat, I thought. The trouble was, the traps on my plant were so small and so quick that I couldn't really see them work.

Well, I decided, I'll just have to find a bigger carnivorous plant.

So I did.

I had to climb a mountain, mind you, and walk through all its boggiest, mossiest places.

But there in the moss were little red plants, shining in the sun. I thought they were covered in dewdrops, but they weren't. They were sundews, and the shiny parts were sticky like honey. I'm sure you can guess what they were for.

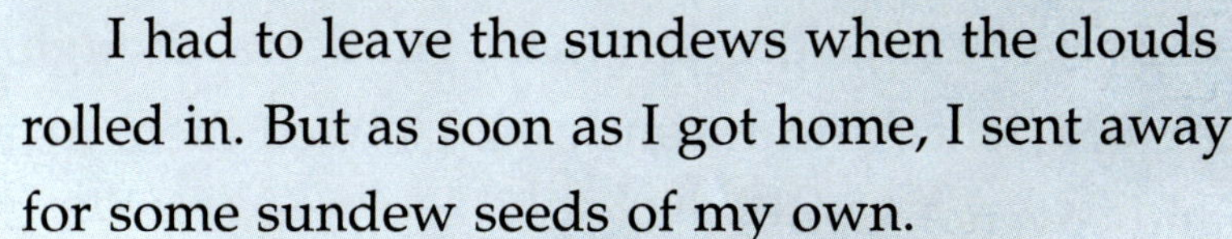

I had to leave the sundews when the clouds rolled in. But as soon as I got home, I sent away for some sundew seeds of my own.

When a bug gets stuck on a sundew, the leaf slowly curls up around it. Then the soft parts of the bug are dissolved by chemicals and eaten. Afterward, the leaf opens up again and the leftover bug parts fall off.

Butterworts are carnivorous plants, too, and often grow in the same places as sundews. They have flat leaves like flypaper. Little bugs stick to the leaves and slowly dissolve.

The seeds weren't just for ordinary sundews, though. They were for Giant African sundews. I sowed them in a pot of moss and covered it with glass.

I watered the pot every day with rainwater straight from the water tank. Soon the seeds started to sprout and I had dozens of baby sundews.

They grew and grew, until they were almost big enough to start catching things.

Then one day I watered them with the wrong kind of water—and every single one died.

There are over 80 kinds of sundews and they are found all over the world.

Giant African sundews are the biggest. Their leaves can grow to be 18 inches long.

My sundews died because I accidentally put fertilizer in the water. All carnivorous plants hate fertilizer.

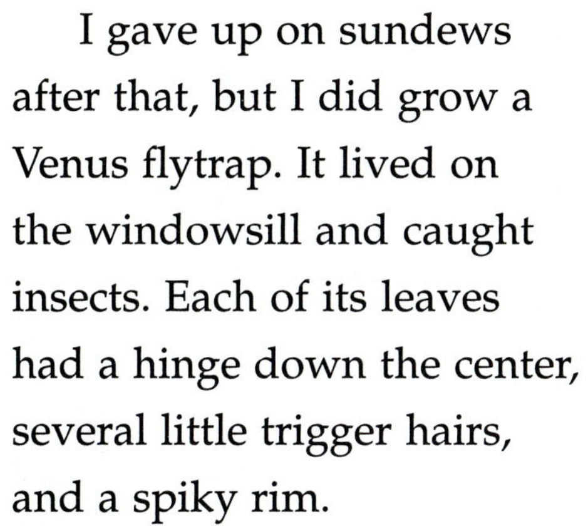

I gave up on sundews after that, but I did grow a Venus flytrap. It lived on the windowsill and caught insects. Each of its leaves had a hinge down the center, several little trigger hairs, and a spiky rim.

When a fly or a wasp walked over a leaf, it was perfectly safe if it didn't touch any of the hairs. It was even safe if it touched just one of the hairs. But if it touched two of the hairs, then . . .

Venus flytraps grow in only one small part of the southeastern United States. They are rare now because people have drained many of the marshes where they once lived.

SNAP!

Small insects such as ants can escape from a Venus flytrap- they're not big enough to be worth eating. But flies and wasps are a different story. Once caught, the more they struggle the tighter the leaf presses together. When the leaf is fully closed, it begins to dissolve its victim.

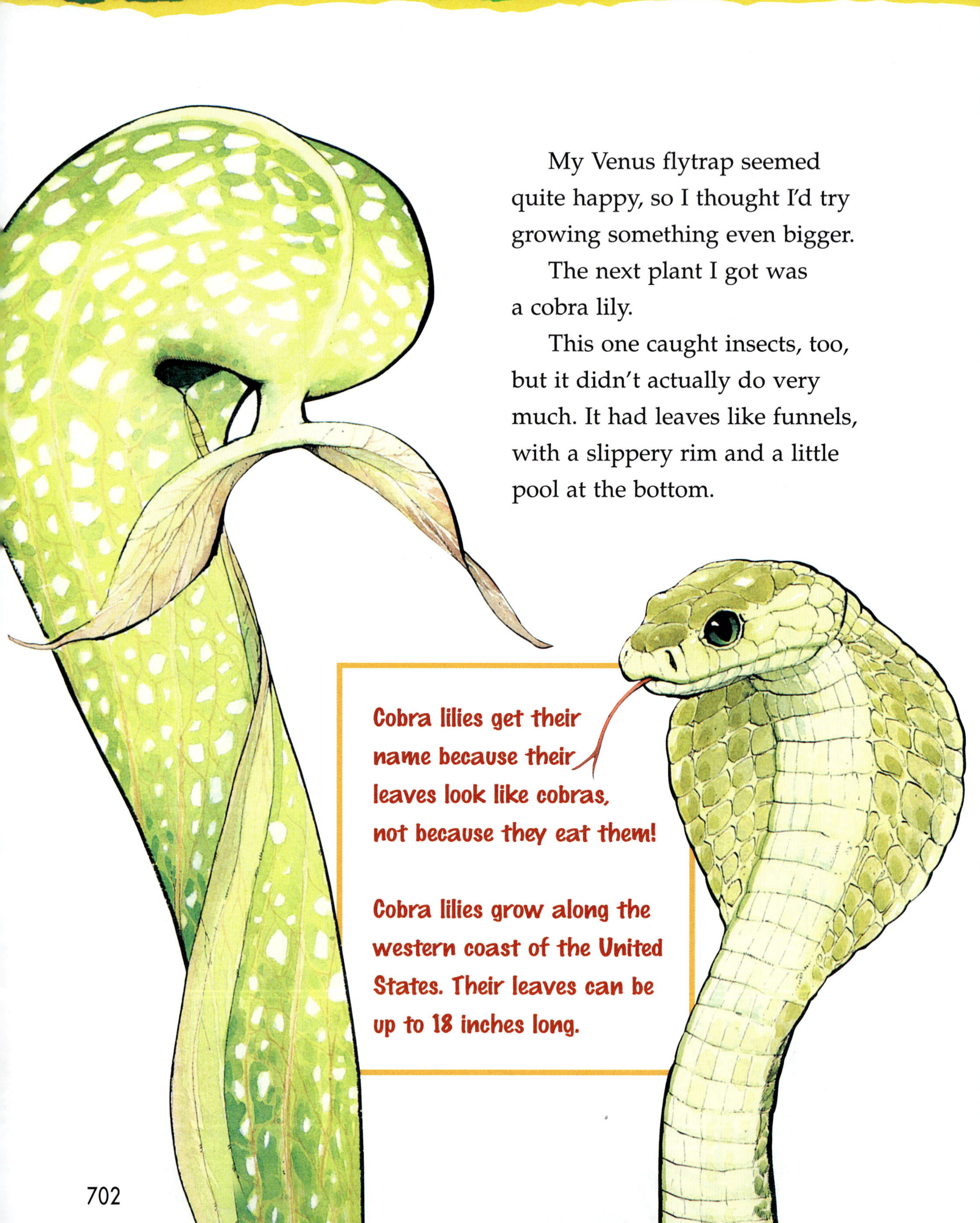

My Venus flytrap seemed quite happy, so I thought I'd try growing something even bigger.

The next plant I got was a cobra lily.

This one caught insects, too, but it didn't actually do very much. It had leaves like funnels, with a slippery rim and a little pool at the bottom.

Cobra lilies get their name because their leaves look like cobras, not because they eat them!

Cobra lilies grow along the western coast of the United States. Their leaves can be up to 18 inches long.

When insects crawled inside, they fell into the pool and couldn't climb out. So they stayed there and became bug soup for the lily.

I was very happy with my cobra lily. Surely it was the biggest carnivorous plant of all. But then my friend told me about pitcher plants.

Pitchers are even bigger, she said, but they are very difficult to grow. In that case, I thought, I'll just go and find some wild ones.

So I went—all the way to Malaysia.

And there, growing up the trees at the edge of the jungle, were hundreds of pitcher plants. Fat red ones, thin yellow ones, curly green ones, all waiting for flies.

I didn't see the biggest pitcher plant of all, though. It's called the Rajah pitcher plant and it grows on the tallest mountain in Borneo.

The pitchers' leaves look like vases, and they catch insects in the same way that cobra lilies do.

There are some kinds of spiders, and even some small tree frogs, that are able to live inside the pitchers. They cling to the slippery sides and grab the insects that fall in.

It has pitchers the size of footballs. People say it can even catch some kinds of squirrels, but I'm not convinced. One day I'll go and see for myself . . .

Think and Respond

1. How are the plants the author describes alike? How are they different?
2. How does the author make the information about **carnivorous** plants interesting and easy to read?
3. How would you describe the tone of this selection and the author's attitude toward the subject?
4. Would you enjoy growing carnivorous plants, as the author did? Why or why not?
5. Where in the selection did you use a reading strategy? How did it help you?

Meet the Author

Martin Jenkins

Martin Jenkins is a biologist who spends most of his time writing "serious things." But in his children's books he takes a light-hearted look at his travels. In *Chameleons Are Cool,* readers experience a trip to Madagascar, where a wild chameleon bit him on the thumb! "I still think they are wonderful," he says, "but tend to leave them alone." Mr. Jenkins calls *Fly Traps!* "absolutely autobiographical."

Meet the Illustrator

David Parkins

David Parkins' amusing people and animals have appeared in many books. Working on *Fly Traps!* brought back memories: "When I first started out as an illustrator, I did a book on wildlife and spent a year tramping around fields drawing berries and birds. So, in a way, this takes me back to my beginnings." Mr. Parkins lives in Lincolnshire, England. His main hobby is singing.

Visit *The Learning Site!*
www.harcourtschool.com

Genre Interview

My Visit to a Dreamy Place

Betsy Mizell

There are few places on Earth that are as special as the Galápagos Islands. As a member of the Young Explorers Club, I was lucky enough to visit these beautiful islands on the equator, about 600 miles west of the coast of South America, this past summer.

Here are some questions that *Dolphin Log* magazine asked Betsy about her trip:

Dolphin Log: What was the best part of the trip?

Betsy: Snorkeling was really fun. At first I was scared, but there were lots of beautiful fish in the water.

Dolphin Log: What was your favorite Galápagos Islands creature?

Betsy: I loved the sea lions, manta rays and sharks, but the sea lions were my favorite.

Dolphin Log: In one of the photos you sent us, you stood right next to the sea lions! Were they friendly?

Betsy: No, not at all. In fact . . . they weren't very nice. They growled at me when I got too close to them. But sea lion pups were cute.

Dolphin Log: Did it rain at all on your trip to the equator?

Betsy: Sometimes it would rain . . . for about one minute. Then it was as hot and sunny as before.

Dolphin Log: Did you know anything about the Galápagos Islands before your trip?

Betsy: My mom told me a little bit about them, and where they were. I knew that they were formed by volcanoes . . . but I didn't know they were underwater volcanoes! That was a surprise.

Dolphin Log: Tell us something else you learned on your trip.

Betsy: I learned a lot of stuff! But the most interesting, I think, was about Galápagos tortoises. I didn't know they were threatened. It's important that people take care of them.

Dolphin Log: Did you eat anything new and different on your trip?

Betsy: One night they served something called gazpacho . . .

Dolphin Log: That's a cold soup . . .

Betsy: With little shrimp in it . . .

Dolphin Log: How was it?

Betsy: Eeew. I wouldn't try it. My mom did, though. She said it was okay.

Think and Respond

What new things did Betsy Mizell learn on her trip?

Galápagos Islands

South America

Pacific Ocean

▲ Fly Traps!

Making Connections

Text to Self • Text to Text • Text To World

Compare Texts

NC STANDARDS: ELA 1.04h increase vocabulary/examine author's craft, 2.04c identify main idea/details, 3.01e interpret/evaluate text/draw inferences/conclusions, 3.02 interpret/evaluate text/analyze/compare texts

1. Why does the author of "Fly Traps!" want to travel to distant lands? INTERPRETATION / EVALUATING

2. What do the illustrations in "Fly Traps!" add to the text? Give examples. INTERPRETATION / KNOWLEDGE

3. How are the authors' experiences different in "Fly Traps!" and "My Visit to a Dreamy Place"? CONNECTIONS / ANALYZING

4. How might "Fly Traps!" be different if the author had written a textbook about carnivorous plants instead of a narrative? COGNITION / EVALUATING

5. Besides carnivorous plants, what other topics were mentioned in "Fly Traps!" that you might like to learn more about? INTERPRETATION / EVALUATING

Write an Explanation

In "Fly Traps!" you read about the ways in which different carnivorous plants capture insects. Choose one carnivorous plant that you read about, and write a paragraph explaining how it captures insects. You may want to use a graphic organizer like the one shown here to organize your ideas.

NC STANDARD: ELA 3.06 conduct research using a variety of tools

Make an Illustrated Chart

Science CONNECTION

Insects are helpful in many ways. Of about one million species of insects in the world, fewer than one percent are harmful. Research the topic of insects. Then make an illustrated chart showing some helpful and harmful insects. Tell how or why each insect is helpful or harmful. A particular insect may be both helpful and harmful, depending on your point of view.

Create a Travel Guide

Social Studies CONNECTION

The author of "Fly Traps!" tells about taking a trip to Malaysia to see pitcher plants. Research Malaysia, and create a travel guide to give visitors facts and information about it. Include a map to show the location of Malaysia. You should also include on your map the major cities and points of interest in Malaysia.

NC STANDARD: ELA 3.06 conduct research using a variety of tools

▲ Fly Traps! Plants That Bite Back

Word Relationships

 NC STANDARD: ELA 1.03 use strategies for key word meanings/relationships

You can use what you know about word relationships to understand the meanings of words that you read. You might look for a synonym or antonym to help make the meaning of a word clear to you. If a word is a multiple-meaning word or a homograph, use the context of the sentence to interpret the meaning. Here are some examples from "Fly Traps! Plants That Bite Back."

Selection Words	Relationship to Other Words	How to Use Context
leaves p. 694	has more that one meaning: • "plant parts" • "goes away" • "pages in a book"	Decide which meaning makes sense in the sentence. ("plant parts")
through p. 696	homophone of *threw*	Look at how the word is spelled.
straight p. 698	has more than one meaning: • "not curved" • "in a row" • "direct"	Decide which meaning makes sense in the sentence. ("direct")
flies p. 701	has more than one meaning: • "moves through the air" • "moves very fast" • "small, two-winged insects"	Decide which meaning makes sense in the sentence. ("small, two-winged insects")

How are the underlined words in this sentence related?

When insects get too close to a Venus flytrap, the leaf may close with a snap.

Visit *The Learning Site!* www.harcourtschool.com

See *Skills and Activities*

Test Prep
Word Relationships

NC STANDARD: ELA 1.03 use strategies for key word meanings/relationships

▶ **Read the passage. Then complete the items.**

Insects: Friends or Foes?

Insects are found just about everywhere on earth. Steamy tropical rain forests are home to numerous insects, but so are frigid polar regions. We tend to think of insects as pests that destroy our crops, carry germs, and bite humans and animals. The use of insecticides to kill harmful insects is often necessary, but we need to be careful that the poisons do not also cause damage to helpful insects. Because insects are a major food source for birds, fish, and other animals, our planet would be a very different place without them.

COGNITION / ORGANIZING

1. What word relationship helps make clear the meaning of *frigid*?

A It is a synonym for *rain.*

B It is a synonym for *polar.*

C It is an antonym of *regions.*

D It is an antonym of *forest.*

Use the context of the sentence to identify a synonym or antonym that helps make clear the meaning of *frigid*.

COGNITION / ORGANIZING

2. The word *place* in this passage means—

F to finish in a certain position

G space or area

H to put in a particular position

J a short street

In two of the answer choices, *place* is a noun. Look closely at the meanings of the nouns.

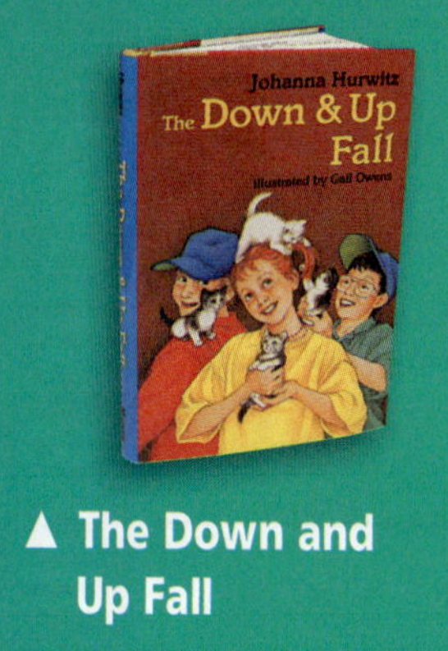

▲ The Down and Up Fall

Vocabulary Power

In "The Down and Up Fall," some students decorate a room in their school for a very special purpose. The following scene is also about people who decorate a room for a good reason.

- corridor
- apparently
- enthusiastically
- investigate
- transformed
- decor

[SETTING: Two men are standing in the **corridor** of an office building. Music and laughter can be heard coming from an office at the other end of the long, narrow hallway.]

RAY: Listen to all that noise! **Apparently** there's a party going on!

FRED: It does sound like a party. I wonder why we weren't invited.

RAY: (He speaks **enthusiastically**, with excitement in his voice.) Come on! Let's go down there and **investigate**. I want to find out what's happening.

FRED: (He speaks without enthusiasm.) Okay, but we shouldn't go in if we weren't invited.

[They walk down the corridor and knock on the door. Suddenly the door bursts open.]

ALL EXCEPT FRED: Surprise! Happy birthday, Fred!

FRED: (He is shocked and amazed.) Wow! Thanks, everyone. You've **transformed** this office. It looks completely different. The balloons and streamers make the **decor** of this room perfect for a party. You all did a great job decorating. Now let's have some birthday cake.

Vocabulary-Writing CONNECTION

Write a paragraph describing the **decor** of your classroom. Remember to use vivid words to describe the way your classroom is decorated.

The Down

by
Johanna Hurwitz
illustrated by
Jenny Tylden-Wright

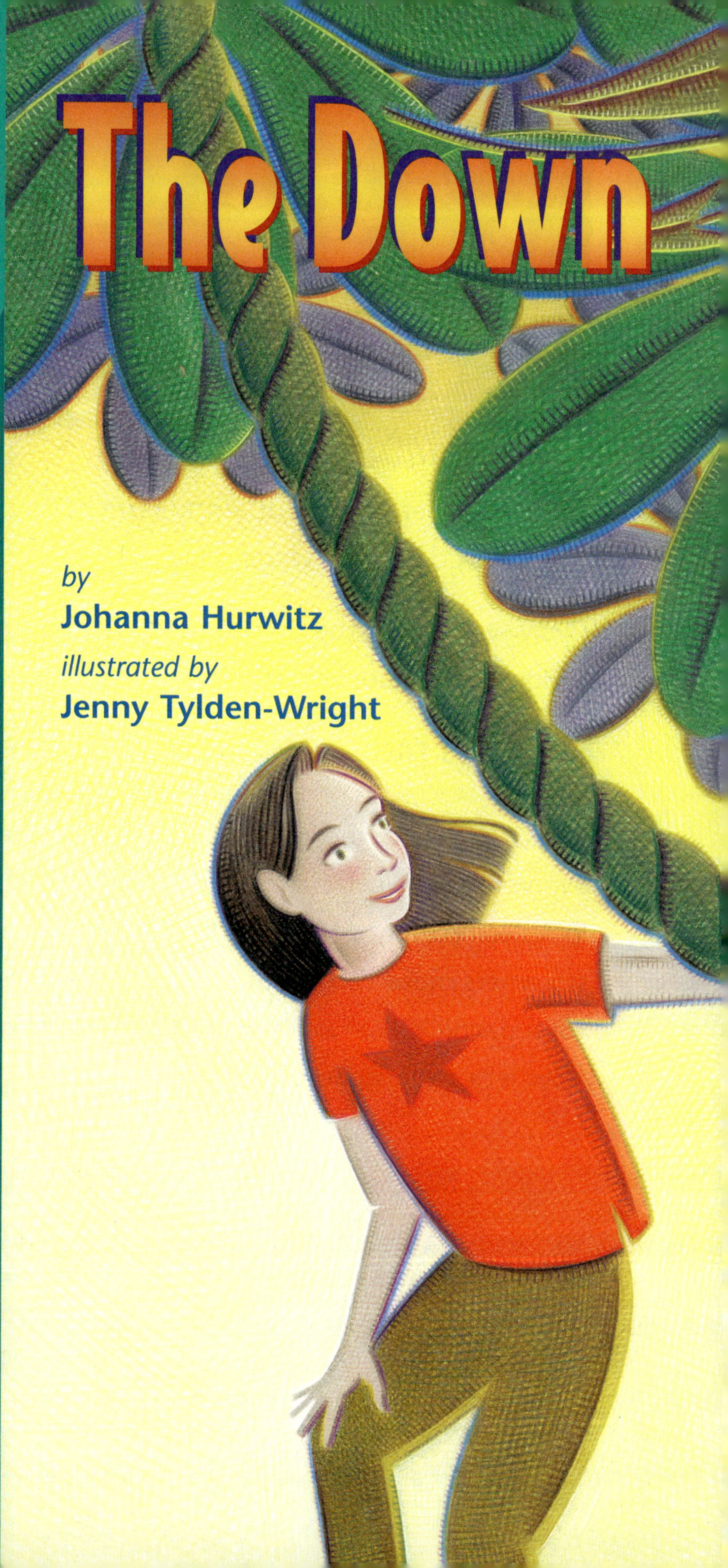

Genre

Realistic Fiction

Realistic fiction tells about characters and events that are like people and events in real life.

In this selection, look for

- **Characters who have feelings that real people have**
- **Details that help the reader picture the setting**

Bolivia Raab is staying with her aunt and uncle, the Goldings, for six months while her parents are working in Turkey. One afternoon her friends —Rory, Derek, DeDe, and Aldo— come over to see her parrot, Lucette. They say she should take the bird to the "rain forest" that the school nature club has set up in a classroom. Bolivia thinks this may be too much excitement for her pet, but she agrees to think about it.

On Monday, as soon as they finished eating their lunches, Aldo took Bolivia to peek inside the room that the nature club had transformed into its rain forest. Even though neither the humidifier nor the heater was turned on when she arrived, Bolivia could still feel the dampness and smell the earthy odor in the air. There was a soft cushion of soil underfoot as she walked inside the room.

Mr. Peters, the adviser to the club, was there, busily watering the rubber plants.

"Hello," he said to them. "Have you come to investigate another corner of the world?"

"This is a girl from my homeroom named Bolivia Raab," said Aldo, introducing his classmate to the teacher. "She's got a real live parrot at home. I asked her to bring it to our club tomorrow."

"A parrot? That's fantastic!" exclaimed Mr. Peters. "What type is it?"

"She's a green Amazon parrot from South America," Bolivia explained. "I've had her since I was very young, and I've taught her to speak a little."

"Wonderful!" said Mr. Peters enthusiastically. "I bet she'd feel right at home here in our rain forest. Will you bring her to school tomorrow?"

Bolivia really was intrigued by the idea of Lucette visiting the rain forest. It seemed only fair that the bird should be given the experience. She had lived for so many years away from the tropical environment that was a parrot's natural habitat. Nevertheless, Bolivia worried that a whole day at school was more than Lucette needed. It was stressful enough for a student. Imagine how it would be for a bird!

Bolivia thought about all the students who would try to touch Lucette during the day when she wasn't around to protect her. There was bound to be some wise guy who would poke the parrot and possibly hurt her.

Mr. Peters seemed to guess what she was thinking. "We'd be very careful that no harm comes to your bird," he reassured her.

"Let me see if my uncle can drive her over to school in the afternoon in time for your club meeting," Bolivia offered. That seemed the perfect compromise. An hour and a half in the afternoon should be enough rain forest adventure for Lucette.

"Wonderful!" Mr. Peters exclaimed again. "I'll tell Kenny to bring his snakes to school tomorrow too. And I'll announce over the public address system that the rain forest will be open to the entire school."

Bolivia knew that most of the time no one paid any attention to the announcements. Otherwise she would have been worried about a thousand students trying to squeeze into the rain forest.

"Neat," said Aldo as a bell interrupted the conversation. He turned to Bolivia. "We'd better go," he said. "Our lunch period is over."

"Okay," Bolivia said. "See you tomorrow," she called to the science teacher.

Mr. Golding was perfectly willing to deliver Lucette to the middle school the next day. "It's been a long time since I was inside a school," he commented. "Do you think they'll let me take some pictures of that rain forest?"

"Why not?" asked Bolivia. "I bet they'll be thrilled. And then I could send a picture to my parents too."

The next afternoon, just at the time when school was being dismissed, Bolivia's uncle Lou arrived there with Lucette. It was a day as warm as summer, so Bolivia hadn't worried about the outdoor temperature being too cold for her parrot. But her uncle was the cautious type. He had Lucette's traveling cage wrapped in a big blanket when he met Bolivia in the school lobby.

Rory and Derek were waiting with Bolivia.

"Poor Lucette," Rory said. "Having to go to school at her age."

"What is her age?" asked Derek.

"She's older than we are," Bolivia responded. "She's about twenty years old."

"What's in there?" asked a boy passing by in the hall. In a moment they were surrounded by a group of students curious about the large bundle in Mr. Golding's arms.

"Stand back. Stand back," Bolivia shouted. "This is my parrot, Lucette, and she's going to make a visit to the rain forest upstairs. If you want to see her, you'll have to wait in line outside the science room. Too many people at once will scare her."

Luckily at that very moment Mr. Peters joined them, and he too announced to the students that the only way to see the parrot was to visit the rain forest.

Then Bolivia, Rory, Derek, Mr. Golding (holding the parrot in the wrapped cage), and Mr. Peters (holding back the crowd) made their way up the flight of stairs and toward the room that housed the rain forest. Outside the doorway of the forest stood Aldo, DeDe, and several students Bolivia didn't know.

Mr. Peters unlocked the door, and they all went inside. The science teacher turned on both the humidifier and the electric heater.

"This is amazing," gasped Mr. Golding, marveling at the room's decor. "Look at that." He pointed to some pieces of rope that had been painted green and hung from the ceiling. "They look just like wild vines."

"It even smells like a rain forest, doesn't it?" Bolivia asked her uncle.

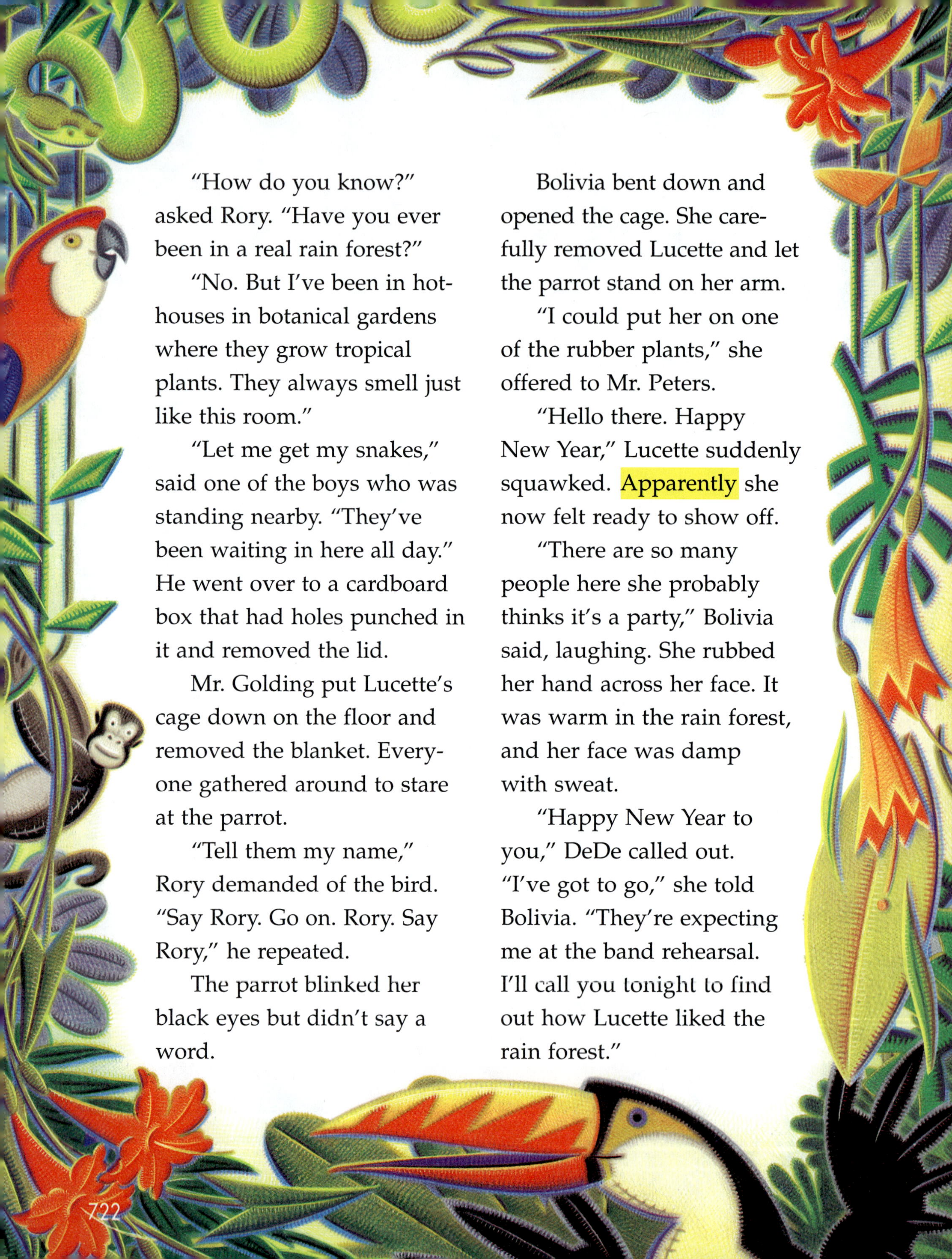

"How do you know?" asked Rory. "Have you ever been in a real rain forest?"

"No. But I've been in hothouses in botanical gardens where they grow tropical plants. They always smell just like this room."

"Let me get my snakes," said one of the boys who was standing nearby. "They've been waiting in here all day." He went over to a cardboard box that had holes punched in it and removed the lid.

Mr. Golding put Lucette's cage down on the floor and removed the blanket. Everyone gathered around to stare at the parrot.

"Tell them my name," Rory demanded of the bird. "Say Rory. Go on. Rory. Say Rory," he repeated.

The parrot blinked her black eyes but didn't say a word.

Bolivia bent down and opened the cage. She carefully removed Lucette and let the parrot stand on her arm.

"I could put her on one of the rubber plants," she offered to Mr. Peters.

"Hello there. Happy New Year," Lucette suddenly squawked. **Apparently** she now felt ready to show off.

"There are so many people here she probably thinks it's a party," Bolivia said, laughing. She rubbed her hand across her face. It was warm in the rain forest, and her face was damp with sweat.

"Happy New Year to you," DeDe called out. "I've got to go," she told Bolivia. "They're expecting me at the band rehearsal. I'll call you tonight to find out how Lucette liked the rain forest."

"So long," Aldo said to DeDe.

"Who's in charge of the sound effects?" asked Mr. Peters.

"It's my turn," one of the girls told him. She went over to a corner where there was a cassette player half-hidden behind a rubber plant. She turned on a switch, and at once the room was filled with tropical noises. There was the sound of dripping water. And there were many birdcalls. In fact, it seemed as if the room was filled with tropical birds.

"Hello there," squawked Lucette.

"She must think she's listening to real birds," said Derek.

"Watch out," warned Kenny, the owner of the two grass snakes. "You almost stepped on Jefferson."

Bolivia looked down. There was a green snake moving in front of her just as if she were walking in a real rain forest.

Mr. Golding took the blanket and the birdcage and placed them in the hallway outside the room. They didn't belong inside a rain forest. Then he took his camera out of the case around his neck and began to take pictures of one of the more realistic toy monkeys climbing on a plant. "I wish people could smell these pictures when they're developed," he told the science teacher. "You've done a fantastic job here."

Bolivia noticed Rory turning the dial on the electric heater. She hoped he was lowering the heat. She was really feeling uncomfortably warm.

"Hello. Can I come in or do I need a passport?" a woman's voice called out at the doorway.

Bolivia turned to see who had entered the room. It was Dr. Osborne, the assistant principal of the school.

"Come in. Come in," called Mr. Peters. "We have everything here except mosquitoes."

"This is lovely. Just lovely," Dr. Osborne told the teacher.

"The nature club has done a lot of hard work to create all this," Mr. Peters informed her proudly.

"Happy New Year!" Lucette squawked from her perch on a rubber plant.

"Happy New Year?" Dr. Osborne walked toward the corner where Bolivia and Lucette were stationed.

"Watch your step!" shouted Kenny as the assistant principal narrowly missed trampling on one of his snakes.

Dr. Osborne looked down and gave an amazingly loud shriek. It was much louder than the one that Bolivia's aunt Sophie had given when she'd seen the mouse in the kitchen.

At that moment Bolivia felt a few drops of rain on her face. Then it started raining harder. She looked up at the ceiling. How in the world had Mr. Peters and his students arranged that?

Some of the students in the room began to rush out the door, but others remained, lifting their faces toward the water and enjoying the unexpected shower.

"It's just a little grass snake. He won't hurt you," said Kenny, but the assistant principal was already out the door. Bolivia wondered if she was looking to get out of the rain or to put more distance between herself and Kenny's snake.

"Get the blanket," she shouted to her uncle. The cool water felt good on her skin, but she thought she'd better protect Lucette.

"Where's this water coming from?" Aldo asked Mr. Peters. Apparently he was just as surprised as Bolivia by the rain.

"It's the sprinkler system," Mr. Peters answered. "The heat in the room seems to have triggered it." He had unplugged the electric heater. Now he was busily opening the windows, which were hidden behind painted backdrops.

"I never heard of having windows in a rain forest," Rory said. His eyeglasses were spattered with water drops, and his hair looked as if he'd been interrupted in the middle of a shower.

"Go and get the custodian," Mr. Peters instructed Aldo. "He'll know how to shut off the sprinklers."

Dr. Osborne returned to the classroom, holding an umbrella over her head. "Where's that snake?" she asked nervously.

"Here," called out Kenny, holding up his grass snake. "This is Jefferson. You scared him."

"I scared him? He scared *me*," the assistant principal said.

"Then you'd better watch out for Washington, my other snake. He's hiding under one of the plants."

"You mean, there are *two* snakes in this room? Snakes are not in my job description." Dr. Osborne looked anxiously down toward her feet.

"Happy New Year, RoryDerek!" squawked Lucette from under the blanket that Bolivia had thrown over her. This was very unusual. Generally Lucette was silent when she was covered up.

The entrance to the science room was jammed with students and teachers from the other clubs that had been meeting along the corridor. Everyone was curious about the screams and the water puddles that had oozed out of the science room.

The custodian arrived, shaking his head in dismay. "First it was dirt," he mumbled. "Now this." He carried a ladder, which he climbed on to reach a switch near the ceiling. The rain stopped as suddenly as it had begun, but the air was more humid than ever. Just the way the air should be in a rain forest, Bolivia realized as she pulled at her wet T-shirt. She looked down at her jeans, which were spattered with mud.

Dr. Osborne closed her umbrella. Mr. Peters smiled at her. "This is how we keep education alive and exciting," he explained. "These students will always remember about rain forests now."

"You can say that again," said the assistant principal. "I'll never forget this afternoon or the snakes."

"Jefferson is harmless," Kenny reassured her. "And so is Washington. Nothing bad could have happened to you." He broke into a grin. "But I am saving up for a boa constrictor."

"If you get one, don't ever bring it to school," Dr. Osborne said firmly.

"They don't eat people. Just mice," Kenny said.

The assistant principal turned to the science teacher. "This was a wonderful display," she said. "I'm sure everyone has learned a great deal from this. But perhaps it's time for you to move on to another area of study."

"Good idea," said the custodian. "I can't wait to get the dirt out of this school."

"Oh, I have plenty of other plans," Mr. Peters told Dr. Osborne. "I thought we'd turn this room into a moonscape. There are no snakes on the moon," he added.

Think and Respond

1. How and why does Dr. Osborne's opinion change about the room that the nature club **transformed**?
2. Why do you think the author included snakes and a parrot in the rain forest display?
3. Why do you suppose Lucette keeps saying, "Happy New Year"?
4. Do you agree that projects like the rain forest display "keep education alive and exciting"?
5. How did using a reading strategy help you understand the story?

Meet the Author

Johanna Hurwitz

As a child, Johanna Hurwitz loved books so much that by the age of ten, she had decided to become a librarian someday and to write books of her own. After graduating from college, she did become a librarian. She also married and had two children. During this time, she wrote hundreds of letters to friends and relatives. She feels that these letters were good training for writing books.

Johanna Hurwitz has published more than forty books for children. She remembers her own childhood very well. She says that everything in her books comes from real life. For example, Derek and Rory are based on her son and his friend. She really met someone who had a daughter named Bolivia and decided to use the name for one of her characters. Some of her friends' pets have appeared in her books, too.

Johanna Hurwitz

Visit *The Learning Site!*
www.harcourtschool.com

Genre
Magazine Article

Amazon River
SOUTH AMERICA

RIO MAR VI

Amazon Adventure

FROM *RANGER RICK* MAGAZINE
BY SUSAN GOODMAN

Cruising down the Mighty Amazon, exploring deep in the rainforest.

How lucky can some kids get?

"Check it out!" Kevin shouted, pointing to something swimming in the world's largest river, the Amazon.

From the deck of a river boat, Kevin and his friends watched rare river dolphins flash past.

Then the kids looked toward shore—at the houses on stilts, the banana plants, and the palm trees. This place was so different from home!

Who were these lucky kids, and what were they doing in the Amazon rainforest? They were junior high students from Michigan. And they were taking part in a Children's Rainforest Workshop.

All through the school year they had studied rainforests. They also worked hard earning money to help pay for the trip. Now all their learning would come to life as they spent a week in a small corner of the world's largest rainforest.

Life in the Forest

After flying to the city of Iquitos, Peru, the kids cruised 50 miles (80 km) down the Amazon. The boat finally docked at a jungle hideaway called Explorama Lodge. Right away the kids could see that life here would take getting used to!

Lots of rain made the air very humid, so wet clothes took days to dry. Kerosene lamps took the place of electric lights. (No videos or hair dryers here!) Mosquito netting kept creepy-crawlies out of their beds.

Look, but don't touch! This tree's long spines keep hungry animals away.

And to go to the bathroom, the kids had to walk down a long path to an outside toilet.

"I miss hamburgers and pizza," said April, "but I've tried some neat new foods—like fried bananas, black beans, and manioc root."

The kids didn't have to go far for animal-watching. While swinging on hammocks, they watched hummingbirds sip nectar from flowers. They shared their showers with huge moths and weird katydids. Once they even had to step over a column of marching army ants to get to the dining room.

A Living Lab

All week, the kids explored the river and the rainforest. While paddling down the Amazon in canoes, they learned that the river contains more species (kinds) of fish than the entire Atlantic Ocean.

Near their camp, one of the kids spotted a two-toed sloth crawling along a thin tree branch.

The most exciting part of the trip was a walk through the treetops.

By catching some of those fish in a net, Jake made another discovery. "These are the same kinds of tropical fish I have in my aquarium at home!" he said.

By hunting for tarantulas, butterflies, and foot-long walking sticks, the kids learned a lot about nature. But exploring the canopy walkway was the trip's high point—in more ways than one.

Getting Above It

The canopy walkway is like a narrow trail through the treetops. It starts at the top of a tower and

zigzags through the rainforest canopy. (That's the top level of the forest.) It ends 1600 feet (480 m) away at another tower.

The kids knew the walkway was safe. But that first step onto it was still a little scary. Sarah said it was "fun, exciting, wonderful, frightening, and every other word that describes my mixed feelings!"

Scientists have known for a long time that tropical rainforests have more species than any other place on Earth. But, until a few years ago, they had no idea *how* many. Now they're sure that *millions* of unknown species live overhead without ever coming near the ground.

Discovering an unknown species would have been neat. But the kids were happy just seeing what they did. Some creatures that were hard to spot from the jungle floor were now right before their eyes.

Instead of seeing just a flash of bright feathers, the kids stood eye to eye with some incredible birds. Instead of just hearing a weird howl, they nearly shared the same branch with a howler monkey.

The sights were amazing, but what Emily liked best was her second trip on the walkway—in the black of night. "We got to see glow-in-the-dark mushrooms up there. It was *so* neat!"

Good-Bye—For Now, Anyway

By week's end, all the kids were ready to see their families—and modern toilets! Still, the kids were sorry to leave. Tim said he was going to be "rainforest sick" instead of homesick. Erica said that although she hoped the forest would always be the same, "I know I'll never be."

Colorful birds, such as this macaw, came so close that the kids could almost touch them.

Think and Respond

What did the students learn in the Amazon rainforest that they couldn't have learned in school?

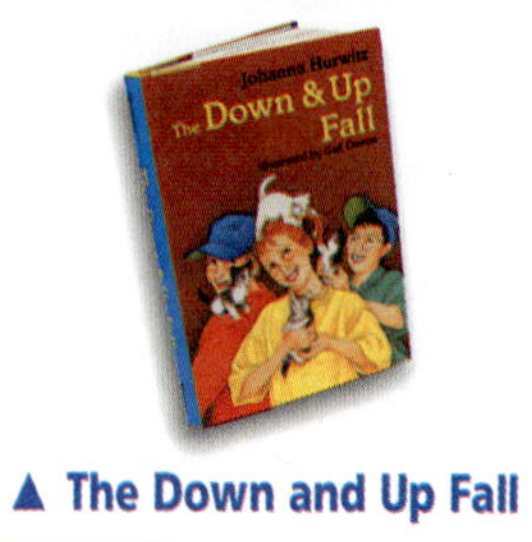

▲ The Down and Up Fall

Making Connections

Text to Self • Text to Text • Text To World

Compare Texts

NC STANDARDS: ELA 2.04b identify theme, 2.07 evaluate usefulness of content, 3.01d interpret/evaluate text/analyze differences among genres, 3.02 analyze/compare texts

1. How does the story "The Down and Up Fall" relate to the theme New Lands? INTERPRETATION / EVALUATING
2. How is the classroom like and unlike a real rain forest? CRITICAL STANCE / ANALYZING
3. Readers learn facts about rain forests from "The Down and Up Fall" and from "Amazon Adventure." Which selection do you think is a better source of information, and why? COGNITION / EVALUATING
4. Think of another selection you have read about events that take place in school. Which selection tells about events that seem more realistic to you? Explain. INTERPRETATION / KNOWLEDGE
5. If you could choose between researching parrots, snakes, or tropical plants, which topic would you choose, and why? CRITICAL STANCE / EVALUATING

Write a Persuasive Speech

Writing CONNECTION

Think about how Mr. Peters might persuade Dr. Osborne to allow him to turn his room into a moonscape. Write a speech to persuade Dr. Osborne to allow Mr. Peters and the students to create the moonscape. Use a graphic organizer like this one to plan the speech.

Opinion:
Reason 1: Examples/details:
Reason 2: Examples/details:
Opinion restated/action requested:

NC STANDARD: ELA 2.01b use strategies to clarify text/vocabulary/use other sources

Draw a Diagram

Science CONNECTION

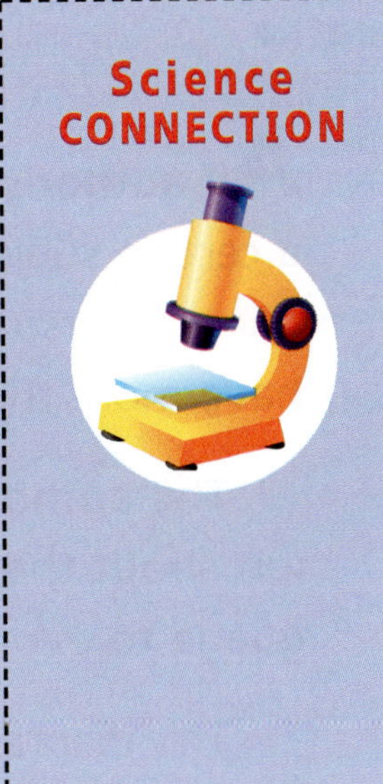

The plants, animals, bacteria, and nonliving elements present in a real rain forest are all parts of an ecosystem. Research the ecology of the Amazon rain forest. Draw a food chain or a food web that shows how one group of rain forest plants and animals connect with each other.

NC STANDARDS: ELA 2.04c identify main idea/details, 3.06 conduct research using a variety of tools

Write a Report

Social Studies CONNECTION

The characteristics of the rain forest affect the lives of people in that region. How do characteristics such as water, landforms, vegetation, and climate affect people's lives in the region where you live? Do research to find answers to this question. Then write a report to share the information you found. Include illustrations and diagrams.

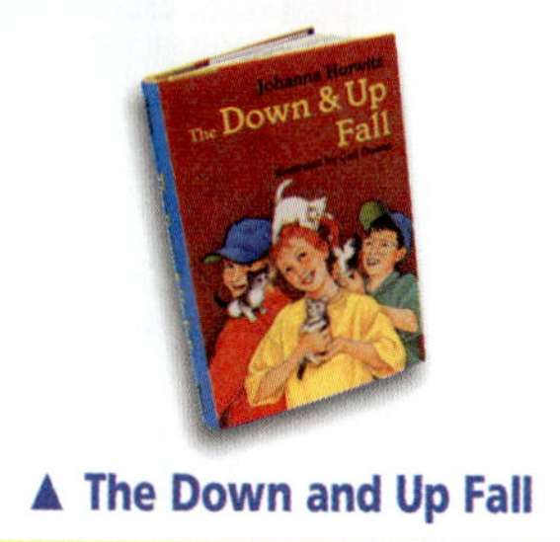

▲ The Down and Up Fall

Author's Purpose

NC STANDARDS: ELA 1.04h increase vocabulary/examine author's craft, 3.05 use graphs/charts/maps to expand understanding

An **author's purpose** is his or her reason for writing about a certain subject. The most common purposes are to entertain, to persuade, or to inform. Sometimes an author may have more than one purpose.

The **author's perspective**, or viewpoint, is his or her opinion about the subject. Authors choose details and use language to express their feelings about their subjects.

This diagram shows how using details and language can help you determine the author's purpose and perspective in "The Down and Up Fall."

Details
- The students are excited about the rain forest display.
- Funny things happen, such as the unexpected sprinkler shower.

Language

The author uses words such as *enthusiastically*, *fantastic*, *amazing*, *marveling*, and *exciting*.

Author's Purposes
- To entertain
- To persuade readers that school and science can be fun

Author's Perspective
- School and science can be fun and exciting.

Visit *The Learning Site!*
www.harcourtschool.com

See *Skills and Activities*

Test Prep
Author's Purpose

NC STANDARD: ELA 1.04h increase vocabulary/examine author's craft

Focus Skill

▶ **Read the passage. Then complete the items.**

Brianna had almost finished her homework when her friend Kerri came over. "We're going to shoot some baskets," Brianna told her mom.

When she got home, Brianna couldn't find her homework paper. Her puppy, Bootsie, kept getting in her way, wanting to play.

"Not now, Bootsie!" Brianna said, and then she gasped. A torn, chewed piece of paper was hanging from Bootsie's mouth.

"Oh, no!" Brianna wailed. "I can't believe I was so careless!" With a sigh, she took out another sheet of paper to start over.

COGNITION / EVALUATING

1. The author probably wrote this passage in order to

A persuade readers to do their homework

B entertain readers with a funny story

C explain how to train a puppy

D inform readers about how puppies behave

Think about the author's purpose. What was his or her main reason for writing this passage?

COGNITION / EVALUATING

2. Which statement best expresses the author's perspective?

F Puppies are bad pets.

G Being careless can lead to extra work.

H Students should not make up excuses.

J Homework is very important.

Does the main character blame Bootsie for what happened, or does she take responsibility?

Writer's Handbook

Contents

Planning Your Writing

Using References and Resources: Reading Functional Texts

Organizing Information

Polishing Your Writing

Presenting Your Writing

Planning Your Writing

Purposes for Writing

Each time you write, you have a reason. You may want to give information, respond to something you read, share an experience, or persuade someone to agree with you. The reason you write is called the **purpose for writing.** What you write depends on your purpose and on the people who will read your writing. These people are called the **audience.**

- **Expository writing** gives information. Expository writing includes how-to essays, literary responses, research reports, comparison and contrast essays, and explanatory essays.

    Sample prompt: *Compare and contrast dogs and wolves.*
    Think about *the ways dogs and wolves are alike and different.*
    Now write *about how dogs and wolves are alike and different.*

Tips for Expository Writing

- Write a topic sentence that tells the main idea.
- Organize your details or steps in a logical order.
- Use transition words or sequence words, such as *first* and *finally*.
- Summarize the main idea in your conclusion.

When you **respond to literature**, your purpose is to demonstrate an understanding of what you have read.

Sample Prompt: *Explain the theme of "The Emperor and the Kite." Use details from the selection to support your ideas.*

Tips for Literary Response

- Write a topic sentence that tells your main idea.
- Use details from the literature and your prior knowledge to support your topic sentence.
- Summarize the main idea in your conclusion.

- **Expressive writing** tells a story or entertains. Stories and personal narratives are both examples of expressive writing.

  Sample prompt: *Imagine you are going to visit the Amazon rainforest.* ***Think about*** *what you might do there.* ***Now write*** *a story about visiting the Amazon rainforest.*

- **Persuasive writing** gives an opinion. When you write to persuade, you try to convince your audience to agree with your opinion and to take action.

  Sample prompt: *Is it better to live in the city or the country? Why? Try to persuade other students to agree with you.*

Tips for Persuasive Writing

- Begin by getting your audience's attention and telling your opinion.
- Explain at least three supporting reasons.
- Give your strongest reason last.
- Support each reason with facts and details.
- Use emotional words to persuade your reader.
- Write a conclusion that restates your opinion and calls readers to take action.

Try This

Identify the audience and purpose for each of these writing tasks: tell a younger child how to play a new game; tell why you think your school should have a book fair; tell why you like mysteries better than science fiction books; present an oral report about tigers.

The Writing Process

A finished piece of writing does not simply happen. Writers go through a series of steps to complete their work and present a finished product. The amount of writing time spent on each step can vary. Here are the five basic steps in the **writing process:**

Prewriting

Before you begin to write, think about your purpose and audience. Decide what form your writing will take. Do research, and collect the information you need. Then **prewrite** by organizing your notes in an outline or another type of graphic organizer.

Drafting

Once you have a plan, you are ready to write. A **draft** is your first try at the finished story, essay, or other piece of writing. After you have finished your draft, you will still have to change parts of it to better fit your purpose and your audience.

Revising

Revising is the first step in the editing process. In this step, go over your draft to make sure that it fits your purpose and audience. Here are some things to do when you revise:

- Use an interesting opening sentence and a clear introduction.
- Add, delete, combine, or rearrange the text in your draft to make your writing more understandable to your audience.

- Make sure your writing follows a logical order from beginning to end.
- Use sequence words to help your audience follow your thoughts.
- Use words and ideas that your audience can understand.

It is often helpful to discuss your writing with a partner or in a small group. You can use what others say about your writing to revise it.

Proofreading

Proofreading is the second step in editing. When you proofread, you correct mistakes and polish your writing. Look for and correct errors in grammar, punctuation, capitalization, and spelling.

Publishing

After you have completed the first four steps, you are ready to **publish** your work, or to present it in its final, polished state. Depending on your purpose and audience, you may publish your writing as a speech, a video, or part of a class book. You may want to add pictures or other visual aids to enhance your work.

Try This

Write a paragraph to describe a person you know well. Follow the five steps in the writing process. On which step did you spend the most time?

How to Get Ideas

All writers must find ideas and topics. Writers think about everyday experiences and events and look for ways to write about them. They might ask themselves why an event made them feel a certain way. They might ask what they learned from an important or unusual experience. They might ask what they would like to learn more about or what they would like to teach others.

Writers use prewriting strategies like these to get ideas and to decide what to include in their writing.

Keep a Journal

You may want to carry a small notebook to write down interesting things you see or hear, unusual or meaningful things people say, and descriptions of people or places. You can refer to your notebook for writing topics later.

Search

If the topic you must write about is unfamiliar to you, **search** first on the Internet or in an encyclopedia. Newspapers and magazines may also have information on your topic. If you don't know how to begin your research, ask a librarian to help you find information on your topic.

Brainstorm

When you **brainstorm,** you write down everything you can think of about your idea or topic. Give yourself about ten minutes to do this. Then read what you wrote and look for only those ideas you think you can really use. Sometimes it helps to brainstorm with a group and to share ideas.

Make a Web Diagram

In a **web diagram** you write your topic in a circle. Then you draw spokes around the circle and write words or phrases about your topic at the end of each spoke.

Ask Questions

Ask questions to guide your thinking and writing about your topic. If you were writing a personal narrative, you could use questions like these as your guide.

- **Who** are the characters, besides yourself?
- **Where** and **when** does the narrative take place?
- **What** happens first? Next? Last?

Interview

Other people are often good sources of information and ideas. Talk with your teacher or your family about who you could interview and how you could contact that person. Always arrive on time for an interview, have questions prepared, and take careful notes.

Try This

Choose strategies you would use to get ideas for an essay about an important job in your community. How would you use each of the strategies you chose?

Encyclopedia

An **encyclopedia** has information on many subjects. The information about a subject is called an **article.** Some encyclopedias are on CD-ROM. Most encyclopedias come in a set of books. Each book in the set is called a **volume.** The volumes are numbered and arranged in alphabetical order.

Guide words appear at the top of every page. They name the subject of the first article on a left-hand page and the last article on a right-hand page.

Chimpanzee 537

Chimpanzees ar... Chimpanzees share more characteristics with human beings than any other animals do. They are intelligent, playful, curious, and easy to train. They are related to three other kinds of apes: gibbons,

Key words within articles may be printed in **bold type** or *italic type*. Key words are terms that are important to know about the subject. Key words themselves may be the subject of a separate article.

Victoria in the east to Gambia in the west. Scientists divide this species into three subspecies: the upper Guinean chimpanzee, the

Guinean chimpanzee, and the eastern, or long-haired, chimpanzee. The second main species, known as the pygmy chimpanzee, or *bonobo*, only lives

Cellos are large instruments that belong to the violin family. They are played with bows. The cello is about 48 inches tall. Like the violin, the cello has four strings, but because of its large size, the cello produces a deep sound.

See also **Orchestra; String quartet.**

References to other articles within the encyclopedia may appear within the article or at the end.

Almanac

An **almanac** is a book of facts. It has facts about people, places, weather, sports, entertainment, history, and events. A new edition of the almanac comes out every year.

An almanac gives information about **places.**

Florida

Population: 15,111,244

Total Area: 59,928 sq. mi.

Land Area: 53,937 sq. mi.

Chief Industries: tourism, agriculture, manufacturing

Capital: Tallahassee

Nickname: Sunshine State

State Flower: orange blossom

An almanac gives information about **history.**

Presidents of the United States

George Washington	1789–97
John Adams	1797–1801
Thomas Jefferson	1801–9
James Madison	1809–17
James Monroe	1817–25
John Quincy Adams	1825–9

Every almanac has an **index.** It lists all the subjects in the almanac and shows the page numbers on which to find the information you need.

Try This

In an encyclopedia and an almanac, look up a famous person, a state in the United States, or one of the oceans. Compare and contrast the information you find in the two resources.

CD-ROM Resources

Encyclopedias and other reference works are available on **CD-ROM.** This is a compact disk that is read by a computer.

After you open a CD-ROM, you will see the **home screen** first. It will tell you how to get to the instructions for using the reference work.

The home screen for this CD-ROM encyclopedia shows the major resources available through it. Click on the section that you want to use.

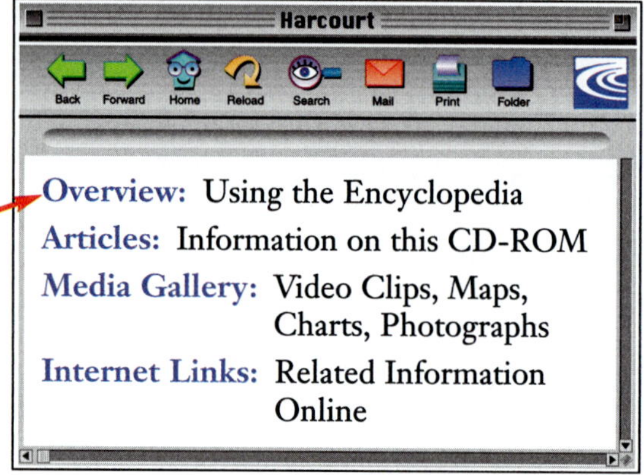

Use the articles section to research a topic. It should have guide words to help you. Use keywords as you would on the Internet. Your search will result in a list of articles that contain your keywords. Click on an article title to display the article. Move between articles by clicking the Back button.

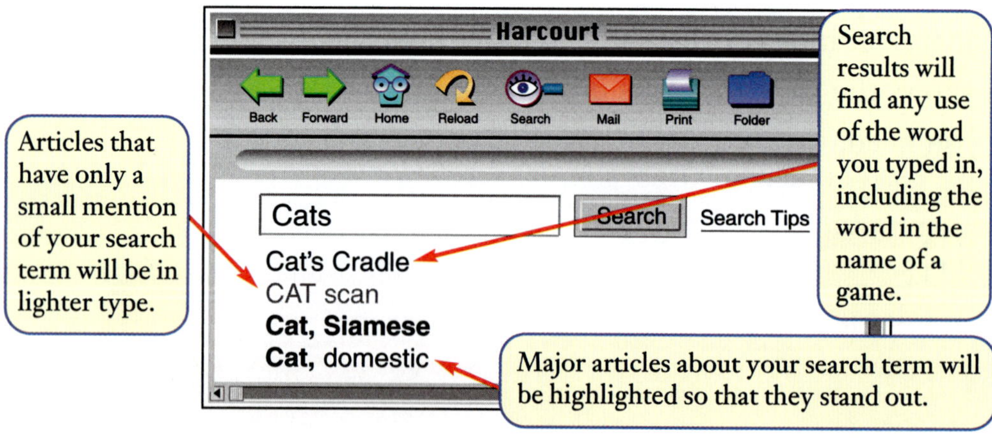

The Internet

The **Internet**—often called the Net—is a network that connects computers all over the world. A **network** is a group of computers that are linked electronically. The Internet is the largest computer network of all.

The Internet is an especially good resource for finding recent information about a topic. You can find specific information by using a **search engine.** A search engine matches your request for information with relevant websites. Follow these steps to get information from the Internet.

- Choose a search engine on the Internet.
- Type in a **keyword** about your topic. The more specific you are, the more exact your information will be. If your keyword is *cats*, you will find a variety of websites on cats. You might get websites about lions or tigers, about adopting kittens, or about the musical *Cats*.
- If you need to narrow your search, enter a more specific keyword or phrase such as *domestic cats*. Look through the list of websites and decide which will be useful. Click twice on each website to open it and to read the information it contains.
- To exit a website and return to the list, click on **Back** at the top of the screen.

Try This

At the library, do an Internet search for information about a pet you would like to have. Then check a CD-ROM encyclopedia. Which source gives you more information?

Using a Dictionary

A **dictionary** is a reference book that lists words in alphabetical order and gives their definitions. A dictionary also gives information about how a word is spelled, how it is pronounced, how it is divided into syllables, and what part of speech it is.

Guide words are at the top of each page. Guide words indicate the first and last entry word on a particular page.

The **phonetic spelling** is used to show how words are pronounced. There may be more than one way to pronounce a word.

lectern **legal**

lec • tern [lek 'tərn] *n.* A stand having an inclined top on which a speaker may put books or papers to read from.

lec • ture [lek' chər] *n.*, *v.* **lec • tured, lec • tur • ing 1** *n.* A speech on a particular subject, usually given to instruct or inform. **2** *v.* To give a lecture or teach by lectures. **3** *n.* A long or severe scolding. **4** *v.* To scold. —lec' tur • er *n.*

led [led] Past tense and past participle of LEAD: I *led* the dog home.

The **part of speech** is usually shown by an abbreviation after the word.

A **definition** tells what the entry word means. Often a word will have more than one definition.

Example sentences and phrases show how a word is used.

Using a Thesaurus

A **thesaurus** gives **synonyms**—words that mean the same or nearly the same as another word. A thesaurus also gives **antonyms**—words that have opposite meanings. Use a thesaurus to find words that will make writing more interesting or more precise. A thesaurus is usually arranged in alphabetical order.

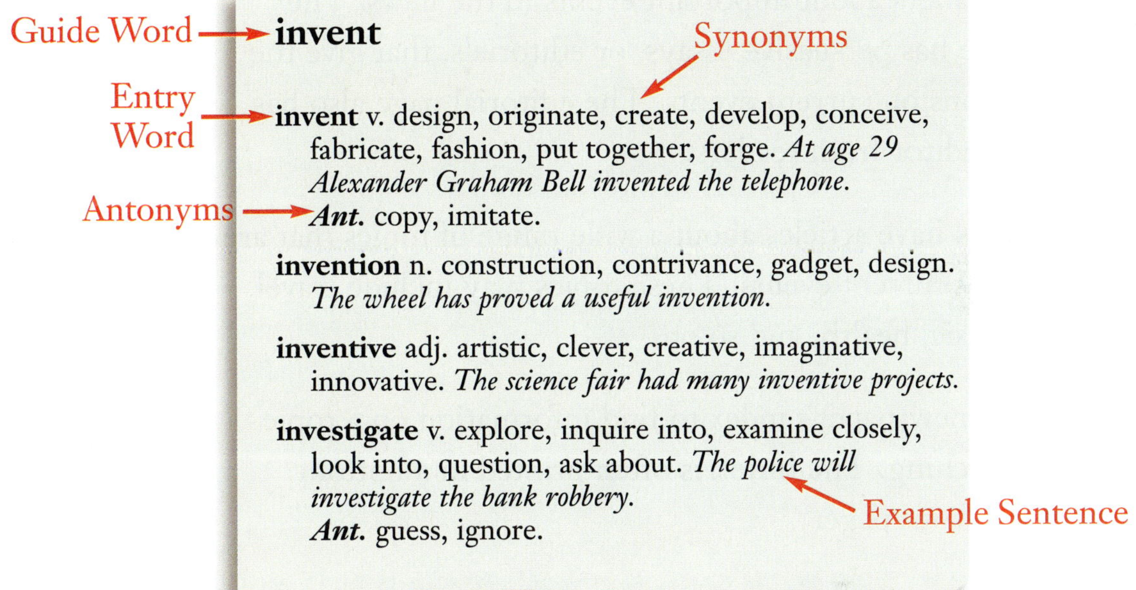

invent

invent v. design, originate, create, develop, conceive, fabricate, fashion, put together, forge. *At age 29 Alexander Graham Bell invented the telephone.*
Ant. copy, imitate.

invention n. construction, contrivance, gadget, design. *The wheel has proved a useful invention.*

inventive adj. artistic, clever, creative, imaginative, innovative. *The science fair had many inventive projects.*

investigate v. explore, inquire into, examine closely, look into, question, ask about. *The police will investigate the bank robbery.*
Ant. guess, ignore.

Try This

Compare and contrast a dictionary entry and a thesaurus entry for the words *draw*, *expensive*, and *laugh*. Which resource would you use to find the definition of a word? Which resource would you use to find a synonym for a word?

Newspapers and Periodicals

A **newspaper** is one of the best places to find information about current events. Most newspapers are published every day. They are usually arranged in the same way and have a **front page,** an **editorial page,** and **feature pages.**

The **front page** is the first page of a newspaper. It has articles that inform readers about important events in the news. The **editorial page** has persuasive essays, or editorials, that give the writers' opinions on current events. The editorial page also has letters to the editor from readers.

Feature pages have articles about a wide range of topics that are not necessarily current events. These topics may include travel, education, music, health, and so on.

You can use a newspaper's index to find information on a topic you are researching. The **index** is often printed in a bottom corner of the front page.

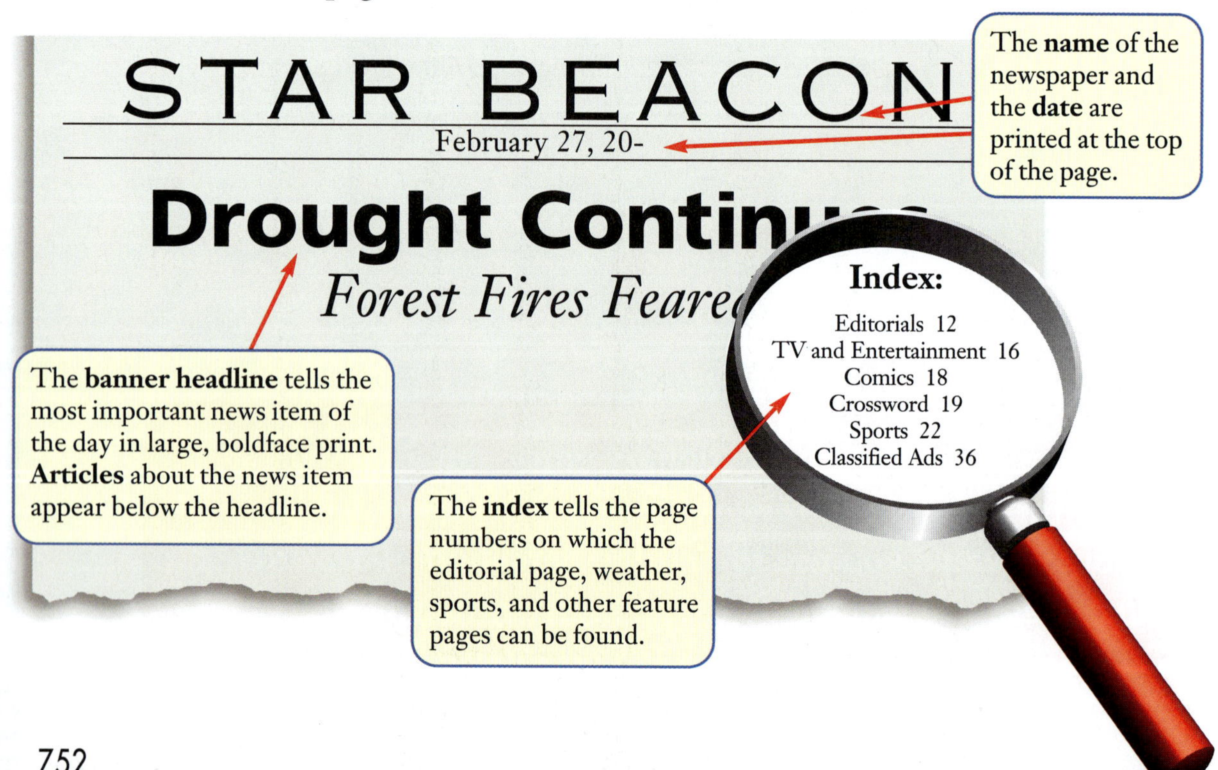

Periodicals are works that are published at regular times, or periodically, during a year. Newspapers are one type of periodical. Magazines are another type. Periodicals may be published once a week, once a month, once every few months, or once a year. Some periodicals print articles about one subject, such as health, sports, or travel. Others print articles on a range of subjects.

The three main parts of a periodical are the **cover,** the **table of contents,** and the **articles.** You can use the table of contents to find information on a topic you are researching.

The **name** of the periodical and the **date** when it was published are printed on the cover page.

A **cover title** in large, bold print tells about the **cover story**. The cover story is the most important story in the periodical.

The table of contents lists the title of every article in the periodical. It also lists the page number on which each article begins. The table of contents is printed near the front of the periodical.

Table of Contents

Each article tells about one topic. In most periodicals, the purpose of the articles is to inform readers about the topics.

Try This

Look in a newspaper and a news magazine published at the same time for an article about a recent sports or cultural event. What differences in the information do you find?

Note Taking

Taking notes can help you understand and remember information. If you take notes on cards, you can rearrange the cards to organize the information you need for writing.

1. Use one card for each idea. Write a subject heading on each card.
2. Write only two or three facts on each card. Number each card to keep your ideas in order.
3. List each source of information on the appropriate card. Include the following:
   - the name of the author (if there is one)
   - the name of the book, magazine, or newspaper; the name of the article or Internet site
   - the page numbers of the source

Early life:
1. born in 1451 in Genoa, a seaport in Italy
2. real name in Italian: Cristoforo Colombo
3. always dreamed of going to sea

Family:
1. father: Domenico Colombo, a wool weaver
2. mother: Susanna Fontarossa, daughter of a wool weaver
3. Cristoforo: eldest of 5 children

from: The Life of Christopher Columbus by Jennifer Alden,
pp. 77–85

Citing Sources

An important part of research and note taking is **citing sources,** or keeping a written record of where you got your information. When you write a report, you include a **bibliography** at the end. A bibliography is a list of the books, periodicals, and other resources that you used to find your information.

Book

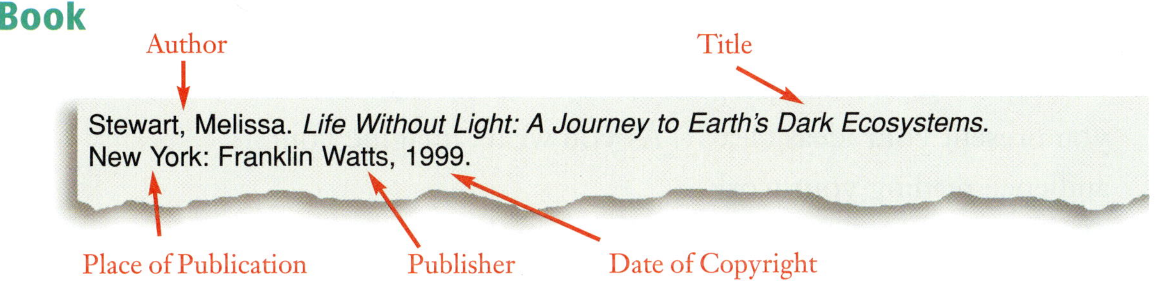

Newspaper or Magazine Article

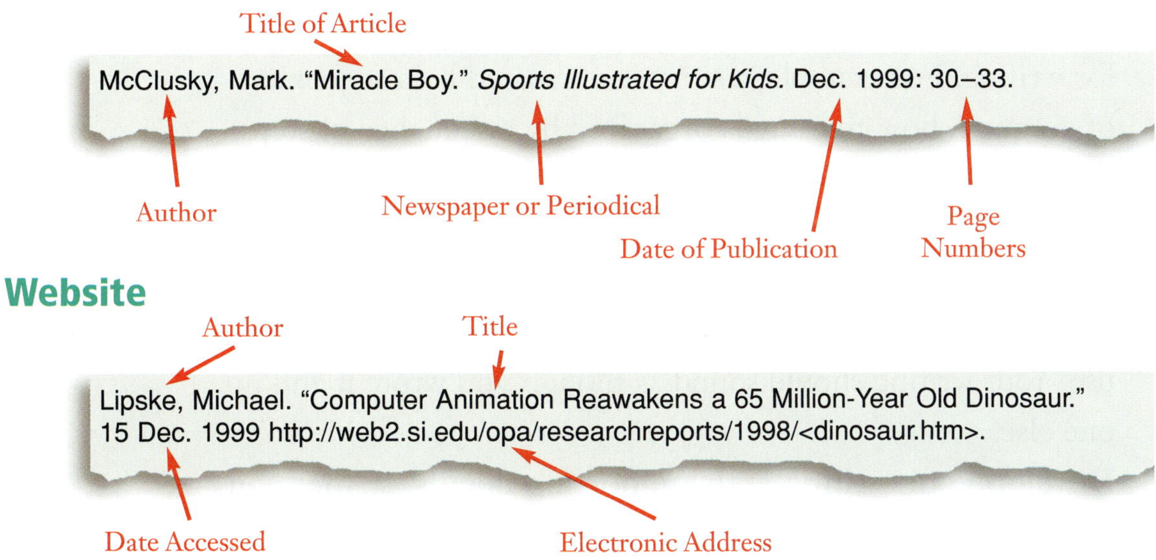

Try This

Select a page in this handbook. Take notes, and list this book as an entry in a bibliography.

Polishing Your Writing

Traits of Good Writing

All good writing has certain characteristics, or **traits**. Use these strategies to make your writing the best it can be.

- **Make your focus and ideas clear.** Select a focus for your writing, based on your purpose and audience. Make sure that you present your ideas clearly. As you write, imagine your audience reading your work.
- **Organize your writing in a logical way.** You may organize your writing in one of several ways. Unless a pattern for organization has been assigned by your teacher, you should select one that best suits your topic and your purpose for writing. For example, a story is organized by a sequence of events. A how-to essay is organized by a sequence of steps. A research report is organized by topics and subtopics.
- **Express your personal voice.** Your interest in your topic should be clear in your writing. Personal voice is shown in your tone, or attitude, and in the words and expressions you use. Your writing should sound as though you wrote it and no one else.
- **Develop your writing with supporting details.** After you have introduced your main idea, support it with simple facts, details, and explanations. If you are writing a persuasive essay, provide details and reasons to support your opinion.

- **Think about vivid word choice.** Vivid words will make your writing interesting for your readers. Precise verbs and strong adjectives help readers picture in their minds what you have written about. A thesaurus is an excellent resource for vivid and exact words.
- **Use effective and varied sentences.** Using a variety of sentence structures will hold your audience's attention much better than using the same kinds of sentences over and over. Short sentences are effective when you want to make important points. Long sentences are effective for providing descriptions and details. Try to use a variety of declarative, imperative, interrogative, and exclamatory sentences.
- **Check your writing for errors.** Make your best effort to fix any errors in your writing. Proofread for errors in grammar, spelling, punctuation, and capitalization. If you pay attention to these details, your writing will be easier to read.

Try This

Choose a magazine article or a newspaper article on any topic. As you read the article, look for as many traits of good writing as you can find.

Using a Rubric

A **rubric** is a checklist or a set of guidelines that you can use to evaluate your writing. Your teacher may give you a special rubric for a writing assignment. That rubric may tell you what you need to include in your writing. It also will tell you what you can do to get your best score. Use the rubic **before, during,** and **after** writing.

My Best Score

The composition fits the purpose for writing. The audience it was written for will understand it, enjoy it, learn from it, or think differently because of it.

The composition has a clear beginning, middle, and end. It is easy to understand how one idea connects to the next.

The topic of the composition is supported by important and interesting details.

The writer's personal voice is clear in the composition.

The composition has clear, exact words and is interesting to read.

The sentences are written in a variety of ways. Each sentence flows smoothly into the next.

The composition has few errors in spelling, grammar, and punctuation.

Peer Conferences

When you participate in a **peer conference,** you meet with a partner or in a small group to read and discuss one another's writing. Getting feedback on your work will help you become a better writer.

Use these tips when you participate in peer conferences:

- Bring a clean copy of your composition for each group member including yourself.
- Use the feedback you get from your partner or group members to revise or proofread your composition. You can also use a rubric to check your work.
- When you look at the work of others, read carefully to find the main ideas. Then read to see whether you can follow the organization easily. Next, look at the sentence variety and word choice. Finally, check for errors.
- Tell your partner or group members what you liked about their work first. Then discuss with them any problems you noticed.
- Be helpful and polite. Work together to suggest ways you can all improve your writing.

Try This

Exchange compositions with a partner. Check your partner's work against the rubric on page 758.

Oral Presentations

One way of publishing your writing is to present it orally. Follow these steps to publish your composition as a speech.

- Write your main ideas or topic sentences on note cards. Keep the notes short and neat so they are easy to read. Add short notes to remind you about details so that you can talk about them without having to read directly from your notes.

- Number your note cards to keep them in order.

- Think about visual media that would make your speech more interesting and clear. You might use pictures, charts, graphs, diagrams, maps, or other media such as music or film. Remember to write on your note cards when to use your visual media.

- Underline or highlight your most important points in your notes. As you speak, emphasize those points. Remember to speak slower, louder, and with expression.

- Practice your speech before you present it. Speak slowly, clearly, and loud enough for everyone to hear. Remember to make eye contact with your audience during your speech.

Multimedia Presentations and Graphics

Multimedia presentations are oral presentations in which you use visual or auditory aids.

- Think about your audience and your purpose. Would photographs, drawings, diagrams, videotapes, or music help the audience understand your information or make it more interesting?
- Ask your teacher about using equipment such as a videocassette player, a CD player, or an audiotape player.
- Design appropriate visual aids by hand, or use a computer to create graphics such as charts, tables, or graphs.

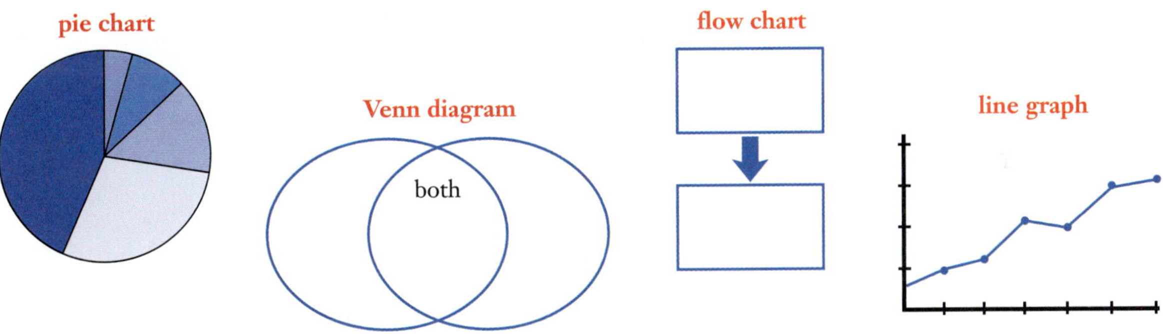

Try This

Think of all the subjects about which you have written compositions or given presentations. Use information on these subjects to complete one of the four graphic organizers on this page. Make sure the information you use is appropriate for the graphic organizer you choose.

Using the Glossary

Like a dictionary, this glossary lists words in alphabetical order. To find a word, look it up by its first letter or letters.

To save time, use the **guide words** at the top of each page. These show you the first and last words on the page. Look at the guide words to see if your word falls between them alphabetically.

Here is an example of a glossary entry:

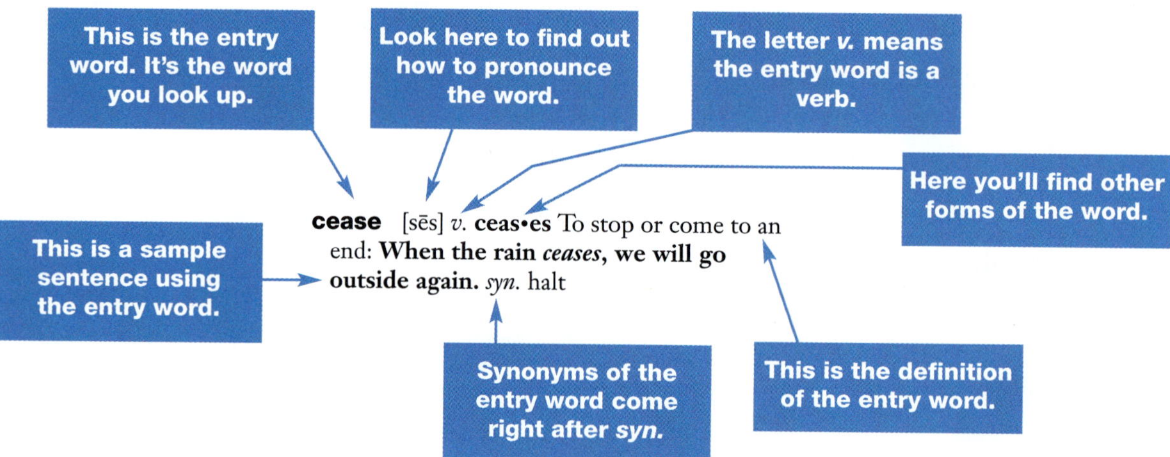

Word Origins

Throughout the glossary, you will find notes about word origins, or how words get started and change. Words often have interesting backgrounds that can help you remember what they mean.

Here is an example of a word origin note:

paddock *Paddock* comes from the Old English word *pearruc*, which means "an enclosed area." *Pearruc* is related to the word *park*.

Pronunciation

The pronunciation in brackets is a respelling that shows how the word is pronounced.

The **pronunciation key** explains what the symbols in a respelling mean. A shortened pronunciation key appears on every other page of the glossary.

Pronunciation Key*

a	add, map	m	move, seem	u	up, done
ā	ace, rate	n	nice, tin	û(r)	burn, term
â(r)	care, air	ng	ring, song	yo͞o	fuse, few
ä	palm, father	o	odd, hot	v	vain, eve
b	bat, rub	ō	open, so	w	win, away
ch	check, catch	ô	order, jaw	y	yet, yearn
d	dog, rod	oi	oil, boy	z	zest, muse
e	end, pet	ou	pout, now	zh	vision, pleasure
ē	equal, tree	o͝o	took, full	ə	the schwa, an unstressed vowel representing the sound spelled *a* in *above* *e* in *sicken* *i* in *possible* *o* in *melon* *u* in *circus*
f	fit, half	o͞o	pool, food		
g	go, log	p	pit, stop		
h	hope, hate	r	run, poor		
i	it, give	s	see, pass		
ī	ice, write	sh	sure, rush		
j	joy, ledge	t	talk, sit		
k	cool, take	th	thin, both		
l	look, rule	t̶h̶	this, bathe		

Other symbols

- • separates words into syllables
- ʹ indicates heavier stress on a syllable
- ʹ indicates light stress on a syllable

Abbreviations: *adj.* adjective, *adv.* adverb, *conj.* conjunction, *interj.* interjection, *n.* noun, *prep.* preposition, *pron.* pronoun, *syn.* synonym, *v.* verb

a•ban•doned [ə•ban′dənd] *adj.* Deserted or left behind: **The empty house seemed *abandoned.*** *syns.* discarded, cast aside

a•bun•dant [ə•bun′dənt] *adj.* More than enough: **The garage has *abundant* room for the many boxes we store there.** *syn.* plentiful

ac•cept•a•ble [ak•sep′tə•bəl] *adj.* Permitted, as an action that is allowed: **Blue jeans are not *acceptable* clothes for a wedding.**

ac•ci•den•tal•ly [ak•sə•dent′lē] *adv.* By mistake; without meaning to: **I *accidentally* let Josh know about his surprise party.** *syn.* mistakenly

ac•cor•di•on [ə•kôr′dē•ən] *n.* A musical instrument that sounds like a small organ: **Kaitlyn plays tunes on the *accordion* without looking at the keyboard.**

accordion

Fact File

accordion The word *accordion* came into use in the 1820s. It comes from the Italian word *accordare*, which means "to be in tune." A related word is *accord*, which means "to agree" or "to harmonize." *Accord* comes from the Latin word *cordis*, which means "heart." The harmony of music and feeling is related to the heart.

ac•quaint•ance [ə•kwānt′əns] *n.* Knowledge of someone or something: **I made the *acquaintance* of Mikaila's mother on the class trip.**

ad-lib [ad′lib′] *v.* To make up lines or music on the spot: **The actor had to *ad-lib* when she forgot her lines.** *ants.* rehearsed, planned

a•dore [ə•dôr′] *v.* To love something or someone dearly: **The puppies *adore* their owner.**

a•larm [ə•lärm′] *v.* **a•larmed** To frighten suddenly: **The noise *alarmed* the ducks and they flew away.** *syn.* startle

Word Origins

alarm The word *alarm* comes from the Italian word *all'arme*, which means "to arm" as in battle. This call to arms is a call to defend oneself.

al•i•bi [al′ə•bī′] *n.* A reason or an excuse for not doing something or not being in a certain place: **Dan's *alibi* was that he was in his room when the window was broken.** *syns.* explanation, defense

anx•ious [angk′shəs] *adj.* Eager: **Dan was *anxious* to find out if he had been chosen for the school play.**

a•pol•o•gize [ə•päl′ə•jīz] *v.* **a•pol•o•gized** To express regret over doing something wrong; to say one is sorry: **Ann *apologized* to her mother for coming home late.**

ap•par•ent•ly [ə•pâr′ənt•lē] *adv.* Seemingly easy to observe and understand: **You are *apparently* too big to ride a tricycle anymore.** *syn.* clearly

ap•pe•tiz•ing [ap′ə•tī′zing] *adj.* Delicious-looking: **The fresh fruit salad plate looked *appetizing.*** *syn.* appealing

ap•pre•ci•a•tion [ə•prē′shē•ā′shən] *n.* Recognition for good qualities; gratitude for something good: **He received an award in *appreciation* of his work.** *syn.* gratefulness

ar•bor [är′bər] *n.* A place that is shaded by trees or shrubs: **We rested on a bench in the cool, shady *arbor.***

as•sent [ə•sent′] *v.* To agree or approve: **I will *assent* to the plan.** *syn.* consent

at•ten•tive•ly [ə•ten′tiv•lē′] *adv.* With great interest and with careful attention: **Juan listened *attentively* to the directions.** *syn.* intently

bar•be•cue [bär′bə•kyo͞o] *n.* A party or picnic where meat is cooked outdoors over coals: **Our family's *barbecue* is held every July 4.** *syn.* cookout

barbecue

beck•ons [bek′ənz] *v.* Attracts or lures by tempting with something desirable: **The ocean *beckons* scientists to explore its mysteries.** *syns.* entices, summons

bel•low•ing [bel′ō•ing] *n.* A loud sound made by an animal; an animal call: **The farm was full of the animals' *bellowing* as feeding time drew near.** *syn.* roar

bic•ker [bik′ər] *v.* To have a minor argument: **Phillip and his sister often *bicker* over where to sit at the dinner table.** *syn.* squabble

bil•low [bil′ō] *v.* **bil•low•ing** To rise like a wave and push outward: **The sound of the orchestra was *billowing* through the halls and out into the street.** *syn.* swell

bog•gy [bäg′ē] *adj.* **bog•gi•est** Soggy or swampy: **We wore boots to hike through the *boggiest* part of the trail.** *syn.* marshy

Word Origins

bog *Bog* is an old Gaelic word meaning "soft and moist," like the wet spongy ground in a bog or swamp. To get bogged down in something is to become stuck in it, as one's feet would become stuck in mud.

bond [bänd] *v.* **bond•ing** To form a close relationship: **The mother and baby are *bonding* whenever they spend time together.** *syn.* link

bri•gade [bri•gād′] *n.* A group of people who work together to accomplish a task: **The volunteers formed a window-cleaning *brigade* and got the job done quickly.** *syn.* squad

brisk [brisk] *adj.* Cool and stimulating, as weather can be: **I wore a jacket when I went outside in the *brisk*, cool weather.** *syn.* chilly

brush [brush] *n.* Low bushes and shrubs that grow close together: **The young deer leaped over rocks and *brush* as it ran.** *syn.* undergrowth

bur•rows [bûr′ōz] *n.* Holes or tunnels that an animal digs in the ground to live in: **Snakes shelter in their *burrows* to protect themselves from the hot sun.** *syn.* nests

car•niv•o•rous [kär•niv′ə•rəs] *adj.* Meat-eating, or, in the case of certain plants, insect-eating: **To survive, *carnivorous* plants need insects.**

cease [sēs] *v.* **ceas•es** To stop or come to an end: **When the rain *ceases*, we will go outside again.** *syn.* halt

cer•tain•ty [sûr′tən•tē] *n.* The state of being sure about something: **I know with *certainty* that the book is good.**

cer•tif•i•cate [sûr•tif′ə•kit] *n.* An official piece of paper that shows one has met certain requirements: **Arthur got a *certificate* showing that he had completed a first-aid course.** *syn.* document

chem•i•cal [kem′i•kəl] *n.* **chem•i•cals** A substance that has certain properties: **The students wear safety glasses when mixing *chemicals* in science class.**

chil•e [chil′ē] *n.* A kind of stew that includes beans, chile peppers, and other ingredients: ***Chile* and salad make a tasty meal.**

chor•tle [chôr′təl] *v.* To laugh heartily: **Grandpa would grin and *chortle* whenever Connie told a joke.** *syn.* chuckle

Fact File

chortle The word *chortle* was coined in the 1800s by Lewis Carroll, the author of *Alice's Adventures in Wonderland* and *Through the Looking Glass*. *Chortle* is probably a combination of the words *chuckle* and *snort*.

cir•cu•lar [sûr′kyə•lər] *adj.* In the shape of a circle: **The wheel turned with a *circular* motion.** *syn.* round

cir•cum•stance [sûr′kəm•stans] *n.* **cir•cum•stanc•es** Any fact or event, especially as it relates to a larger event: **The *circumstances* of the accident were very unusual.**

com•pro•mise [käm′prə•mīz′] *v.* To settle a disagreement by having each party give in on certain points: **Sam and Bob agreed to *compromise* on how much they would spend.**

conch [känk] *n.* A sea animal of the mollusk family and the shell in which it lives: **We found a large pink *conch* during our vacation at the beach.**

conch

a add	e end	o odd	o͞o pool	oi oil	th this	ə = *a* in *above*
ā ace	ē equal	ō open	u up	ou pout	zh vision	*e* in *sicken*
â care	i it	ô order	û burn	ng ring		*i* in *possible*
ä palm	ī ice	o͝o took	yo͞o fuse	th thin		*o* in *melon*
						u in *circus*

con•fet•ti [kən•fet′ē] *n.* Bits of colorful paper that are thrown during celebrations to make them more festive: **The guests tossed *confetti* as the bride and groom passed by.**

Fact File

confetti The first *confetti* was actually small candies, which people would throw during carnivals and other celebrations. Then plaster candies were used. Finally, bits of paper took the place of plaster. The word *confetti* comes from the Italian word *confetto*, which means "candy." The English word *confection* also means "candy."

co•or•di•na•tion [kō•ôr′də•nā′shən] *n.* The act of working together smoothly for a purpose: **The movements of the dancer's arms and legs showed graceful *coordination*.**

cor•ri•dor [kôr′ə•dər] *n.* A long passageway or hall: **Our classroom door opens onto the *corridor*.** *syn.* hallway

cou•ra•geous [kə•rā′jəs] *adj.* Brave: **The *courageous* firefighter saved a child from the smoky room.** *syn.* fearless

cul•ture [kul′chər] *n.* The customs and way of life of a group of people: **Music, food, and literature are some of the ways a *culture* expresses itself.** *syn.* civilization

cur•few [kûr′fyo͞o] *n.* A time, usually in the evening or at night, after which people must be home or may not gather publicly: **During the emergency, no one was allowed outside after *curfew*.**

de•com•pose [dē′kəm•pōz′] *v.* **de•com•pos•es** To decay: **A pile of fallen leaves *decomposes* and becomes part of the soil.** *syn.* rot

de•cor [dā•kôr′] *n.* The way a room is decorated: **The room was done in Early American *decor*.** *syn.* design

de•cree [di•krē′] *v.* **de•creed** To make an official order, such as from a ruler or a government: **The queen *decreed* a holiday in honor of her birthday.**

ded•i•ca•tion [ded′ə•kā′shən] *n.* Great loyalty or devotion: **The cellist feels great *dedication* to his music, so he practices four hours every day.** *syn.* commitment

des•per•ate•ly [des′pər•ət•lē] *adv.* With great need for help; with almost no hope: **The swimmer held on *desperately* to his rescuer.**

de•vice [di•vīs′] *n.* A piece of equipment that was designed to do a certain task: **The telephone is a communication *device*.** *syn.* tool

dis•a•bil•i•ty [dis′ə•bil′ə•tē] *n.* **dis•a•bil•i•ties** A condition, such as an illness or injury, that interferes with normal activity: **The Special Olympics is a sports event for athletes with *disabilities*.** *syn.* handicap

dis•ap•point•ment [dis′ə•point′mənt] *n.* The feeling that something did not meet expectations: **After I had seen the toy again and again in ads, actually owning it was a *disappointment*.** *syn.* letdown

dis•card [dis•kärd′] *v.* **dis•cards** To toss away as something without value: **Valerie *discards* the gift wrap after she opens a present, but Kayla saves it.**

dis•pleas•ure [dis•plezh′ər] *n.* The feeling of being annoyed: **The librarian showed his *displeasure* when he saw that the book cover was torn.** *syn.* irritation

dis•po•si•tion [dis′pə•zish′ən] *n.* The character of a person; the way an individual usually acts: **He has a pleasant *disposition*.** *syn.* nature

dis•solve [di•zälv′] *v.* To break up into tiny parts and become part of a liquid: ***Dissolve* some sugar into the lemonade so it will taste sweet.** *syn.* melt

doc•u•ment [däk′yə•mənt] *n.* A printed or written record that contains information: **A passport is a *document* that allows you to travel from one country to another.**

eaves•drop [ēvz′dräp] *v.* **eaves•drop•ping** To listen secretly to someone else's private conversation: **Shana was *eavesdropping* to find out what her birthday present would be.**

Word Origins

eavesdrop *Eavesdrop* is an old term for the water that drips from the eaves, which are the edges of a roof. An eavesdropper may have been a person who would sit under the eaves of a roof in order to listen to someone else's conversation.

e•lat•ed [i•lā′tid] *adj.* Filled with joy or pride, as over success or good fortune: **Mark was *elated* when his soccer team won the championship.** *syns.* thrilled, overjoyed

el•e•gant [el′ə•gənt] *adj.* tasteful, stylish, and beautiful: **Grandma's lace tablecloth and fine china made her dining room table look *elegant*.** *syns.* lovely, appealing

el•e•va•tions [el′ə•vā′shənz] *n.* Heights above the ground or sea level: **The helicopter rose to higher *elevations* on its trip up the mountain.** *syn.* altitudes

en•cir•cling [in•sûr′kling] *v.* Forming a circle around; surrounding: ***Encircling* the farm was a white picket fence.** *syns.* enclosing, surrounding

en•dan•gered [in•dān′jərd] *adj.* Being in danger of no longer existing as a species: **The bald eagle is no longer an *endangered* species, as its numbers have increased.**

en•rich [in•rich′] *v.* To improve something by increasing its value, importance, or effectiveness: **Marsha will *enrich* her vocabulary if she looks up the words she doesn't know.** *syn.* enhance

en•thu•si•as•ti•cal•ly [in•thōō′zē•as′tik•lē] *adv.* In a way that shows intense or eager interest: **The audience clapped *enthusiastically* when the conductor walked onstage.** *syn.* spiritedly

e•quiv•a•lent [i•kwiv′ə•lənt] *n.* Having the same meaning or worth: **One hundred pennies is the *equivalent* of a dollar.** *syn.* counterpart

ex•am•in•er [ig•zam′ə•nər] *n.* Someone whose job is to give official tests: **The *examiner* gave Sarah her driver's test.**

ex•cit•a•ble [ik•sīt′ə•bəl] *adj.* Easily stirred up or provoked: **Paul has an *excitable* nature, so break the bad news gently.**

fa•cial [fā′shəl] *adj.* Having to do with the face: **Her *facial* features are almost the same as her mother's.**

fa•mine [fam′ən] *n.* A period of time when there is not enough food, such as during a crop failure: **The lack of rain caused many crops to die, which resulted in a *famine*.** *syn.* hunger

fares [fârz] *n.* Money paid for rides in a ship, bus, train, or airplane: **Bus *fares* cost more today than they did twenty years ago.** *syns.* fees, charges

fas•ci•nate [fas′ə•nāt′] *v.* **fas•ci•nat•ed** To interest very much: **The baby was *fascinated* by bright colors.** *syns.* captivate, attract

fate•ful [fāt′fəl] *adj.* Leading to an important outcome, often by chance: **Marta's *fateful* meeting with the program director led to a career change.**

fer•tile [fûr′təl] *adj.* Able to support growth of plants: **Crops grew well in the *fertile* soil.** *syn.* fruitful

fer•til•iz•er [fûr′təl•ī′zər] *n.* Something spread on the soil, such as chemicals, to make it richer and able to produce better crops: **After we added *fertilizer*, the plants grew better.**

flam•ma•ble [flam′ə•bəl] *adj.* Able to catch on fire: **Tamara made sure there were no *flammable* objects near the stove before she turned it on.** *syn.* burnable

flammable

gadg•et [gaj′it] **gadg•ets** *n.* A small instrument or tool: **The *gadgets* Sue took camping included a hand-held can opener.**

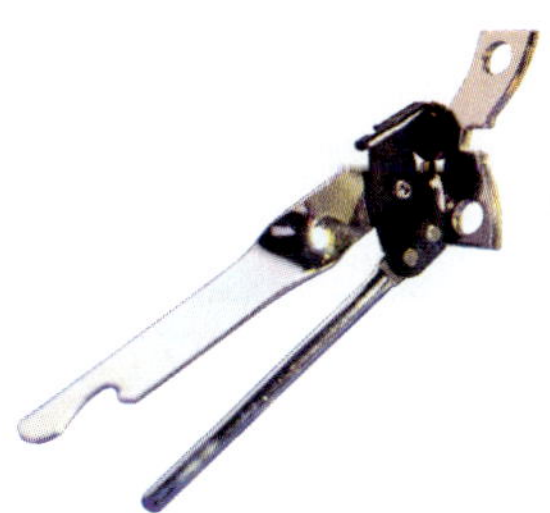

gadget

gen•er•ous [jen′ər•əs] *adj.* Large, more than enough: **The restaurant gives *generous* portions of dessert.** *syn.* plentiful

Word Origins

generous *Generous* is related to the Latin word *genus*, meaning "origin" or "birth," and refers to people born into the aristocracy. Such people were expected to have a high standard of behavior. Being *generous* was one of the character traits they were expected to display.

glum•ly [glum′lē] *adv.* With a gloomy feeling or expression: **The cat gazed *glumly* at its empty bowl.** *syn.* sadly

grudge [gruj] *n.* Long-lasting bitterness or anger that one feels as a result of another's action: **Carlos held a *grudge* against Neil because Neil had never chosen him for the team.** *syn.* resentment

a add	e end	o odd	ōō pool	oi oil	th this	ə = *a* in *above*
ā ace	ē equal	ō open	u up	ou pout	zh vision	*e* in *sicken*
â care	i it	ô order	û burn	ng ring		*i* in *possible*
ä palm	ī ice	ŏŏ took	yōō fuse	th thin		*o* in *melon*
						u in *circus*

hab•i•tat [hab′ə•tat′] *n.* The place where something or someone lives: **A pond is a *habitat* for many kinds of plants, animals, and insects.** *syn.* environment

har•mo•ny [här′mə•nē] *n.* Two or more musical tones sung or played at the same time as a chord; pleasant musical sounds: **The choir sang in *harmony*.**

haze [hāz] *n.* Air that appears foggy because it contains small particles of dust, water, or pollutants: **This morning you can barely see the skyline through the *haze*.** *syn.* mist

haze

heart•i•ly [härt′əl•ē] *adv.* With much enthusiasm and energy: **The food was delicious and we were hungry, so we ate *heartily*.**

hys•ter•i•cal•ly [his•ter′ik•lē′] *adv.* With uncontrolled emotion: **The sad news caused the children to weep *hysterically*.** *syn.* wildly

im•mi•grant [im′ə•grənt] *n.* **im•mi•grants** A person who comes to live in a new country: **In our school are *immigrants* from Spain, Russia, and Haiti.** *syn.* newcomer

im•plore [im•plôr′] *v.* **im•plored** To ask in a pleading way: **Joan *implored* Coach Ames to let her run the race.** *syn.* beg

im•pose [im•pōz′] *v.* To force on someone: **We don't want to *impose* our opinions on you.** *syn.* force

in•dif•fer•ent [in•dif′ə•rənt] *adj.* Showing no interest: **Simon walked calmly, *indifferent* to the activity around him.**

in•dig•nant•ly [in•dig′nənt•lē] *adv.* Being angry about something that does not seem right or fair: **Susan reacted *indignantly* when her sister received a bigger dessert than she did.** *syn.* angrily

in•hale [in•hāl′] *v.* **in•haled** To take a deep breath in order to smell something: **Madison *inhaled* the fresh morning air.**

in•jus•tice [in•jus′tis] *n.* An unfair act: **It was an *injustice* when the innocent man was punished.**

in•sig•nif•i•cant [in′sig•nif′ə•kənt] *adj.* Lacking in importance, meaning, size, or worth: **The minor detail seemed *insignificant* compared to the larger problem.** *syns.* trivial, unimportant

in•stinc•tive•ly [in•stingk′tiv•lē] *adv.* With an action that is automatic and not thought out in advance: **While training, the athlete knew *instinctively* when to run and when to rest.** *syn.* naturally

in•ter•pret•er [in•tûr′prə•tər] *n.* A person whose job is to translate spoken words from one language to another: **Someone who enjoys learning languages may choose a career as an *interpreter*.** *syn.* translator

in•ves•ti•gate [in•ves′tə•gāt′] *v.* To search out and study the facts in order to find the truth about something: **Joel's doctor had to *investigate* the cause of his rash.** *syn.* examine

ir•ri•ga•tion [ir′ə•gā′shən] *n.* An artificial way to water the soil so that plants will grow: ***Irrigation* allows farmers to grow crops when there isn't enough rain.**

irrigation

ir•ri•ta•bly [ir′i•tə•blē] *adv.* With annoyance or anger: **The boy answered his friend *irritably* but later was sorry.** *syn.* crossly

jeal•ous [jel′əs] *adj.* Resentful of someone's relationship with another person: **Lloyd was *jealous* of his brother for having so many friends.** *syn.* envious

lav•en•der [lav′ən•dər] *n.* A pale shade of purple: **The sunset colored the sky orange, pink, and *lavender*.** *syn.* orchid

lavender

lei•sure [lē′zhər] *n.* Time free from work or other duties: **Summer vacation is a time of *leisure*.** *syn.* relaxation

Word Origins

leisure The word *leisure* comes from an Old French word meaning "something that is permitted, or freedom to do something." Now its meaning has changed to "free time."

loathe [lōth] *v.* To dislike very much: **On the playing field, the teams act as if they *loathe* each other.** *syn.* despise

log•i•cal [läj′i•kəl] *adj.* Naturally expected based on what has already happened: **A good math grade is the *logical* result of studying.** *syn.* reasonable

loy•al [loi′əl] *adj.* Constant and faithful to people or ideals: **The *loyal* dog stayed with the family and never ran away.** *syn.* devoted

loy•al•ty [loi′əl•tē] *n.* Faithfulness to a person or thing: **The citizens showed their *loyalty* to the mayor by reelecting her.**

lux•u•ry [luk′shər•ē] *n.* Anything of value that gives comfort or pleasure but is not necessary for life or health: **A diamond ring is a *luxury*, not a necessity.** *syns.* extravagance, frill

mar•veled [mär′vəld] *v.* Became filled with awe or wonder: **We *marveled* at the sight of the magnificent waterfall.** *syn.* stood in awe

mes•quite [mes•kēt′] *n.* A thorny tree or shrub common in the southwestern United States and in Mexico: **The ranch was surrounded by *mesquite* bushes.**

Fact File:

mesquite *Mesquite* wood has a pleasant aroma that is used to add flavor to barbecued meat. Some commercially made barbecue sauces use it.

mesquite

min•i•a•tures [min′ē•ə•chərz] *n.* small-scale models of larger things: **Scott kept his collection of airplane *miniatures* in a shoebox.** *syns.* replicas, models

mod•est [mäd′ist] *adj.* Not showy; proper and quiet in manner: **Pat is *modest* about his art ability, but he is actually very talented.** *syns.* unassuming, humble

mod•i•fy [mäd′ə•fī] *v.* To change slightly: **Since it is raining, we will have to *modify* our plans for the class picnic.** *syn.* alter

mul•ti•cul•tur•al [mul′ti•kul′chər•əl] *adj.* Showing the varied customs, religions, or beliefs of different people: **The *multicultural* feast had food from many countries.** *syn.* diverse

mu•ral [myŏŏr′əl] *n.* A large picture painted on a wall: **The artist painted a *mural* in the lobby of the office building.**

mural

mut•ter [mut′ər] *v.* **mut•tered** To speak in an unclear way and in a low voice, usually in anger: **Debbie *muttered* a complaint that her sister did not hear.** *syn.* grumble

nectar [nek′tər] *n.* A sweet liquid found in flowers: **The bee drank *nectar* from the flower.**

neg•lect•ed [ni•glek′tid] *v.* Failed to care for or attend to: **The lawn is overgrown because Jason *neglected* to mow it.**

nes•tle [nes′əl] *v.* **nes•tles** To hug or pull close to give affection: **The child *nestles* her puppy in her arms.** *syn.* snuggle

o•blige [ə•blīj′] *v.* **o•bliged** To do a favor for someone: **Sal *obliged* his fans and played another song.**

oc•ca•sion•al•ly [ə•kā′zhən•əl•ē] *adv.* Happening now and then: **Walter *occasionally* plays ball after school, but usually he practices chess.** *syn.* sometimes

out•spo•ken [out′spō′kən] *adj.* Bold or honest in speech: **The *outspoken* man firmly stated his opinion.** *syns.* blunt, straightforward

o•ver•whelm [ō′vər•hwelm′] *v.* To overpower: **Don't *overwhelm* a new puppy with too many commands or you will confuse it.** *syn.* overburden

pad•dock [pad′ək] *n.* A small, fenced field next to a stable, where horses can exercise: **The horse and the pony grazed together in the *paddock*.**

Word Origins:

paddock *Paddock* comes from the Old English word *pearruc*, which means "an enclosed area." *Pearruc* is related to the word *park*.

paddock

pag•eant [paj′ənt] *n.* A performance in honor of an important event or holiday: **Sasha played the part of a general in the town's history *pageant*.** *syn.* show

pas•time [pas′tīm′] *n.* **pas•times** An enjoyable activity one does in one's free time: **Reading and hiking are Raul's favorite *pastimes*.** *syn.* entertainment

perch [pûrch] *v.* To sit or settle on a high or dangerous spot: **The bird was about to *perch* on the tree branch.**

perch

per•se•ver•ance [pûr′sə•vir′əns] *n.* Trying to do something no matter what difficulties arise: **Through his *perseverance*, he earned a place on the baseball team.** *syns.* steadfastness, determination

pe•ti•tion•er [pə•tish′ən•ər] *n.* **pe•ti•tion•ers** One who makes a written request of those who are in charge: **The *petitioners* asked the king to lower their taxes.**

pi•o•neer [pī′ə•nir′] *n.* A person who explores and settles new land in a faraway area: **A *pioneer* had to struggle to survive on the frontier.**

Fact File

pioneer The idea of a *pioneer* has come to mean someone who explores the unknown, not only on land. We refer to *pioneers* as leading the way in fields such as science, medicine, and space.

pit•e•ous•ly [pit′ē•əs•lē] *adv.* Causing feelings of sadness: **The puppy howled *piteously* the first night, so Sheila sat up with it.** *syn.* touchingly

plen•ti•ful•ly [plen′ti•fəl•ē] *adv.* With nothing lacking; with more than enough: **The art supplies closet was *plentifully* stocked with brushes, paper, paints, and clay.** *syn.* abundantly

plot•ting [plot′ing] *v.* Planning in secret to do something, often something evil: **The bank robber was *plotting* his next crime.** *syn.* scheming

pos•si•bil•i•ty [päs′ə•bil′ə•tē] *n.* **pos•si•bil•i•ties** Something that has a chance of happening: **There are many job *possibilities* for an educated person.** *syn.* likelihood

prac•ti•cal [prak′ti•kəl] *adj.* Useful or sensible: **It is *practical* to have a spare set of house keys.** *syns.* reasonable, wise

priv•i•lege [priv′ə•lij] *n.* A special benefit , favor, or right enjoyed only under special circumstances: **It is a *privilege* to vote in this country.** *syn.* advantage

prof•it•a•ble [prof′it•ə•bəl] *adj.* Bringing advantage or monetary gain: **The artist's business was so *profitable* that she became a millionaire.** *syns.* beneficial, rewarding

pros•thet•ic [präs•thet′ik] *adj.* Having to do with a replacement body part, such as a tooth, an eye, or a limb: **With her *prosthetic* hand, Hilda could draw.**

pro•trude [prō•tro͞od′] *v.* **pro•trud•ed** To stick out: **The dock *protruded* thirty yards into the water.** *syns.* extend, bulge

ras•cal•ly [ras′kəl•ē] *adj.* Mischievous, dishonest: **The *rascally* hamster escaped from its cage and hid in the house for two days.** *syn.* impish

ra•tion [rash′ən] *n.* A limited amount; a part of the whole: **Each soldier got a small daily *ration* of food and water.** *syns.* measure, share

rec•og•nize [rek′əg•nīz′] *v.* **rec•og•niz•ing** To know someone or something by details such as appearance or sound: **My dog is capable of *recognizing* the sound of my footsteps.** *syn.* identify

re•hears•al [ri•hûr′səl] **re•hears•als** *n.* Preparation and practice before an actual performance: **The actors read their lines during *rehearsals*.** *syn.* drill

re•pent•ant [ri•pent′ənt] *adj.* Showing sorrow and regret for past actions: **Noreen's *repentant* letter about the broken window led her neighbor to forgive her.** *syn.* remorseful

re•sound [ri•zound′] *v.* **re•sound•ed** To echo or to fill a place with sound: **The last notes of the symphony *resounded* in the hall.**

rest•less [rest′ləs] *adj.* Unable to rest or relax: **The cattle were *restless* as they sensed the coming storm.** *syns.* nervous, uneasy

re•tire [ri•tīr′] *v.* To leave a job because one has reached one's goals or has reached an advanced age: **The star athlete's decision to *retire* from basketball shocked his fans.** *syn.* withdraw

re•tort [ri•tôrt′] *v.* **re•tort•ed** To answer in an arguing way: **Jane *retorted* angrily when I said the mistake was her fault.**

ro•guish [rō′gish] *adj.* Full of mischief; likely to stir up trouble: **The child's *roguish* smile led his mother to suspect that he had made the mess.** *syn.* sneaky

rug•ged [rug′id] *adj.* Having a rough, uneven, or broken surface: **The farmer had to smooth out the *rugged* strip of land.** *syn.* irregular

rus•tle [rus′əl] *n.* A swishing sound: **The *rustle* of leaves in the trees means the wind is getting stronger.** *syn.* whisper

sal•a•ry [sal′ə•rē] *n.* The amount of money that a person gets for doing a job: **Josh receives his *salary* every Friday.** *syn.* pay

Fact File

Salt is necessary for life. Because it keeps food from spoiling, it was considered very valuable in times and places where there was no refrigeration. In ancient Rome, soldiers were paid in salt! The Latin word *salarium* means "salt money" and is the root of the word *salary* that we use today.

schol•ar•ship [skäl′ər•ship] *n.* The quality and character of a serious student: **Ray's high grades showed good *scholarship*.** *syn.* studiousness

script [skript] *n.* The words of a play, including stage directions: **Each actor got a copy of the *script*.**

scrounge [skrounj] *v.* **scroung•ing** To hunt around for what is needed: **We saw a raccoon *scrounging* around in the trash.** *syn.* search

sculp•tor [skəlp′tər] *n.* An artist who carves wood or stone or who shapes clay: **The *sculptor* makes drawings before she carves.**

sculptor

shame•fa•ced•ly [shām′fā′səd•lē] *adv.* In a way that shows shame for having done something bad: **Robert *shamefacedly* told his mother that he broke her favorite vase.** *syns.* guiltily, sorrowfully

shift•less [shift′lis] *adj.* Showing lack of ambition or energy: **The *shiftless* hare slept under the tree while the tortoise won the race.** *syn.* lazy

a	add	e	end	o	odd	o͞o	pool	oi	oil	th	this
ā	ace	ē	equal	ō	open	u	up	ou	pout	zh	vision
â	care	i	it	ô	order	û	burn	ng	ring		
ä	palm	ī	ice	o͝o	took	yo͞o	fuse	th	thin		

ə = *a* in *above*, *e* in *sicken*, *i* in *possible*, *o* in *melon*, *u* in *circus*

skid [skid] *v.* **skid•ded** To slide in an unexpected direction: **The car *skidded* on the icy road before it stopped.**

smug•gle [smug′əl] *v.* **smug•gled** To take something secretly: **The diamond was *smuggled* out in an empty soda can.** *syn.* sneak

soft•heart•ed [sôft′härt′id] *adj.* Kind; full of mercy: **Paul is so *softhearted* that he kept the stray kittens.**

spin•y [spī′nē] *adj.* Covered with thorns or needles: **A porcupine's *spiny* quills keep enemies away.** *syn.* sharp

spiny

sports•man•ship [spôrts′mən•ship′] *n.* Conduct, such as fair play, expected of an athlete: **The losing team showed good *sportsmanship* by cheering for the winning team.**

spruce [sprōōs] *v.* **spruc•ing** To fix something up: **The scouts are *sprucing* up the campsites as part of their community service.**

star•struck [stär′struk] *adj.* Full of stars: **She looked up at the *starstruck* sky.**

starstruck

steel•y [stē′lē] *adj.* Like steel, as in strength, hardness, or coldness: **The athlete lifted the heavy weight with a *steely* grip.** *syns.* strong, vise-like

straight•a•way [strāt′ə•wā′] *adv.* Without delay: **The ambulance came *straightaway*.** *syn.* immediately

strand [strand] *v.* **strand•ed** To leave behind without help: **The tourist was *stranded* when his plane took off without him.** *syn.* abandon

strength•en•ing [streng(k)th′ən•ing] *adj.* Adding more force and growing in power: **The darkening skies and *strengthening* wind meant a storm was on the way.** *syn.* increasing

sulk•i•ly [sulk′ə•lē] *adv.* With a withdrawn, unpleasant attitude: **The small child sat *sulkily* on the rug after her crayons were taken away.** *syn.* gloomily

sur•ren•der [sə•ren′dər] *n.* The act of giving up: **Generals from both sides met to work out the terms of the *surrender*.**

sym•pa•thet•i•cal•ly [sim′pə•thet′ik•lē] *adv.* With the same feelings as another person has: **The coach talked *sympathetically* after the player sprained his ankle.** *syn.* understandingly

teem [tēm] *v.* **teem•ing** To be very full: **The rain forest is *teeming* with animals.** *syn.* overflowing

thrift•y [thrift′ē] *adj.* Careful about saving money, or doing things to make it last longer: **The *thrifty* family found ways to use all the leftovers from meals.**

top•ple [täp′əl] *v.* To make fall over: **Rahaili liked to make a big block pile and then *topple* it with the tiniest push.** *syn.* collapse

trag•e•dy [traj′ə•dē] *n.* A very sad event that brings suffering: **The fire was a *tragedy* for the families who lost their homes.** *syn.* disaster

trans•form [trans•fôrm′] *v.* **trans•formed** To undergo a change, either in appearance or in character: **The schoolyard was *transformed* into fairgrounds for Family Appreciation Day.**

tre•men•dous [tri•men′dəs] *adj.* Very large: **The diver in the shark cage saw only the shark's *tremendous* open mouth.** *syn.* enormous

trick•le [trik′əl] *n.* A thin, slow stream of something, such as water or sand: **A *trickle* of raindrops slid down the windowpane.**

trickle

tri•um•phant•ly [trī′um′fənt•lē] *adv.* In a way that indicates success or victory: **We sang *triumphantly* all the way home after winning the championship game.**

trop•i•cal [träp′i•kəl] *adj.* Having to do with the hot area of the earth: **A *tropical* storm can develop into a hurricane.**

Fact File

tropical The area known as the *Tropics* extends from 23.5 degrees north latitude to 23.5 degrees south latitude. Within these boundaries, the sun's rays shine directly on earth. Because the area receives so much direct light, it is warm all year.

tropical

trou•ble•some [trub′əl•səm] *adj.* Causing difficulty and worry: **Carl's odd behavior was *troublesome* to his parents.** *syn.* bothersome

tun•dra [tun′drə] *n.* A flat, treeless region near the Arctic Circle: **Summer in the *tundra* is brief and cool.**

tundra

tu•tor [tōō′tər] *v.* To teach privately: **Luis is home with his leg in a cast, so his mother and father *tutor* him every day.** *syn.* instruct

twined [twīnd] *v.* Twisted around: **The machine *twined* the wires around each other to make a cable.** *syns.* twisted, wound

un•doubt•ed•ly [un•dout′id•lē] *adv.* Surely; proven beyond question: **Science was *undoubtedly* her best subject.** *syn.* definitely

un•eas•y [un•ē′zē] *adj.* Nervous or troubled: **Jan was *uneasy* every time she had to go down into the dark basement.** *syn.* worried

un•in•hab•it•ed [un′in•hab′it•id] *adj.* Unoccupied; empty: **The old cottage stood *uninhabited* for years.**

un•yield•ing [un•yēl′ding] *adj.* Constant and never-ending, not giving way: **Her desire to become an astronaut was *unyielding* throughout her life.** *syn.* uncompromising

va•cant [vā′kənt] *adj.* Empty, having nothing in it: **A new family has rented the *vacant* apartment.**

val•u•a•ble [val′yōō•ə•bəl] *adj.* Having great worth and meaning, either in terms of money or in personal terms: **A good education is a *valuable* tool for reaching one's goals.** *syn.* precious

ven•ti•late [ven′təl•āt′] *v.* To bring fresh air into a place: **In order to *ventilate* the house, open all the windows.** *syn.* freshen

Word Origins

ventilate The word *ventilate* comes from the Latin word *ventus*, meaning "wind." Another related meaning of *ventilate* has to do with "airing" feelings or points of view — discussing things in an open way.

ven•ture [ven′chər] *v.* To risk moving from a safe place: **The mouse sniffs the air before it will *venture* from its nest.**

vic•tim [vik′təm] *n.* A living thing that is harmed: **The mouse was the *victim* that became the snake's lunch.**

wind•break [wind′brāk] *n.* A fence or line of trees that breaks the force of the wind: **The farmer planted a *windbreak* to protect his crops.** *syn.* barrier

wist•ful•ly [wist′fəl•ē] *adv.* With a thoughtful, wishful feeling for something: **Papa sighed *wistfully* as he shared his childhood memories.** *syn.* longingly

a add	e end	o odd	ōō pool	oi oil	th this
ā ace	ē equal	ō open	u up	ou pout	zh vision
â care	i it	ô order	û burn	ng ring	
ä palm	ī ice	ŏŏ took	yōō fuse	th thin	

ə = *a* in *above*, *e* in *sicken*, *i* in *possible*, *o* in *melon*, *u* in *circus*

Index *of* Titles

Page numbers in color refer to biographical information.

Acknowledgments

For permission to reprint copyrighted material, grateful acknowledgment is made to the following sources:

Atheneum Books for Young Readers, an imprint of Simon & Schuster Children's Publishing Division: From *My Name Is María Isabel* by Alma Flor Ada, cover illustration by K. Dyble Thompson. Text copyright © 1993 by Alma Flor Ada; cover illustration copyright © 1993 by K. Dyble Thompson.

Rowan Barnes-Murphy: Cover illustration by Rowan Barnes-Murphy from *Cricket* Magazine, September 1996.

Boyds Mills Press, Inc.: "Geography" from *Baseball, Snakes, and Summer Squash: Poems About Growing Up* by Donald Graves. Text copyright © 1996 by Donald Graves. "My Village" from *The Distant Talking Drum* by Isaac Olaleye, illustrated by Frané Lessac. Text copyright © 1995 by Issac Olaleye; illustrations copyright © 1995 by Frané Lessac.

Robert Byrd: Illustrations by Robert Byrd from "Kite Tales" in *Ranger Rick* Magazine, April 1999.

Candlewick Press, Cambridge, MA: Fly Traps! Plants That Bite Back by Martin Jenkins, illustrated by David Parkins. Text © 1996 by Martin Jenkins; illustrations © 1996 by David Parkins.

Children's Better Health Institute, Indianapolis, IN: "Wings of Hope" by Marianne J. Dyson from *U. S. Kids, a Weekly Reader* Magazine, April/May 1998. Text copyright © 1998 by Children's Better Health Institute, Benjamin Franklin Literary & Medical Society, Inc.

Children's Book Press, San Francisco, CA: From *In My Family/En mi familia* by Carmen Lomas Garza. Copyright © 1996 by Carmen Lomas Garza.

Children's Press, Inc.: Saguaro Cactus by Paul and Shirley Berquist. Text copyright © 1997 by Children's Press®, a division of Grolier Publishing Co., Inc.

Cinco Puntos Press: From "In the Days of King Adobe" in *Watch Out for Clever Women!*, folktales told by Joe Hayes, cover illustration by Vicki Trego Hill. Published by Cinco Puntos Press.

The Cousteau Society, Inc.: From "My Visit to a Dreamy Place" in *Dolphin Log* Magazine, January 1998. Text © 1999 by The Cousteau Society, Inc.

Crabtree Publishing Company: From *The Gold Rush: Life in the Old West* by Bobbie Kalman, illustrated by Barbara Bedell and Bonna Rouse. Copyright © 1999 by Crabtree Publishing Company.

CRICKET Magazine: From "It's Math-Not Magic" (Retitled: "It's Just Math") by Linda O. George in *CRICKET* Magazine, Vol. 24, No. 1, September 1996. Text © 1996 by Linda Olsen George.

Dial Books for Young Readers, a division of Penguin Putnam Inc.: "I Love the Look of Words" by Maya Angelou, illustrated by Tom Feelings from *Soul Looks Back in Wonder* by Tom Feelings. Text copyright © 1993 by Maya Angelou; illustrations copyright © 1993 by Tom Feelings.

Barbara Emmons: Illustrations by Barbara Emmons from "It's Math-Not Magic" (Retitled: "It's Just Math") by Linda O. George in *CRICKET* Magazine, September 1996.

Farrar, Straus & Giroux, LLC: "Chester" and "Harry Cat" from *The Cricket in Times Square* by George Selden, illustrated by Garth Williams. Copyright © 1960 by George Selden Thompson and Garth Williams; copyright renewed © 1988 by George Selden Thompson. *The Gardener* by Sarah Stewart, illustrated by David Small. Text copyright © 1997 by Sarah Stewart; illustrations copyright © 1997 by David Small.

Susan Goodman: From "Amazon Adventure" by Susan Goodman in *Ranger Rick* Magazine, October 1994. Published by the National Wildlife Federation.

Harcourt, Inc.: Lou Gehrig: The Luckiest Man by David A. Adler, illustrated by Terry Widener. Text copyright © 1997 by David A. Adler; illustrations copyright © 1997 by Terry Widener. "Saguaro" from *Cactus Poems* by Frank Asch, photographs by Ted Levin. Text copyright © 1998 by Frank Asch; photographs copyright © 1998 by Ted Levin. Text and illustration from "Berries and Birds" by Lynne Cherry and cover illustration by Greg Shed from *Down to Earth*, compiled by Michael J. Rosen. Text and illustration copyright © 1998 by Lynne Cherry; cover illustration copyright © 1998 by Greg Shed; compilation copyright © 1998 by Michael J. Rosen. *The Garden Of Happiness* by Erika Tamar, illustrated by Barbara Lambase. Text copyright © 1996 by Erika Tamar; illustrations copyright © 1996 by Barbara Lambase.

HarperCollins Publishers: From *Donovan's Word Jar* by Monalisa DeGross, cover illustration by Michael Hayes. Text copyright © 1994 by Monalisa DeGross; cover illustration © 1998 by Michael Hayes. *Look to the North: A Wolf Pup Diary* by Jean Craighead George, illustrated by Lucia Washburn. Text copyright © 1997 by Julie Productions, Inc.; illustrations copyright © 1997 by Lucia Washburn. *A Very Important Day* by Maggie Rugg Herold, illustrated by Catherine Stock. Text copyright © 1995 by Maggie Rugg Herold; illustrations copyright © 1995 by Catherine Stock. From *The Down & Up Fall* by Johanna Hurwitz, cover illustration by Gail Owens. Text copyright © 1996 by Johanna Hurwitz; cover illustration copyright © 1996 by Gail Owens. "The Hen and the Apple Tree" from *Fables* by Arnold Lobel. Copyright © 1980 by Arnold Lobel. From *Sarah, Plain and Tall* by Patricia MacLachlan, cover illustration by Marcia Sewall. Text copyright © 1985 by Patricia MacLachlan; cover illustration © 1985 by Marcia Sewall. From *Stealing Home* by Mary Stolz, cover illustration by Pat Cummings. Text copyright © 1992 by Mary Stolz; cover illustration copyright © 1992 by Pat Cummings. *I Have Heard of a Land* by Joyce Carol Thomas, illustrated by Floyd Cooper. Text copyright © 1998 by Joyce Carol Thomas; illustrations copyright © 1998 by Floyd Cooper.

Houghton Mifflin Company: Nights of the Pufflings by Bruce McMillan. Copyright © 1995 by Bruce McMillan.

Kalmbach Publishing Co.: Red Writing Hood by Jane Tesh and cover from *Plays: The Drama Magazine for Young People*, November 1997. Text and cover copyright © 1997 by Plays, Inc. This play is for reading purposes only; for permission to produce, write to Kalmbach Publishing Co., 21027 Crossroads Cir., P. O. Box 1612, Waukesha, WI 53187-1612. *The Baker's Neighbor*, adapted by Adele Thane, with cover from *Plays from Favorite Folk Tales*, edited by Sylvia E. Kamerman. Text copyright © 1987 by Sylvia K. Burack. This play is for reading purposes only; for permission to produce, write to *Plays* Magazine, 21027 Crossroads Cir., P. O. Box 1612, Waukesha, WI 53187-1612.

Lerner Publications Company: From *The Kids' Invention Book* by Arlene Erlbach. Copyright © 1997 by Arlene Erlbach.

National Wildlife Federation: "Caring for Crocs" by Lyle Prescott from *Ranger Rick* Magazine, August 1995. Text copyright 1995 by the National Wildlife Federation. From "Kite Tales" and "Kite Festivals" in *Ranger Rick* Magazine, April 1999. Text copyright 1999 by the National Wildlife Federation. "Kites! Kites! Kites!" (Retitled: "Paper Fold Kite") from National Wildlife Federation Internet website. Copyright 1999 by National Wildlife Federation.

Dorothy Hinshaw Patent: "Wagon Train Adventure" from *Spider* Magazine, June 1996. Text © 1996 by Dorothy H. Patent.

Suni Paz: "The Candles of Hanukkah" by Suni Paz. Copyright © 1990 by Suni Paz (ASCAP).

Philomel Books, an imprint of Penguin Putnam Books for Young Readers, a division of Penguin Putnam Inc.: "Moon of Falling Leaves" and cover illustration by Thomas Locker from *Thirteen Moons on Turtle's Back* by Joseph Bruchac and Jonathan London. Text copyright © 1992 by Joseph Bruchac and Jonathan London; cover illustration copyright © 1992 by Thomas Locker. *The Emperor and the Kite* by Jane Yolen, illustrated by Ed Young. Text copyright © 1967 by Jane Yolen; illustrations copyright © 1967, 1988 by Ed Young.

Puffin Books, a division of Penguin Putnam Inc.: Cover illustration by Robert Barrett from *Blue Willow* by Doris Gates. Illustration copyright © 1990 by Robert Barrett.

Random House Children's Books, a division of Random House, Inc.: "Paul Bunyan and Babe the Blue Ox" from *Larger Than Life: The Adventures of American Legendary Heroes* by Robert D. San Souci, illustrated by Andrew Glass. Text copyright © 1991 by Robert D. San Souci; illustrations copyright © 1991 by Andrew Glass. From *Encyclopedia Brown and the Case of Pablo's Nose* by Donald J. Sobol, cover illustration by Eric Velasquez. Text copyright © 1996 by Donald J. Sobol; cover illustration © 1996 by Eric Velasquez.

Scholastic Inc.: One Grain of Rice: A Mathematical Folktale by Demi. Copyright © 1997 by Demi. Published by Scholastic Press, a division of Scholastic Inc. From *Fire!* by Joy Masoff, principal photography by Jack Resnicki and Barry D. Smith. Copyright © 1998 by Joy Masoff. Published by Scholastic Reference, an imprint of Scholastic Inc. "Horned Lizard" from *This Big Sky* by Pat Mora, illustrated by Steve Jenkins. Text copyright © 1998 by Pat Mora; illustrations copyright © 1998 by Steve Jenkins. Published by Scholastic Press, a division of Scholastic Inc. *Amelia and Eleanor Go for a Ride* by Pam Muñoz Ryan, illustrated by Brian Selznick. Text copyright © 1999 by Pam Muñoz Ryan; illustrations copyright © 1999 by Brian Selznick. Published by Scholastic Press, a division of Scholastic Inc.

SPIDER Magazine: Cover illustration by Michael Chesworth from *Spider* Magazine, Vol. 3, No. 6, June 1996. Illustration copyright © 1996 by Carus Publishing Company.

Viking Penguin, a division of Penguin Putnam Inc.: From *Blue Willow* by Doris Gates. Text copyright 1940 by Doris Gates, renewed © 1968 by Doris Gates.

Walker and Company: From *How to Babysit an Orangutan* by Tara Darling and Kathy Darling. Copyright © 1996 by Tara Darling and Kathy Darling. From *Two Lands, One Heart: An American Boy's Journey to His Mother's Vietnam* by Jeremy Schmidt and Ted Wood. Text copyright © 1995 by Jeremy Schmidt and Ted Wood; photographs copyright © 1995 by Ted Wood.

Wesleyan University Press: "If flowers want to grow" (originally titled: "The City") from *Poems 1934-1969* by David Ignatow. Text © 1970 by David Ignatow.

Zheng Xu: "Grandfather Is a Chinese Pine" by Zheng Xu.

Every effort has been made to locate the copyright holders for the selections in this work. The publisher would be pleased to receive information that would allow the correction of any omissions in future printings.

Photo Credits

Key: (t)=top; (b)=bottom; (c)=center; (l)=left; (r)=right

Page 44-45, Jim Reigel; 50, Spencer Grant / PhotoEdit; 51(t), Tom Stewart / Corbis Stock Market; 51(b), Superstock; 71(l), Dennis Brack / Black Star; 71(r), Kelly Culpepper; 96, Dale Higgins; 102, Superstock; 103, Paul Barton / Corbis Stock Market; 140, Peter Stone / Black Star; 141, Lisa Quinones / Black Star; 142-143, Justin Meyer / Challenge Air; 196, Jason Semple; 254-267, Tara & Kathy Darling; 288, Rick Friedman / Black Star; 317, courtesy, Mary Stolz; 343, courtesy, Farrar Strauss Giroux; 350, Spectrum / H. Armstrong Roberts; 351, George Haling / Photo Researchers; 352-367, Ted Wood; 372(t), John Warden / Alaska Stock; 372(b), B&C Alexander / Photo Researchers; 373(t), Mark Stouffer / Animals Animals; 373(b), Don Enger / Animals Animals; 388, Rick Falco / Black Star; 400(t), Keith Bedford / AP Wide World Photos; 400(b), Fabrice Coffrini / AP Wide World Photos; 401(t), The Granger Collection, New York; 401(b), Corbis; 449, Black Star; 455, Tony Freeman / PhotoEdit; 523, Michael St. Sheil / Corbis; 538(both), Lisa Quinones / Black Star; 544-545, Paul Berquist; 546-547, Ellis Nature Photography; 548-560, Paul Berquist; 561, Ellis Nature Photography; 602-603, Dale Higgins; 612, Mike Norton / Earth Scenes; 613, David Lawrence / Corbis Stock Market; 635, Bettman Archive / Corbis; 662-663, courtesy, Random House; 682, Dale Higgins; 707(t), David Levenson / Black Star; 707(b), courtesy, Walker Books; 729, Black Star; 730, Minden Pictures; 730(inset), Jim Cronk; 731, Jim Cronk; 732(l), Gail Shumway; 732(r), Jim Cronk; 733(b), Brian Kenney.

Illustration Credits

Larry Moore, Cover Art; Margaret Kasahara, 4-5, 18-19; Fabian Negrin, 6-7, 148-149; Mary GrandPré, 8-9, 272-273, 152-169; Gerard Dubois, 10-11, 398-399; Margaret Chodos-Irvine, 12-13, 500-501; Frank Ybarra, 14-15, 610-611; Ethan Long, 16-17, 121, 145; Steve Björkman, 20-21; David Small, 22-45; Shelley Hehenburger, 52-71; Tom Feelings, 72-73; Steve Snider, 75, 323; Jackie Snider, 78-79, 203, 249; Jose Ortega, 80-97; Terry Widener, 104-117; Erika LeBarre, 124-125; Brian Selznick, 126-141; Karen Stralecki, 150-151; Ed Young, 176-197; Jennifer Thermes, 206-207; Karen Oppatt, 230-231; Barbara Lambase, 232-245; Lynne Cherry, 246-247; Karen Lee, 252-253; Beata Szpura, 269, 369; Jonathan Combs, 274-275; Craig Spearing, 276-289; Lisa Carlson, 300-301; Cedric Lucas, 302-319; Kunio Hagio, 320-321; Sarah Hollander, 326-327; Garth Williams, 328-345; Lucia Washburn, 374-391; Steve Johnson/Lou Fancher, 392-393; Leslie Wu, 422-423; Matthew Archambault, 424-431; Anne Cook, 438-439; Gerardo Suzan, 440-449; Bethann Thornburgh, 456-467; Chad Cameron, 472-473; Demi, 474-493; Barbara Emmons, 494-495; Catherine Stock, 524-539; Neverne Covington, 568-569; Robert Crawford, 570-583; Tracy Mitchell, 590-591; Carmen Lomas Garza, 592-603; Stephan Daigle, 604-605; Steven Noble, 638-639; Floyd Cooper, 640-663; Yan Nascimbene, 668-669; Andrew Glass, 670-683; Joe Cepeda, 684-685; Tuko Fujisaki, 690-691; David Parkins, 692-707; Christine Schneider, 714-715; Jenny Tylden-Wright, 716-729.

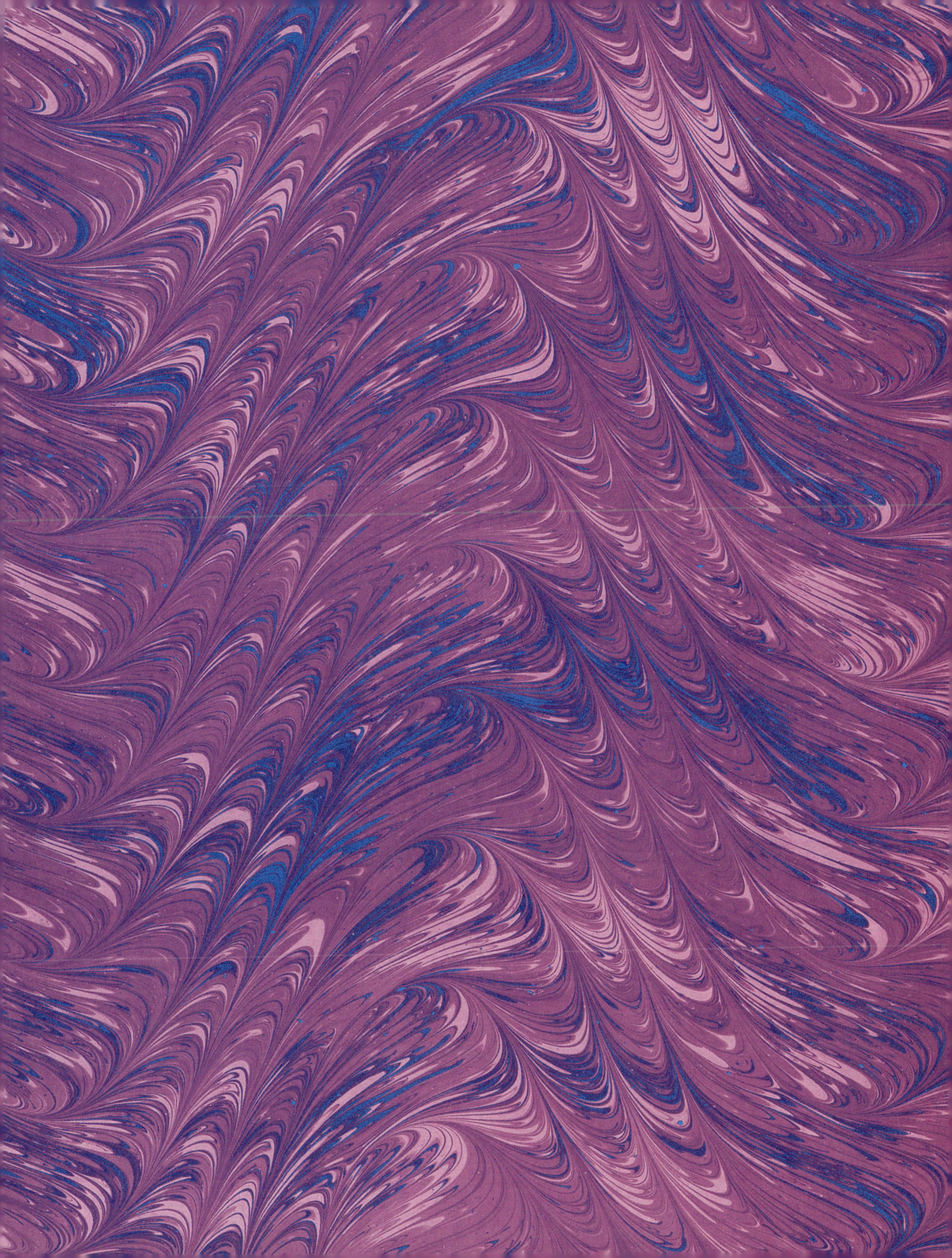

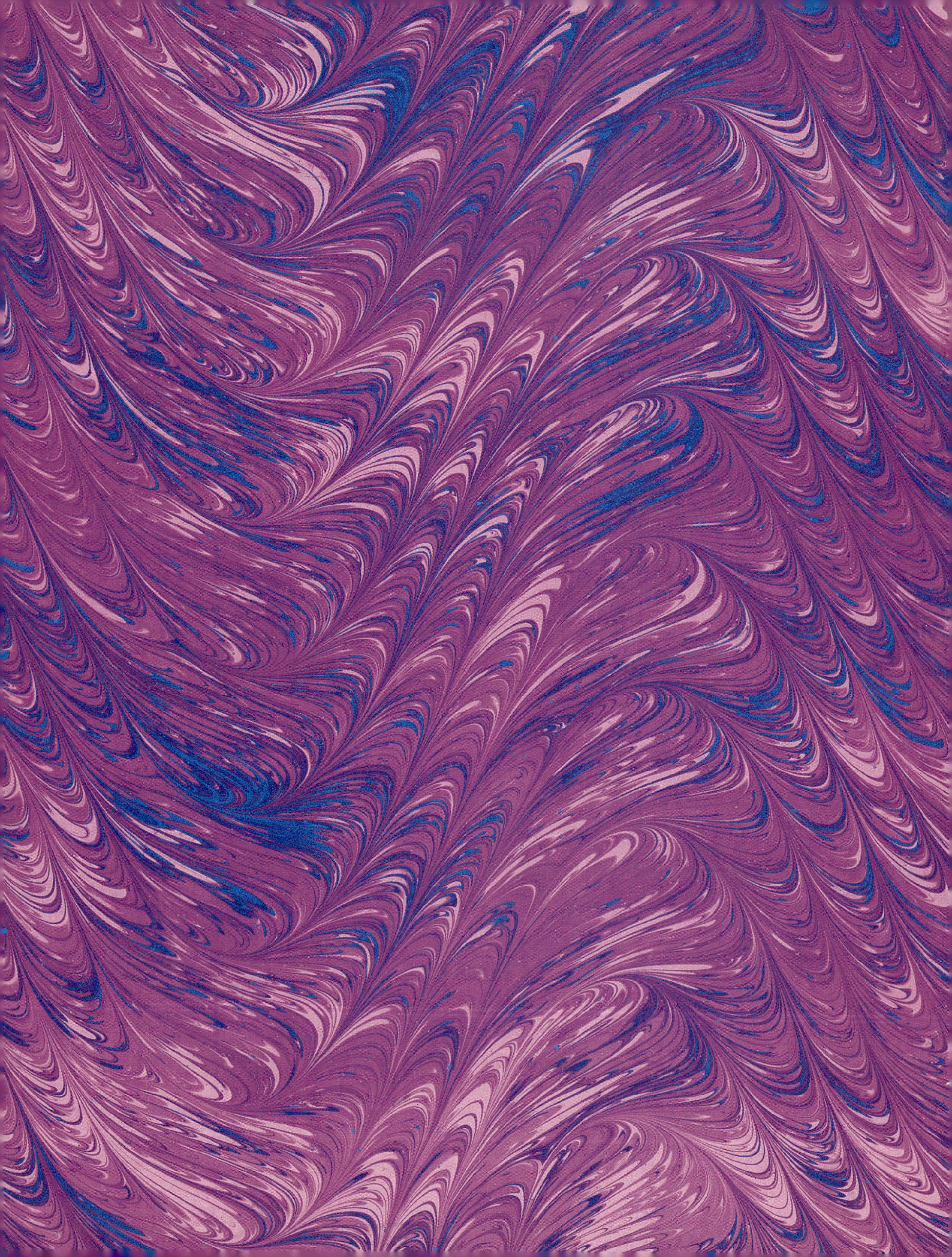